# A CRISIS OF GOVERNANCE:
# ZIMBABWE

# A CRISIS OF GOVERNANCE:
# ZIMBABWE

Jacob Chikuhwa

Algora Publishing
New York

© 2004 by Algora Publishing.
All Rights Reserved
www.algora.com

No portion of this book (beyond what is permitted by
Sections 107 or 108 of the United States Copyright Act of 1976)
may be reproduced by any process, stored in a retrieval system,
or transmitted in any form, or by any means, without the
express written permission of the publisher.
ISBN: 0-87586-284-5 (softcover)
ISBN: 0-87586-285-3 (hardcover)
ISBN: 0-87586-286-1 (ebook)


Library of Congress Cataloging-in-Publication Data

Chikuhwa, Jacob W. (Jacob Wilson), 1940-
  A crisis of governance : Zimbabwe / Jacob Chikuhwa.
     p. cm.
  Includes bibliographical references (p.   ) and index.
  ISBN 0-87586-284-5 (trade paper : alk. paper) — ISBN 0-87586-285-3 (hard
cover : alk. paper) — ISBN 0-87586-286-1
  1. Zimbabwe—Politics and government—1980- I. Title.

JQ2925.C47 2004
320.96891—dc22
                        2004006344

Printed in the United States

This book is dedicated to all the people who were tortured and those who died for the liberation and for the democratic process underway in Zimbabwe.

I also dedicate the book to those who are campaigning to make Zimbabwe a truly democratic society.

# ACKNOWLEDGEMENTS

I would like to thank my wife Raisa, my son Tonderai-Wilson and his wife Assiati and my daughter Eleonora-Ngwarai, and all my friends and acquaintances who have directly or indirectly made the task of writing this book more easy, bearable and even pleasurable.

These include pastors Doug and Jodi Fondell, who provided me with material and moral support when I had just returned to Sweden at the end of April 2002. Their hospitality and kindness, at a time I was receiving trauma therapy, gave me the encouragement I needed to start all over again and to continue with writing this book. My heartfelt appreciation goes to Lars Gyllenswärd for the IT technical assistance and advice that enabled me to compile the final version of this book. For information and advice on style and content, I am grateful to Prof. Regi Austin. Further, my deepest appreciation to Marie and Daniel Grout, of Rhodia Sverige AB, and to Lennart Simonsson, of the Nordic Outlook on Development Assistance, Business and the Environment, for the reports and research material provided.

I would like to express my sincere gratitude for the enthusiasm and assistance provided by the many and necessarily anonymous interviewees and the organizations that provided vital information.

Paragraphs and pages of this book immeasurably benefited from intense editorial consulting from Andrea Secara and other editorial members of staff at Algora Publishing. Their art of critically reading and polishing a sentence, a paragraph, is such an example of the highest craftsmanship that it enriched my literal intellect. My heartfelt gratitude go to them for making the publication of this book a reality.

# LIST OF ABBREVIATIONS

| | |
|---|---|
| AAC | Anglo American Corporation |
| AAG | Affirmative Action Group |
| ACP-EU | African Caribbean Pacific-European Union |
| AIDS | Acquired Immune Deficiency Syndrome |
| AIPPA | Access to Information and Protection of Privacy Act |
| BBC | British Broadcasting Corporation |
| BSAC | British South Africa Company |
| BSAP | British South Africa Police |
| CABSA | Canadian Alliance for Business in Southern Africa |
| Campfire | Communal Areas Management Programme for Indigenous Resources |
| CAZ | Conservative Alliance of Zimbabwe |
| CBZ | Commercial Bank of Zimbabwe |
| CFU | Commercial Farmers' Union |
| CMED | Central Mechanical Equipment Department |
| COMESA | Common Market for Eastern and Southern Africa |
| COSATU | Congress of South African Trade Unions |
| CSC | Cold Storage Company |
| CSO | Central Statistical Office |
| COTTCO | Cotton Company of Zimbabwe |
| CZI | Confederation of Zimbabwe Industries |
| DDF | District Development Fund |
| DRC | Democratic Republic of Congo |
| DZL | Dairyboard Zimbabwe Limited |
| EFZ | Evangelical Fellowship of Zimbabwe |
| EPZ | Export Processing Zone |
| ESAF | Enhanced Structural Adjustment Facility |
| ESAP | Economic Structural Adjustment Programme |
| ESSA | Enterprise Services for Southern Africa |
| EU | European Union |
| FAO | Food and Agriculture Organization |
| Finhold | Financial Holdings |
| FPZ | Forum Party of Zimbabwe |
| FROLIZI | Front for the Liberation of Zimbabwe |
| GDP | Gross Domestic Product |
| GMB | Grain Marketing Board |
| GNP | Gross National Product |
| GPAWUZ | General Plantation and Allied Workers Union of Zimbabwe |
| GTB | Government Tender Board |
| HIPCs | Heavily Indebted Poor Countries |
| HIV | Human Immunodeficiency Virus |

| | |
|---|---|
| IBDC | Indigenous Business Development Centre |
| IBWO | Indigenous Business Women's Organization |
| IDA | International Development Association |
| IDC | Industrial Development Corporation |
| IFC | International Finance Corporation |
| IUSY | International Union of Socialist Youths |
| JAG | Justice for Agriculture |
| MBOs | Management buy-outs |
| MDC | Movement for Democratic Change |
| MIEC | Movement for Independent Electoral Candidates |
| MISA | Media Institute of Southern Africa |
| MMD | Movement for Multi-party Democracy |
| NAGG | National Alliance of Good Governance |
| NCA | National Constitutional Assembly |
| NCC | National Convention for Change |
| NDP | National Democratic Party |
| NECF | National Economic Consultative Forum |
| NEPAD | New partnership for Africa's Development |
| NERP | National Economic Revival Programme |
| NGO | Non-governmental organization |
| NIT | National Investment Trust |
| NITZ | National Investment Trust of Zimbabwe |
| NOCZIM | National Oil Company of Zimbabwe |
| NORAD | Norwegian Agency for International Development |
| NRZ | National Railways of Zimbabwe |
| NSSA | National Social Security Authority |
| OAU | Organization of African Unity |
| PAZ | Privatization Agency of Zimbabwe |
| POSA | Public Order and Security Act |
| PTC | Posts and Telecommunications Corporation |
| PTRAZ | Posts and Telecommunications Regulatory Authority of Zimbabwe |
| RBZ | Reserve Bank of Zimbabwe |
| RENAMO | Resistencia Nacional de Mocambique |
| RTG | Rainbow Tourist Group |
| SADC | Southern Africa Development Community |
| SDR | Special Drawing Rights |
| SIDA | Swedish International Development Co-operation Agency |
| SMEs | small-medium enterprises |
| SSB | Salaries Service Bureau |
| TTL | Tribal Trust Land |
| UCLAF | Unité pour la Coordination de la Lutte Anti Fraudes |
| UDI | Unilateral Declaration of Independence |
| UK | United Kingdom |

| | |
|---|---|
| UN | United Nations |
| UNCTAD | United Nations Conference on Trade and Development |
| UNIP | United National Independence Party |
| UNDP | United Nations Development Program |
| USAID | United States Agency for International Development |
| UNIP | United National Independence Party |
| VCCZ | Venture Capital Company of Zimbabwe |
| VID | Vehicle Inspection Depot |
| WFP | World Food Program |
| WIB | Women in Business |
| ZANLA | Zimbabwe African National Liberation Army |
| ZANU | Zimbabwe African National Union |
| ZANU (PF) | ZANU (Patriotic Front) |
| ZAPU | Zimbabwe African People's Union |
| ZBC | Zimbabwe Broadcasting Corporation |
| ZCTU | Zimbabwe Building Constructors' Association |
| ZESA | Zimbabwe Electricity Supply Authority |
| ZIANA | Zimbabwe Inter-Africa News Agency |
| ZIDCO | Zoram Industrial Development Co-operation |
| ZIMASCO | Zimbabwe Mineral and Steel Company |
| ZIMCORD | Zimbabwe Conference on Reconstruction and Development |
| ZIMPREST | Zimbabwe Programme for Economic and Social Transformation |
| ZIMRA | Zimbabwe Revenue Authority |
| ZIMRE | Zimbabwe Reinsurance Corporation |
| ZINATHA | Zimbabwe National Traditional Healers' Association |
| ZIPRA | Zimbabwe People's Revolutionary Army |
| ZISCO | Zimbabwe Iron and Steel Company |
| ZNCC | Zimbabwe National Chamber of Commerce |
| ZSE | Zimbabwe Stock Exchange |
| ZUD | Zimbabwe Union of Democrats |

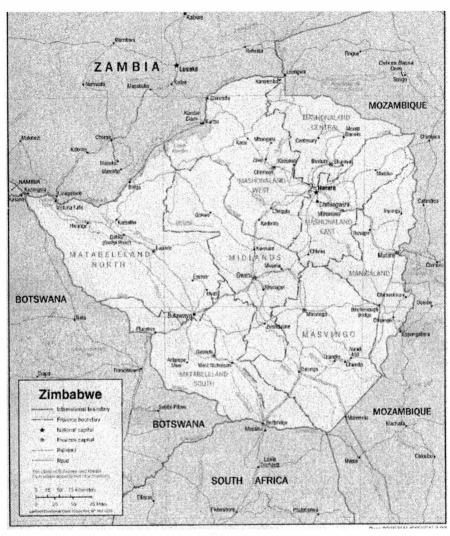

Zimbabwe, showing provincial boundaries.

# TABLE OF CONTENTS

INTRODUCTION                                                                    1

PART I. CONSTITUTIONAL DEVELOPMENT                                              5
CHAPTER 1. SOCIO-POLITICAL SYSTEMS                                             5
Pre-Historic Social Structures                                                5
Pre-Colonial Political Systems                                                9
Colonial Incursions and the Early Constitutions                              12
The Chimurenga War                                                           14
The 1923 Constitution                                                        16
The 1961 Constitution                                                        17
The Unilateral Declaration of Independence (UDI)                             19
The 1965 Constitution                                                        21
The 1969 Constitution                                                        24
CHAPTER 2. THE NEED FOR CONSTITUTIONAL CHANGE                                 27
Settlement Talks                                                             27
The 1979 Constitution                                                        30
The Lusaka Accord and the Lancaster House Constitution                       32
Countless Amendments to the Lancaster House Constitution                     35
Retention of Colonial Laws                                                   49
Cultural Expression and Repression                                           65
Special Legislation and Rights Infringements                                 67
The Clamor for a Homegrown Constitution                                      69
Mugabe's Constitutional Commission                                          75
The Commission's Draft versus the Popular Will                              80
Ramming It Through                                                          86
CHAPTER 3. THE FOLLY IN A DE FACTO ONE-PARTY DEMOCRACY                       91
Harassment of the Opposition                                                91
Growing Discontent                                                         109
Cracks within the Ruling Party                                             137
The Roots of Corruption                                                    157
One-party political systems                                                160
Allocation of Resources to the Less-privileged                            168
Aid Programs                                                               179

Centralized Allocation of Assets and Projects 183
Potential investors are bound to be put off by such shenanigans. 187
Commodity Shortages and National Disasters 191

PART II. ECONOMIC EMPOWERMENT 205
CHAPTER 4. THE INDIGENIZATION POLICY 205
Prerequisites for Indigenous Investment 205
The Economic Empowerment Lobby 213
Political Patronage 235
CHAPTER 5. ECONOMIC REFORMS 244
The Land-Reform Program 244
Economic Liberalization 263
Parastatal Privatization 277
Industry and Export Promotion 288
What Lies Ahead 319

APPENDIX I. THE PRESIDENCY AND MINISTERS' SALARIES 327

APPENDIX II. GOVERNMENT COMPOSITION 329

BIBLIOGRAPHY 337
Books 337
Reports 339
Periodicals 340

INDEX 343

# INTRODUCTION

*A Crisis of Governance* is a detailed analysis of Zimbabwean socio-economic history and development since the nation achieved independence from Great Britain in April 1980, with a focus on recent events under President Robert Mugabe and the ZANU (Patriotic Front).

It is one thing to break free of colonial tutelage; it is quite another to recover from the legacy of colonialism and implement the macroeconomic changes that would lay the basis for a self-sustaining economy. The crisis of governance in Zimbabwe (then known as Rhodesia) had begun with the occupation of Mashonaland by the British South Africa Company (BSAC) in 1890.[1] Self-rule and the subsequent British-sponsored constitutions did not much improve the situation, and the 1965 Unilateral Declaration of Independence only aggravated it.

Writing an analysis of the political and socio-economic development of a country is an exercise fraught with pitfalls, more so in an era like ours which puts a scholarly premium on narrow specialization. Analyses are usually suspect as indulgences of naive retiring scholars, purveyors of simplistic models or grand theories. Nevertheless, the importance of analyses cannot be over-emphasized. They are a means of taking stock of the academic capital accumulated at various

---

1. Since no census was taken after the 1890 occupation, the number of African inhabitants at that time is not known; however, to give some sense of the ratio of indigenous to white population, one may note that some contemporary demographers believe that there were about 34,000 Kalangas, 24,000 Ndebeles, 320,000 Karangas, 350,000 Zezurus and 300,000 Manyikas, giving a total of 1,028,000. The first government census was taken in 1901, but only the settler population was counted. The African population was merely estimated, at about 600,000, versus an estimated 1,500 European residents in 1891. This figure rose to 11,000 in 1901; 49,900 in 1931; and 69,000 in 1941.

moments in the development of scholarship. Ideally, they provide signposts of where a subject is, and possible directions for future research. Ignorance of the research results and trends in areas or disciplines outside one's own field of specialization often breeds fatuous generalizations and futile re-inventions of the wheel. Analyses capture the interconnectedness of social processes and economic realities often obscured in micro-studies. An analysis is like the "dissection" of a forest that gives shape to the distinctive trees and grass, animals, birds and insects that are found in it. It is not a substitute, but an indispensable complement, of primary and micro-research.

In the last several years, Zimbabwe's socio-economic history has come of age. One only needs to compare the tentative and anaemic reviews on the subject written in journals and books during the early 1980s with the self-assured and comprehensive surveys of the 1990s to see this. In the space of nearly two decades, Zimbabwe's socio-economic history has become a vast international enterprise, dominated by no single national or methodological tradition. While this heterogeneity has a drawback of permitting a wide range of scholarly standards, it also guarantees an openness to new ideas and it acts as a protection against the dominance of a single orthodoxy. This has made socio-economic historians of Africa in general much more interdisciplinary than other socio-economic historians.

Thematically, *A Crisis of Governance* is divided into two parts. Part I examines constitutional development in Zimbabwe, with Chapter One examining political systems, putting emphasis on the origins of its socio-political systems and colonial constitutions. Chapter Two examines the history of constitutional change in Zimbabwe, taking particular interest in settlement talks with the different British governments, amendments to the Lancaster House Constitution, retention of colonial laws, and the urgent need for a homegrown constitution. Chapter Three looks at the folly in a *de facto* one-party democracy with emphasis being centered on harassment of the opposition, growing discontentment, cracks within the ruling party and the roots of corruption.

Part II looks at economic empowerment, dealing with the indigenization policy in Chapter Four. Here, due emphasis is put on the prerequisites for indigenous investment, the economic empowerment lobby and the role of political patronage. In Chapter Five, the research concentrates on economic reforms, particularly the thorny question of land reform, the process of economic liberalization, the need for a transparent approach to parastatal privatization, and industry and export promotion.

Through out the book, I outline the roles played by Mugabe and his clan in the prevailing corruption, lawlessness and economic mismanagement.

I examine both the advantages and disadvantages of Economic Structural Adjustment Programs (ESAP). They are essential, provided they are properly interpreted and managed; but I describe the unrealistic goals set for the implementation of ESAP and show how both the government and the IMF failed to make allowance for the short-term negative effects of liberalization.

My emphasis on the need for privatization is not meant to encourage a wholesale disposal of assets to foreign companies. Strategic enterprises must be safeguarded; but there are cases where technological partnership or strategic partnerships in which foreign companies are allowed to buy shares (perhaps in the range of 40%) could foster a technological transfer. I also encourage 5-10% employee ownership and the offering of shares in parastatals to Zimbabwe citizens.

*A Crisis of Governance* offers no grand theory or interpretation. Its aims and objectives are far more modest. Both socio-economic history and development studies are about people, how they produce and reproduce their daily lives in their households, communities, societies, regions, districts, and within a country as a whole. The material and social conditions of production and reproduction are molded by a complex interplay of nature and society, men and women, rulers and ruled, locals and foreigners, the past and the present. This work was undertaken in the conviction that socio-economic historians and development economists can pull together their knowledge and resources to produce analyses that would be a valuable instrument to both government and development agencies.

# PART I. CONSTITUTIONAL DEVELOPMENT

## CHAPTER 1. SOCIO-POLITICAL SYSTEMS

How far back can we trace the roots of Zimbabwe's tribal rivalries, and what does history tell us of its people, technology and economy? Africa saw the earliest developments of mankind; a historical introduction of a few pages will give us a better backdrop against which to consider more recent events.

### Pre-Historic Social Structures

Historians have dated the existence of modern man or *Homo Sapiens* as far back as 100,000 years, and his hominid antecedents in Africa go back perhaps a further million years. Many Early Stone Age tools have been found in Zimbabwe, indicating that the area was populated even in the pre-*Homo Sapiens* era, from the very earliest pebble and flaked-stone tool users to the first fire users in about 40,000 or 30,000 BC.

Zimbabwe has more than 6,000 known rock art sites. Archaeologists have turned up important artifacts of the Middle Stone Age (which ended in 10,000 BC) in the Matobo Hills and in Bindura near Harare. The dominant Late Stone Age within present Zimbabwe is also associated with Zimbabwe's prolific rock paintings.

Every known archeological site in Zimbabwe has produced positive evidence of Shona occupation, and perhaps several phases of occupation. There is general agreement that the innovations of the original phase of occupation were introduced by immigrants who may have been the predecessors of the present Shona-speaking peoples. These are the Early Iron Age cultures of the Gokomere people in Masvingo, the Leopard's Kopjé people in Matabeleland and the Ziwa people in Manicaland and Mashonaland. Their settlements were built of stone, as demonstrated by the excavations at Great Zimbabwe near Masvingo; Khami, near Bulawayo; and Nyanga, north of Mutare.

In *Topographia Christiana*, written in about AD 547, a merchant-traveler from Alexandria by the name of Cosmos notes that the Abyssinian king of Axum regularly sent naval expeditions to Sasos (the name given to the country now known as Zimbabwe), to barter in oxen, salt, cloth and iron for gold. This trading took place during the period when Great Zimbabwe was being built, around in the year AD 211. The Shona are recorded to have moved southwards into Zimbabwe during the late first millennium, about AD 850.

Shona is considered part of central, eastern and southern Africa, where we find the Bantu language cluster. Every known ruin has positive evidence of Bantu occupation. The origin of these Bantu inhabitants is thought to have Congo connections. The Portuguese of the 17th century thought that they came from the Great Lakes (Tanganyika and Victoria), which they believed to be the source of both the Nile and Zambezi Rivers. The Congo Valley became the gathering place of various branches of the people we know now as Bantu.

Bantu tribes spread far to the west into the Congo Basin and southward through the central plains. The languages of the tribes of eastern and southern Africa show many similarities. For example, the Shonas call a person *munhu*, the Xosas, Zulus and the Rwandese — *umuntu;* the Sothos say *mutu*, while in Uganda they say *omuntu.* Father is *papa* in Rwanda, *baba* in Kenya and Zimbabwe. And water is *amazi* in Rwanda and Uganda, while they say *amanzi* in Zimbabwe (Ndebele) and South Africa (Zulu).

The similarity of the linguistic evidence is paralleled by the archaeological evidence. All cultural features that can be observed in Early Iron Age sites correspond more or less closely to cultural features of the Bantu-speaking peoples.

The new arrivals intermixed and employed their predecessors as cattle herders and ironworkers. The population gradually increased and the Bantu-speaking people spread into the south and southeast of the country towards the Limpopo Valley. Armed with the mining knowledge of their more experienced indigenous Iron Age neighbors, they located copper and gold deposits, producing ornaments for their own use. This appears to be confirmed by al-Masudi, the great Mohammedan voyager and historian who, in AD 943, gives account of Oman sailors traveling as far as "Sufalah" for gold trade. Idris, an Arabian who was appointed court geographer by the Norman king Roger XI of Sicily, also wrote accounts connected with gold trading between the Arabs and the Bantu. In 1150, about two hundred years after al-Masudi, Idris states that even in the 12th century much gold was brought from Sofala (the Sofala or Sufalah of Arab tradition and Portuguese record was the whole hinterland between the Zambezi and Limpopo Rivers, which includes the territory now known as Zimbabwe).

Archaeological evidence suggests that the first gold mines were started by the early Iron Age peoples, presumably in response to a demand for the precious metal by pioneering traders from the East Coast. Gold production may have approached one and half million ounces per annum. More reliable estimates for the 16th and 17th centuries range from 53,125 to 25,571 ounces per annum, respectively. Specific figures — rather than estimates — for the port of Sofala in a twenty-year period at the beginning of the 16th century give a much lower average of about 930 ounces per annum.[2] These figures declined drastically during the 18th century. Shona rulers were obviously conscious of the need to conserve their resources and often restricted production.

Iron was mined since at least AD 200. Pre-colonial workings are numerous, but almost all were small; production in local Shona societies was generally limited to weapons and tools. No significant long-distance trade in iron goods seems to have developed, in contrast to that for gold and copper.

Copper has been mined in the country almost as long as iron. Almost all modern copper mines are sited over old Shona workings, more than 150 of which have been identified.

The elephant population in the Zambezi River valley was substantially reduced by the demand for ivory from Arab traders based on the Indian Ocean coast. From early times, ivory ranked only second behind gold as a Shona export item to Muslims on the east coast. The Portuguese continued the trade from the 16th century, but allowed it gradually to taper off until the early 19th century.

Cloth was a very well-established import by about 1500 and had been imported far earlier. The actual techniques of spinning and weaving were imported along with the cloth. By the 14th century, spinning was going on at several sites on and near centers like Great Zimbabwe, Khami and Nyanga, and by the 16th century the growing of cotton and the weaving of cotton cloth were well established. Moreover, before long the technique of weaving had been applied to the fibers that came from the bark of certain trees, like the *mupfuti*.

Agricultural activity apparently began with the arrival of Iron Age peoples early in the first millennium AD. The Ziwa people, builders of what are now the Nyanga Ruins, constructed irrigation ditches, some of which still function. Endless kilometers of hillside terraces clearly indicate that agriculture of a high order was the mainstay of an enormous population.

The Iron Age economy, like today's in Zimbabwe, was based on agriculture, but the variable climate often led to what the Shona called *shangwa*, drought or disaster: the rains might come too late, too abundantly, or not at all,

---

2. I.R. Phimister, 'Precolonial Goldmining in Southern Zambezia: A Re-assessment', African Social Research (1976) [III], xxi, 1-30.

or locusts or other unexpected pests could all ruin the crops, in perhaps one year out of five. This basic weakness underlay the whole economy of the Iron Age people, and made their remarkable efforts in export production and trade understandable. Their escape from the threat of *shangwa* did not lie in gold-mining or elephant-hunting, however, but in pastoral farming. Livestock lived longer than grain could be stored; and they reproduced themselves, and could be looked after by the boys of the village. Not only could the animals be eaten in time of famine, but they could be traded with neighbors who still had grain. Goats were the main livestock, and even in the 19th century there were usually at least twice as many goats as cattle in Shona communities.

The Shona fully exploited these economic activities as they intermixed with the Gokomere, Leopard's Kopjé and Ziwa peoples. Historically, the Shona have tended to identify themselves as members of either dialects or clusters such as Karanga, Manyika, and Zezuru, or smaller groupings such as Shavasha, and Korekore. Shona speakers also pervade Matabeleland in the west and some spill over into Botswana. Individuals, families, ruling dynasties and even whole communities have historically moved about the country frequently.

The modern Shona community is a complex ethnic amalgam, within which several distinct dialect clusters are generally recognized as a meaningful division. These correspond, at least broadly, to recognized ethnic divisions. Korekore-speakers live in the north; Zezuru live around Harare; Manyika are in the east; Ndau in the southeast; Karanga in the south; and Kalanga in the far west. A seventh recognized branch, the Rozvi, are found throughout the country, confounding attempts at neat regional classifications. It is the Rozvi who had a profound political influence in the pre-colonial Zimbabwe.

Besides being in contact with other neighboring tribes, the Rozvi kings had established good trading relationships with the Arabs who were well established at Sofala by the beginning of the 15th century. The Arabs had set up a network of trading stations throughout Shona country. Their interest was to furnish themselves with an effective umbrella under which they could expand their commercial operations in an atmosphere of political stability. It is thus most probable that it was these Arab traders and their Shona agents who fostered the empire-building ambition of the Rozvi. By astute political maneuvering, the Rozvi leader established an overlordship over a loose confederacy of vassal chieftains, who paid him tribute in ivory and gold dust.

The Shona were controlled through the Rozvi king, who maintained careful control of the *Mwari* (God) cult and ruled by means of a council of prominent citizens and by strategically placed regiments of warriors. Individual chiefs and events begin to enter the picture in about 1440, when the Rozvi king Mutota launched a major military campaign to secure a vast region of southern Africa, bounded by the Indian Ocean, the Limpopo and the Zambezi Rivers and the Kalahari Desert. This Mutota Nyatsimba is credited with the founding of the Munhumutapa Empire.

### Pre-Colonial Political Systems

Little is known about the political systems of the Shona before about the 14th century. By then, the first large-scale state system (including tributary areas) had arisen among the Karanga branch of Shona.

Only four Shona political units appear to have been able to compel the allegiance of tributaries at any distance over any significant period of time, largely by the threat of military force. The first state was centered in the southeast at Great Zimbabwe, and was emulated by a number of competing dynasties. Three of these dynasties seem to have achieved hegemony over an area of roughly the same size as that dominated by the rulers of Great Zimbabwe.

The first of these dynasties is the Munhumutapa, or Mutapa "master pillager" — a name his successors adopted as a dynastic title. This was the creation of a ruling group which, with its followers, moved northwards off the plateau in the early 15th century to conquer and dominate the Tawara peoples of the southern side of the middle Zambezi valley between Tete and Zumbo. The Munhumutapa state was established in the Dande region by Mutota Nyatsimba, the son of a Shona ruler from the southern, Guruhuswa region. The background to this migration, and indeed to the emergence of the other rival dynasties such as those of Changamire and of Torwa, may well have been some considerable economic and political disruption on the plateau. It has been suggested that this may have been connected, in some way, with the Sotho groups who at this time were moving southwards between the highlands and the Kalahari. However, it is perhaps more likely that it was the result of one or more natural disasters, such as droughts (shangwa), crop failure or cattle epidemics, in a situation where the growth of human or cattle populations may have been putting critical pressures on the resources of the land.

Nevertheless, the more specific explanation for the particular movement of the Munhumutapa dynasty towards the Zambezi lies with the tradition that the dynasty wanted to make better contact with the important Arab-Swahili controlled main trade artery along the Zambezi. The significance of long-distance trade to the Zimbabwe successor states is illustrated by the history of the Changamire dynasty, the second of the three distinctive dynasties at that time. It was first heard of in the 1490s, when it attempted to challenge the power of the Munhumutapa in the southern Zambezi lowlands, but was defeated. Later on, in the late 17th century, the Changamire reappear as the successful challengers for the power and wealth of the Torwa, the third dynasty, which from the late 15th century onwards had developed hegemony over the substantial area of the plateau known as Guruhuswa to the southwest of the old center at Great Zimbabwe, an area which was being fertilized by trade routes running to and from the coastal emporium which the Arabs had developed at Sofala, and which the Portuguese had occupied in 1505.

Thus, the Changamire state rapidly developed into an empire that dominated more of the country than did any other pre-colonial state system. The Changamire rulers became known as Rozvi and their empire, like its predecessor state, was really more a confederation than a centralized polity. It comprised a collection of tribute-paying chiefdoms with their own dynasties. The tendency toward local autonomy was persistent, and by the late 18th century, the empire was disintegrating.

The Torwa dynasty, like the Changamire a result of a rebellion against Munhumutapa Chikanga in the 1490s, retreated to the south, establishing an independent state in the Guruhuswa region. Recent research has indicated that the Torwa state may have been responsible for introducing Khami culture to the region now known as Matabeleland, and that Khami itself was built as a Torwa center. The Changamire dynasty appears to have displaced the Torwa dynasty in the late 16th century, after Munhumutapa Neshangwe expelled the Changamire people from the Mbire region in the northeast.

From an early date, the Portuguese used the power of the Munhumutapa to gain access to the wealth of all the northern Shona, and they were still using their treaties with the Munhumutapa to this end in the 1890s.

While the Munhumutapa empire disintegrated following active Portuguese penetration between about 1575 and 1666, the Changamire dynasty, possibly in alliance with Muslim traders operating further up the Save valley, prospered and gained ground, and eventually, at the end of the 17th century, expelled the Portuguese from their interior trading fairs in the highlands.

Meanwhile, tributary provinces broke away, forming autonomous states. The most prominent of these were the Mutasa dynasty in the east of the country (early 16th century); the Makoni dynasty in the Maungwe District (early 17th century); the Mangwende dynasty in the Murewa District (early 18th century); the Svosve dynasty of the Zezuru cluster of Shona (early 18th century); and the

Chinamora dynasty just northeast of Harare (in the mid-18th century). Another factor which accelerated the disintegration of the Munhumutapa empire was the Mfecane invasions of the 1830s. Afterwards, there were more than 100 independent Shona chiefdoms, many of which had to struggle for autonomy against the raids and tribute executions of the newly arrived Ndebele and Gaza kingdoms.

Even during the peak periods of the large-scale Shona states, Shona societies remained rooted in subsistence agriculture and animal husbandry. State systems emerged partly as a response to competition for control of ivory and gold trades with the east coast.

Generalizations about Shona political structures are difficult to make, but their lack of uniform systems of political succession stands out clearly. Shona social structure is patrilineal, and family power blocs often developed quickly. Competition for political succession among rival families was — and still is — a major feature of Shona politics.

*The Political Structure:*

KING (Mambo)

↓

ROYAL COURT (Dzimbahwe)
(5-10 courtiers/cabinet members)

↓

ROYAL ENTOURAGE (Dare)
(Number varied between 100 and 140 members)

The King was the head of state and government. Europeans referred to the King as the "Chief," because they wanted to avoid equating African kings with European kings. However, they were kings in the truest sense of the word and most of them could trace their lineage back more than a thousand years.

The Royal Court was responsible for cabinet-like matters such as military affairs, justice, finance (tribute collection), royal health and personal security (herbalists and fortune tellers), and administration. They consulted with the King on fairly a regular basis. They were not just a policy-making body, but they also sat in court to hear and render judgment on appeal cases arising from the districts. Immediately below the Royal Court was the Royal Entourage, numbering between 100 and 140 functionaries. These included a master of the hunt, a master of storytellers, and a keeper of oral traditions; the rest were headmen. These were the equivalent of members of parliament. They came to the Royal Court once in a while, especially when marking certain national occasions.

Fission occurred frequently within dynasties and was a major cause of the proliferation of autonomous states. A typical example is the era of intermittent warfare between the Mutasa and Makoni dynasties, *Hondo ye paMhanda* (the Battle of Mhanda, 1865-1889). Rivalries among neighboring states were often intense, accounting for the relative ease with which the Ndebele dominated the western part of the country in the nineteenth century as well as contributing to the failure of the Shona to mount an effective resistance against the British in the 1890s.

## Colonial Incursions and the Early Constitutions

During the 1880s, European imperial powers (especially the British) started to scramble for a stake in the regions above the Limpopo River. At that time, European entrepreneurs and adventurers known as "concessionaries" beleaguered African rulers throughout southern Africa for concessionary rights to mine, to monopolize trade, to cut timber, and to hunt, especially for the elephant. The Transvaal Boers signed a treaty with Lobengula on July 30, 1887. The Grobler Treaty was a one-sided document reaffirming the treaty a certain A.H. Potgieter was said to have made with Mzilikazi in 1853. Following this, J.S. Moffat signed a treaty with the Ndebele king on February 11, 1888. The document, later to be known as the Moffat Treaty, merely reaffirmed the terms of the Mzilikazi's 1836 treaty of friendship with the British government; however, this treaty made an endeavor to exclude any other European nation from claiming possession of Lobengula's territory by making the king pledge eternal Ndebele amity with the British and promise not to sign treaties or land grants with any foreign power without first obtaining permission of the British High Commissioner for South Africa.

Finally, on October 30, 1888, the Rudd Concession was signed by Lobengula and by C.D. Rudd, F.R. Thompson and J.R. Maguire as agents of Cecil Rhodes. Acquisition of the Concession by a syndicate comprising Rhodes, Rudd and Thompson led directly to the formation of the British South Africa Company (BSAC) and its Royal Charter in 1889. The signing of this document was used to conclusively exclude European imperial competitors from the territory north of the Limpopo River.

There were two versions of the concession. The first and more important was the one written in English and fully accepted by the BSAC and the British Government of the day. The second was an oral version communicated to the Ndebele by the interpreter C.D. Helm, who also signed the written version as a witness. As it turned out, the two versions differed greatly, but this was of no consequence for the colonialists, for their purpose had been achieved.

Besides excluding other colonial seekers from the territory, the written document (concession) also granted the British South Africa Company "exclusive charge over all metals and minerals" in all of Lobengula's domain. Although Ndebele occupation did not include Shona territory (Mashonaland), Rhodes and his associates exaggerated the boundaries. The document also gave the grantees power to exclude other mineral prospectors and concessionaires from the region, and the right of veto over any future Ndebele concessions.

So as not to compromise British claims of Ndebele sovereignty over Mashonaland as a whole, upon which the British right of occupation was allegedly based through the Rudd Concession, the occupation of the country was carried out without reference to the rights of the Shona, with the exception of the Manyika ruler Mutasa.

The Manyika kingdom had long been the focus of Portuguese-British rivalry; Mutasa Chifambausiku was pressured to accept Portuguese sovereignty during the 1870s. In the late 1880s, however, British prospectors entered the country and established mines at Penhalonga in 1889. To expel any claim the Portuguese may have had, A. Colquhoun obtained a treaty from Mutasa on September 14, 1890. Notwithstanding, Portuguese agents J.C.P. d'Andrada and da Sousa tried to lay claim to Manicaland but were arrested by P.W. Forbes at Bingaguru on November 15 of the same year. Finally, the Anglo-Portuguese Convention of 1891 resolved these European differences, and the Manyika kingdom was partitioned between Southern Rhodesia and Portuguese East Africa, with the center of the kingdom lying on the British side.

Rhodes' rivals soon alerted Lobengula to the existence of two documents and the discrepancies between them; the political crisis brought scuffles that resulted in the death of *induna* Lotshe Hlabangana and his relatives. Because the *induna* had openly favored Lobengula's signing of the Rudd Concession, he became the scapegoat when Lobengula realized that the concession had been badly misrepresented. On Lobengula's authority, Lotshe was killed in early September, 1889. In the meantime, Lobengula publicly repudiated the concession and sent Babayane and Mshete to London to protest. Although the

BSAC continued to regard the concession as a valid agreement, Rhodes sent L.S. Jameson to Bulawayo several times to renegotiate it.

After the BSAC occupied Mashonaland with its Pioneer Column in September 1890, the validity of the Rudd Concession became less important, as British occupation was an accomplished fact. However, in violation of the concession, Lobengula was persuaded to sign the Lippert Concession in 1891, thinking he was dealing with a rival European party. In actual fact, he was dealing with BSAC's agents, which used his various concessions to build a legal justification for the Ndebele War of 1893.

After the conclusion of the war in 1894, a land commission was formed by the BSAC administration to investigate the problem of relocating the Ndebele people. This commission created two large reserves in Matebeleland, establishing the principle that African needs had to be met before land could be alienated to Europeans. In 1898, a British Order-in-Council reiterated this principle and made the BSAC administration responsible for assigning land to Africans. Nevertheless, no guidelines for determining African land needs were established. Thus, the administration simply passed its responsibility on to its district commissioners to enforce. The result was piecemeal allocation of African reserves, based on situations pertaining in individual districts. This is the origin of the policy of land segregation.

### The Chimurenga War

It is precisely because of these land encroachments and cattle seizures that the Shona peoples and their allies waged a war (Chimurenga) against the BSAC between June 1896 and October 1897. Although the Ndebele had capitulated in 1894, the BSAC had not effectively disarmed or broken up the quasi-military *ibuto* organization. Aggrieved by their humiliation and by the company's continuing seizures of cattle, the Ndebele started their uprising in March 1896. To try to defuse the situation, Rhodes conducted the first "*indaba*" with the Ndebele southern leaders on August 21, 1896. The northern leadership was ignored, but the general situation had deteriorated so much for the Ndebele that virtually all major leaders surrendered by December 1896.

Attempts at negotiation with the Shona peoples in January 1897 proved fruitless. The Shona had even less of a central command structure than the Ndebele. The British were thus hard pressed to know exactly whom to strike, or with whom to deal, to achieve significant results. Because of superior fire power and ruthless dynamiting of Shona strongholds in the caves, virtually all major

Shona leaders had either been killed or captured by October 1897. Shona independence came to a decisive end, and since then Shona chiefdoms have survived merely as government-sanctioned administrative units in Communal Lands.

Although the Shona, the Ndebele and other tribal tributaries like the Lemba, Birwa, Rozvi, Kalanga, and Dumbuseya waged essentially separate revolts, they rose up for much the same reasons and roughly at the same time. When the dust had finally settled, Britain introduced representative government in Southern Rhodesia on October 20, 1898, with the creation of a Legislative Council. In May 1899, the council had its first session. There were four elected "unofficial" members and five "official" members nominated by the BSAC.

*Table 1: The Legislative Council ("Legco")*

| Representation | Method of Choice | No. of Seats |
|---|---|---|
| "Unofficial" Members | Elected | 4* |
| "Official" Members | BSAC Nominees | 5 |
| TOTAL | | 9 |

*By 1920, there were 13 elected seats.

The BSAC administrator presided over the Executive Council with a British resident commissioner sitting on the council as a non-voting member. He was responsible for reporting on Legco decisions to the high commissioner for Southern Africa. The BSAC responded to persistent settler demands for increased representation by periodically increasing the unofficial seats to Legco. By 1908, elected members held a majority, and by 1920 there were 13 such members. As time went on, Legco played an increasingly important role in law-making, but the elected members' majority was held in check by built-in restrictions on Legco's range of powers and by the administrator's power to veto legislation relating to revenue generation or to BSAC land rights.

Nevertheless, Legco became the first formal arena of settler politics, especially after Charles Coghlan was elected in 1908. By the late 1910s, the dominant issues the Council faced pertained to the constitutional status of the territory following the planned termination of BSAC rule. As there was virtually no organized African opposition (about 60 Africans were then eligible to vote) during the campaign for "responsible government," a referendum on October 17, 1922 approved the idea by 8,774 voters, while 5,989 voted for union with South Africa. When Responsible Government was launched in 1923, Legco was replaced by the Legislative Assembly.

## The 1923 Constitution

For more than three decades, Zimbabwe was ruled by a private company owned by Cecil John Rhodes, from whom the country derived its name. During that period, no constitution governed the affairs of the country. It was not until September 12, 1923 that Southern Rhodesia was declared a British Crown Colony and Coghlan was sworn in as first premier on October 1, with J.R. Chancellor the first Governor. This entailed that Southern Rhodesia had a legislature of its own, based on the Buxton Committee recommendation.

From 1924 to 1965, the country's main government body became known as the Legislative Assembly, modeled after the British House of Commons. An important clause in this "Responsible Government Constitution" was that the British Government reserved the same powers over legislation affecting African rights that it held over the BSAC regime. In addition, this Constitution formalized the African reserves created by the BSAC; the 1930 Land Apportionment Act enlarged the reserves' total area slightly, with the result that they accounted for about 22.4% of the whole country.

While the British Crown recognized the Assembly as Southern Rhodesia's primary law-making body, it reserved the right to block any legislation it disapproved. It further limited the Assembly's competence to purely internal affairs. In practice, however, the Assembly and its Prime Ministers gradually broadened their range of competence and never had legislation vetoed by the British Government. When faced with local legislation such as the Land Apportionment and Industrial Conciliation acts, Britain tended to amend the Letters Patent upon which its reserved powers were based, thereby legitimizing the Assembly's actions. It is important to note that while the British Government had the sole right to select governors, in practice it consulted with the leaders of the local settler government. In 1942, such consultation was formalized, and by the 1950s the local Prime Ministers were nominating the governors themselves.

Between 1924 and 1961, the Legislative Assembly comprised 30 members elected for a five-year term, with the elections being conducted on party lines. Although the Assembly was unicameral, power existed to create an Upper House. Members of the Assembly were elected by a technically color-blind franchise, but high property qualifications for voters left the settler community with an overwhelming majority through 1957. In that year, new franchise qualifications created a special voters' roll for Africans.

In an effort to expand its influence in the southern African region, the British created the Federation of Rhodesia and Nyasaland in 1953. Ignoring African objections, the British Parliament approved a federation constitution in March 1953. On April 9, a Southern Rhodesian referendum ruled in favor of federation by a vote of 25,580 to 14,929. Only a few hundred Africans were able to vote on the issue. In September, the Federation of Rhodesia and Nyasaland was inaugurated with Huggins as Federal Prime Minister; Gafield Todd succeeded Huggins as Southern Rhodesian Prime Minister. Under the Federation, Southern Rhodesia preserved her status, although certain powers hitherto exercised by the Government relating to external affairs, defense, the regulation of commerce and industry, immigration, European agriculture, and education were then transferred to the Federal Government. The Southern Rhodesia Government continued to be responsible for "native" administration, education and agriculture, local government and housing, internal security and industrial relations.

After a decade of amalgamation, the Federation was dissolved on December 31, 1963 after Northern Rhodesia (Zambia) and Nyasaland (Malawi) gained responsible governments. In October 1964, following the independence of Zambia, the Southern Rhodesia Government dropped the prefix "Southern."

## The 1961 Constitution

It was not until 1961 that a new constitution for Southern Rhodesia was hammered out. The British Foreign Office organized a constitutional conference under the Commonwealth Secretary, Duncan Sandys. The constitution, drafted by a convention held in London and Salisbury (now Harare) in 1960-61, made sure that Britain retained ultimate sovereignty while relinquishing her reserved powers over local legislation. Settler representatives sought to safeguard their control of the government, while African nationalist representatives fought unsuccessfully for majority rule. In July 1961, the constitutional proposal was the subject of a referendum, when it was accepted by 41,949 to 21,846 votes.[3]

Although the reformist politician Joshua Nkomo accepted the constitution, it was denounced by the hard-core leadership of the National Democratic Party (NDP). In an effort to persuade his colleagues, Nkomo originated the theory of "two burning fires." It was his conviction that it was essential to "plant" some African representatives in Parliament so that they would raise African concerns and represent their interests, i.e. burn from within. At the same time, mass

---

3. *The Europa Year Book 1962*, Vol.II, London, 1962.

protests against repressive legislation would be intensified from outside Parliament. However, nationalist attitudes towards settler rule were hardening. Whereas the African National Congress (NDP's predecessor) advocated constitutional reforms, time was ripe for a direct attack on the constitutional basis of minority rule. The NDP concentrated more on demanding majority rule than on seeking reforms for specific grievances

As it was, the constitution created separate voter rolls, giving Africans their first seats in an Assembly of 65. This meant a complex voting system with "A" and "B" rolls, where "A" roll voters had higher educational, property, and income qualifications than "B" roll voters. The "A" roll elected 50 European Assembly members from 50 "constituencies." The "B" roll voters elected African members from 15 "electoral districts."

*Table 2: The Legislative Assembly*

| Representation | Voters' Roll | No. of Seats |
|----------------|--------------|--------------|
| European | "A" | 50 |
| African | "B" | 15 |
| T O T A L | | 65 |

To be registered as a voter, one had to be an adult citizen of Southern Rhodesia or a citizen of Rhodesia and Nyasaland, who had been resident in the Federation for any continuous period of two years, and who possessed the prescribed educational and means qualifications, which fell into five groups as follows:

(a) Income of not less than £720 per annum and the ability to complete, without assistance, the form of claim for registration. The alternative was ownership of immovable property valued at £1,500 or more and that same ability to complete the form unaided; or

(b) Income of not less than £720 per annum or the ownership of immovable property valued at £1,000 or more and, in either case, completion of a full course of primary education; or

(c) Income of not less than £300 per annum or the ownership of immovable property valued at £500 or more and, in either case, completion of a course of four years secondary education; or

(d) Income of not less than £240 per annum and the ability to complete the form without assistance; or

(e) Income of not less than £120 per annum and the completion of a course of two years secondary education.

In every case in which an income qualification was claimed, the claimant should have received the income during each of the two years immediately preceding the date of the claim for his or her registration as a voter. When the number of voters registered under groups (d) and (e) equaled 20% of the total number of voters registered under groups (a), (b) and (c), no further registration under the two former groups would be permitted.

In place of the British oversight, the constitution contained a Bill of Rights and created a Constitutional Council meant to safeguard African rights. The Constitutional Council (comprising 11 members) was supposed to report to the Governor and the Speaker of the Legislature on all Bills (except money Bills) passed by the Legislature and to inform them whether the Bill conflicted with the provisions of the Declaration of Rights. This was to be done within 30 days after the passing of the Bill, unless an extension was granted. In the event of a conflict with the Declaration of Rights, the Bill could only be presented to the Governor for assent after a two-thirds majority vote in the legislature, or after a simple majority vote together with a delay of six months.

In other words, the constitution contained checks and safeguards designed to be operated by the people of Southern Rhodesia themselves. However, existing legislation that contradicted the new bill of rights was unaffected, and the settler-dominated Assembly effectively nullified the Constitutional Council, which it was empowered to overrule with a two-thirds majority vote on any challenge. The British Privy Council remained the ultimate court of appeals. The November 1964 referendum on the issue of independence was held under the auspices of this 1961 constitution. With only a white electorate voting, 58,091 voted in favor of independence, with 6,906 against. During the Unilateral Declaration of Independence (UDI) — November 1965 to December 1979, Britain and most other nations regarded the 1961 document as the legal constitution for the country.

## The Unilateral Declaration of Independence (UDI)

Firing the first shot in the lead up to the achievement of independence, Ian Smith and his Rhodesian Front Government proclaimed the Unilateral Declaration of Independence (UDI) in November, 1965, to pre-empt a possible move by the British who had been relinquishing control in neighboring colonies in favor of the indigenous blacks. The country was plunged into a bitter war between the Rhodesia Front Government and the nationalist forces (freedom fighters) spearheaded by the Zimbabwe African National Liberation Army

(ZANLA) and the Zimbabwe People's Revolutionary Army (ZIPRA). In the communal lands (set aside by the British for the indigenous people) where almost 80% of the population resided, homes were destroyed and livestock perished; people were forced into protected villages (*makeep*); innocent civilians were randomly murdered by soldiers on both sides in the conflict while others were killed by land mines; refugees were chased into neighboring countries and massacred by Rhodesian Selous Scouts.

While the nationalists were determined to end the crisis of governance in Zimbabwe, there were conflicts within their ranks. In the nationalist training camps in Mozambique, Tanzania and Zambia, freedom fighters were subjected to torture and murder. Nationalist leaders controlling these camps were not safe, either. The assassination of Herbert Chitepo on March 18, 1975, was just one example of many. With the liberation struggle gaining the upper hand inside Zimbabwe, especially after the collapse of the Portuguese colonial empire in Africa in 1974, political feuding became rampant. Leaders in exile began to feel the breeze of political power, especially from the eastern border with Mozambique, where the Rhodesian forces had virtually lost control to the ZANLA forces. For the leaders in Lusaka, capital city of Zambia where the freedom fighters' headquarters were situated, control and command of these forces became their primary target. Thus, a tribal struggle ensued.

Back home, internal forces were playing their part. Ian Smith, using "divide and rule" tactics, had managed to hoodwink Bishop Abel Muzorewa and chief Jeremiah Chirau into joining his camp. At one time, even the astute Joshua Nkomo, the leader of the Zimbabwe African People's Union under whose command fell ZIPRA, abandoned his base in Lusaka and joined them, but later he recognized his error. In an effort to neutralize the ever ascendant ZANU forces, Smith managed to bring the Rev. Ndabaningi Sithole into his internal settlement negotiations — not realizing that the ailing reverend had lost credibility within the militant ZANU (at that time led by Robert Mugabe from the Mozambican capital of Maputo).

In his book, *The Great Betrayal*, Ian Smith paints a picture of a Zimbabwean people satisfied with his regime and at peace with his racial policy. "Rhodesia was an oasis of peace and contentment. Visitors to the country invariably commented on 'the happiest black faces we have seen'," he writes.[4] Although he boasts of providing the best education for blacks, he still argues in his book that the blacks were not mature enough to understand what an election or

---

4. *The Great Betrayal*, by Ian D. Smith, Blake, London, 1997.

referendum was. Writing about the British demand for "a test of acceptability" for the 1971 Anglo-Rhodesian Settlement Proposals, he states ".... it would be impossible to obtain an honest assessment of our black people, since the vast majority of them had never exercised a vote in their lives, could neither read nor write, did not understand the meaning of the word 'constitution,' and were completely bemused by all the talking and maneuvering going on around them."

In his interviews with the BBC and other Western media organizations, Smith talks of Zimbabweans who approach him in the streets to say that they feel they were better off during his rule than at present. It must be noted that Smith thus tries to project a false picture of the people's attitude: he overlooks the economic meltdown, for which he is partially culpable. The public does not doubt that the Rhodesian Front had a virulent racist policy, the overtones of which are still perceptible. There was nothing special in Ian Smith's racist Rhodesia that would make any right-minded Zimbabwean look back with nostalgia. Rather, there are many Zimbabweans, whites included, who hold him responsible for having taken the country to war and having refused negotiated compromises that would have ended the violence that cost about 35,000 lives.

### The 1965 Constitution

The 1965 constitution, promulgated shortly after UDI, was essentially a modification of the 1961 constitution. At the same time, the Legislative Assembly was re-designated as the "Parliament," with 65 members, 15 of whom were elected on a Lower Roll.

*Table 3: The Parliament*

| Representation | Voters' Roll | No. of Seats |
|---|---|---|
| European | Higher | 50 |
| African | Lower | 15 |
| TOTAL | | 65 |

While still recognizing Queen Elizabeth II as the country's sovereign, the 1965 constitution replaced the British Governor with an "Officer Administering the Government." It also eliminated all vestigial British reserved powers. In other words, provisions under the Southern Rhodesia Order-in-Council, 1961, were held to be of no effect. The Constitutional Laws Validity Act, 1961, and the Powers of Disallowance and the Reservation of Bills were repudiated under the new Constitution. Orders in Council and royal instructions through the Governor were likewise repudiated.

The form of government remained a constitutional monarch, with Her Majesty the Queen represented as Head of State by the Officer Administering the Government. Executive powers in him included the appointment and accreditation of diplomatic representatives, the ratification of international treaties, the proclamation of martial law or state of emergency, the declaration of war and peace and the conferment of honors and precedence. Temporary provisions gave the Officer Administering the Government complete freedom of constitutional amendment for the first six months of UDI.

The Legislature was made the Sovereign Legislative power in and over Rhodesia, and no Act of Parliament of the UK was held to extend to Rhodesia unless extended thereto by Act of the Legislature of Rhodesia. The Legislature had power to amend the constitution by a two-thirds majority of the total membership of Parliament, without the need of referenda among the four racial groups (African, European, Asian and Colored), as stipulated in the 1961 Constitution.

In respect of the Delimitation of Constituencies and Electoral Districts, the 1965 Constitution followed closely the 1961 Constitution. The new Constitution had removed some of the safeguards on judicial independence, however, and appeals to the Judicial Committee of the Privy Council were no longer provided for. Ultimate appeal under the Declaration of Rights was to the Appellate Division of the High Court of Rhodesia, not to the Judicial Committee of the Privy Council as before. It was no longer provided that two of the members of the Constitutional Council be African. In regard to the TTL Board, agreement by the four principal racial communities to changes in the powers and terms of trust was no longer needed, such changes being subject to a two-thirds vote of Parliament, the Senate's certificate, and the assent of the Officer Administering the Government.

The following Emergency Regulations were in force: Maintenance of Law and Order; Censorship of Publications; Postal and Radiocommunications; Dissemination of Information; Control of Goods and Services; African Affairs; Control of Government Employees. These gave the Government powers of intervention in a wide range of private and public affairs.

By mid-1965, Europeans constituted 95% of the 97,284 "A" roll voters, while Africans constituted 92% of the 11,577 "B" roll voters. The impact of African voters was further diluted by an effective nationalist boycott of the general elections in 1962 and 1965. The Rhodesian Front led by Ian Smith was the first European political party to develop a broad-based organization among Europeans. Earlier European political parties were little more than transient

22

bodies mobilized by top leadership before each general election. Because of this broad-based support, the RF won all 50 European parliamentary seats in the general elections of 1965, 1970, 1974, and 1977. The party was also able to win all the seats reserved for whites in the 1979 and 1980 general elections.

Meanwhile, immediately after the Unilateral Declaration of Independence, the Queen, acting through her representative the Governor, dismissed the Government of Rhodesia and the British Parliament passed the Southern Rhodesia Act, which declared that Southern Rhodesia (the legal name of the country then, although "Rhodesia" remained in common usage) continued to be part of Her Majesty's dominions and that the Government and Parliament of the United Kingdom continued to have responsibility and jurisdiction for and in respect of it. The Southern Rhodesia Order 1965 which was made under the Act declared that any constitution which the regime in Rhodesia may have purported to promulgate was void and of no effect. The Order also prohibited the Legislative Assembly from making laws or transacting any other business and declared any proceedings in defiance of this prohibition void and of no effect. It also suspended the ministerial system, empowered the Governor to exercise his functions without seeking ministerial advice and empowered a Secretary of State as well as the Governor to exercise the executive authority of Rhodesia on her Majesty's behalf.

In their approach towards the problem of granting Rhodesia independence, successive British Governments were guided by five principles, to which the Labour Government added a sixth:

1. The principle and intention of unimpeded progress to majority rule, already enshrined in the 1961 Constitution, would have to be maintained and guaranteed.

2. There would also have to be guarantees against retrogressive amendment of the Constitution.

3. There would have to be immediate improvement in the political status of the African population.

4. There would have to be progress towards ending racial discrimination.

5. The British Government would have to be satisfied that any basis proposed for independence was acceptable to the people of Rhodesia as a whole.

6. It would be necessary to ensure that, regardless of race, there was no oppression of majority by minority or minority by majority.

In September 1966, the Constitution Amendment Act became law, having passed all the parliamentary stages by two-thirds majorities. Under its terms, the Rhodesian government was given power to detain or restrict individuals in the interests of defense, public safety or public order, without recourse to proclamation of a state of emergency. These powers were held not to contravene the human rights explicitly protected under the 1961 Constitution. Persons detained in special centers could be obliged to perform tasks of forced labor. Other powers granted under the Act included the control and regulation of the publication of information about restricted persons and detention camps; the ability to detain individuals without a special order, pending consideration of the issue of such an order; and the ability to acquire property in satisfaction of any tax, rate or due.

The widening of the powers of the tribal courts was a further feature of the new Act. Customary law was made applicable to all Africans in Rhodesia, whether or not indigenous to the country, while the tribal courts were held to be non-discriminatory, even when members of the court were interested parties.

### The 1969 Constitution

With specific terms of reference, a five-men commission was set up in February 1967 to advise the Government on "the constitutional framework best suited to the sovereign independent status of Rhodesia and which is guaranteed to protect and guarantee the rights and freedoms of all persons and communities in Rhodesia and ensure that harmonious development of Rhodesia's plural society, having regard to the social and cultural different systems of land tenure and to the problem of economic development."

Two years later, in a referendum held on June 20, 1969, the Rhodesian Front constitutional proposals were approved by 54,724 votes to 20,776. At the same time, the predominantly white electorate also approved the proposal to declare Rhodesia a republic, by a vote of 61,130 to 14,327.[5] The necessary constitutional legislation was enacted in November 1969. The constitution also reconstituted Parliament as the House of Assembly — the lower chamber of a new bicameral Parliament, with the Senate created as an upper chamber following the South African system. The House of Assembly had 66 seats, including 50 Europeans, elected by 260,000 whites, Asians and Coloreds, and 8 Africans (four from Mashonaland and the other four from Matabeleland) elected by 4.5 million African voters, with another 8 Africans (again drawn equally from Mashonaland and Matabeleland) elected indirectly by tribal electoral colleges (chiefs, headmen and representatives of African district councils who were government-appointed officials). Africans on the "A" roll were transferred to the

---

5. *The Europa Year Book*, London, 1970.

African roll. The income and property qualifications for both African and non-African rolls were raised above those for the "A" and "B" rolls.

*Table 4: The House of Assembly*

| Representation | Voters' Roll | No. of Seats |
|---|---|---|
| European | White, Asian and Colored (260,000 inhabitants) | 50 |
| African: | 4.5m inhabitants | |
| Mashonaland | 80 % | 4 |
| Matabeleland | 20 % | 4 |
| Tribal Chiefs: | Tribal Electoral Colleges | |
| Mashonaland | | 4 |
| Matabeleland | | 4 |
| T O T A L | | 66 |

The Constitutional Council was replaced by a Senate of 23 members including 10 Europeans elected by the 50 white members of the House of Assembly, 10 Africans elected by an advisory Council of Chiefs (five of these African chiefs were from Mashonaland and the other five from Matabeleland). The remaining three members (of any race) were appointed by the President.[6] Members of both houses served for up to five years.

*Table 5: The Senate*

| Representation | Electoral College | No. of Seats |
|---|---|---|
| European | 50 White MPs | 10 |
| Tribal Chiefs: | Council of Chiefs | |
| Mashonaland | | 5 |
| Matabeleland | | 5 |
| Non-Racial | Presidential Nominees | 3 |
| T O T A L | | 23 |

A republic was declared on March 2, 1970, and the first elections under the new constitution were held that April, with the Rhodesian Front winning all 50 seats on the European roll. This constitution created the office of President and instituted loyalty oaths for government officials. The President was a constitutional Head of State appointed for a five-year term on the nomination of the Executive Council (Cabinet). The Council was responsible to the legislature.

---

6. *Ibid.*, London, 1978.

The President appointed the Prime Minister, and on the latter's recommendation, other ministers. For the first time, voter rolls were defined on an explicitly racial basis, and the possibility of eventual majority rule was denied by a stipulation in the constitution. The provision of the Republican Constitution included, *inter alia*, an increase in African representation tied to the increase in the proportion of income tax paid to the Exchequer by Africans. When the aggregate of income tax assessed on the income of Africans exceeded sixteen sixty-sixths of that assessed on the income of Europeans and Africans, then the number of African members in the House of Assembly would increase in proportion — but only until the number of African members equaled that of the European members. The government was granted still wider powers to restrict civil rights, and the power of the judiciary to rule on the constitutionality of legislation was given to the legislature itself.

In 1976, the constitution was amended to allow the Prime Minister to appoint ministers who would not be members of the House of Assembly.

One of the landmarks identified with the promulgation of the 1969 constitution was the land law that replaced the Land Apportionment Act of 1930. Despite the fact that most European farms were clearly under-utilized, the Land Tenure Act sought a solution to the European agricultural problem by expanding the amount of land available to white farmers, while more rigidly segregating African and European areas. This Act converted most existing "unreserved land" into European areas, but otherwise made only minor changes in designated boundaries. The Act divided the country into three basic categories of land: European, African, and "national" — the last comprising most of the national parks and game reserves. Under this Act, European and African lands were equalized, with African lands, designated as Tribal Trust Lands (TTLs), fixed at 16,151,520 hectares, or 41.4% of the total land in the country (40% was made available to European farms and settlements). Most of the remaining African lands (3.8%) were divided into non-communally owned Purchase Areas (*Kumatenganyika*).

One result of the Act was to fragment African lands into more than 160 units, which were generally the least productive agricultural lands and were overpopulated by both people and cattle. Promulgation of the law was followed by more vigorous government efforts to evict African "squatters" from European areas. Exchange of land between one area and the other was controlled by two Boards of Trustees, one to watch over the interests of Europeans and the other for Africans.

## CHAPTER 2. THE NEED FOR CONSTITUTIONAL CHANGE

### Settlement Talks

By the time a republic was declared (1970), four years of a real people's war, triggered by the Chinhoyi Battle, had gone by, with the subsequent establishment of permanent guerrilla bases in the northeast and east of the country. About five months after UDI, British officials had already begun visiting Salisbury to discuss a reopening of formal constitutional negotiations. The first formal negotiations held after UDI were the December 2-4, 1966, talks aboard the British cruiser HMS Tiger, just off Gibraltar. Two years after the abortive agreement produced by their "Tiger Talks," Ian Smith and British Prime Minister Harold Wilson met again between October 9-13, 1968, off Gibraltar, this time aboard the warship HMS Fearless, in talks that became known as the "Fearless Talks." Although Britain dropped the demand for a return to "legality," no agreement was reached.

However, in early 1971 British officials began holding secret talks with Rhodesian officials in Salisbury. By September, news of these talks was public and Lord Goodman was openly visiting Rhodesia as a special emissary. As a result, in mid-November 1971 Alec Douglas-Home, the British Foreign Secretary and former Prime Minister, met with Ian Smith in Salisbury. On November 24, an agreement was signed. Known as the "Anglo-Rhodesian Settlement Proposals," it called for immediately increased African representation (at that time 16) in Parliament, as more Africans met voting qualifications, until it equaled the Europeans' 50 seats. The creation of new African seats was to depend on the growth of a new higher African electoral roll, the qualifications being the same as those for Europeans. Two seats would be added for each 6% rise in the higher African roll, but half the new seats would be filled by indirect election by the College of Chiefs. When 50-50 parity was achieved, an independent commission would recommend whether or not 10 Common Roll seats should be added, to be voted for by all on the European and higher African rolls. By this time, both rolls should have about the same numbers. As more Africans qualified, they could out-vote the Europeans and produce an African majority in the Assembly. An agreed blocking mechanism would prevent retrogressive legislation. An independent commission would examine racial discrimination. Britain and Rhodesia would join a £100 million development and educational program and Africans would get more land. Once the British Government was satisfied by Rhodesian action on the franchise, discrimination and detainees, Parliament would be asked to grant Rhodesia independence and to end sanctions.

In contrast to earlier British settlement proposals, the 1971 agreement was based upon modification of the 1969 Constitution, not that of 1961. Britain held firm on one principle — that the proposals undergo a "test of acceptability" by the people of Zimbabwe as a whole before they would be implemented.

In pursuit of that principle, the British Government commissioned what became known as the "Pearce Commission" to investigate the acceptability of the proposals. Having arrived in the country in the third week of January 1972, the commission completed its work on March 10 and issued its formal report in late May. The Commission reported wide acceptance of the proposals among European settlers, mixed reactions among Asians and Coloreds, and 97% negative responses from the more than 100,000 Africans polled. On May 23, 1972, the Pearce Commission report was presented to the House of Commons by the Foreign Secretary. The Commission concluded that "the people of Rhodesia as a whole did not regard the proposals as acceptable as a basis for independence." The Anglo-Rhodesian proposals were then officially abandoned by Britain and the 1969 Constitution remained in force.

In the meantime, Muzorewa and Ian Smith continued to hold secret negotiations, which they openly acknowledged in 1973. More talks were held between Rhodesian government officials and African nationalist leaders in Lusaka in December 1974. In February 1975, Smith met with Nkomo, Muzorewa, Ndabaningi Sithole and others to set up a formal constitutional conference. After prolonged disagreement over the site of a conference, Smith and his top aides met with Abel Muzorewa, Ndabaningi Sithole, Joshua Nkomo, James Chikerema and others in a railroad dining car atop the Victoria Falls Bridge on August 25-26, 1975. South African Prime Minister John Vorster and Zambian President Kenneth Kaunda, who both gave support to *détente*, attended the first session of talks. The conference broke down the very next day, however, when Smith refused to consider allowing nationalists who were wanted by the Rhodesian police for "terrorist" activities to participate freely in politics within Zimbabwe.

After the collapse of the Victoria Falls Conference, Nkomo denounced Sithole and James Chikerema and returned to Salisbury as the head of the "internal" African National Council (ANC). On December 15, 1975, Smith and Nkomo began weekly talks (which were abandoned on March 19, 1976). On September 19, Ian Smith met with U.S. Secretary of State Henry Kissinger in Pretoria, after which he announced willingness to bring about African majority rule within two years. Joshua Nkomo, who was in Salisbury, announced his willingness to participate in a new round of constitutional talks based upon the proposals made by Kissinger.

This cordial atmosphere led to the Geneva Conference convened on October 28, 1976. The first major attempt at a negotiated constitutional settlement after the abortive August 1975 Victoria Falls Conference and the first settlement attempt in which Britain was directly involved after the 1972 Pearce Commission, the Geneva Conference was the product of a direct American diplomatic initiative. Under the chairmanship of the British UN Ambassador Ivor Richards, five delegations attended: Smith's government; Ndabaningi Sithole's branch of ZANU; Abel Muzorewa's branch of the ANC; Joshua Nkomo's wing of the ANC and Robert Mugabe's branch of ZANU. The latter two organizations had announced the formation of a "Patriotic Front" on the eve of the conference. In the second week of December, the conference adjourned for Christmas holidays without having achieved any substantial accords. In January 1977, the British government attempted to reopen the conference, but the Smith government refused to participate.

In order to appease the British and the outside world, the Rhodesian legislature amended the Land Tenure Act. The Act regulated the ownership, leasing and occupation of land in all areas and preserved the special status of TTLs within the African area. The Land Tenure Amendment Act, which came into force on April 1, 1977, removed racial restrictions on the ownership and use of all agricultural land, together with urban land zoned for industrial and commercial purposes in the former European Area (comprising 46.5% of the country). Racial restrictions were ended on the use of national parks and forests, but residential areas continued to be segregated.

On April 13, 1977, a new British initiative was made by Foreign Secretary David Owen, in Cape Town, where he met Ian Smith. Immediately after that, on April 16, Owen consulted with Smith in Salisbury, becoming the first British cabinet-level official to visit the country in six years. As a result of these consultations, on September 1, 1977, David Owen and American UN Ambassador Andrew Young met with Smith and local nationalist leaders in Salisbury to discuss new Anglo-American proposals and on September 24, the Frontline Presidents group endorsed the proposals. On September 25, Smith and two ministers flew secretly to Lusaka to confer with Kaunda and on September 28 Britain presented an Anglo-American plan to the UN Security Council.

As pressure for a constitutional settlement mounted, Smith announced, on November 24, conditional acceptance of the principle of "one man, one vote" for

Zimbabwe. On December 2, Smith opened a new round of internal negotiations with Muzorewa, Ndabaningi Sithole and Jeremiah Chirau of Zimbabwe United Peoples' Organization. Meanwhile, in January 1978, the leaders of the Patriotic Front met in secrecy on the island of Malta with the British Foreign Secretary David Owen and the US UN Representative Andrew Young. At the conclusion, Owen announced that the "Malta Talks" had resulted in the two PF leaders' acceptance of the idea of independently observed and supervised elections to end the war, but that they demanded the PF play a substantial role in any transition governing body during the period leading up to those elections. Smith and the "moderate" nationalist leaders inside the country, who were at that time engaged in negotiations, rejected the proposals.

## The 1979 Constitution

By this point in time, the tempo of events was stepping up considerably. On February 15, 1978, after the 37th session of internal settlement talks, Smith and the nationalist trio announced agreement on an eight-point plan calling for universal adult suffrage and a 100-member parliament with 28 seats reserved for whites. The agreement gave whites veto over legislative decisions for 10 years and maintained white control of the military, civil service, police and judiciary. In total, the constitution included more than 120 "entrenched" clauses which, in effect, guaranteed the continued political and economic control of the country by Europeans. The President was appointed by an electoral college consisting of members of the Senate and the House of Assembly. His term of office was six years, with a second term allowed. The President could be removed from office only by a vote of at least two-thirds of the members of the Senate and the House of Assembly.

The House of Assembly consisted of 100 members: 72 blacks elected by voters on a Common Voters' Roll; 20 whites, elected on a preferential voting system; and 8 additional whites, elected from 16 candidates nominated by the 20 white members of the House of Assembly.

*Table 6: The House of Assembly*

| Representation | Voters' Roll | No. of Seats |
|---|---|---|
| Common | Universal Adult Suffrage | 72 |
| Reserved (White) | Preferential System | 20 |
| Reserved (White) | Elected by 20 White MPs | 8 |
| TOTAL | | 100 |

The Senate was made up of 30 members: 10 white, 10 black and 10 chiefs elected by the Council of Chiefs.

*Table 7: The Senate*

| Representation | Electoral College | No. of Seats |
|---|---|---|
| African | 72 MPs in House of Assembly | 10 |
| Reserved (White) | 28 MPs in House of Assembly | 10 |
| Tribal Chiefs | Council of Chiefs | 10 |
| TOTAL | | 30 |

At the end of ten years or after the second Parliament, whichever was the longer, a Commission would be established to review the question of retaining the 28 white seats; it was to report to the House of Assembly. All citizens who were 18 years or over were eligible to be enrolled on the Common Voters' Roll. In addition, all whites who had attained the age of 18 were eligible to be enrolled on the White Voters' Roll. A minister or deputy minister who would not be a member of the Senate or House of Assembly could not hold office for longer than four months unless he became a member of either House.

The Declaration of Rights was enforceable by law and the High Court had powers to declare any law which was in contravention of the Declaration of Rights to be *ultra vires*. Existing laws were exempted from the provision of the Declaration of Rights for ten years, although this could not preclude the amendment or repeal of any such law. The amendment of entrenched provision of the Constitution required the affirmative votes of at least 78 members of the House of Assembly. The amendment of any other provision of the Constitution required the affirmative votes of two-thirds of the total membership of the House of Assembly. Any Bill to amend the Constitution also required the affirmative votes of two-thirds of the total membership of the Senate but if this could not be obtained, the Bill would, after a period of 180 days, be sent to the President for his assent despite the failure of the Senate to approve it.

Note, however, that this internal settlement was quickly rejected by the Patriotic Front and on March 14, the UN Security Council voted 10-0 to condemn the settlement (with the US, UK, France, Canada and West Germany abstaining). Following this, on April 2, US President Jimmy Carter, while visiting Nigeria, called for all-parties Rhodesian talks. In defiance, the multi-racial government on April 5 announced a cabinet composed of nine ministries with African and European co-ministers. Between April 14 and 15, US Secretary of State Cyrus Vance, UK Foreign Secretary David Owen, Robert Mugabe and Joshua Nkomo met in Dar es Salaam, but no agreement was reached. Nevertheless, on April 17 Vance and Owen met with the Executive Council in Salisbury in an effort to bridge the gap.

On February 28, 1979, Smith dissolved the Rhodesian Parliament, officially ending 88 years of minority white rule. After the election held April 17-21, the 1979 constitution was passed in accordance with provisions of the existing Constitution on the recommendation of the Constitution Commission established in March 1978 by the transitional government.

Produced as a result of the Internal Settlement agreement, the 1979 constitution created the Republic of Zimbabwe-Rhodesia. The office of President and the Executive Council (Cabinet), which held actual authority, were retained from the 1969 Constitution. The first general elections in which Africans voted for government officials were held April 17-21, with Bishop Abel Muzorewa's ANC collecting 51 seats of the 72 African seats; 12 seats went to Ndabaningi Sithole's ZANU and 9 to Chief K. Ndiweni's United National Federal Party.[7]

## The Lusaka Accord and the Lancaster House Constitution

After Margaret Thatcher became the new British Prime Minister in May 1979, Britain renewed efforts to end the constitutional conflict. During the bi-annual Commonwealth meeting in Lusaka in August 1979, the Lusaka Accord was signed, calling for a new constitution, free elections and independence. Within a week of the end of that conference, the British Foreign Secretary, Lord Peter Carrington, had issued invitations to all parties concerned with the resolution of the war and the future independence of the country.

Negotiations for a settlement began at Lancaster House in London on September 10, 1979. The Lancaster House Conference was the first all-parties conference held since the failed October 1976 Geneva Conference. The Zimbabwe-Rhodesia government delegation was led by the Prime Minister, Abel Muzorewa and Ian Smith, who in effect represented the country's European community. The Patriotic Front delegation was led by Robert Mugabe of ZANU and Joshua Nkomo of ZAPU. Lord Carrington represented the British government and was the chairman of the conference.

---

7. *Zimbabwe: The Rise to Nationhood*, Minerva Press, London, 1998.

The conference began by the tabling for discussion of a draft constitution written by British officials. This contained plans for a parliamentary system of government, guarantees for representation of the European minority following independence and acceptance by the new government of existing government debts and obligations, particularly those of civil servants. Surprisingly, this draft constitution contained quite a substantial number of similarities to the contested "Zimbabwe-Rhodesia" constitution. For example, there were reserved seats for whites; a declaration of human rights; no land nationalization; entrenched clauses. After protracted negotiations, a parliamentary form of government with reserved 20% representation for the European community for a period of seven years in a Parliament of 100 seats was accepted by both sides. They also agreed that entrenched clauses could only be legally amended by a two-thirds vote of Parliament.

On land redistribution, it was required that the new independent government pay full compensation for all land acquired by the government for redistribution and would guarantee minority rights. The parties agreed to the new constitution on October 18, 1979, almost a month after the convening of the conference. The final Lancaster House Agreement was signed on December 21, 1979.

The Lancaster House Agreement also called for a short transition period of three to four months and the appointment of a British governor who would exercise full executive and legislative authority. During the transition period, free elections, which would implement the new constitution, would be held. Muzorewa initially balked at the idea of new elections, but eventually agreed.

In the wake of the final agreement, the Zimbabwe-Rhodesia House of Assembly voted on December 12, 1979 to cease to exist as an independent state and return to colonial status under a British-appointed governor. Later that day, Lord Soames arrived in Salisbury and took over responsibility for governing the country and Zimbabwe-Rhodesia officially ceased to exist.

The Lancaster House Constitution took effect on April 18, 1980, with the independence of the Republic of Zimbabwe. The Constitution provided for a Declaration of Rights guaranteeing the fundamental rights and freedom of the individual, regardless of race, tribe, place of origin, political opinions, color, creed or sex. The following rights and freedoms were protected: the right to life; the right to personal liberty; protection from slavery and forced labor; protection from inhuman treatment; protection from deprivation of property; protection from arbitrary search or entry; the right to protection of the law; freedom of conscience; freedom of expression; freedom of assembly and association; freedom of movement; freedom from discrimination.

In addition, the Constitution called for the protection of minority rights and was entrenched for a period of 10 years. It also provided for special legislative representation of 20 seats out of 100 for Europeans for a period of seven years. It guaranteed that all government obligations of previous regimes would be respected, and that fair compensation would be paid for any land acquired by the new government for resettlement.

This constitution also retained the office of the President and a parliamentary form of government. Before it was amended, the Constitution provided that each candidate for the Presidency was to be nominated by not fewer than ten members of the House of Assembly; if only one candidate was nominated, he would be declared to be elected without the necessity of a ballot. Otherwise, a ballot would be held amongst an Electoral College consisting of the members of the House of Assembly and the Senate. The President would hold office for six years and would be eligible for re-election. The President would be Head of State and Commander-in-Chief of the Defense Forces.

The Parliament consisted of a Senate and a House of Assembly. The Senate consisted of 40 senators: 14 elected by an electoral college of those members of the House of Assembly elected by voters registered on the common roll and ten by those members elected by voters on the separate white roll; five were chiefs in Mashonaland, elected by an electoral college consisting of those chiefs in Mashonaland who were members of the Council of Chiefs, and five were chiefs in Matabeleland, similarly elected; the remaining six members were to be appointed by the President.

The House of Assembly consisted of 100 members, elected by universal adult suffrage from 80 common roll constituencies and 20 white roll constituencies. The life of the Parliament was ordinarily to be five years.

*Table 8: The House of Assembly*

| Representation | Voters' Roll | No. of Seats |
|---|---|---|
| Common | Universal Adult Suffrage | 80 |
| Reserved (White) | White, Asian and Colored | 20 |
| TOTAL | | 100 |

Table 9: The Senate

| Representation | Electoral College | No. of Seats |
|---|---|---|
| Common | 80 MPs in House of Assembly | 14 |
| Reserved (White) | 20 MPs in House of Assembly | 10 |
| Tribal Chiefs: Mashonaland Matabeleland | Council of Chiefs | 5 5 |
| Non-Racial | Presidential Appointees | 6 |
| T O T A L | | 40 |

Amendments to the Constitution had to be voted by not less than two-thirds of the members of the Senate and not fewer than 70 members of the House of Assembly. In addition, amendments to entrenched clauses relating to the representation of whites required the approval of all the members of the House of Assembly.

Executive authority was vested in the President, who acted on the advice of the Cabinet. Before the Constitution was amended, the President appointed as Prime Minister the person who, in his opinion, was best able to command the support of the majority of members of the House of Assembly. The President, acting on the advice of the Prime Minister, appointed other Ministers and Deputy Ministers, to be members of the Cabinet.

The Constitution also provided for an Ombudsman, appointed by the President, acting on the advice of the Judicial Service Commission, to investigate complaints against actions taken by employees of the Government or of a local authority. Chiefs were appointed by the President and formed a Council of Chiefs from their number, in accordance with customary principles of succession. Other provisions related to the Judiciary, Defense and Police Forces, public service and finance.

## Countless Amendments to the Lancaster House Constitution

The Lancaster House Constitution was modelled on the Westminster style of democracy. Its major weaknesses were that it implied a winner-takes-all status and that it was basically a transitional document. Because of the problem with delimitation of constituencies in a country that had just gone through many years of armed conflict, the first elections were contested on proportional representation. Therefore, when ZANU (PF) won the elections in 1980, it used the opportunity to form a coalition with other minority parties represented in both houses of parliament. On the face of it, there seemed nothing sinister about it. This was a time for reconciliation; the country had undergone a devastating civil war that pitted not only blacks against whites but also blacks against blacks.

When the nationalist forces went to Lancaster House to confer on the future of Zimbabwe, then known as Zimbabwe-Rhodesia, there were three main stakeholders in the conference proceedings: the British Government as the colonial power, the Zimbabwe-Rhodesia Government with Bishop Abel Muzorewa as Prime Minister and Ian Smith representing white interests, and the Patriotic Front represented by Robert Mugabe's ZANU and Joshua Nkomo's ZAPU.

As soon as a settlement was reached and a date for elections sat, the Patriotic Front split into its former two hostile factions and decided to contest the elections as independent entities. The hostility between ZANU and ZAPU was well known. For decades, the parties had been at each other's throats, much to the satisfaction of the Rhodesian Government. Thus, when ZANU (PF) gained 57 seats out of a possible 80 (since 20 seats were reserved for the white minority), reconciliation and unity was the logical policy for the party to promote. It is to be remembered that the Lancaster House Constitution required a two-thirds majority if the government of the day wanted to change any clauses in the document. Of course, it is understood that there were some entrenched clauses which could not be repealed until after a stipulated period, for example, seven years in the question of the 20 reserved seats.

Slowly, but in a calculated manner, the independence government was able to change some non-controversial clauses in the constitution with the help of Joshua Nkomo's Patriotic Front-ZAPU. One example is the electoral law whereby the government was able to choose members of both the Delimitation and Electoral Supervisory Commissions. The fact that Zimbabwe did not have an effective opposition in parliament was in part a result of changes made in the Lancaster House Constitution, fashioned to serve the one-party state ambitions of the ruling ZANU (PF) party. Thus, Zimbabwe found itself in a situation where she could change the constitution without an effective opposition in parliament and the country could not have an effective opposition in parliament unless it amended or repealed those aspects of the constitution and those offending pieces of legislation which stood in the way of a truly democratic disposition. Any chance of a voluntary reform of the constitution that would amount to an erosion of the political establishment's current sweeping powers appeared remote.

The Lancaster House Constitution got its first face-lift in 1981. Amendment No. 1 (Act 27 of 1981) dealt with qualifications for legal practitioners in Zimbabwe and appointments of members of the Senate Legal Committee, a key organ that would be a guardian of the constitution. Entry qualifications, particularly the number of years spent in practice in Zimbabwe, were lowered to allow quick entry for black Zimbabweans, some of whom had been practicing abroad.

Instead of having the general and appellate division of the High Court, the government introduced the High Court and Supreme Court while references to advocates and attorneys were removed and the term "legal practitioners" introduced instead. The position of Chief Justice was created to head the judiciary and the Supreme Court.

In the face of the war against dissidents in Matabeleland and parts of the Midlands, the legislature passed the Emergency Powers (Security Forces Indemnity) Regulations 1982. This was to exonerate the Fifth Brigade for atrocities committed. Thus, after the signing of the unity accord in December 1987, both the ZIPRA guerrillas and all government forces were excused for their actions.

During 1983, the Government took measures to prevent subversive activity; Matabeleland was placed under curfew. In addition to the deployment of the Korean-trained Fifth Brigade in Matabeleland, new laws were introduced in September, providing for further press censorship and granting the security forces greater powers under the state of emergency introduced by Ian Smith's regime in 1965. In November 1983, Bishop Muzorewa was arrested on suspicion of having subversive links with South Africa. The state of emergency was renewed every six months from 1984.

The 2nd amendment of the constitution (Act 1 of 1983) revised qualifications for membership of the Judicial Service Commission and the Electoral Supervisory Commission. The third amendment of the constitution also took place in 1983. Amendment Act No. 3 allowed for the appointment of a minister without the person being a member of Parliament although he/she was required to become a member of either of the two chambers, at the time, within three months of such an appointment. Under the same amendment, the term "tribal trust lands" which used to designate the waste lands where most blacks were concentrated was replaced by "communal lands."

Another amendment to the constitution came in 1984. Amendment Act No. 4 gave the President flexibility in appointing an acting judge or appointments to the Judicial Service Commission by reducing the period the person was required

37

to have practiced in Zimbabwe from seven to five years. It also introduced direct political control by allowing the President to appoint judges, the Ombudsman, Director of Prisons, Police and Defense Forces officers and the Comptroller and Auditor-General.

In December 1985, the government enacted legislation barring Zimbabweans from holding dual citizenship, which affected the European community to a much greater extent than Africans. This Act also removed the automatic right of former Rhodesians to Zimbabwean citizenship if they had become citizens of other countries, unless they renounced the other citizenship. A landmark amendment to the constitution came during the same year when Amendment Act No. 5 introduced provincial governors with ministerial status in each of Zimbabwe's eight provinces.

Canaan Banana, the only candidate, was sworn in for a second term of office as President in April 1986. In anticipation of the abolition of the 20 seats reserved for whites in the House of Assembly (as permitted by the Constitution, subject to a majority vote in the House), three white independent MPs joined ZANU (PF) in July 1986 and four CAZ members defected to ZANU (PF) in August.

Meanwhile, in April 1987, Ian Smith was suspended from the House of Assembly for one year, owing to verbal denigration of ZANU (PF) leadership and the support that he had given to white South Africa, which was threatened by economic sanctions. In May of the same year, he resigned as leader of the CAZ.

Among the most far reaching changes to the Lancaster House Agreement were two amendments to the Zimbabwe Constitution in 1987. On August 21, the government introduced legislation to abolish the reserved white seats and it met unanimous approval in Parliament. In September, the Senate approved the bill (amendment number six) abolishing the European-reserved seats (20 in the House of Assembly and 10 in the Senate). This section had been entrenched for seven years to safeguard white interests during the initial phase of majority rule. Thus, in the following month, the 80 remaining members of the House of Assembly elected 20 candidates who were nominated by ZANU (PF), including 11 whites, to fill the vacant seats in the House of Assembly until the next general elections, to be held in 1990. Candidates who were also sponsored by ZANU (PF), including four whites, were elected to the vacant posts in the Senate by the new 100-member House of Assembly. (No members of PF-ZAPU were elected.)

Amendment No. 6 also authorized the Prime Minister to appoint a Delimitation Commission at intervals of less than five years.

In October of the same year, Parliament adopted another major constitutional amendment, whereby the ceremonial presidency was to be replaced by an executive presidency. The post of Prime Minister was to be incorporated into the presidency. The 7th Constitution of Zimbabwe Amendment (Act 23 of 1987) provided for an Executive Presidency to be elected by the House of Assembly and then by the electorate in the next general election. The executive presidency would combine the roles of head of state, head of government and commander-in-chief. It authorized the President to appoint the Commissioner of Police, Defense Force Commander, Attorney-General, Permanent Secretaries and their deputies. The amendment also provided that presidential prerogatives could not be challenged in court.[8]

In December, Prime Minister Robert Mugabe was nominated as sole candidate for the presidency, and President Banana retired shortly afterwards. On December 31, 1987, Mugabe was inaugurated as Zimbabwe's first Executive President. Two days later, President Mugabe announced a new Cabinet, with extensive changes and an increased membership, which included several PF-ZAPU officials. Joshua Nkomo was appointed as one of the three Senior Ministers in the President's Office who were to form a "super cabinet" to oversee policy and review ministerial performance, in association with the President.

Meanwhile, the long-awaited unity agreement was finally signed on December 22, 1987 by Prime Minister Robert Mugabe and Joshua Nkomo. The accord was later ratified by both parties in April 1988.

The state of emergency (which had been renewed every six months since Zimbabwe's independence) remained in force, owing to incursions into eastern Zimbabwe by Mozambican Renamo rebels.

In October 1988, student unrest resulted in the temporary closure of the University of Zimbabwe and in the arrest of several students; the Secretary-General of the Zimbabwe Congress of Trade Unions (ZCTU) was also detained temporarily, owing to his criticism of the Government's methods at suppressing the unrest. In the following month, the Government was accused by the Supreme Court of failing to respect court decisions.

The 8th amendment (Act 4 of 1989) fine-tuned the new presidential powers. It allowed a vice-president to act for the President and confirmed and expanded the role for the office of the Attorney-General as the principal legal adviser to the government, with permission to sit in both Cabinet and

---

8. As Minister of Justice, Legal and Parliamentary Affairs at that time, Eddison Zvobgo is blamed for having created the dreaded Executive Presidency.

Parliament, but with no voting powers. It also gave him power to direct police investigations. In essence, the AG can stop police investigations against a minister or any Executive appointee. Legal experts believe that this exposes the AG's office to undue influence and compromise from cabinet colleagues.

By June 1996, corruption seemed to have become so chronic that it was necessary to amend the Prevention of Corruption Act to prohibit public employees from accepting gifts from people with whom they do official business. Under the amendment, public servants would also be required to account for any assets they may possess beyond what is commensurate with their lawful incomes.

During the general elections of March 1990, legislation (that had been passed in late 1989) came into effect abolishing the Senate and increasing the number of seats in the House of Assembly from 100 to 150. One hundred and twenty seats were to be directly elected, 12 were to be allocated to presidential nominees, 10 were to be allocated to traditional Chiefs and eight were to be allocated to Provincial Governors, also directly nominated by the President.

*Table 10: The Parliament*

| Representation | Voters' Roll | No. of Seats |
|---|---|---|
| Common | Universal Adult Suffrage | 120 |
| Traditional Chiefs | Council of Chiefs | 10 |
| Non-Partisan | Presidential Appointees | 12 |
| Provincial Governors | Presidential Appointees | 8 |
| TOTAL | | 150 |

Constitutional Amendment No. 9 also had a provision whereby members of Parliament defecting or expelled from their parties would lose their seats, but those appointed by the President would be under no such obligation. This Act also allowed the constitution, including the Bill of Rights, to be amended by a two-thirds parliamentary majority.

1990 also witnessed two amendments to the constitution. Amendment No. 10 (Act 15 of 1990) provided for the appointment of not more than two vice-presidents. Following the unity accord between former ZANU (PF) and PF-ZAPU and the general elections, it had been found politically necessary to create a senior position for former PF-ZAPU leader, Joshua Nkomo. This amendment took effect on August 3, 1990. During the same month, at a meeting of the politburo of the ruling ZANU (PF), a majority of the members announced their opposition to a proposal by President Mugabe for the introduction of a one-party political system.

In October 1990, after 25 years, the state of emergency was repealed. However, Zimbabwe remains in a permanent state of emergency because of the existence of the Presidential Powers (Temporary Measures) Act which allows the President to assume legislative powers on behalf of Parliament even in circumstances that do not warrant decrees. Using these powers on November 27, 1998, the President suspended parliamentary powers for six months and amended the Labour Relations Act to make strike action illegal. This was after the ZCTU had organized highly successful job stayaways on November 11 and 18. The amendment stipulates that any employer, organization, trade union or its federation found guilty of recommending, encouraging, or inciting employees in any way to embark on illegal protests faces the prospect of losing its license. It would then be illegal to collect or pay dues to the banned organizations. Furthermore, the Act deems that all employers who recommend their staff to join such actions, or help them to facilitate such action, shall be found guilty of a criminal offence and be either fined up to Z$100,000 (US$2500) or jailed for up to three years, or both. The same penalties can be meted out to officials and union officers.

In addition, those who recommend, incite or organize unlawful collective action can be sued for damages by those who have lost property or been injured as a result of the action. Owners of commuter omnibuses who facilitate unlawful collective action will lose their transport licenses. Withdrawing services will be considered facilitating such action.

Parliament, the Politburo and the Cabinet, most of whose members have been cowed into submission, could be counted on to rubber stamp all that the President says and does. As the President continued to consolidate his powers, the 11th amendment signaled the beginning of the feud between the Judiciary and the Executive. After a Supreme Court ruling that corporal punishment was "inhuman and degrading" and therefore violated the constitution, a ruling applauded internationally, the Executive went to Parliament and sought an amendment to Section 15 to allow for corporal punishment on people under 18 years by a competent authority or by a parent. This amendment also formally established Zimbabwe as a republic, incorporated customary law into the legal system and authorized the acquisition of land for resettlement. The legislation that permitted the compulsory acquisition of land by the Government was approved by the House of Assembly in March 1992. This was expected to facilitate the redistribution of land ownership from Europeans (who owned about one-third of farming land in 1992) to Africans.

Following this, two more amendments of the constitution were made in 1993. Amendment No. 12 (Act 4 of 1993) excluded courts from inquiring into compensation of acquired land while it also unified the defense forces command structure. Sensing that the Supreme Court could soon abolish the death penalty on the grounds that hanging was inhuman and degrading, the Executive also reinforced this aspect by inserting a clause which confirmed the constitutionality of hanging. Amendment No. 13 (Act 9 of 1993) allowed for the delay in carrying out executions as not being inhuman and degrading. This amendment was triggered by the Supreme Court's decision in the case involving the Catholic Commission for Justice and Peace, on the one hand, and the Attorney-General and others, on the other: the Court had ruled that long delays in execution had infringed the rights of four people who were to be hanged. The death sentences were later commuted to life imprisonment.

Earlier in August 1992, the House of Assembly had flexed its muscles when several ZANU (PF) MPs denounced the creation (in the July reorganization) of the new Ministry of National Affairs, Employment Creation and Cooperatives, claiming that it was superfluous. This ministry took over the functions of the controversial Ministry of Political Affairs through which ZANU (PF) acquired funding for its political activities (including the building of its party headquarters at Rotten Row). In the following month, however, the House of Assembly approved legislation which granted government funding to any party with at least 15 seats in the Assembly (in effect only ZANU PF); the opposition strongly contested this measure, accusing the Government of misappropriating public funds during a period of national economic hardship.

The Political Parties (Finance) Act came under scrutiny in the Supreme Court when Bishop Abel Muzorewa's United Parties filed an application, in July 1997, contesting against Zimbabwe's Electoral Act and the funding of political parties under the Act. During the hearing, the question that took center stage was whether continued funding of the ruling ZANU (PF) by treasury disadvantaged other political parties. Also debated was the control over the electoral process by the government of the day. Justice Mcnally, in his contribution, said: "The more I think about it, the more I cannot see its relevance; the criterion by seats is not reasonable."[9]

---

9. Panafrican News Agency, 30 July, 1997.

On September 5, 1997, the Supreme Court delivered a stunning blow to President Robert Mugabe's ruling ZANU (PF) by preventing the party from taking all the state subsidy intended to encourage multi-party democracy. A full bench of the country's highest court ruled that the Political Parties (Finance) Act violated voters' constitutional rights to hear the views of the other parties, and that the minimum qualification of 15 seats in Parliament was too high, making it virtually impossible for other parties to mount a meaningful challenge in elections. Sitting with judges of appeal Ibrahim, Mcnally, Korsah and Muchechetere, the Chief Justice Anthony Gubbay said that the present financing of political parties made it impossible for new parties to come on stream. "The system should give a chance for some sort of basis with which to put forward one's views," he said.[10] The court noted that while in the 1990 elections, opposition parties took 20% of the vote, in the past two elections they have captured just three seats.

For the past five years to 1997, the ZANU (PF)-dominated Parliament had voted millions of dollars to itself on the grounds that no other party made the minimum cut off of 15 seats. The Act had been a major source of concern among opposition political parties; the high threshold gave the ruling party Z\$32 million per annum (US\$1 = 12.5 zimdollars), an unfair advantage that violated freedom of expression.

The government took no time to amend the Political Parties (Finance) Act in order to change the threshold for parties to get public funding. Without issuing a White Paper or consulting with opposition parties, taxpayers or other civic organizations, Minister of Justice, Legal and Parliamentary Affairs Emmerson Mnangagwa introduced an amendment which was based on the threshold of votes cast, not the number of seats. This meant that other political parties would then qualify and benefit from public funding even if they failed to get seats. While the opposition ZANU (Ndonga) welcomed government's move to amend the Act, the independent Harare South MP Margaret Dongo accused the ruling party of changing goal posts whenever it was defeated in court. United Parties felt that while they concurred with the Supreme Court that there was nothing wrong with the funding of political parties, it was improper to amend the Act without proper consultations.

Following the amendment, the threshold for financial support would be 5% of votes with allocation of funds being proportional to votes garnered. For

---

10. *Ibid.*

example, a party which receives 60% of the ballot cast would be entitled to 60% of the funds allocated under the Act.

The Supreme Court's judgment was further proof that in the absence of durable democratic institutions and with Parliament powerless to stop blatant infringement of the law by the Executive, the judiciary remained one of the few custodians of the constitution. However, political analysts wondered how long the Executive would allow the judiciary to erode its powers with its unadulterated interpretation of the law. It was felt there would come a time, if it had not come already, that appointments to the judiciary would be made with an eye to favorable determinations from the bench. Many found that the checks and balances that should be the norm in a tripartite democracy were increasingly being canceled out as the executive assumed disproportionate powers.

Notwithstanding, the challenge to the Political Parties (Finance) Act by the United Parties was a breath of fresh air in an era of political apathy and indifference. It was a living example of what was possible in a functioning democracy when political parties with a clear vision execute their mandate on behalf of the electorate. With effective opposition in Parliament, such self-serving legislation would be consigned to the House's dustbin, thus avoiding the time and money wasted in litigation (at the taxpayer's expense) each time the government lost its case.

The Electoral Act itself leaves a lot to be desired. According to the Electoral Act, the office of the Registrar-General is the principal agency responsible for conducting all aspects of elections. In carrying out the duties of this office, the Registrar-General (Article 15(2)), "shall not to be subject to the direction or control of any person or authority other than the Election Directorate, but shall have regard to any report or recommendation of the Electoral Supervisory Commission." However, according to the ESC, this had not been the case. While the Electoral Act makes the Registrar-General the primary person responsible for the conducting of elections, the President is given sweeping powers to control the election process. Article 158 specifically empowers the President to suspend or amend any provision of the Electoral Act and to alter any time period specified by the Electoral Act.

The election authorities, particularly the Registrar-General, are the subject of considerable controversy. Opposition political parties and civil society organizations consistently express concerns over the lack of credibility and independence of election authorities; a partisan bias in the work of election authorities; lack of transparency in the election preparations; and a lack of institutional coordination. Questions were raised in particular about the recruiting of polling officials. In the past, primarily teachers staffed the polling stations. Some political parties and civic organizations expressed concern that war veterans could be recruited for these posts during the June 24-25, 2000 elections.

In an apparent attempt to improve Government's standing with the public, a list of 70 commercial farms (covering some 190,000 ha) was published in May 1993, detailing those properties allocated for acquisition by the State under the Land Acquisition Act. However, publication of the list provoked a strong protest from the white-dominated Commercial Farmers' Union, which challenged the proposed acquisitions on the grounds that they contravened a previous undertaking by the Government that only land that was idle or derelict would be acquired for redistribution. In September, six white farmers took the issue to the High Court, where they sought a declaration that the acquisition of their land would be unconstitutional; the Government contested their action.

In February 1994, in anticipation of a possible influx of whites from South Africa, following the general election to be held there in April, the Zimbabwean Government drafted a bill which would make immigration laws significantly more stringent and would lengthen — to 10 years — the qualifying period of resident status. The bill was also designed to deprive former "Rhodies" of their automatic right to return and settle in Zimbabwe.

A new law, the Private and Voluntary Organizations Amendment Act No. 14, passed in July 1995, enabled the government to sack outspoken board members of any independent charitable organization or non-governmental organization (NGO) and replace them with government-blessed appointees. Under the new law, the Ministry of Social Welfare acquired powers to remove NGO officials and blacklist any NGO in the "national interest," thus preventing them from operating in the country. However, the Supreme Court, in the matter of Sekai Holland and others versus the Minister of Public Service, Labour and Social Welfare, struck down section 21 of the Act. The section, which empowered the minister to suspend a member of the executive committee of an NGO, was held to be *ultra vires* section 18(9) of the present constitution of Zimbabwe in that it deprived an individual of the right to a fair hearing.

The government had another setback in August 1995, when the High Court nullified the election result in one Harare constituency (Harare South) on the grounds that the number of votes polled exceeded the total number of registered electors.

In 1996, the 15th amendment to the Lancaster House Constitution barred discrimination by gender. Specifically, it did away with any preferential right to enter and stay in Zimbabwe for foreign husbands of Zimbabwean women and for foreign wives of Zimbabwean men who were entitled to pass on Zimbabwean citizenship to their children.

Nearly 95% of a total of 340 changes in the constitution involved real constitutional provisions, with the rest representing definitions. Since 1980, there were amendments to nearly 200 sections, sub-sections or paragraphs. More than 60 new parts were inserted, over 50 were modified while at least 30 parts, including Part 2 Chapter V and the whole of Chapter VI, were replaced by new laws.[11]

The new telecommunications law, highly indicative of the government's attitude, was presented for review in the 1998 Parliamentary session. The Zimbabwe Communications Bill led to the formation of the Independent Broadcasting Authority (IBA), whose powers specifically excluded the granting of broadcasting licenses. Clause 33 (2) provided that only the Zimbabwe Broadcasting Corporation (ZBC) shall operate, or have in its possession or control, a broadcast station. This clause effectively retains the ZBC's monopoly over the airwaves. The Zimbabwe chapter of the Media Institute of Southern Africa was worried that by providing for this monopoly and establishing an authority appointed by the Minister of Information, Posts and Telecommunications in consultation with the President, the bill would undermine attempts to free the airwaves and create an independent authority appointed to regulate broadcasting and telecommunications activities in the public interest. The draft Bill also retained monopoly in telecommunications services, with the exception of cellular phone services, for a successor company of the existing Posts and Telecommunications Corporation (PTC). All shares in the successor company would be held by persons nominated by the Minister of Information on behalf of the state.

Clause 95 gave the President the power, in the interest of public security or the maintenance of law and order, to give a postal and telecommunications licensee direction to intercept any postal article or communications transmitted by means of a telecommunication service. It empowers the President to order a postal or telecoms licensee to:

intercept or detain a postal article and deliver it to an employee of the state to be disposed of in such a manner as directed by the President;

or intercept or monitor any telecoms service; or

suspend any telecoms service or service to a named person.

---

11. Institute of Directors Zimbabwe, Direct Report, Vol. 4 No.3, June 1999-September 1999

It also allows a police officer to order that a postal article be detained under suspicion that it may contain evidence, without the requirement of a court order. In addition it provided for a fine of up to Z$2,500 and/or imprisonment of up to six months for making a phone call with the purpose of causing annoyance, inconvenience or needless anxiety.

The law, passed in February 2000, also gave the President power to suspend any telecommunication services established, maintained or worked by the telecommunications licensee. Generally, the new bill gave considerable power to the Minister of Information, Posts and Telecommunications who would, in consultation with the state President, appoint board members of the Authority (clause 6). The minister would also be in charge of all hiring and suspensions of IBA staff (clauses 8; 10; 11 and 12). This effectively voided the freedom of the press.

As further evidence of its displeasure with criticism, the Zimbabwean government proposed a new information Bill in November 2001. The proposed legislation, the Access to Information and Protection of Privacy Bill, was designed ostensibly to make public officials and institutions they represent more accountable to the taxpayer, protect personal privacy and regulate Zimbabwe's media operations. The Bill was designed to give enormous powers to the Minister of Information and Publicity in the President's Office.

It was a great relief to Zimbabweans when the Parliamentary Legal Committee, at the end of January 2002, was able to press for amendments to remove all the unconstitutional clauses from this draconian law. The bill included provisions that effectively would have meant that access to public information would be worse off than previously. The Zimbabwe Chapter of the Media Institute of Southern Africa resolved to set up a network of lawyers under a legal defense fund (The Media Defense Fund) for media practitioners and the possibility of setting up an editors' forum.

Land reform was addressed just before the Fourth Parliament of Zimbabwe was dissolved in April 2000. A controversial bill was passed empowering the government to seize white-owned farms to resettle landless blacks, without paying adequate compensation. The Zimbabwe constitution amendment (No. 16) compels Britain, Zimbabwe's former colonial master, to honor a pledge it made at independence in 1980 to fund the transfer of white-owned farms to peasant black farmers. "The former colonial power has an obligation to pay compensation for agricultural land compulsorily acquired for resettlement through a fund established for the purpose," the bill, enacted on April 6, 2000, states. "If the former colonial power fails to pay compensation through such a fund, the government of Zimbabwe has no obligation to pay compensation for agricultural land compulsorily acquired for resettlement," it added.

The amendment was voted into law with the minimum 100 votes, exactly two-thirds, although President Mugabe had 147 ZANU (PF) MPs — an indication that the President did not carry all his members on this issue.

In the meantime, Britain said it could not be bound by the constitutional amendment, arguing that a country cannot shift its legal obligations to another sovereign country. However, Britain has repeatedly pledged support for the land reform program as long as it was done in a transparent and orderly manner.

Those whose farms are taken by the government under the 16th amendment could still challenge the acquisition in court and demand compensation. The government did not have the power to compulsorily acquire land without paying compensation, as they would have to amend Section 20 of the Land Acquisition Act first — the Land Acquisition Act (enacted in 1990 and amended in 1992) required compensation and also provided for farmers to object to the acquisition of their farms in court.

Surely, if the government was serious about solving the land issue through constitutional means, it could not have dissolved Parliament without amending the Land Acquisition Act. Or, maybe President Mugabe was so pleased with the passing of the constitutional amendment that he forgot to amend the Act before dissolving Parliament.

Legal and political observers interviewed said the failure to amend the Act showed that the constitutional amendment was just a political gimmick by the government ahead of the elections due in June 2000. Professor Ncube, who is also the secretary-general of the country's biggest opposition party, the Movement for Democratic Change (MDC), said, "Part of the incompetence of this government can be seen in its handling of the land issue. It does not even know what it is supposed to do in order to take land without compensation. That constitutional amendment does not give the government exclusive powers to take land without compensation, contrary to what the government is telling people." David Coltart, a prominent lawyer, observed, "What the government just did shows what a gimmick all this is. It does not help to amend the constitution without amending the underlying Land Acquisition Act and they cannot do that now because Parliament has been dissolved and cannot be reconvened. So the government would have to wait for the next Parliament to be elected."

Agreeing with David Coltart, Professor Ncube said, "Although the President can use the Presidential Powers (Temporary Measures) Act to amend the Land Acquisition Act, this would only be valid for six months upon which it would have to be passed by the new Parliament."[12]

The 16th constitutional amendment also included a provision for the formation of an anti-corruption commission. The independence of the proposed commission is, however, questionable given that it is appointed by the President and can only prosecute culprits through the Attorney-General's office. What it means is that if the AG decides not to prosecute, there is nothing that the commission can do. Moreover, given that the AG is a presidential appointee, sits in Cabinet and is not answerable to Parliament, the proposed commission is likely to have a credibility problem.

On February 13, 2004, President Mugabe used his presidential powers[13] to fast-track a new law that allows the police to hold suspects accused of economic crimes for up to four weeks without bail. (The constitution allows police to hold suspects for only 48 hours. After the period expires, they have to be brought to court where they may ask for bail.) The regulations violate the presumption of innocence contained in Section 18 subsection 3 of the constitution.

A growing trend towards Marxist-Leninist authoritarianism was confirmed by a number of events in Zimbabwe during the 1980s and 90s. Firstly, virtually all of the constitutional amendments passed by the legislature thus far have been self-serving and restricted rather than enhanced public liberties. Secondly, there was a growing resort to the judicial process by ordinary citizens and/or company executives and farmers who felt that their rights have been violated by state structures and public officials. Thirdly, there was a growing trend of abuse of public office for personal benefit and self-preservation at the expense of the common good. Lastly, but not least, there was increasing violation of laid down procedures in the government tender system — the awarding of public projects aimed at benefiting the destitute and disadvantaged in society, with some of the benefits being looted by the "chefs" themselves.

Under amendments to the Road Traffic Act (early 2003), it is even punishable for Zimbabweans to gesture at the presidential motorcade.

### Retention of Colonial Laws

One of the main targets of the nationalist movements of the 1950s was the campaign for the abolition of "pass" laws (which required that all adult African

---

12. *The Zimbabwe Standard*, 23-29 April, 2000.

13. The Presidential Powers (Temporary Measures) (Amendment of Criminal Procedure and Evidence Act) regulations, contained in Statutory Instrument (SI) 37 of 2004, also specifically disallow courts from granting suspects bail for seven days.

males carry registration certificates at all times). It was in 1936 that Godfrey Huggins personally introduced the Native Registration Act, which required African men in towns to obtain additional documentation certifying that they were employed or seeking employment. Later legislation modified many rules, but the basic law was not abolished. Mustering mass support in both urban and rural areas throughout the country, the African National Congress used strictly constitutional means to protest against pass laws.

After independence in 1980, these pass laws were left intact. Today, the police have authority to demand that people produce their National Registration Cards (a thin aluminum disk) on demand or face going to jail for a maximum of one year. The police frequently swoop on hundreds of people at a time and cart them off to the police station for deposit fines for not having their IDs with them. In March 1997, Chief Justice Gubbay noted that the law was tougher on people without identity cards than it was on drivers without licenses, even though the car was "a lethal machine." In a ruling, the full bench of the Supreme Court concurred that for police authorities to require that people produce their IDs on demand violated the constitutional right to freedom of movement.

Many of the unpopular practices of the Smith regime, including "emergency powers" and the detention of political opponents, have continued since independence. Both Smith and Nkomo were detained briefly during the 1980s, and several ex-ZAPU activists were actually arrested and imprisoned, and remain in prison up to now.

The notorious 1960 Law and Order (Maintenance) Act was the centerpiece of black oppression under colonial rule. This exceptionally tough security law was introduced by Edgar Whitehead's government in October 1960 after government arrests of leaders of the National Democratic Party, which provoked bloody urban rioting. According to Chief Justice Robert Tredgold, who resigned his post to protest the law, the measure "outrages every basic human right." The act enabled the police to declare any group of three or more people an unlawful assembly. It imposed heavy prison sentences for participation in proscribed gatherings, and it generally provided for the suppression of political dissent. The Dominion Party also supported the bill when it was tabled in Parliament, and its successor, the Rhodesian Front, repeatedly amended and toughened the law after coming to power in late 1962, making it the primary tool for suppressing African nationalist political activity.

Ironically, on coming to power, the ZANU (PF) government never found it necessary to repeal this diabolical law. Instead, it was the judiciary that found it repugnant that this law should be kept on the statute books almost 14 years after independence. Consequently, in February 1994, the Zimbabwean Supreme Court ruled that the 34-year-old section of the Law and Order (Maintenance) Act that prevented opposition members from holding peaceful public demonstrations without prior permission from the authority was in conflict with the Zimbabwean Bill of Rights and should therefore be repealed.

It is in reaction to this challenge that the independence government, in July 1997, tabled the Public Order and Security Bill to replace the Law and Order (Maintenance) Act. Comparatively, the new bill dropped most of the acrimonious clauses from the previous law it seeks to repeal. At least seven harsh sections have been removed. Notable changes include Section 18, which gave the state power to ban any publication, and Section 24, which made civic activities including lobbying the public to boycott government events or engage in civil disobedience punishable by life imprisonment. The old law also gave police the power to tamper with all postal mail, while holding public gatherings on Christmas Day could have earned one a five-year jail term.

However, civil and human rights groups in the country objected to the retention of at least six clauses in the revised bill. The six clauses had direct infringements on freedoms of assembly and association, movement, and freedom of expression. These included clauses 14:5 and 16 that required all Zimbabweans to give a mandatory seven-day notice to the police before exercising their right to assembly. The police would have the discretion to approve or block the assembly on grounds of public security. Human rights groups argued that this right was still meaningless as long as it remains at the grace of a police officer. They also said that seven days was too long a notice to allow citizens to respond to urgent issues. Under this law, a magistrate of a court would also have sweeping powers to ban all forms of assembly in designated areas.

Clause 16, which was one of the six objectionable clauses, would give a police officer of the rank of Inspector powers to impose curfews and restrict public movement outside the approved hours. He would not be obliged to give reasons or prior warning of the impending curfew. The police officer also would have power to cordon off any public gathering or area and disperse people. In clause 12, the new bill would make it a criminal offence for any individual or media to utter, publish or distribute news deemed by the state to be subversive. It did not, however, define what would constitute a subversive statement. In the previous law, that included harsh criticism of the President. Persons found in contravention of this clause would be sentenced to a fine of up to US$2,500, or five years' imprisonment, or both.

Civil society and human rights groups also objected to the inclusion of secret service officials in the definition of the law enforcement agencies that could arrest or disperse assemblies in accordance with this bill. It was felt that since the intelligence services were not in the constitution, they were not accountable to the public while the police were.

At this stage of Zimbabwe's political development, it seemed as though it mattered very little how the new legislation differed from the previous version. It was said to be an "improvement." It might have appeared to be an improvement simply because the political circumstances had changed — the color of the oppressors is now black. Therefore, there was no way the two could have been identical. The previous act was authored to protect the privileges of a white minority who did not need the black vote to remain in power. The current one was aimed at protecting the privileges of a black minority dependent on black voters for sustenance. But the spirit of the Bill remained identical. It was an instrument for the repression and denial of opportunity to the politico-economically-powerless majority.

No surprise then that the Minister of Home Affairs, Cde Dumiso Dabengwa, decided to withdraw the Bill, saying that it had undergone too much "panel beating" and could not be brought to the House in its state. Nonetheless, after some cosmetic changes, the controversial Bill was passed by Parliament on October 19, 1998.

This Public Order and Security Bill was obviously not targeted at those with the means of survival or those with choices. Neither was it targeted at those who can choose to abide by the rules and nightly retreat to the safety of their fortresses. Ironically, the enactment of the Law and Order (Maintenance) Act in 1960 became the main catalyst for the liberation struggle. Instead of instilling a sense of fear in the people, the new act actually fuelled their desire to be free.

Many were surprised that despite the fact that the Bill was passed by Parliament, the President took his time to assent (and in the end, refused to assent). It is only in early June 1999 that he refused to sign this bill, together with the War Veterans' Amendment Bill — the first time he had done so since independence, in 1980. According to authoritative government sources, the President sent a letter to Parliament advising the Speaker of the House, Cde Cyril Ndebele, that he was withholding his assent because the security bill had inadequacies in so far as it dealt with the media, particularly the publication of unsubstantiated stories which endanger the security of the country.

Political analysts felt that the President's move was designed to facilitate the trial of the two *Zimbabwe Standard* journalists being charged under the Law and Order (Maintenance) Act. Legal experts said the gazetting of the new bill would have automatically repealed the Law and Order (Maintenance) Act, which would have effectively weakened the charges being pressed against *Standard* editor Mark Chavunduka and his reporter, Ray Choto. This development was also seen as an effort by the government to silence and tighten its grip on the privately run media.

On May 22, 2000, in a landmark judgment upholding the right to freedom of expression, the Supreme Court unanimously struck down the legal provision under which the tortured journalists were charged. Rather than responding to the charges, Chavunduka and Choto challenged their validity with a direct appeal to the Supreme Court. The Court declared that section 50 (2) (a) of the Law and Order (Maintenance) Act was unconstitutional. On the provision prohibiting the publication of any false statement that is likely to cause fear, alarm or despondency among the public, the Court noted that, "Were this provision to be actively applied, it would exert a significant chilling effect on freedom of expression," holding that this represented "a fair and realistic summation of the harsh impact" of the provision.[14]

In another landmark judgment by Chief Justice Godfrey Chidyausiku, on November 20, 2001, the full Bench of the Supreme Court unanimously declared that the terrorism and sabotage charges leveled against Morgan Tsvangirai, the MDC leader, by President Mugabe's government were unconstitutional. The State had alleged that when Tsvangirai addressed a rally at Rufaro Stadium in Harare to mark the first anniversary of the founding of the MDC, in September 2000, he had said Mugabe should leave office peacefully if he was to avoid a violent removal.

The Supreme Court ruled that sections 51 and 58 of the Law and Order (Maintenance) Act were a flagrant violation of the Constitution and inconsistent with democratic values. The judges sharply criticized the Act as a colonial piece of legislation, which should have been changed when the country gained independence from Britain in 1980. "It was bitterly criticized by the leaders of the nationalist movements, many of whom are in leadership positions in present-day Zimbabwe. It was widely expected that it would be replaced after independence," the judges noted. In the judgment written by Chidyausiku and delivered by McNally, the court said: "It is declared sections 51 and 58 of the Act are in contravention of Section 18 of the Zimbabwe Constitution and are accordingly invalid and of no force."[15]

---

14. *The Zimbabwe Standard*, 4 June, 2000.

Not surprisingly, the Public Order and Security Bill was "panel beaten" and gazetted on December 14, 2001 to become even more draconian than the Law and Order (Maintenance) Act. Among other provisions, the Act now authorizes defense force members to assist the police in suppressing any civil commotion or disturbances in any police district. In addition to providing the police with wide-ranging powers, the Act allows them and persons assisting them to kill while in the process of dispersing an unlawful public gathering.

Clause 29 allows a police officer to disperse or apprehend persons attending an unlawful gathering. "And, if any such person makes resistance, the police officer or the person assisting him may use such force as is reasonably justifiable in the circumstances of the case for overcoming any such resistance," reads the clause. "If a person is killed as a result of the use of reasonably justifiable force, where the force is directed at overcoming that person's resistance to a lawful measure, the killing shall be lawful."

The Act allows the police to detain people before they appear in court for up to a week. (Its predecessor limited lawful detention to not more than 48 hours.) Under the Act, the courts will not entertain bail for suspects facing treason, murder, rape, armed robbery, kidnapping, arson or theft charges. It also requires members of the public to carry an identity document on their person for presentation when requested by the police.

No Zimbabwean questions the government's imperative duty to rigorously safeguard law and order in the country, but it should not do so by bringing back emergency rule through the back door. The deployment of heavy armor and troops in Harare's high-density suburbs in November 1998, first to crush violent (but popular) protests against sharp fuel-price rises and then to intimidate workers during their Wednesday stayaways, marked the latest chapter in Zimbabwe's inexorable descent into a new tyranny.

For the generation that has memories of colonial tactics of quashing African nationalism during the 1960s, this may signal the beginning of another war of liberation. History has it that the presence of the troops in the former townships merely toughens and does not weaken the people's resolve to press on with their demands. It can also be recalled that at the end of October 1998, the President summarily dismissed the feuding heads of the CIO (Shadreck Chipanga and his deputy Lovemore Mukandi), rapidly replacing them with the military (two army brigadiers Elisha Muzonzini and Happyson Bonyongwe) in a clear sign of where the country was headed: back to the martial law which ended

---

15. *The Daily News*, 21 November, 2001.

with the defeat of the tyrannical rule of the Rhodesian Front government. With troops removing roadblocks on November 11, 1998, observers noted that November 11 was the anniversary of Ian Smith's ill-fated 1965 Rhodesian Unilateral Declaration of Independence.

To emphasize the point that Zimbabwe was a military dictatorship, the Military Police arrested the editor of *The Zimbabwe Standard* weekly, Mark Chavunduka, after a story of a foiled military coup had appeared in the weekly on January 10, 1999. High Court judge Justice George Smith then granted an order on January 13 for the unconditional release of Chavunduka from military barracks at Cranborne. While the Ministry of Defense defied the ruling, the Attorney-General Patrick Chinamasa dissociated himself from the illegal act by the military officials. Ray Choto, the reporter who wrote the article, was also later arrested. If one takes a close look, the *Zimbabwe Standard* got it right — there was actually a coup d'état, because the defiance of a High Court order is consistent with a coup. The military violated the rules of justice by refusing to carry out the instruction of the court and in normal circumstances should be prosecuted for their defiance.

The Defense Act, which prescribes the laws governing the functions of the military, does not give the Military Police the power to arrest civilians. The Military Police has powers to arrest and interrogate members of the defense forces only. Military courts are, however, still subject to supervision by the Supreme Court — military law can never be supreme to the law of the land. It is logical to conclude, therefore, that there was a de facto military coup in Zimbabwe.

Confronted by the obvious disregard by the military and/or the police for the Constitution of Zimbabwe, Supreme Court judges Justice Wilson Sandura, Justice Simbarashe Muchechetere, Justice Nicholas McNally and later High Court judge Justice Ishmael Adam sent a petition to President Robert Mugabe urging him to re-affirm the rule of law by making a public statement, following four contempt of court orders for the release of the two *Standard* journalists. However, in an emergency address to the nation on February 6, 1999, the President launched a scathing attack on the judges, describing their stand as "an action of utter indiscretion,.... an outrageous and deliberate act of impudence." The President lectured the judges on the provision of the Constitution saying, "The Presidency in the first place arises from the Constitution of the country and its incumbent emerges as a result of national presidential elections. I am that incumbent and as head of state I am also the head of the Executive. Accordingly, I have the right to appoint judges in the manner prescribed by the Constitution and due laws of the country. In accordance with our constitution and the principle of the separation of powers, the judiciary has no constitutional right whatsoever to give instructions to the President on any matter as the four judges purported to do."[16]

One thing was crystal clear, according to the President himself: "....It is a matter that has now brought about confrontation between the Judiciary and the Executive." While the President must necessarily appoint the judges in the context of the legalities that spell out their separate powers and functions, it cannot be said that the judges should remain beholden to any government and that they cannot and must not interpret the Constitution for an orderly and smooth running of the country and a just enforcement of its laws. The Executive cannot place itself above the law. Indeed, under the Constitution, it is not empowered to do so; it must subject itself and all its actions to the directions of an independent and impartial judiciary, which interprets and enforces the Constitution of the land. The President cannot be the legislator of the laws, the prosecutor and the judge all in one.

The act of writing the petition to the President was not unprecedented. Indeed, in 1965 when the Smith regime made its unilateral declaration and overthrew the constitutional order of the day by subverting the very idea of legality and the rule of law, many of the Rhodesian judges took similar action. The irony will not be lost on students of history, who will record that the reaction of President Mugabe's government is hardly distinguishable from that of Ian Smith's. The circumstances of UDI were serious and extraordinary, and clearly justified judicial reaction. The circumstances which prompted the reaction of the Supreme Court and High Court judges were also serious and in many respects extraordinary. First, the military, clearly without lawful authority, had arrested civilian journalists and detained them for a whole week. In so doing, it was subverting legality and simultaneously usurping the powers of the police. The Lancaster House Constitution, notwithstanding its numerous amendments (imperfections), clearly provides that the duty of the armed forces is to defend Zimbabwe against external aggression while that of the police is to maintain internal order and security. Thus, there can be no doubt that the army has neither business nor lawful authority to investigate any breaches of the internal law of Zimbabwe, let alone to arrest and detain civilians.

Secondly, at one point the unlawfully arrested and detained journalists had found their way into police custody and yet the police had amazingly and

---

16. *The Sunday Mail*, 7 February, 1999.

seemingly helplessly handed them back to the military or the CIO, where they were apparently severely tortured in violation of the complete ban on torture imposed by both the Constitution of Zimbabwe and international law (which has characterized the practice of torture as an international crime). Although the authorities denied the torture (saying "they scratched themselves"), there was overwhelming evidence.

Thirdly, the High Court had issued no fewer than three orders declaring the detention of Mark Chavunduka to be unlawful and ordering his release, and yet those to whom the orders had been directed had either refused or had avoided being served with the court orders, in what the Supreme Court judges described as playing a cat and mouse game with the courts. More importantly, they had defied the orders by refusing to release Chavunduka. Clearly, all this conduct was not only contemptuous of the courts but also undermined both their legitimacy and effectiveness as custodians of the rights of the people of Zimbabwe as enshrined in law.

Fourth, at least one senior civil servant to whose ministry the court orders had been directed was quoted in the press as declaring that the military was above the law and that the courts could not give him orders; and hence he and the military would move at their own pace. Elsewhere in the world where democracy and the rule of law prevail, the civil servant would have been dismissed. And yet here he had remained in office, with not even a reprimand.

A situation where court orders are ignored and defied by those sworn to defend and uphold the laws of the country opens the judicial system to ridicule and contempt. That makes it difficult (if not altogether impossible) for the judiciary to operate effectively and meaningfully. Thus, the cumulative effect of all the above led the judiciary to petition the President. In their request (not "instruction," as the President chose to misrepresent it), the judges' concerns were legitimate; they were concerned about their dignity, as they clearly wanted the government to re-affirm that it still upheld the rule of law as a necessary ingredient of a democratic Zimbabwe, and to confirm that the power to arrest and detain persons reasonably suspected of breaking the law was vested in the police, working with the courts.

However, although the President addressed the nation, he did not respond to the judges' concerns. Instead, in a clear reference to pending appeals by 841 farmers who had received notices their farms will be nationalized and the ZCTU High Court hearing against the ban on stayaways, the President declared: "Let those judges concerned now decide which way they want to go, because their impartiality in regard to cases that affect the incident has vanished and we, as the State, cannot trust them any longer to pass a fair judgment on cases that may arise relating to the incident involving *The Standard* and perhaps to any others which may arise in the future involving the Executive."[17]

Human rights activists were stunned — while the President rounded on the judges and lashed out at human rights organizations and the independent media, he notably refused to condemn torture of journalists by the army, and he did not promise an investigation. Besides taking a stand against an outrageous mockery of the law, the judges were rightly concerned to bring to the Executive's attention the very public excesses and illegality of the actions of its members (the refusal to obey court orders, if nothing else). In the circumstances, the people of Zimbabwe expected the Executive to respond by ensuring that lawful court orders were swiftly enforced and illegal action rapidly stopped and punished. Surely, neither the expression of concern nor the request for assurances nor the manner, method or language of the expression could be described as judicial indiscretion, let alone as an act of "deliberate and utter impudence." The judges had the responsibility and indeed the duty to express their concerns to the Executive in the interest of upholding the integrity of the courts.

The first referendum in a post-independence Zimbabwe revealed the characteristics of Zimbabwe's rulers. Just before the February 12-13, 2000 referendum, the Law and Order (Maintenance) Act (LOMA) was taken down from the shelf and dusted off. The irony of such an Act, implemented before a referendum on a proposed new "democratic" constitution for Zimbabwean society, will go down in history as the definitive expression of the trend in Zimbabwe, and just how desperately Zimbabweans need change.

On April 27, 2000, Police Commissioner Augustine Chihuri invoked special powers under the same LOMA to restrict political meetings. It became illegal for parties to ferry members to political gatherings unless the presidents of parties addressed them. Observers saw this as giving an advantage to President Mugabe and his beleaguered ZANU (PF). At least 30 people —including four farmers, farm workers and political party supporters — died of political violence in the run-up to the 2000 elections. The violence was exacerbated by farm invasions by government-sponsored militias, comprising largely ex-combatants and youths recruited from Harare townships.

It is obvious Zimbabweans no longer enjoyed the protection they had fought for and were being transported back to the worst days of colonial rule

---

17. *Ibid.*

when arbitrary measures by state agents removed unwanted voices like Edison Sithole (who simply disappeared, on October 15, 1975). Sithole was one of the leaders of the People's Movement (an internal ZANU organization). The police refused to intervene to protect the two journalists and others threatened by the military police; they brought charges against the journalists, because they were told to do so. Progressive forces in and outside the continent have watched with increasing dismay as the learned guerrilla-turned-statesman regressed over the years from a staunchly nationalistic but realistic leader into an intolerant, profligate and short-tempered autocrat. President Robert Mugabe has lost the down-to-earth touch that endeared him to many and appears to be out of touch with the restless and impoverished masses of Zimbabwe. The independent media and High Court and Supreme Court judges have stood up in the face of intimidation, harassment and violence.

Other oppressive colonial laws which the independence government has retained, such as the Censorship and Entertainment Control, the Official Secrecy, the Protected Areas and the Privileges and Immunities Acts, work against freedom of expression. After the establishment of the BSAC administration in Mashonaland in 1890, the various European governments of Rhodesia were sensitive to criticism. It is said that Cecil John Rhodes threatened W. E. Fairbridge with deportation shortly after the latter had started the forerunner of the *Rhodesia Herald* in 1891. Fairbridge then toned down his editorial criticisms of the administration. Until the Rhodesian Front came to power in 1962, the European press tended to identify closely with the interests of the government, so overt censorship was rarely a problem. By contrast, the majority African population, whose interests have almost always conflicted with those of the government, have never established anything like an independent press. Papers such as the *African Daily News*, *Chapungu*, the *Zimbabwe Sun* and others were quickly suppressed when they expressed overtly African nationalist sentiments.

Shortly before UDI in 1965, Ian Smith's government promulgated emergency regulations allowing for wide press censorship. Censorship was directed mainly against the Argus Group newspapers that editorially opposed UDI. Censorship prevailed in the country throughout the period of the Rhodesian Front rule, full censorship coming into force under the Emergency Powers (Censorship of Publications) Order which accompanied the independence declaration on November 11, 1965. In December 1967, the government established a permanent Board of Censorship to examine publications and films of all kinds. It frequently banned importation of foreign materials for political or moral reasons.

The government embarked upon a direct take-over of radio and television broadcasting, justifying such action on the basis of restoring a balance with what it termed the "monopoly press" — the newspapers belonging to the Rhodesian Printing and Publishing Company. It criticized the European press for its lack of support for government policies. However, although these newspapers were known to be opposed to an illegal declaration of independence, they displayed no open hostility to the government as such.

Therefore, the situation inherited by the independence government of Zimbabwe in 1980 was one in which all the main newspapers were owned by the Rhodesian Printing and Publishing Company, which had become subservient to Smith-Muzorewa pressure and which, as a subsidiary of the Argus Press, was subject to South African influence and control. At independence, there was no immediate fundamental change in the tenor and emphasis of newspapers in Zimbabwe. Thus, the ruling ZANU (PF) established in January 1981 the Zimbabwe Mass Media Trust (ZMMT), a non-profit-making organization run by a Board of Trustees. The ZMMT took over 45.24% of South African shareholding in Zimbabwe Newspapers (the new name of the Rhodesian Printing and Publishing Company) and established the Zimbabwe Institute of Mass Communication. The ZMMT went on to own 51% of the shares of Zimbabwe Newspapers. The Mass Media Trust was given responsibility to create editorial policy and to make senior editorial appointments. Generally, although this increased the number of African staff members on the papers, there was never any criticism of the independence government. In other words, the media continued to reflect its colonial image.

The independence government has been known for its intolerance of criticism in its media institutions. As early as 1983, the first black editor of the *Sunday Mail*, the late Willie Musarurwa, was fired for what was clearly deemed a too-independent editorial line, although the official reason given was his membership of PF-ZAPU. Musarurwa's fall from favor followed hard on the heels of the "promotion" of the first black editor of the *Herald*, Farai Munyuki, who went to Zimbabwe Inter-Africa News Agency (ZIANA) as editor-in-chief, after a front-page editorial had denounced the Botswana government following revelations that Botswana was harboring Super ZAPU anti-government elements at Dukwe camp near Francistown. Munyuki was replaced by Tommy Sithole, previously editor of the *Chronicle* in Bulawayo. Sithole was in turn replaced at the *Chronicle* by Geof Nyarota, who was "reassigned" after he spearheaded reports into the Willowgate scandal, which led to the Sandura Commission of inquiry in 1988.

Henry Muradzikwa, who took over from Musarurwa at the *Sunday Mail*, was fired from the post in 1985 and promoted to special projects manager of the group after publishing a story on Zimbabwean students suffering from AIDS being repatriated from Cuba. The article was deemed harmful to Zimbabwean-Cuban relations. Zimbabwe had not renounced its socialist ideology and was a strong ally of Fidel Castro's Cuba, where Zimbabwean student teachers had been sent for training.

Although the media has traditionally been "forced" to be a faithful ally of Zimbabwe's entrenched political establishment, it adopted an unusually critical tone during the December 1997 national protests and the January 1998 food riots. The Executive was not amused by the Zimbabwe Broadcasting Corporation's television coverage of protests organized by the ZCTU against tax hikes. While the ZBC managers followed orders handed down by the Ministry of Information, Posts and Telecommunications blaming protesters for the subsequent violence, footage screened showed police firing teargas at random to prevent people gathering for a peaceful demonstration in the Harare city center. Furthermore, when the Ministry declared that white industrialists and farmers were behind the protests, viewers saw a church-based human rights activist describing the government's conspiracy theory as "absolute rubbish." Callers to ZBC's Radio 3 agreed. As veteran talk-show host Gerry Jackson warned listeners to avoid trouble spots, many called in to dispute the official view that the unrest was the product of whites bent upon avenging President Mugabe's land grab. Jackson paid for her indiscretion, as she was dismissed four days later.

Later in 2000, Gerry Jackson fought and won a legal battle in the Supreme Court to set up Zimbabwe's first independent radio station, Capital FM, and began broadcasting with a transmitter set up on a hotel roof in Harare. Within six days it was raided by soldiers wielding AK47s. They smashed the studio equipment while Jackson's two employees escaped in the hotel lift. Jackson decided then to broadcast from outside Zimbabwe and after a year raising funds and putting a team together, moved to London, launching SW Radio Africa (The Independent Voice of Zimbabwe) in December 2001.

Among buildings hit by teargas was Herald House, headquarters of the government's press empire. Tommy Sithole, editor of the flagship *Herald* daily since 1983, described riot police as "trigger happy" and "over-zealous." "In many instances the targets were innocent people trying to go about their duties," he wrote in an outspoken editorial. The *Herald*, or rather Sithole, was even more severe in response to the riots against food-price rises which rocked the capital on January 19, 1998. "If someone has been maliciously pumping up prices, then something is wrong with our monitoring systems. We have allowed this to happen and yesterday we saw the results," Sithole wrote in rare openness. "Now is the time for Zimbabwe to stop reacting to crises, as we have been doing for the past few months...... We all know that things cannot go on the way they are," he said. "Inflation is killing us.... Yesterday was the end of the era of business as usual. Today we must start fixing the underlying problems facing our country or watch disaster unfold."[18]

In an apparent swipe at Minister of Information Cde Chenhamo Chimutengwende's renewed accusation that whites were to blame for the unrest, Sithole commented, "If the demonstrations were spontaneous, as seems certain, then both the ruling party and the government are in trouble..... Anyone wanting to wag a finger at the ZCTU or hurl abuse at ethnic groupings in the mistaken belief that the problem will go away is deluding himself." After reading Sithole's editorial comment, Chimutengwende is reported to have remarked, "His days are numbered!" Sure enough, he soon lost his post.

The ZCTU mass labor stay-away on March 3-4, 1998 provided a test ground for the newly appointed *Herald* editor. In the aftermath, the state-controlled *Herald* ran articles describing the mass stay-away as a huge failure and generally downplayed the event. The independent media, namely the *Zimbabwe Independent*, the *Financial Gazette* and the *Zimbabwe Mirror*, on the other hand, told the opposite story. Meanwhile, the ZBC journalist who had planned to have ZCTU secretary-general Morgan Tsvangirai and Labour Minister Florence Chitauro on his live phone-in program on the last day of the stay-away was told at the last minute to drop the labor leader from the program.

No sooner had Cde Charles Chikerema taken control of the *Herald* than the daily newspaper was nicknamed "Pravda," after the Soviet Union's Communist mouthpiece. Unfortunately, it looks as though Cde Chikerema's health could not cope with the pressures at Herald House. At the end of April 1998, just some nine weeks after occupying his editorial position, Chikerema collapsed at his desk and later died at the Avenues Clinic. It could not have been easy for him to come up with an editorial (on a daily basis) to please the decaying dictatorship his uncle had created. As a devout Marxist, Cde Chikerema had mounted the podium on behalf of the "povo" (common or poor people). He was portrayed as the champion of the underprivileged, the Marxist who had championed the cause of the poor blacks when they were being exploited by the rich white men. However, he seemed unwilling to see any government or party culpability in the

---

18. *The Herald*, 21 January, 1998.

poverty in which the majority of the Zimbabwean people were drowning. Now, he found himself in the unenviable position to champion a black government that was exploiting the same poor blacks.

As if to emphasize this point, President Robert Mugabe showered praise on the late editor at his funeral and burial at Kutama village in Zvimba, saying that "Charles had criticized the party for deviating from its original Marxist-Leninist principles," the principles to which every Zimbabwean knew ZANU (PF) gave lip service. While he praised Chikerema's editorial policies, saying they should be emulated by young journalists, he reserved harsh words for black journalists working for private establishments, attacking them for being used by whites and wondering whether some of the scribes were true Zimbabweans. This outburst against black journalists in the independent media, coming soon after his call for a purge of *varoi* (witches) within ZANU (PF), raised questions among journalists on whether the President accepts any views contrary to his own.

It is no wonder Zimbabwe's press was rated as "not free" by a prominent United States-based media watchdog organization in its report for 1998. Freedom House, which monitors the press around the world, said it had classified Zimbabwe's press from "partly free" to "not free" in the year under review. The report's ratings are based on legal restrictions, the degree to which the media freedom is determined by the political interests, the degree to which economic factors inform news content and the frequency and severity of violations against journalists. In Zimbabwe, the law does not protect a journalist's sources — the courts still retain the power to force a journalist to choose between revealing a source or going to jail.

In a clear lesson for Zimbabwe, the survey reported that government constraints on the news media contributed to the Asian financial crisis in May 1998. The report said that "pervasive and institutionalized press controls allow corruption, cronyism and bad economic policy to flourish while the public remains ignorant of and unprepared for impending consequences."

On April 25, 1999, in an interview with the state-owned *Sunday Mail*, President Robert Mugabe said he was going to broaden state powers against the country's press. "The government will strengthen laws of criminal libel so that journalists will not be able to use their pen as a bloody sword....on individuals they think they don't like. That we shall do, not to prevent journalists from doing their work, but from going beyond the scope of their powers in assassinating people they don't like," the President said.[19]

---

19. Africa News Online, May 25, 1999.

The Paris-based freedom of expression group Reporters sans Frontieres (RSF) expressed concern about this threat to reinforce defamation laws. RSF noted that the Zimbabwean Constitution already permitted legal action for damages in case of defamation. Section 20(1)(b)(i) includes, "protecting the reputations, rights and freedoms of other persons or the private lives of persons concerned in legal proceedings." The Zimbabwean Constitution already included a long list of restrictions on freedom of expression in Article 20 (2), and Zimbabwean law also provided for criminal defamation, which RSF considered unjustified.

Further on the subject of the clampdown on the free flow of information, Mugabe (still chafing after his ban from the just-ended Commonwealth summit in Nigeria) was afforded the opportunity to position himself as a champion of developing countries in their fight against domination by the developed world. Speaking at the World Summit on the Information Society in Geneva on December 9, 2003, he attacked Britain and the United States for using their superiority in information technologies to destabilize Zimbabwe and other small and poor states. However, Mugabe's laws on information management are completely contrary to the spirit of the UN's WSIS, which is "to promote the urgently needed access of all countries to information, knowledge and communication technologies for development." Fourteen people were arrested in mid-November under harsh new state security laws for exchanging e-mail messages that were not flattering to President Mugabe.

Law historians will find striking similarities and continuities between Rhodesia and Zimbabwe in respect of the political leadership's relationship and attitude towards the law and legality, wherein the law is seen and consistently used as a tool of political and social repression and also is frequently manipulated to grant wide discretionary powers to executive organs. It is quite conspicuous for a president of a country who took an oath to uphold and defend the Constitution and other laws of the country to change that same Constitution to suit his political ambition and go against court rulings by using the Presidential Powers (Temporary Measures) Act. The cumulative effect of this systematic undermining of the rule of law has been so overwhelming that it has become evident that there is one law for the "povo" and another for the political elite. When the allies and friends of the political elite are prosecuted and convicted by the courts, the presidential power of pardon is used to place them beyond the reach of the law or punishment.

Conversely, where the courts have ruled against an abuse of human rights by the government, the president has intervened to overturn the rulings. Take the case of the three Americans who were accused of sabotage. In July 1999, President Mugabe invoked the Presidential Powers (Temporary Measures) Act, to make new prison regulations which gave the Commissioner of Prisons power to determine the allocation of cells to prisoners. This move came hot on the heels of a Supreme Court order compelling prison authorities to relax the conditions under which the three Americans were being held so they could interact with each other within their cell block. The President used his powers to effectively overturn Chief Justice Anthony Gubbay's ruling, and had the Commissioner of Prisons allocate separate cells to the Americans to ensure they did not communicate with each other. The Prison (General) Regulations also gave the Commissioner of Prisons the power to classify all prisoners and prisons.

Constitutional lawyers in Zimbabwe felt the use of presidential powers to reverse a Supreme Court ruling was illegal because the President could not overturn a Supreme Court ruling without making amendments to the Constitution itself. Arguably, in one move the President took over the legislative function from Parliament.

## Cultural Expression and Repression

Earlier in the year, the state-run broadcasting station removed a Ndebele television drama called Stitsha, after showing seven of the ten episodes which it had commissioned in 1997. The removal of Stitsha from the screen sparked angry reactions from television viewers. The first Ndebele drama to be removed was Sinjalo. Sinjalo (Ndebele for "we are like that") was removed following political interference by the ruling party's heavyweights, who felt that it was too political. Activities of the notorious Fifth Brigade troops, accused by human rights organizations of committing atrocities in Matabeleland and the Midlands, were highlighted in the program. Refusing to be intimidated, Amakhosi Productions (one of southern Africa's most dynamic theater and music companies) later came up with another controversial play, "Attitudes," exposing the hypocrisy of the country's political leaders and members of parliament. The play proved to be a hit with both Harare and Bulawayo viewers.

When corruption in the corridors of power finally came out in the open in 1988, the father of Chimurenga music (named for the war of 1896-97 in which the Shona and Ndebele revolted against the British colonists), Thomas Mapfumo, composed a piece of music which became a hit. The lyrics of "Corruption" related directly to current events, suggesting that one cannot expect to go into business without bribery, typified by the tender system scams. Combining a highly danceable melody with a political message, Mapfumo is quick to remind those involved in these and other corrupt activities that "you cannot run away from justice." This did not sit well with the "chefs" in Harare, who immediately banned the music from the air-waves and confined the disc to the music archives. Although other albums were routinely banned from the airwaves, it did not deter Mapfumo.

Chimurenga Explosion, released in December 1999, contains scathing songs, all critical of the government's policies which are blamed for having reduced the majority of the people to paupers. *Mamvemve* portrays the country as having been reduced to rags.

The politically-pregnant Chimurenga Rebel had eight of its songs banned. Released just before Christmas in 2001, the album is heavily laden with potent lyrics that attack bad governance, abuse of human rights, and misguided policies, and brings to the fore the wailing voices of victims of political violence in Zimbabwe. The same can be said of Oliver Mtukudzi. His cassettes and compact disc (CDs) were confiscated in 2001 by the police and members of the CIO because of the "offensive" songs on the album *Bvuma/Tolerance*. At one time, engineer Steven Schadendorff was arrested by detectives from the Law and Order Section for repeatedly beaming the spotlight on Mugabe's portrait at the Harare International Conference Centre as Tuku sang *Wasakara* (You're Finished).

Continuing with his fearless and relentless attack, Mapfumo released yet another hot potato in December 2002. Toyi Toyi has ten hot songs, none of which has been played on radio.

It is to be noted that this was not the first time "Mukaya" had fallen out of favor with authorities. During the 70s, at the height of the liberation war, he encouraged both the young and the old to participate in the struggle. With the Acid Band, he blended popular and traditional *mbira* music, coupled with politically inspired lyrics which, although covertly expressed, rallied people to the guerrillas' cause and instilled a sense of national pride in his audience. Attendance at his shows rose to unprecedented levels and word went out to the racist regime that Thomas Mapfumo was promoting Chimurenga. To curb his influence, the authorities locked him up in prison.

*Special Legislation and Rights Infringements*

As the war progressed, it was not enough for the Smith regime to rely on draconian and sweeping laws like the Emergency Powers, Law and Order (Maintenance); it decided to legislate specific statutes of impunity, like the infamous Indemnity and Compensation Act of 1975. When the Catholic Commission for Justice and Peace documented the terror of the Rhodesian Front regime during the 1970s, the Indemnity and Compensation Act indemnified all government officials from prosecution for acts committed "in the line of duty." The regime even had the audacity to make the Act retrospective to 1972, to the start of the people's liberation war, to excuse the human rights violations of earlier years. The ZANU (PF) government reverted to similar legislation as the RF government under the Emergency Powers Act — the Emergency Powers (Security Forces Indemnity) Regulations 1982, specifically to cover atrocities committed in Matabeleland and the Midlands during the war against dissidents.

Another piece of legislation promulgated by the Rhodesian Parliament in 1976 is the Criminal Procedure and Evidence Act, which allowed a Cabinet Minister to issue a certificate barring the disclosure of certain information in public. The Minister of State for National Security, in an unprecedented move on February 10, 2003, issued a certificate to protect a key State witness from disclosing details of the agreement between his firm and the government, citing national security concerns. This was at the treason trial of the leader of the Movement for Democratic Change, Morgan Tsvangirai, and two senior party officials, Welshman Ncube and Renson Gasela, during which the independence government was seeking to prevent defense lawyers from cross-examining Ari Ben-Menashe on the nature of the contract he signed with the government.

This legislation was promulgated specifically to deal with cases involving freedom fighters during the 1970s war of liberation. The High Court judge, Judge President Justice Paddington Garwe said, "In the Rhodesian context, the intention was to prevent any further enquiry on the part of the court, but the situation has now changed. The Constitution of Zimbabwe now has a Bill of Rights.... I am satisfied that in appropriate cases the court can make inquiries and order proceedings to be held in camera." Thus, the judge ordered that the cross-examination of Ari Ben-Menashe, the head of Canadian-based consultancy firm Dickens & Madison, should proceed in camera. Observers saw this as a compromise between the demands of the State and the defense lawyers.

One law that makes a mockery of the needs of local people is the Precious Stones Act. Enacted during the colonial era, the Act prohibits unlicensed dealers from processing specified precious stones. Of specific reference is the Mberengwa district in the Midlands, where there is an abundance of emerald stones. The green mineral can be picked down stream of rivers passing through two licensed Sandawana and Masaga mines. Because it is mined as a "pure" precious stone, it is one of the most lucrative stones. Other less valuable minerals like chrome, iron and asbestos are exempted from the stiff regulation of the Act. Mberengwa is the only district in the world that produces first-grade emeralds, and yet its residents have reaped little benefit from them as mining is confined to licensed and financially sound companies. It is deplorable that the independence government did not repeal or relax the regulations of the Act to allow people to make a living from what is around them. If someone is found with the green stone, he is bound to be sentenced to three years behind bars without the option of a fine. Because of the strict regulations and despite the stiff penalty, a lucrative black market has developed. Thousands of Mberengwa families live on the mineral. Illegal mining from deserted pits has attracted school children and smuggling by mine employees is prevalent. A lucrative market for the emeralds is in South Africa, where one can earn thousands of rands, or barter, with a commuter omnibus. Observers feel that the government must overhaul the Act by setting less stringent measures to pave the way for other local mining aspirants.

Quite a good number of other laws passed during the colonial days have remained on the statute books, e.g. the Prevention of Constitutional Act, and the Liquor Licensing Act that criminalizes the brewing of traditional beer by peasant women in the rural areas, thus making criminals of Zimbabweans going about their usual business.

It is quite clear that not only has the independent government of ZANU (PF) retained colonial laws, it has also introduced repressive laws and is guilty of gross human rights abuse against opposition political parties, the judiciary and the independent Press. Ironically, it is even in violation of the 1991 Harare Declaration wherein member states of the (British) Commonwealth made a commitment to the promotion of human rights, democracy, the rule of law and the independence of the judiciary. Zimbabwe has plunged further into more severe manifestations of dictatorship than that of the Rhodesia Front regime. This stems from the birth of obnoxious pieces of legislation like the Public Order and Security Act (POSA) and the Access to Information and Protection of Privacy Act (AIPPA).

*The Clamor for a Homegrown Constitution*

There is growing national consensus, even among members of the ruling ZANU (PF) itself, on the need to overhaul Zimbabwe's constitution. The current Lancaster House Constitution is perceived by many Zimbabweans as foreign and irrelevant to the realities of the nation today. The 1980 constitution was a compromise document adopted in a war situation. In May 1997, a forum of various interest groups was set up. The National Constitutional Assembly (NCA), created by various civic society groups involving the labor movement, human rights associations, lawyers' associations, the student movement, women's organizations and other civic groups, was designed to mobilize the general public towards changing the country's constitution. The forum, which had already secured financial support from local as well as international donors, was expected to serve as the launching pad for nationwide activities that would culminate in a national constitutional convention that would draft a new constitution for Zimbabwe.

Although the Government had over the past six years spurned calls by opposition parties and civic groups for a national constitutional conference, the heated ZANU (PF) annual national conference held in Mutare in December 1997 adopted a resolution calling for constitutional changes. In addition, the ZANU (PF)-dominated Parliamentary Reform Committee, which in January 1998 completed a tour of the country's provinces, issued its report in May 1998. The committee, made up of 27 MPs (among whom were four Cabinet Ministers) and chaired by Chimanimani MP Mike Mataure, set out in remarkable detail precisely what needed to be done to transform Zimbabwe's legislature from an instrument of the ruling party into the public watchdog it was supposed to be. The report's conclusions were derived from extensive consultation with grassroots opinion at home and expert opinion abroad. Besides visiting 28 centers in nine provinces, the committee studied the workings of parliaments in Britain, Australia, New Zealand, South Africa, Namibia, Uganda and Germany. Together with evidence from civil society stakeholders who had well-considered positions on the role of Parliament, the consultation exercise gave the report a clear ring of authenticity and credibility.

Among the recommendations were the strengthening of portfolio committees, the canvassing of opinion through pre-legislative white papers and the taking on board of the views of civil society in drafting Bills. It was understood that this was designed to enhance accountability and make the process of law-making more representative. "A reform system of parliamentary committees lies at the very heart of effective parliamentary democracy in Zimbabwe.... Energetic and well-resourced committees 'give teeth' to parliament's efforts to fulfill its duties," the report says. It noted that the committee system was the "engine room" of South Africa's new parliament. It recommended that parliamentary committees be empowered to examine the government's policies, a function that President Robert Mugabe saw as a preserve of the executive and his ruling ZANU (PF) party.

It paid particular attention to the roles of the Public Accounts Committee, the Comptroller and Auditor-General, and the Ombudsman, with recommendations to make the last two independent, for instance by transferring the right to make the appointments from the presidency to Parliament. The Auditor-General Mr. Eric Harid, in evidence to the committee, had noted that his staff was drawn from the Ministry of Finance, one of the ministries he was supposed to scrutinize. In the countries the reform committee visited, the executive works alongside parliamentary Public Accounts Committees to make financial controls more open and effective, the report noted.

The report also called for the appointment of all senior officials, including permanent secretaries and ambassadors, to be approved by Parliament and recommended that the Government Tender Board should be renamed the "Public Procurement Board"; it should be appointed through, funded by and report directly to Parliament. In regards to Zimbabwe's electoral system, the report recommended that the Electoral Supervisory Commission (ESC) should be provided with a full complement of administrative personnel and research expertise in order for it to fulfill its constitutional role. It said the ESC should be funded from appropriations specifically made in order to enhance its independence from the executive and to submit its reports directly to Parliament to emphasize its accountability to the people.

The committee encountered strong concerns throughout Zimbabwean society about corruption, financial waste and mismanagement. "Unless clear steps are taken to address such concerns," the report warned, "there is a danger of increasing disillusionment with the political process which will pose a threat to stability." The report looked beyond Parliament itself to the wider issue of constitutional reform. Recommending the setting up of a constitutional committee, the report said, "A parliamentary constitutional committee should be established to safeguard the observance and promote the progressive development of the constitution on an on-going basis, scrutinize constitutional Bills and generally serve as a democratic forum on constitutional issues to all citizens irrespective of their political persuasions." The report went on to say that, "The constitutional committee should initially investigate, specifically, constitutional provisions having a bearing on the recommendations of this Parliamentary Reform Committee and, generally, into the reform of the Constitution and report to the House."

This is a logical outcome to the committee's work. Issues raised in the report (such as executive accountability to Parliament, the appointment of non-elected MPs, presidential powers, proposals for a second chamber, the status and number of vice-presidents and ministers, and the electoral process) were all matters that could only be addressed if parliamentary reform proceeded hand-in-hand with wider constitutional reform to redress the balance between executive and legislative powers.

On the basis of the report, Parliament was considering a resolution that President Robert Mugabe undertake a review of the country's constitution, whose many amendments had entrenched his authority. The resolution that went to Parliament as a motion by controversial MP Dzikamai Mavhaire, with an amendment by Mhondoro MP Mavis Chidzonga, read: "Whereas honorable members are aware of the original history, inadequacies and other shortcomings inherent in the present Zimbabwe constitution, now, therefore, this House resolves to call upon the Executive (President Mugabe and Cabinet) to put in place a mechanism for the purpose of undertaking such a review (and) to ensure that all segments of society have access to such a mechanism in order to participate fully in the review proceedings." The amendment to Mavhaire's motion by Chidzonga represented a significant contribution to Parliament's call for a review. The Mhondoro MP said that the House should call upon President Mugabe to convene a constitutional conference to be attended by representatives of government and civil society — including political parties, trade unions, churches, NGOs, civil servants, the legal fraternity, academia, students and women's groups. The MP said that the terms of reference for the conference should be the setting up of an independent constitutional commission, which would report to the conference and the President.

The resolution was widely hailed as timely. Although it was dominated by the President's party and Mavhaire had been suspended from the ruling ZANU (PF) party, Parliament had not yet shown signs of a climb down on the issue. However, its authority was so limited it could not force the President to accede to its demands. Fears were emerging the President would not heed calls from Parliament but instead would choose to work with his party on an internal program to thwart measures that would curb his sweeping powers. On May 20, 1998, the ruling party's supreme decision-making organ, the Politburo (which is chaired by President Mugabe himself), was understood to have discussed recommendations drafted by the party's legal affairs supremo, Cde Eddison Zvobgo, on how the party could chart the way forward on constitutional reforms. Party sources said that the Politburo agreed to start the process of reforming the Constitution. It was understood that a new homegrown national Constitution was to be in place before the next general elections in the year 2000.

The privately-sponsored NCA initiative for a homegrown constitution was already debating the need for wide-ranging constitutional changes. It is interesting to note, however, that already in February 1998 members of Parliament had proposed the setting up of a mechanism to review the 1980 British-crafted constitution. They pointed out that the review must focus on presidential powers and terms of office. Parliamentarians underscored the fact that, in the fourteen amendments already made to the constitution, the rights of the people were taken away and given to the executive. The deputies said that it made no sense to claim that "Parliament had powers to pass a vote of no confidence in the President" when at the same time the "President himself could dissolve Parliament" whenever he wished.

Pressure groups and political parties also felt that the 14 amendments made to the 1980 Constitution by the Government since independence had given President Mugabe too much power. The Constitution was amended to suit ZANU (PF)'s ideals of a one-party state. Scrutinizing some of the clauses, one discovers that the constitutional amendments made the President higher than the law itself. For example, paragraph 31 (k) of Chapter Four of the Constitution states, *inter alia*, "Where the President is required or permitted by this Constitution or any other law to act on his own deliberate judgment, a court shall not, in any case, inquire into any of the following matters:

- whether any advice or recommendation was tendered to the President or acted on by him; or
- whether any consultation took place in connection with the performance of the act; or
- the nature of any advice or recommendation tendered to the President; or
- the manner in which the President has exercised his discretion."

It is no wonder that convicted criminals who were ruling party members were given presidential pardon and that, in some cases, there was political interference with the judiciary.

Besides, one of the main concerns is the relationship between the Executive and the legislature. Parliament feels that it was not being accorded its proper status of checking the Executive. In all but one of the constitutional amendments, the general public was never consulted. The process involved a decision being made by the ZANU (PF) Politburo, then adopted by the Cabinet and rubber-stamped by Parliament. Some have also argued that the number of times that the Constitution had been amended bore testimony to its fragility, particularly when some countries like Australia have only changed their constitution about five times in about one hundred years. Developments in neighboring countries like Namibia and South Africa, which consulted widely and came up with their own constitutions, have put more pressure to change the Zimbabwean Constitution.

Even President Robert Mugabe, who initially took a swipe at some legislators who he accused of jumping the gun by pushing for constitutional reforms outside the party system, agreed there should be extensive constitutional consultation and that the process should be expedited. Opening the fourth session of the fourth Parliament on July 14, 1998, the President said that it was now glaringly evident that the Constitution did not augur well for the needs and aspirations of the majority of Zimbabweans. "I do hope, therefore, that the House will be able during this session to begin in earnest to debate this matter thoroughly so that the final agreed constitution will truly reflect the wishes of our people.... This exercise should ensure that the debate genuinely takes on board the values and aspirations of the generality of our people," he said. While President Mugabe had previously insisted that ZANU (PF) should take the lead in preparing the draft constitution, he now spoke of the importance of involving everyone in the reform debate and parliamentarians were now seeking to entrench popular participation in the constitutional review process.

Thus, the Zimbabwean legislators moved for the setting up of an independent constitutional commission tasked with holding extensive nationwide consultations and preparing a draft constitution. The parliamentarians wanted the commission to be headed by an independent retired judge and to be composed of legal experts, insisting that every political party, including the ruling ZANU (PF) party, should be involved in the review process, by way of invitation as a stakeholder only. One MP said, "The process we are embarking on is not to draw up a ZANU (PF) constitution, but a national one which transcends political affiliation. We want to have a constitution which will reflect and address the needs of the people, even after the reign of ZANU

73

(PF)." The MPs further insisted that in their proposal they did not want the exercise to be spearheaded by senior members of the ruling party, but that these (like all other stakeholders outside ZANU PF) make their input to the constitutional commission.

The stance adopted by the legislators dovetailed with the process proposed by the NCA. In its resolutions during their session of July 11-12, 1998, the NCA said that it was the duty of the incumbent government to facilitate a constitution-making process without seeking to control and dominate the exercise. "Government of the day formulate and implement policies and laws, but the formulation of a constitution, the basic law of the land, and even its amendment, is exclusive preserve of the sovereignty of the people.... No single political party, however dominant, has the right to make a constitution for the people, and no group or segment of society, however small or weak, should be left out or marginalized in the constitution-making process," the NCA said.

The Parliamentary reform program seemed hopeful. Parliament was the only institution in the land that could make laws in a comprehensive manner. The prevailing judicial determinations resulted in piecemeal changes; judges made laws on the hoof whenever they interpreted laws. Apart from stopping bad laws from being enacted, it was hoped that a reformed Parliament would be receptive to public petitions to expunge existing bad laws from the country's statutes.

As it was, there were three "parties" competing for the right to write the constitution. The ZANU (PF) government claimed that it must "lead the campaign to review the constitution"; the NCA felt that it was the best representative of various interest groups; and Parliament regarded itself as the representative of the people in the country's constituencies. The ZANU (PF) Government was now taking the initiative, but one must wonder why it should have taken nearly 20 years to realize that the constitution needed to be reviewed. Besides, political analysts asked whether it was not the same ZANU (PF) government that had defaced the constitution in the first place by making the controversial amendments. It seemed likely that the ZANU (PF) (the Politburo) was insincere about constitutional change and its move was rather an attempt to take away the initiative from the opposition. The Lancaster House Constitution may not have been the evil document that it was being made out to be — the most undemocratic features were created by amendments by the same ZANU (PF) government.

By March 1999, the constitutional reform process had deteriorated into a political stand-off between the ruling ZANU (PF) and the NCA. Mugabe and his party insisted that they should be responsible for nominating 300 commissioners (including the 150 MPs) that should be charged with drafting the constitution. Under the Commissions of Inquiry Act (Chapter 10:07), Mugabe was expected to appoint the other 150 commissioners. However, civic organizations insisted that the fact that commissioners were going to be hand-picked by the government (in the person of Dr. Eddison Zvobgo) negated the very principle of inclusion and participatory democracy which was understood to be lacking in the discredited amended constitution. The civic organizations contended that the process of appointing a commission was flawed: the commission would be put in place under the terms of a law that upheld sweeping executive powers to modify, amend or reject altogether all findings of the commissioners. The organizations emphasized that involvement by the government should be facilitative and not determinative, because the formulation of a constitution was the exclusive preserve of the sovereignty of the people.

### Mugabe's Constitutional Commission

Brushing aside the NCA, Mugabe appointed a 395-member Constitutional Commission on April 28, 1999. According to Proclamation No. 6 of 1999 in Statutory Instrument 138 A of 1999, published in a Government Gazette Extraordinary, all members of the commission automatically became Members of Parliament. In the Proclamation, the President said, "I direct the said Commissioners to compile a report of their findings after the said inquiry, which report must be submitted to me not later than the 30th November 1999, although they will be at liberty to report their proceedings to me from time to time."

Besides all mayors who were members of the ruling party, the Commission included ZANU (PF) provincial chairmen and a number of central committee members nominated from provinces. The ruling party also had 147 out of the 149 MPs (who included cabinet ministers and top government officials) who were part of the 395 commissioners. Prominent ZANU (PF) fund-raisers in the business sector were also nominated.

The commission comprised nine thematic committees with 43 commissioners each. These included the separation of powers committee convened by Rita Makarau; executive organs convened by Dzinotyiwei; pillars of democracy — Mushayakarara; fundamental rights — Canaan Dube; separation of governments — Dr. Themba Dlodlo of the National University of Science and

Technology; public finance and management — Eric Bloch; customary law — Professor Rudo Gaidzanwa; transitional mechanisms — Honour Mkushi; and legal committee — Patrick Chinamasa. There were also the executive and the coordinating committees, which were chaired by Justice Chidyausiku and Professor Kamba, respectively. The coordinating committee had two subcommittees: finance and administration, chaired by Dr. Ibbo Mandaza, and the media and public relations subcommittee, chaired by Moyo.

Critics suggested that the fact that virtually all convenors of committees were independent commissioners was a camouflage to cover up the hegemony of the ruling party — an obvious "cheap strategy to sway public opinion."

Harare South independent MP and leader of Zimbabwe Union of Democrats (ZUD), pulling out of the presidential commission, said, "I didn't sign and I'm not going to sign those nomination papers given to all MPs because I don't want to be part of such a commission. The appointment of commissioners is tantamount to fraud because most of the people (241) were hand picked and imposed on us." Of the 241 appointed commissioners, more than three quarters belonged to ZANU (PF). Other leading Zimbabweans who refused to participate because they were not consulted or simply saw the panel as too partisan were Edgar Tekere and Prof. Masipula Sithole.

An NCA spokesperson, Professor Welshman Ncube, asked, "How can a commission be democratic when it is composed of people drawn from a party which has been failing to come up with a democratic constitution for many years?"

The NCA refused to be part to the commission. At a three-day convention, which was convened on June 18, 1999 in Chitungwiza Town, the NCA was supported by traditional chiefs in opposing the Chidyausiku Constitutional Commission. The spokesman for the traditional leaders, Chief Samanga of Honde Valley in Manicaland, said, "There is something drastically wrong with the government's approach. People participating in this exercise should come from the people and not be appointed from above. We need change in the country because our children are dying of hunger...." One other chief added, "Our children have now turned to stealing in order to escape the hunger brought by this government's policies. And yet even after 18 years in control, the government does not seem prepared to relinquish power or share it with others." The participation of traditional chiefs at the NCA convention indicated growing public disillusionment with the government and its policies.

However, the ZANU (PF) government, known for its knack for pulverizing opponents, unceremoniously elbowed out other groups that had already started the exercise. Opposition parties for years had called for changes to the constitution, particularly the laws governing elections, and for trimming presidential powers. The Zimbabwe Unity Movement, formed in April 1989, played a significant role in helping to prevent ZANU (PF) from declaring a one-party state. Then, in September 1995, the Multi-Party Consultative Conference (comprising some seven opposition parties) started to agitate for constitutional changes. It might also be noted that by boycotting both the 1995 parliamentary and the 1996 presidential elections, the opposition parties brought pressure to bear on the ZANU (PF) government to recognize the need for constitutional reform. Furthermore, in 1997, the ZANU (PF)-dominated Parliament created a Parliamentary Reform Committee which visited 28 centers in nine provinces and studied the workings of parliaments in countries such as Britain, Australia, South Africa and Namibia. And then in May 1997, the NCA joined the mobilization of the general public towards changing the country's constitution. To add to the growing aspirations of the people of Zimbabwe for a new constitution, opposition parties formed the National Convention for Change (NCC) at the end of 1998 and were able to publish a draft constitution in early 1999.

One must be quick to point out that the independent press also articulated its opposition to the authoritarianism of the Mugabe regime. Since the advent of the independent press in Zimbabwe at the beginning of 1994, the institution has been busy exposing corrupt activities in high places and fostering a new political culture.

Thus, the President and his Cabinet basically told these stakeholders to go to hell. Cde Eddison Zvobgo, who was personally responsible for handpicking some 240 commissioners, did not mince words:

> Anybody can sit down under a tree and write his or her own constitution and it may even be a stimulating exercise. But the result of that exercise does not become a national constitution.... Our position is that we are going to consider no other document except the one that is going to be produced by the commission appointed by the government. We will not take notice of the draft constitution produced by the NCA or any other such group. Such drafts are just political essays on constitution making and they are only useful to get good grades at universities and not for national constitution making.[20]

---

20. *The Financial Gazette*, 6 April, 1999.

Those opposed to the handpicked commission argued that while the 120 elected MPs represented and were accountable to clearly defined constituencies, and while it was fair to assume that the ten traditional chiefs who were members of the House represented the chiefs' council, it would be hard to say what mandate, if any, the 240 or so remaining commissioners represented.

The NCA, for example, made the point that it would have been fair to allow recognized social groupings elect or nominate representatives who would have been accountable to their "constituencies" throughout the commission's work. These socio-political groupings included religious organizations, the trade unions, farmers' organizations, political parties, women's organizations, youth organizations, human rights organizations, business organizations that embrace industry and commerce, various professional associations such as the Legal Resources Foundation, civil service bodies such as the Public Service Association and the Zimbabwe Teachers' Association, disabled persons' organizations, and various others.

There are essential clauses and sub-sections in a constitution that can only be contested by given associations/organizations. Take, as an example, aspects of the Bill of Rights dealing with the workers' rights to strike; and women's rights to inheritance or the termination of pregnancy. It is one thing for the commission to go out and gather opinions, but it is another to interpret the submissions. Indeed, workers or women's groups may express different opinions and sometimes contradict each other. It is the business of their elected commissioners to interpret these submissions and make choices between and among various positions on any issue. This is where the representation of all stakeholders is vital.

A report by the civil liberties group African Rights also questioned the credibility of Zimbabwe's government-appointed constitutional reform process, saying, "If it is to be meaningful, constitutional reform must produce accountability at all levels of the government, and reduce the political and economic advantages now enjoyed by ZANU (PF)." The report, "Zimbabwe: In the Party's Interest?" released on June 11, 1999, noted that although there is a broad agreement on the need for reform, the government's decision to go ahead with a process "regarded as unacceptable by many civil organizations and almost all opposition parties is unfortunate." It pointed out that, "The domination of the commission by ZANU (PF) members and supporters is a major handicap that will inevitably compromise the work of the commission," and "As long as members of the ruling party promote ethnic or racial divisions; license the accumulation of wealth by a growing elite and turn a blind eye to corruption, they will obstruct necessary change."[21]

From an economic point of view, the Constitutional Commission drew up a budget amounting to Z$300 million for the six-month period from June to December 1999. According to the proposed budget, a hefty chunk of the money (Z$76.9 million or 35.6%) of the total requirement, would go towards the payment of honorariums for over 300 people who would be paid about Z$6,000 per day for a 45-day work period. Support staff were allocated Z$9.2 million, with 50 senior staff getting Z$5.13 million and 100 junior staff Z$4.1 million, for 180 days' work. The commission budgeted Z$30 million for the purchase of twenty 25-seat minibuses. Five desktop computers valued at Z$95,000 each, 15 Y2K-compliant laptops at Z$76,000 each and two printers at Z$76,000 each would also be purchased. Three fax machines, valued at Z$38,000 each and two photocopiers at Z$152,000 each were budgeted for.[22]

The commission also set aside Z$3.3 million for five commissioners to visit regional and overseas countries to "study and learn from experiences of countries that have gone through similar exercises." Regional countries targeted were South Africa, Ghana, Uganda and Kenya, while India and countries in Europe and North America would also be visited.

A parliamentary constitutional review committee went through the same process, and also visited the nine provinces and almost the same regional and overseas countries. The Parliamentary Reform Committee presented its report in May 1998. It is quite obvious nothing had changed either in the countries visited or the opinions of the people of Zimbabwe. Not much return on the taxpayers' investment, here.

Given the prevailing aggressive mood, with the people reeling under harsh economic conditions, one thing was clear; whoever wrote the new constitution was expected to make sure it was a constitution of the people and not one imposed upon them. All Zimbabweans were agreed on the minimum requirements, namely that there must be:

(a) limitations on presidential terms and powers;

(b) an end to presidential nomination of MPs;

(c) accountability of the Executive branch to Parliament;

(d) a senate to trim bills rather than allowing them to "sail" through the House;

---

21. UN Integrated Regional Information Network (IRIN), June 11, 1999.
22. *The Zimbabwe Independent*, 16 July, 1999.

(e) independent delimitation and electoral supervisory commissions; and

(f) a clear separation of powers between the executive, judiciary and legislature.

In early November 1999, after a protracted outreach program, the Constitutional Commission proclaimed, "The people have spoken." However, in an article in the *Sunday Mail* of November 14, 1999, Commission spokesperson Professor Jonathan Moyo ventured to say that the so-called process of gathering evidence from the people was simply meant "to legitimize" the Commission's own views on the constitution. "It is unreasonable and dishonest for anyone anywhere to think or suggest that expressing a view is the same thing as making a decision — what the people have spoken does not amount to a decision. Put simply, the people have said different things, some of them quite contradictory."[23]

### The Commission's Draft versus the Popular Will

One wonders how contradictory the people's expressed wish to have a non-executive head of state could be. The committee on the separation of powers clearly indicated that six out of ten administrative provinces did not want an executive president. The six provinces were Mashonaland Central, Mashonaland East, Manicaland, Matabeleland South, Matabeleland North and Bulawayo. The report showed that there was a split in Harare with some people suggesting that there should be a prime minister as head of government answerable to Parliament while others wanted an executive president who shared power with other important arms of government. Mashonaland West, Masvingo and the Midlands recommended the retention of the current system, with checks and balances, and the curtailing of the president's powers.

Various interest groups (which included the Zimbabwe National Chamber of Commerce, the Confederation of Zimbabwe Industries, Zimbabwe People's Convention, Transparency Front, and the Democratic Front) also wanted a ceremonial president.

Furthermore, all the 10 provinces agreed that the offices of governors should be abolished. However, the draft constitution featured elected governors as proposed by ZANU (PF). The draft recommended the constituency-based winner-take-all system while the committee on separation of power report said that most provinces wanted proportional representation. "Six of the 10 provinces indicated that they preferred proportional representation in

---

23. *The Sunday Mail*, 14 November, 1999.

parliamentary elections. That position was also supported by two political parties and a number of interest groups," the report said. "Three provinces and one political party favored the constituency-based winner-take-all system. One province preferred a simple majority."

Most of the ruling party's constitutional proposals to the Commission got the nod ahead of submissions made by the general public, opposition political parties and other interest groups. ZANU (PF) again triumphed over the will of the people. The ruling party, dragged into constitutional reform kicking and screaming, showed again its contempt for the electorate. The Constitutional Commission succumbed to ZANU (PF)'s seduction. The draft constitution was an imposition from above, and did not even begin to approximate the people's written and oral submissions.

The 106-page draft constitution presented to President Robert Mugabe on November 29, 1999 rejected major proposals contained in the survey report to restrict the powers of the presidency. The NCA, which boycotted the government's reform process, said the commission was "always a ZANU (PF) affair" and the independent commissioners who "thought they had a say are left licking their wounds."[24]

The major principles of the draft constitution as against the evidence of what the public said they wanted in the constitution can be summed up as follows:

- The Commission's own reports show that the people wanted both lower and upper age limits for persons holding presidential office, 40 years and either 65 years or 70 years, respectively. Only the lower limit of 40 years was implemented.

- The majority of the people who spoke to the Commission clearly demanded that the constitution should implement a ceremonial presidential system. Instead, an executive presidential system was augmented with a ceremonial Prime Minister.

- The public wanted the powers of the executive to be reduced drastically. Instead, the same powers continued to be invested in the executive president, including the power of appointing cabinet ministers, judges, ambassadors, members of all commissions ("independent" or otherwise), permanent secretaries, the attorney-general, etc.

---

24. UN Integrated Regional Information Network (IRIN), 30 November, 1999.

- The power to dissolve Parliament at any time was retained, as was the power to pardon convicted criminals and the power to declare a state of emergency. Indeed, now the specific power was added to deploy troops as and when and to wherever the president wished, including in foreign countries.

- The public also categorically demanded an executive which was not above the law and which was not immune to legal process. Instead, the executive presidency enjoys legal immunity such that while he/she remains in office the president would not be amenable to the law.

- The public demanded a professional and impartial Attorney-General who has responsibility for non-partisan and professional prosecutions.

- The public also demanded independent commissions for the administration and management of elections; monitoring and setting regulatory standards for the media; promoting and defending human rights; combating corruption; controlling and regulating land tenure, acquisition, distribution, planning and use; the processing of judgeship appointments; and for regulating and controlling the national central banking authority.

No independent central banking authority was provided, not even in name. The other independent commissions were, but in name only. In reality, they cannot be independent. All of their members are appointed by the president, albeit subject to Senate approval. There was not even a requirement that any of these members be recommended by independent centers of authority. They are all simple presidential appointees.

Indeed, the *Human Rights and Social Justice Commission* had greater potential for independence than the Electoral Commission, since three of its members were to be appointed on the advice of the Judicial Service Commission — assuming that there would be an independent Judicial Service Commission. However, even here the president could out-number the three by appointing seven others at his own discretion, subject only to Senate approval.

The composition of the *Judicial Service Commission* would be the Chief Justice, the Judge President, the Attorney-General, a member of the Public Service Commission, a chief appointed by the president at his discretion, a law lecturer appointed by the president at his discretion, two other persons appointed by the president at his discretion and one person appointed by the president on the nomination of the Law Society. It is known that the Attorney-General is a party sympathizer and the Judge President falls in the same category; so does the leadership of the chiefs. With the exception of the Chief Justice and the nominee of the Law Society, the rest would have the potential of being party cadres or supporters.

The Supreme Court was emasculated by the creation of a new *Constitutional Court*, which would remove the Supreme Court's existing powers to interpret the constitution. Closer examination reveals that whilst it would comprise present Supreme Court judges and the Judge President, Section 151 (3)(b) of the draft constitution would give Parliament wide powers to pack the court with additional judges. This is a horrendous provision, which completely negates the principle of separation of powers and undermines the independence of the judiciary. Parliament would have the power to add almost a majority of judges, who would then consider the constitutionality of bills presented to the Constitutional Court by the very same Parliament that appointed them in the first place.

The *Independent Electoral Commission's* impartiality was compromised by making its appointment dependent exclusively on the president (Section 199). In terms of Section 204, the president could remove a member of the commission from office on such vague grounds as "misconduct" or "incompetence."

The provisions relating to a *Media Commission* (Section 213) are premised on the obvious deception that journalists themselves may threaten the freedom of the press; all that was required to protect press freedom was to provide a fundamental right to freedom of expression (including press freedom) in the Bill of Rights.

The *Public Prosecutor* created by Section 216 to replace the current Ombudsman was nothing but a change of name for the Ombudsman. Like the current Ombudsman, he/she would have no power to take appropriate action to redress prejudices or injustices discovered by his/her investigations. He/she would not investigate the president's office, as the current position could, because the draft constitution restricted his/her investigative functions to "administrative action taken by a public officer" and the definition of "public officer" in the same draft constitution may not cover the president or even Cabinet ministers.

Participants in the Constitutional Commission had agreed that commissioners on the *Anti-corruption Commission* should be appointed by members of the public, through Parliament, and not by the executive. The final draft revealed that the anti-graft board would have no powers to prosecute any persons suspected of corruption and any suggested prosecution could only be through the Attorney-General (Section 212), who in terms of the same constitution is a member of the Cabinet. In any event, the president's prerogative of mercy was retained in its current uncontrolled manner (Section 101 of the draft) and could therefore be used to pardon persons convicted of corruption.

In another area of great concern, the draft constitution allowed Parliament to "confer legislative functions on any person or authority" (Section 104). This section reproduced, almost word for word, Section 32(2) of the current constitution which has allowed Parliament to delegate its law-making powers so much as to permit the president via the Presidential Powers (Temporary Measures) Act (Chapter 10:20) to make law as he pleases.

The power of Parliament to pass a vote of no confidence in the government is made almost impossible to exercise by insisting that two-thirds of the total membership and not a mere majority is required to pass the motion (Section 99) and by giving the president power to dissolve Parliament even where two-thirds of MPs pass a vote of no confidence in the government.

Constitutional lawyers felt that these restrictions on Parliament's powers show that the framers did not understand the constitutional principles involved. If a prime minister is made a head of government and all that is required to form a government is a simple majority, it should follow that all that is required to remove the government should be a simple majority. This is indeed the position under the Westminster system. In other words, if a majority of MPs can pass a vote of no confidence in the government, it means the Prime Minister is no longer commanding a majority and should go. Why require a two-thirds majority? Further, it does not make sense to give the president the option of dissolving Parliament for passing a vote of no confidence in the government. The president can only be permitted to dissolve Parliament if there is no other person who commands a majority and is able to form a government.

Then there is the power of Parliament to remove the president from office. The National Assembly, which is supposed to be the main representative of the people, has no power to remove the president from office even if all its members vote in favor of that removal. At most, the National Assembly could only make a "request" (Section 84) to the Senate to impeach the president. On the other hand, the Senate could not on its own initiate the removal of the president: it would have to wait for a request from the National Assembly. Constitutional lawyers ask whether the Senate would be obliged to conduct impeachment proceedings on receipt of the "request" from the National Assembly. The wording of Section 84 suggests that it would not. What would happen where the two houses are under the control of different political parties? Furthermore, although the president cannot dissolve Parliament once the impeachment process has started in the Senate, the president has powers to dissolve Parliament during the time that the National Assembly is debating a motion to request the Senate to conduct impeachment proceedings.

Another point of departure in the draft constitution is Clause 5 of Part 11 of the 4th Schedule, which provides that where the Senate has rejected a Bill (proposed law), the two Houses of Parliament shall sit in joint session and vote on the Bill. If at least "half of the total membership of the House" votes in favor of enacting the Bill, it shall be regarded as having been passed. This means that the National Assembly members are empowered to over-rule the Senate by their sheer numbers since a joint sitting will have 200 members of the National Assembly and 60 members of the Senate. Thus, even if all the Senators voted against a Bill at a joint sitting, they will always be a minority. In short, a dispute between the Houses will invariably be resolved in favor of the lower house unless a large number of members of the lower house abandon that house's position in favor of the Senate one. In reality, the National Assembly is given the final word.

While critics conceded the document had some good elements, particularly the widened Bill of Rights, it failed dismally to ensure an accountable executive and to level the political playing field. Because the draft constitution was seen as a replica of that of ZANU (PF), it was unlikely to create a common political culture and a durable democracy.

Eric Bloch, an outspoken critic of the government who only accepted the appointment to the commission after Minister Without Portfolio Cde Eddison Zvobgo promised him in writing that the panel would be allowed to act independently, had this to confess: "I am sorry to all Zimbabweans that I endorsed and agreed to take part in this thing (the Constitutional Commission). All the fears that were expressed by those who opposed this process have come true. I am disillusioned."[25] About 24 commissioners, mostly non-ZANU (PF) members, signed a petition urging President Mugabe to reject the draft because they felt Chidyausiku had bulldozed it through and because it did not represent the people's views.

Since the plenary session to adopt the draft on November 26, 1999, the commission had strongly disagreed on what powers the proposed new constitution should allocate the president and on whether Mugabe should be

---

25. *The Financial Gazette*, 2 December, 1999.

barred from standing for president again. One group, made up of mainly non-ZANU (PF) commissioners, accused the other group, led by top ZANU (PF) officials, of trying to subvert the will of the people to further political party interests. On November 29, 1999, the Commission's chairman, Justice Godfrey Chidyausiku, declared the draft adopted "by acclamation" — instead of by secret ballot, as required by the terms of reference. There were cries of "No! No! No!" from the floor, but the deal had been done.

Thus, the draft constitution was gazetted on December 2, 1999 amid a storm of protest from commissioners and others who felt it had deliberately ignored popular demands — most notably relating to the powers of the president.

### Ramming It Through

However, this did not even deter the commission from perpetuating its life in questionable circumstances and energetically promoting a "Yes" vote, while the state, through its broadcasting monopoly, prevented any sort of reply even though the NCA had paid millions of dollars for advertisements on the broadcaster. Those with divergent views were branded reactionaries who wanted to maintain the 1979 colonial constitution agreed at Lancaster House — ignoring the 15 amendments the ZANU (PF) government made to deface that document.

Analysts felt that the commission's campaign drumbeats were out of tune with its claims of impartiality. By entering the fray alongside partisan groups to campaign for a particular outcome, the commission was admitting that it was also partisan. In any case, the commission had no legal right or authority to campaign for the draft. It was using the state apparatus and public funds to purchase support for its unmarketable product.

It is sad to note that part of the commission's media campaign had racial overtones. An advert entitled "Why You Must Vote Yes" said: "White settlers in this country voted for something they called self-government which excluded the rest of us (Black people). They used this illegality to continue taking away our land without compensation." The commission's advert concludes, "The same white settlers, with the help of the British government and their international friends, are funding sell-out Zimbabweans to buy your rights urging you to vote 'No' to the draft constitution.... Vote 'Yes' in the referendum and make a historic change."

The run-up to the referendum on February 12-13, 2000 was reminiscent of the famous "No" campaign in November 1971, when the country's then disenfranchised majority united to hold mass demonstrations against the Pearce Commission and to reject constitutional proposals that had been worked out by the British government and Rhodesia's Premier Ian Smith. It was not just the NCA that campaigned against the draft constitution, but Zimbabwe's influential churches added their voices to a chorus of national disapproval.

Even as the commissioners took it upon themselves to go back to the people to urge them to vote "Yes" to the draft constitution, the meetings turned into "No" campaigns. Political observers pointed out that meetings were successful in that people managed to have their views heard and managed to tell the commissioners that they were not happy with the draft and were going to reject it if major changes were not made. Many commissioners were reported to have been booed by the audiences before being dismissed and never given a chance to address the people. During all the meetings, people were particularly worried about the presidential powers in the draft constitution, which they said were excessive.

The necessity for the Constitutional Commission to even hold further meetings to ensure that the people did not miss "the historic opportunity to vote yes" was itself an indication that the Constitutional Commission did not carry out thorough civic education before penning its draft. Otherwise, how could they have come up with such unpalatable provisions as the one enabling a president to declare war, with no more check-and-balance provided but that the president's decision had to be ratified at a meeting of the Senate and National Assembly which shall be held within seven sittings of Parliament, and without specifying the period within which the said seven sittings should be held — seven days? seven years? Or proposing a House of Assembly of 200 MPs, a number which could not even be accommodated in the present parliament chamber. This was no doubt taken from Section 8.3 of the ZANU (PF) draft constitutional proposals.

The final document was forced through its final plenary session without a vote of approval from the commissioners themselves. This only reinforced the knowledge that the draft constitution could not serve as the founding law upon which Zimbabwe could claim to be a democratic country. If it were, and if it had been genuinely subjected to national debate, there would have been no need for the feverish efforts to brainwash the nation, and to intimidate, harass and muzzle all those expressing their doubts about its contents.

On the contrary, the commission sought to create the illusion that the constitution had been widely debated when, in actual fact, the final draft was presented to President Robert Mugabe as a *fait accompli* without any debate whatsoever (beyond the howls of protest from every corner).

In December 1999, the government, under pressure to reject the Commission's so-called findings, made "corrections and clarifications" to the draft in an effort to convince Zimbabweans it had captured their views. Legal opinion was that the amendments thus produced went far beyond the boundaries of "clarification," especially the clauses dealing with land acquisition, the declaration of state of emergency, corporal punishment and other topics. One constitutional lawyer called the changes "substantial." If the government wanted to effect the changes legitimately, the logical course would have been to reconvene the Constitutional Commission to debate the changes.

No wonder that in February 2000 (just before the historic referendum), ten commissioners signed a petition distancing themselves from the "corrections and clarifications" made to the draft.

On February 12-13, 2000, Zimbabwean President Robert Mugabe suffered a humiliating defeat in a referendum on the draft constitution, which his opponents said was designed to entrench his 20-year rule. The referendum was a crucial test before general elections in June 2000, in which a new broad-based opposition movement (spurred on by the country's worsening economic crisis) was challenging the government. Final figures announced by Registrar-General Tobaiwa Mudede showed that 697,754 (or 55%) voted against and 578,210[26] in favor of the draft constitution.

Abandoning his customary unyielding posture, Mugabe accepted defeat with apparent grace, saying it consolidated democracy. In a televised address to the nation on February 15, the President said, "Government accepts the result and accepts the will of the people."

The *Daily News* must have been rubbing its hands in glee, because its own poll had indicated this result. The *Herald* had tried to neutralize that poll with one of its own which showed that Mugabe would win comfortably.

Notwithstanding, under referendum legislation, the President was not obliged to respect the outcome of the vote, although he had promised beforehand that he would do so.

Most political analysts believe that in urban centers, black voters angered by unprecedented economic hardships had flocked to the polls to reject the

---

26. *Business Day*, 16 February, 2000, Johannesburg, SA.

proposals by an average three-to-one margin. In rural areas, more voters supported the proposals, but there was a generally low turnout. The rains were nominally blamed for the poor turnout in rural areas; but while the opposition thought the "Yes" vote was in fact boosted by the rural vote which was easier to rig, it must have dawned on the ruling party that the opposition had been working on the rural electorate. Clearly, ZANU (PF) was no longer popular in the rural areas — it was feared. Once the fear was removed, ZANU (PF) had no base.

Celebrations over the result were heightened by the release of opposition figure Tendai Biti and eight of his colleagues who were detained on February 12 while campaigning for a "No" vote. The courts said they had no case to answer.

Analysts thought ZANU (PF) was shaken, not only by the low turnout for the referendum in its traditional rural stronghold, but also by the narrow margin of the "Yes" victory there. Although only 26% of the voters turned up, the figures were also a smack in the face for those who were claiming that whites swayed the vote. The difference of nearly 120,000 was more than the entire white population in Zimbabwe, men, women and children included.

The intensified "Yes" media campaign also revealed one fallacy. People may buy and read newspapers, but they can still read between the lines. ZANU (PF) ought to have understood this because they came to power in 1980 the same way. ZANU (PF) won the 1980 general elections despite a media blackout on the party: its leaders were only allowed back in the country a month or so before the general elections and they received no media coverage other than some negative pieces. As "communist terrorists," the local media claimed the party was even going to scrap Christmas. The party was denied offices in the city center and was only bailed out by Solomon Tawengwa, who offered them offices at his Mushandirapamwe Hotel in Highfield. Mugabe himself survived a bomb explosion in Masvingo, but when it came to poll time, even ZANU (PF) was surprised — not only did they win, but the margin was so wide it could have formed a government on its own. Bishop Abel Muzorewa (who had the backing of all the state media, the country's police and soldiers, helicopters to campaign with, and the backing of Ian Smith and the white community as well as the West), lost dismally, leading some people to joke that he ruled for three months, had three helicopters and ended up with three seats.[27]

In a very stark way, history was repeating itself. The "Yes" campaigners threatened the electorate and threatened the people about the consequences of

---

27. *Zimbabwe: The Rise to Nationhood*, Minerva Press, London, 1998.

voting "No." They did not give the people an option. It was "Yes," or nothing. If they did not accept the new constitution, it meant they supported the Lancaster House one. This was reminiscent of the campaign in favor of the rejected Anglo-Rhodesian Settlement Proposals.

Most political analysts agreed that the referendum was not about the constitution alone, but also was about Mugabe's continued leadership. Some argued that it was not even about ZANU (PF), but about Mugabe himself. He has so personalized the party that the people react to him as a person, rather than the ruling party, per se. Although some critics were trying to play down the numbers, the victory was very significant. For four months before the referendum, Zimbabweans had been bombarded with "Yes" campaign advertising on radio, television and all the country's newspapers while the "No" campaign was only allowed on radio and TV for a month. Prior to that, it had only been carried by the smaller, weekly, private media whose circulation is a tiny fraction of the mainline pro-government newspapers. The campaign was so distorted that some rural voters interviewed by the BBC said they did not know what they were going to vote for except that they had to vote "Yes."

Instead of easing the pressure on his government by withdrawing from the DRC, agreeing an economic rescue package with international donors, and launching a new constitutional reform process with opposition participation, Mugabe unleashed the so-called ex-combatants onto the commercial farming community. By March 15, 2000, 500 farms had been seized nationwide. In fact, there was evidence that Zimbabwe's ruling ZANU (PF) had hired thousands of supporters and unemployed youths to help restive war veterans invade white-owned commercial farms across the country. It was discovered that only between 15 and 20% of the farm invaders were ex-combatants, with the rest of the invaders being ZANU (PF) supporters and urban-based jobless youths who were being paid Z$50 a day for their participation. CFU members also saw government vehicles dropping food supplies on the farms.

Although President Mugabe tried to play up the question of land, especially the fact that the draft constitution allowed the repossession of white-owned farms without compensation, this was not an issue at all with most black voters. Commentators said black Zimbabweans supported Mugabe on the land issue. People wanted land; but they were against the implementation of the program. Mugabe made too many promises which he did not fulfill, and people were no longer buying what he said. The government had failed to deliver over the past 20 years and even though in 1997 it designated more than 1,500 farms, none of these farms had been taken over, except those whose designation was not contested. In the case of the designated farms, Zimbabweans were quite aware that these ended up in the possession of ZANU (PF) politicians and cronies.

Thus, even under the draft constitution, people were convinced that this was just another campaign gimmick. ZANU (PF) was not going to deliver.

## CHAPTER 3. THE FOLLY IN A *DE FACTO* ONE-PARTY DEMOCRACY

### *Harassment of the Opposition*

The experience of de-colonization of Africa and Zimbabwe's own liberation struggles, reflected during Chimurenga I, the "reformist politics" of the 1940s to early 1960s, and finally Chimurenga II show that these sacrifices were inspired by the desire to win democratic rights.

However, from the very early years of independence, ZANU (PF) was quite clear about its intentions to establish a one-party state. The essence of totalitarianism lies in its ideology. It offers a set of self-serving propositions about society and one-sided accounts of history in which the existing order has to be radically overhauled and tries to refashion the economy, society, family life, education and culture in its own image. While democracies allow for a fairly broad parameter of political competition, totalitarian regimes offer forced mobilization or induced participation; they are more restrictive and the will of the ruling party and its leader are often imposed on the people. Whereas democracies try to win the support of civic groups through sound policies, totalitarian regimes try to penetrate, restructure and integrate different interest groups. This is precisely what ZANU (PF) was trying to do.

The 1980 general election supervised by the British Governor, Lord Arthur Soames, was regarded as fair by all the observers on the ground. It should be appreciated, however, how fearful Zimbabweans were of a return to violence, which ZANU (PF) had threatened if it did not win that election — perhaps that is why it won. The results, nonetheless, gave Zimbabwe a government with a strong opposition which was made up mainly of PF-ZAPU with 20 seats and the Rhodesian Front with its reserved 20 seats. The United African National Council (UANC), which had emerged with 51 seats in the 1979 "internal-settlement" election, managed to take home only three seats out of a possible 80.[28] Although ZANU (PF) was the majority party with 57 seats, it did not muster the two-thirds majority needed for changing those provisions in the constitution which were not entrenched. It is understandable, therefore, why ZANU (PF) decided to develop a policy of reconciliation.

It would be foolhardy to underestimate the turbulent political climate which drove ZANU (PF) in choosing priorities in building the first government of an independent Zimbabwe. With a war-torn country and the hatred that had been created between blacks and whites, in addition to the three antagonistic armies that had emerged as a result of 15 years of conflict, the country was in need of stability. Thus, when Prime Minister Mugabe went for national reconciliation and reconstruction coupled with integration of the three armed forces as his main priorities, he was hailed as a statesman. But the coalition government that emerged as a result of the policy of reconciliation did not hold for very long.

When ZANU (PF) called for an increasingly socialist economy for the country, in early 1982, and stated that in future all government policies would first be approved by ZANU (PF), this was immediately denounced by PF-ZAPU's Joshua Nkomo. A new political crisis between the two long-time rival leaders was created. The discovery of arms caches on farms owned by Nitram, a firm owned by about 4,000 former ZIPRA combatants through their demobilization payments, was the straw that broke the camel's back. Joshua Nkomo, who was Minister of Home Affairs, and his other three colleagues in the coalition government were dismissed. Dissident activities in Matabeleland and part of the Midlands made reconciliation between the two parties even more difficult. The government decided to discard the carrot and went for the stick in the form of Operation Gukurahundi. A crack Korean-trained force was sent to suppress the rebellion in Matabeleland. PF-ZAPU was accused of collaboration and banned. Gukurahundi sought to wipe out Joshua Nkomo's opposition in the most brutal manner. Nkomo was forced into exile to avoid the North Korean-trained brigade set on him and his followers by President Mugabe.

The 1985 general election saw the vote split strictly along tribal lines and Prime Minister Mugabe emerged with a powerful majority, winning 76% of the vote, an increase of 12% over 1980. The emerging picture reflected a gradual crumbling of opposition to ZANU (PF). By this time the party had created a youth brigade, which it used to unleash violence on those accused of being members of ZAPU and UANC (*Madzakutsaku*). After the election, a short period of violence against supporters of non-ZANU (PF) parties occurred and some senior PF-ZAPU party officials and recently elected MPs were arrested. After

---

28. *Zimbabwe: The Rise to Nationhood*, Minerva Press, 1998.

Prime Minister Mugabe's "*kugobora zvitsiga*" (uprooting tree stumps) victory speech, the Youth Brigade roamed the high density areas evicting their "enemies" from their homes, looting and destroying their properties. While no law was invoked against them, they were joined by the party's Youth League. This partnership was particularly felt in Kwekwe, where they not only destroyed property belonging to perceived political enemies but also besieged a police station and seized an alleged ZAPU member who had sought refuge there — and murdered that person right there. There were no arrests and no one was ever charged for that murder. In Silobela, Lower Gweru and elsewhere the Youth Brigade were bussed from Gweru and Kwekwe and torched people's huts and granaries. Like Kamuzu Banda's notorious Young Pioneers of Malawi, the Youth Brigade (in their khaki attire with green-collared shirts) was used by the ZANU (PF) politicians before being disbanded after the signing of the unity (peace) agreement on December 22, 1987.

Interesting enough, December 22 has been turned into a national holiday; but for many Zimbabweans, the fact that two parties came together to form one party in their quest to establish a one-party state should not be celebrated. There is no unity in the country. History shows clearly that in 1963 ZANU split from ZAPU, after which an "effort" was made to merge the rival parties in 1971 when the exiled ZANU and ZAPU leaders resident in Lusaka announced the formation of the Front for the Liberation of Zimbabwe (FROLIZI). The titular leaders of the new organization were ousted early in 1972 by James Chikerema, George Nyandoro and Nathan Shamuyarira. Then the parties came together under the African National Council (ANC) "umbrella," in 1974. However, by the end of 1975, Joshua Nkomo had denounced the ANC umbrella and returned to Zimbabwe (then Rhodesia) as leader of an "internal" ANC. That was not the end of the story; Nkomo and Mugabe announced the formation of the Patriotic Front on October 9, 1976. The Frontline Presidents and the Liberation Committee of the Organization of African Unity immediately endorsed the front, which excluded Ndabaningi Sithole and Abel Muzorewa, as the primary Zimbabwe nationalist body. It was not surprising, however, that ZANU and ZAPU split again into ZANU (PF) and PF-ZAPU in the run-up to the February 27-29, 1980 general election.

Even ZAPU political detainees (who were supposed to be affected by the unity accord and the 1988 presidential amnesty), were, at the end of December 1997, reported to be languishing in Khami maximum-security prison on the outskirts of Bulawayo, ten years after the signing of the accord. The prisoners included villagers detained for helping rebel forces in Matabeleland and parts of the Midlands. There were three former guerrillas of ZIPRA, one of who was identified as being Lovejoy Ncube, who originated from Tsolotsho district north of Bulawayo. Ncube was detained in 1985 on allegations that he assisted anti-government rebels in the villages of Matabeleland, the political power base of Nkomo's party. The presidential amnesty was supposed to have covered all ZAPU detainees, fugitives and members of the party's former armed wing. During political disturbances in the two provinces, the ZANU (PF) government detained more than 10,000 Nkomo supporters, former ZIPRA guerrillas and their commanders, and villagers who were accused of assisting dissidents. Moreover, the emergence of pressure groups like Imbovane Yamahlabezulu (one of the Zulu battalions)[29] and Vhukani Mahlabezulu (wake up Zulu nation) and other related organizations cannot be described as a sign of national unity.

The 1998 Unity Day commemoration in Bulawayo was marked by an open rebellion against the ruling ZANU (PF). While the party battled to garner respectable crowds for its ceremonies at Mpopoma High School, political and pressure groups organized functions that directly challenged the legitimacy of the unity accord itself. Imbovane Yamahlabezulu packed the Bulawayo City Hall, which has a capacity of 4,500 people, while ZAPU revivalists also attracted a substantial number of loyalists at White City Stadium and the federalist Liberty Party of Zimbabwe staged a prayer rally in memory of all those who died during the 1980s armed conflict. In the city center, it was business as usual as many shops, cashing in on Christmas late-shoppers, remained open, while in the industrial area some companies operated behind closed doors.

The boycott and the thrust of the three meetings organized by the anti-unity groups were the biggest statement of Matabeleland's open rebellion since the signing of the unity pact. One of the disturbing features of this rebellion is the call for "sovereignty" by some of the Ndebele groups. They want "political autonomy and sovereignty" to govern themselves so they can "practice [their] own culture and honor [their] fallen heroes." They say that they need sovereignty to redress the existing political and economic disparity. They want "total autonomy" in order to bring about total reconciliation between Nguni-speakers and the rest of the ethnic groupings inside Zimbabwe.

People in Matabeleland are unanimous in saying that unity was achieved through force, not the ballot box. PF-ZAPU was forced to surrender. Before the

---

29. Imbovane treasurer Mqondobanzi Magonya said, "This is a reincarnation of Imbovane, we found it there and has always been there dating back to the 17th century. Imbovane started in South Africa during the days of Tshaka and since then, each Ndebele generation has had Imbovane." (*The Zimbabwe Mirror*, 3 July, 1998)

unity accord was signed, Home Affairs Minister Dumiso Dabengwa, who was the chief of ZIPRA, said, "It would be very difficult for both parties, not just the ZAPU leadership, to persuade people to come into a merger in which one of these parties still maintains its name. It could be necessary to find a completely new name without ZAPU or ZANU connotations." As it stands, not only was PF-ZAPU swallowed into ZANU (PF), but ZANU (PF) retained its emblem of a cock while the bull which represented ZAPU was done away with. As if to emphasize this point, the National Railways of Zimbabwe building in Julius Nyerere Way was suitably named "Karigamombe" (Mugabe's nickname, which literally means "the one who brought the bull to its knees").

At Dr. Joshua Nkomo's burial at Heroes Acre, on July 5, 1999, the pleas for unity further proved that the accord was cosmetic. If the number of times ZANU (PF) politicians pronounced the word "unity" were all that was required to achieve it, then Zimbabwe would be the most united nation in the entire world. People expected President Mugabe to take the opportunity of such a national event to apologize for the atrocities committed by the Fifth Brigade. However, what the nation heard was that, "We regret that the conflict resulted in great suffering of civilians." Regretting that the episode took place is scant comfort to the people of Matabeleland and part of the Midlands who live with the scars of that terrible phase of Zimbabwe's independence.

In order to gain and maintain hegemony, ZANU (PF) also used constitutional amendments, reflected particularly in Constitutional Amendment No. 7 of 1987. At this stage, both PF-ZAPU and the whites were co-opted and integrated into the government, thereby losing some of their independent institutional existence. Only ZANU (Ndonga), which had only one seat in Parliament, was able to persistently resist integration and guard its zones of autonomy in Chipinge, despite the fact that many of its middle classes and intellectuals were co-opted into the ruling ZANU (PF). It is common knowledge, however, that many in the white communities and among the Ndebele (and even among the Shona) never quite accepted integration and co-option into the ZANU (PF) authoritarian institutional structures.

During the 1990 general election, Zimbabwe Unity Movement's candidate for Gweru, Patrick Kombayi, was shot and wounded at the height of the elections' campaign. In Chinhoyi, several ZANU (PF) youths unleashed violence on suspected members of ZUM (Zimbabwe Unity Movement). ZANU (PF) registered an overwhelming victory with 117 of a possible 120 seats in a House of 150 (20 seats are presidential nominees and 10 are reserved for customary chiefs).

Like the attackers of Kombayi, the marauding youths were arrested, prosecuted and convicted but they immediately received presidential pardons.

With ZUM represented by just two MPs and ZANU (Ndonga) a single seat, there would appear to have been little need for the governing party to use violent methods to suppress the opposition. Nonetheless, a reported turnout of little over 50% of the registered electorate must have worried the authorities in Harare. During the 1980 election, 94% cast their vote; now, even the most ardent supporters of ZANU (PF) agreed that the low turnout must have been a "protest vote." The country was gradually sliding towards bankruptcy and the lawlessness during general elections was caused by the policies of the government itself, which showed very little respect for democratic principles and the rule of law.

By the 1995 general election, Zimbabwe was reported to have 18 opposition parties, although only a handful were active. The activities of the opposition parties in the ensuing election campaign seemed to have been overshadowed by internal squabbles within ZANU (PF). The general election was actually fought and won or lost during ZANU (PF)'s primaries. Quite a good number of radical candidates, critical of corruption within the Party, were ousted during the primaries. Some stood as Independents during the subsequent election. One such suspended candidate was Margaret Dongo, whose campaign generated interest in Harare. Standing as an Independent and claiming that she had been "rigged" out of the ZANU (PF) primaries by senior party members, Dongo articulated the frustration and impatience of the urban poor as real wages plummeted, health and education services (ZANU's hallmark in the 1980s) deteriorated and ministerial corruption went unchecked. Although at first Dongo lost to a ZANU (PF) candidate, the result was declared null and void in an unprecedented ruling in the High Court in August 1995. Subsequently a by-election was held in the Harare South constituency at the end of November 1995. The campaign was characterized by political mud slinging and the presence of ZANU (PF) "top guns" was almost menacing.

Although just 18% bothered to go to the polls, Margaret Dongo defeated her liberation-war comrade Vivian Mwashita by 3,075 votes to 1,613.[30] This by-election evidently demonstrated that the ZANU (PF) giant could be challenged and defeated by those who were brave enough to do so. It also exposed the electoral process as a farce based on faulty voters' rolls, which clearly extended far beyond the Harare South constituency.

---

30. *The Herald*, 28 November, 1995.

Bolstered by Margaret Dongo's success, independent candidates started challenging ZANU (PF) in local elections. In Mutare, Lawrence Mudehwe stood against a party nominee and swept to victory in the executive mayoral election. Against a background of intimidation and physical attacks, independent candidates plunged in, anyway. Fidelis Mhashu stood in the Chitungwiza town executive mayoral election. In June 1997, when he decided to inspect the voters' list at town house, he found ruling ZANU (PF) supporters waiting for him. He was assaulted in the presence of the Minister of State in the President's Office, Cde Witness Mangwende. The assailants were never arrested. Political analysts suspected that the ruling party gave orders that Mhashu be assaulted to eliminate his chances of winning. Human rights organizations also suspected that people questioned by police for the assault may have implicated top ZANU (PF) officials, who may have given orders to eliminate Mhashu, and this had resulted in the delay in the prosecution of the assailants.

In the aftermath of the nationwide protests against taxes in December 1997, the ZCTU secretary general, Morgan Tsvangirai, was savagely assaulted by intruders who raided his office. Since the secretary general was credited for the successful protest, he may have been targeted as a political threat to the ruling party. Tsvangirai's assailants were still at large in 2004. It should be noted, though, that initially the independence government had enlisted the ZCTU and other civil society organizations into its authoritarian structures or induced them into giving the government acquiescent support, particularly with the patriotic excitement of independence. However, progressively there has been a reclaiming of independent existence and more importantly, the questioning of the politico-economic policies of the ZANU (PF) government.

Zimbabwe was experiencing the rise of the "independent candidates" phenomenon. Margaret Dongo, who had created a zonal autonomy in Sunningdale (the nucleus of the Harare South constituency); from that base, she was able to harass ZANU (PF) hegemony in neighboring areas. Riding on a wave of popularity, Dongo, with the help of the late Kempton Makamure (a University of Zimbabwe lecturer who stood as an independent candidate for the Harare executive mayoral election in 1997), formed a support group called the Movement for Independent Electoral Candidates (MIEC). The MIEC was not a political party, but a support group whose objectives were to help independent candidates and to act as a watchdog against excesses by the government. In that capacity, Margaret Dongo was involved in the Chitungwiza St Mary's constituency by-election.

Joseph Macheka, who was elected Chitungwiza's executive mayor in December 1997, was a Member of Parliament for Chitungwiza's St Mary's constituency. In the by-election campaign, an independent candidate, Marjorie Zenda, was pitted against Patrick Wurayayi Nyaruwata, a ZBC employee contesting on behalf of ZANU (PF). In that connection, Zimbabwe's only independent MP went to Chitungwiza to address a rally organized by the independent candidate in February 1998. While Margaret Dongo and some supporters were at the St Mary's home of Marjorie Zenda, a petrol bomb was thrown directly at Dongo and narrowly missed her. The rally was later abandoned because of the attack. It is no wonder, then, that out of about 35,000 registered voters only 3,430 participated and of these 2,250 voted for the ZANU (PF) candidate with the other 1,180 voting for the Independent.[31]

In a letter to Home Affairs Minister Dumiso Dabengwa, seeking guarantees for her safety, the Harare South constituency MP wrote that ZANU (PF) cadres carried out the attack. She pointed out that police officers who came to the scene of the attack confirmed a petrol bomb had been used, but they refused to arrest the assailants, who were still there and had been pointed out to the officers by witnesses. The MP said that she had experienced politically motivated attacks during election campaigns, but that this had been the worst as it involved a direct attempt on her life. No arrests were made. ZANU (PF) officials and cadres apparently are above the law.

The murder cases of Tichaona Chiminya, Talent Mabika (both MDC activists), and David Stevens (a Marondera farmer) need particular mention here. In early 2001, the High Court ordered the Attorney-General to instruct the police to investigate war veteran Kainos Tom "Kitsiyatota" Zimunya and CIO operative Joseph Mwale after they were repeatedly named as the prime suspects. Andrew Chigowera, the Attorney-General, duly complied and forwarded a request to the police — but this was ignored.

In November 2001, when pressed in Parliament on progress made in the matter, Cde Patrick Chinamasa, the Minister of Justice, Legal and Parliamentary Affairs, made a startling U-turn, accusing the High Court of exceeding its mandate. "The courts have no legal right to order the Attorney-General to prosecute criminals," fumed the Minister. "If a High Court judge did so, he was usurping the powers of the AG because the AG must not take directives or be influenced by the Executive, Parliament or the courts."[32]

---

31. *The Zimbabwe Standard*, 22 March, 1998.
32. *The Daily News*, 27 November, 2001.

Legal analysts thought Cde Chinamasa misdirected himself in this case. Section 137 of the Electoral Act empowers the courts to refer evidence to the AG. Mr. Stevens was dragged out of Murewa Police Station and murdered. Daniel Chitekateka, a Marondera war veteran, was arrested — almost a year later — and released soon afterwards without being charged. It is interesting to note, here, that the State media, as in all the cases involving kidnapping and the murder of assumed government opponents, took no interest in the matter. However, when the Bulawayo war veteran leader Cain Nkala was kidnapped and murdered, the glare of publicity and the pace at which the police arrested suspects left many Zimbabweans wondering. Ironically, the abduction and disappearance in June 2000 of Patrick Nabanyama, the poll agent of Bulawayo South MDC MP David Coltart, never received so much urgency although the late Cain Nkala himself was a suspect in the abduction.

Newspapers and their vendors were not spared by the selective application of justice involving lawlessness in Zimbabwe. In Murewa and elsewhere, *The Daily News* vendors were beaten by so-called war veterans; its offices were bombed followed by the bombing of the newspaper's printing press on January 28, 2001 but no arrests were made. It came as no surprise to political observers when the ZANU (PF) government decided to shut down *The Daily News* on September 12, 2003. And immediately after the closure, warrants of arrest were issued for 45 journalists of the newspaper. Following a ruling in its favor by Justice Michael Majuru on October 24, five directors were arrested on contempt of court charges after *The Daily News* returned to the news stands on Saturday. The Administrative Court had found that the government-appointed Media and Information Commission had wrongly denied the paper a license the previous month, and ordered the paper to be licensed by November 30. On December 18, sitting at the Administrative Court in Bulawayo, Judge Selo Nare, ignoring death threats, granted the paper a publishing license with immediate effect. Hours later, the government defied the court order to allow the paper to resume publishing and sent in riot police to shut down its printing works.

The ANZ registered yet another legal victory against the junior Minister of Information and Publicity, Jonathan Moyo, when High Court judge Tendai Uchena, in his ruling on January 18, 2004, said the police legal representative, Fatima Maxwell, was trying to defend the "indefensible." He compelled the police to vacate the newspaper's premises and stop interfering with its operations.

Shutting down the country's only private daily newspaper was a crude attempt to silence critics amid a deepening economic and political crisis. The

Zimbabwe chapter of the Media Institute of Southern Africa (MISA) said the shutdown of *The Daily News* should be seen as a "severe assault on media freedom." "The closure robs the country of one of the few alternative voices in an increasingly restricted space where Zimbabweans can freely express themselves," MISA said in a statement.

*The Daily News* had been operating without a license in defiance of AIPPA, which was passed soon after Mugabe's controversial re-election in 2002. The newspaper had indicated, however, that it was going to apply for registration, and a High Court ruling had allowed the Associated Newspapers of Zimbabwe to continue publishing while filing for registration as demanded by the Supreme Court. However, the government was not prepared to entertain the rulings by its own courts. While the constitutional challenge, in terms of the Supreme Court judgment, was still pending, not only was the newspaper abruptly closed but its equipment was confiscated by the police. This undermined the efficacy of a constitutional challenge. Taking into account provisions of Section 3 of the Constitution of Zimbabwe, "any law that is inconsistent with the constitution is null and void to the extent of its inconsistency with the constitution even without a declaration of invalidity." The Supreme Court had been too hasty in dealing with the ANZ application and not other challenges to AIPPA (e.g. the Independent Journalists Association of Zimbabwe's application, made in November 2002), raising the suspicion of political factors in its administration of justice, legal groups noted.

This contemptuous attitude towards the law starts at the highest levels of government and has been consistent over the whole period of independence. Ironically, the Rhodesian regime, which was universally accepted as a dictatorship, had the same disregard of legality and the rule of law. The expectation of the public is always that the police will carry out their constitutional duty to preserve law and order impartially and without fear or favor. Failure on the part of the police to live up to this standard and to the public's expectations erodes the public's confidence in law enforcement agencies and ultimately contributes to a breakdown of the rule of law.

In a development following the closure of *The Daily News*, Beatrice Mtetwa was allegedly brutally attacked by police. A senior partner of the local firm Kanto & Immerman, Mtetwa was attacked on October 12, just days before she was to represent the paper in the court hearing. She is also chairperson of the Zimbabwe Law Society Human Rights Committee. The incident shocked the legal fraternity at home and abroad as it came after the assault on *The Daily News* lawyer Gugulethu Moyo by Jocelyn Chiwenga in June — also at a police station.

It is trite to state that the Zimbabwe Republic Police and all other government agencies whose salaries are paid by taxpayers owe it to the Republic of Zimbabwe, and not to a political party, to carry out their duties rapidly, impartially and efficiently. There can be no law and order, or the rule of law, if those charged with its enforcement (including those who make the laws that Zimbabweans must abide by) continue to flagrantly flout or bend the law. This is a recipe for anarchy.

The air of strife in the country blew across the borders into the rest of Africa. The Organization of African Unity (OAU) decided to cancel a proposed meeting of its Central Organ for Conflict Prevention, Management and Resolution scheduled for February 11-12, 1998 in Harare; how could African leaders come to talk about resolving conflict when there was conflict ongoing in the country? The Central Organ on Conflict Resolution was formed in 1993, with Algeria, Angola, Botswana, Burkina Faso, Cameroon, Congo Republic, Gabon, Ghana, Ivory Coast, Kenya, Mauritius, Nigeria, Togo, Tunisia, Uganda and Zimbabwe as its members. It is not far-fetched to conclude that these African leaders were worried about the prospect of renewed civil unrest in the Zimbabwean capital after graphic reports in the international media.

Secondly, the decision by President Clinton to scratch Zimbabwe from his African tour in March 1998, and an unusually robust statement from the US ambassador to Zimbabwe (declaring that the Zimbabwe government was "moving in a disturbing direction") provided further indications of disenchantment by friends who were usually anxious to shower praise. (It was leaked that President Bill Clinton was even prepared to be a little economical with the truth, proposing to utter expressions like "a beacon for Africa.... model democracy.")

Notwithstanding, the problem appears to go beyond the fact that laws are disregarded. The content of some of the major laws of Zimbabwe negate the very idea of law (as opposed to political and executive authority). A nation's laws must be certain and in a democracy must eliminate the exercise of wide executive discretionary powers. In Zimbabwe, Parliament has repeatedly enacted laws which are the very antithesis of the rule of law in that they vest wide discretionary powers in the executive arm of government. The electoral laws themselves amount to a surrender by Parliament of its legislative power. Zimbabwe is a *de facto* one-party state.

Therefore, it appears that the fundamental difficulty in the process of seeking the rehabilitation of not just the law and the rule of law but also the political system is to ensure that elections and electoral processes produce a balanced Parliament which is not excessively dominated by one political party. ZANU (PF) has never been challenged to be imaginative in the economic and political governance of the country. The party has governed with no consultation with the electorate, and has suffered virtually no consequences when it gets things wrong.

This does not mean that no opposition exists in Zimbabwe. The weakness in the opposition is evidenced by the fact that everyone wants to be considered the leader at the expense of the other leaders. In 1994, a fragile unity forged between Bishop Abel Muzorewa's tainted United African National Council and Edgar Tekere's ZUM disintegrated precisely because there were "too many leaders" and "too few followers." Hopes were raised when the Forum Party of Zimbabwe (FPZ) was created out of a former pressure group (Forum Trust, formed in 1990), with former Chief Justice Enoch Dumbutshena at its head. Council seats were won in Harare and Bulawayo, but because everyone wants to be considered "best," at the expense of "friends" and "neighbors," the party just faded away.

In December 1998, the MIEC launched a new party by the name of the Zimbabwe Union of Democrats (ZUD), led by Harare South MP Margaret Dongo. ZUD's political agenda was supposed to focus on the institution of good governance, democracy, respect for the rule of law, and equitable distribution of resources. If elected to form a government, ZUD professed it would reduce the cabinet to just 16 ministers, reduce foreign diplomatic missions to a sustainable level, and cut public expenditure by drastically reducing the defense budget. ZUD acknowledged the need to address the land imbalance but said it would ensure that all land acquired would be given to deserving people — the poor masses in the rural areas. Hardly six months after the birth of ZUD, the country witnessed the birth of the Movement for Democratic Change (MDC) on May 19, 1999. Chaired by the ZCTU president Gibson Sibanda, the MDC comprised a national working group made up of about twenty civic and political bodies that would steer the establishment of provincial and district chapters throughout the country.

Whether these are any different from the numerous ineffective opposition parties that preceded them remains to be seen. However, it appears to be fashionable that each time individuals "quarrel" with ZANU (PF), they decide to resolve their dispute by forming political parties. Zimbabwe is a long way from being able to create a partnership between the government, the opposition, the bureaucrats, the academics, and the people in commerce and industry who could form committees to advise politicians and top bureaucrats, using researched and well-informed data and information.

The National Economic Consultative Forum, for example, instead of being a forum for discussions with the captains of commerce and industry, the trade union and other stakeholders, turned out to be a vehicle for the government to "lecture" on its policies. The party and government use their liberation credentials to claim a monopoly on national wisdom. Over the years, politicians made one bad policy after another. Because there was no vocal opposition from the public, they became more brazen and bad governance became the norm. Many of the "povo," middle and upper class citizens do not even know how to vote. Very few university students bother to participate in elections.

President Mugabe, speaking at the OAU summit in Harare in June 1997, lectured the international audience, saying, "democracy pursued without preparation is a factor for instability rather than stability......African governments have reason to question the motives of those who would stampede our governments willy-nilly to adopt democracy....Indeed," he went on, "these are countries which not only ran completely undemocratic colonial regimes, and even later supported dictatorships for decades where it suited their agendas during the Cold War." He concluded by saying, "African nations should be left alone to evolve our own institutions to sustain the democratic process." However, UN Secretary General Kofi Annan's speech, minutes after, appeared to be a direct rebuke. Criticisms of human rights violations were viewed by some African leaders "as a luxury of the rich countries for which Africa is not ready," he said. "I know that others treat it as an imposition — if not a plot — by the industrialized West....I find these thoughts truly demeaning," the veteran Ghanaian diplomat said, "demeaning of the yearning for human dignity that resides in every African heart.... So I say this to you, my brothers and sisters: that human rights are African rights."

It looks as though the pendulum was not swinging in the Zimbabwe leader's favor. Incensed by blatant human rights violations, the world's largest youth organization, the International Union of Socialist Youths (IUSY)[33], in December 1998 resolved to stage demonstrations against him. The youths also appealed to the UN, Amnesty International, the European Union, and the OAU

---

33. The IUSY has a membership of 100 countries as well as 132 affiliates worldwide. In a document signed by IUSY leaders at their convention in Mexico, the organization points at President Mugabe's unilateral decision to ban demonstrations using the draconian Presidential Powers (Temporary Measures) Act. "We as the IUSY members are worried at the persistent human rights violations the Zimbabwe government is presently engaged in," read part of the document.

to urgently investigate the torture allegedly inflicted on Zimbabwean soldiers who refused to fight in the Democratic Republic of Congo. Concern was also expressed over the use of contingents of the Zimbabwe National Army (ZNA) to crack down on civil unrest, which the youths said was a clear mechanism of a military regime. "IUSY condemns the recent shooting of innocent youths during the fuel price increase demonstrations, as well as the deployment of heavily armed Zimbabwe National Army units around the country, in place of the Zimbabwe Republic Police," the document said.

In at least one respect, Mugabe's overseas tour at the end of November 1998 went horribly wrong. On the last leg of a 16-day tour, which had taken him to Egypt, Libya, France and Italy, a hostile press greeted the President in the British capital. Instead of the usual diplomatic niceties proffered by insufferable official hosts — even for a head of state on a private visit — he was greeted with a barrage of bad publicity and state officials evidently were too embarrassed to be seen entertaining him. He was described in that country as a tyrant, a genocidal maniac, and a faceless dictator whose leadership qualities matched those of former Chilean dictator Augusto Pinochet. It was said that he should have been arrested upon his arrival on British soil for his human rights record. In an article headlined, "Larcen," the *Daily Mail* said: "Mugabe moves around Harare with all the panoply of a dictator....Like others of his sort, he has a weather eye for his own finances, but is oblivious to everyone else's, his cronies excepted. He does not care about the economy. His hold on power is all that counts." The paper went on to ask why President Mugabe should be granted financial aid, "when he is spending half a million pounds a day on a war that has absolutely nothing to do with Zimbabwe? When millions of pounds are being siphoned off by government corruption?"[34]

Meanwhile, Zimbabwe's political climate shifted in September 1999, with the launch of the labor-backed Movement for Democratic Change (MDC). After skillfully maneuvering the ZCTU for two years until it became the country's de facto official opposition, the trade union leaders finally launched Zimbabwe's newest political party on September 11, 1999. Many political analysts contended that the MDC, firmly rooted in the national labor force, had a strong grassroots base from which to launch itself into a formidable force that could wrest political power from ZANU (PF). It appeared the MDC was broad-based enough to garner sufficient votes in a fair poll to pip ZANU (PF).

---

34. *The Daily Mail*, London, 3 December 1998

Besides the strong political platform provided by the national labor constituency, the MDC had everything going its way. One only needed to look at the searing poverty and growing discontent among the populace. The living standard of most Zimbabweans has collapsed; 80% of them now live under the poverty datum line. Their plight has been exacerbated by soaring inflation, which raced to a new record high of 68.8% in August 1999, up more than five percentage points on July's annualized figure, as well as the crushing burden of record high interest rates of 60%.

In its favor, the new party had very strong leaders in Morgan Tsvangirai and Gibson Sibanda. During the MDC's launch at Harare's Rufaro Stadium, ZCTU head Sibanda and his secretary-general Tsvangirai appeared to embrace the challenge, directly appealing to the population to take charge of their lives. Formally declaring the MDC a political party, Sibanda told the 20,000-strong crowd: "We are suffering! We are angry! We are ready for change! The time has come. Today is the day we put an end to silent oppression and become a people inspired again to fight for what is right for Zimbabwe." Amid a welter of excitement from the crowd, the firebrand Tsvangirai declared: "Zimbabwe is at the cross-roads. The nation stands demoralized." He was scathing in his criticism of the past 21 years of ZANU (PF)'s rule, accusing President Mugabe and his party of dragging the country down the path of economic and social ruin. "There is corruption at the highest levels of the ZANU (PF) government and its leadership is unable to provide any leadership. The government's inability to provide solutions to problems affecting the people is a source of national anxiety, torment and despondency. Basic needs like food, health care, shelter and education are no longer within reach of the population."[35]

The basic needs the trade unionists were alluding to are fundamental human rights all over the world. It is no doubt, therefore, that the biggest challenge Africa faces in the new millennium is the attainment and recognition of all basic human rights, for without that, the continent's much talked-about renaissance will remain a pipe dream. Delivering a keynote address at a two-day Africa renaissance conference in Johannesburg at the end of September 1998, South African Deputy President Thabo Mbeki said that people wanted to see an Africa in which citizens participated in systems of governance, a continent where they were truly able to determine their destiny and put behind them the notion that democracy and human rights were peculiar western concepts. "Thus would we assume a stance of opposition to dictatorship, whatever form it may

---

35. *The Financial Gazette*, 16-22 September, 1999.

assume, and assure that when elections are held, these must be truly democratic, resulting in government which the people accept as genuinely representative."[36]

Although the human rights debate has been on the African agenda for decades, critics say most governments continue to pay lip service on the importance of upholding basic principles of democracy. Quite a good number of African states hide behind the OAU Charter that prohibits other African states from intervening in "internal affairs" even when it is obvious something is wrong. At the OAU summit held in Burkina Faso in June 1998, in his key-note speech South African President Nelson Mandela observed (with obvious reference to this), "I believe that we must all accept that we cannot abuse the concept of national sovereignty to deny the rest of the continent the right and duty to intervene when, behind those sovereign boundaries, people are being slaughtered to protect tyranny." Judging from what was happening in countries as far afield as the horn of Africa in Somalia to the Sahara in Algeria, Morocco and the Sudan; on to west Africa in Nigeria, Liberia, Sierra Leone and Guinea Bissau; on to central and east Africa in the Democratic Republic of Congo, the People's Republic of Congo, Rwanda, Burundi and Kenya; right down to southern Africa in Angola, Lesotho, Swaziland and Zimbabwe, it appeared more still had to be done to foster democracy and good governance.

When African historians of the future sit down to write about the tumultuous last decade of the 20th century, they may view the surge of democratic aspirations as having been crucial stimuli of change.

In that vein, it is hoped that the elected substantive leaders of the MDC would enter the political ring aware of the daunting task ahead. The unveiling of the MDC symbol — the palm of the hand[37] — at the Chitungwiza Aquatic Complex on January 29, 2000 was in itself historic. The MDC was the first opposition party to hold a congress since independence in April 1980. The mission of the congress, which attracted about 4,000 delegates from the party's 12 provinces, was to elect a substantive executive as well as map out a strategy for the forthcoming elections. Morgan Tsvangirai and Gibson Sibanda were unanimously elected president and vice-president, respectively, after being nominated by all the party's provinces. University of Zimbabwe law professor Welshman Ncube was elected secretary-general and trade unionist Gift Chimanikire his deputy. Isaac Matongo was voted the party's national chairman with Fletcher Dhlamini as treasurer general.

---

36. *Business Day*, South Africa, 29 September, 1998.

37. According to party officials, the symbol denotes that Zimbabweans "must open up" and end ZANU (PF) 20-year rule.

The inclusion of Learnmore Jongwe, Tendai Biti, Grace Kwinje, David Coltart, Trudy Stevenson, Sekai Holland and Nelson Chamisa as well as Ncube into the MDC's 30-member executive seemed to have vindicated those who had viewed the new party as an extension of the NCA.

There are very few precedents in Africa in which a party formed on the eve of an election went on to win. However, Tsvangirai said his party would unseat ZANU (PF) on the basis of its manifesto that, among other things, advocates for land re-distribution exercise based on transparency. "MDC would ensure that land reform is not isolated from the infrastructure, social service and rural industrialization strategies that must go with it if people's lives were to improve," he said.[38]

In its manifesto, the MDC conceded that even if it won the general elections it would take more than five years to turn round the country's fortunes. "It would be easy to promise quick gains, to win votes. But people want to know the truth....We will have to identify our priorities for the next five years so that we can turn the nation from its impoverished, disempowered and economically weak state towards a firm and stable path, towards meeting people's needs, towards sound governance and towards sustained returns for production."[39]

The MDC also said that, if elected to power, it would immediately set up a truth commission to probe such issues as the wealth amassed by government officials, and the Matabeleland atrocities. An MDC victory would also lead to the reduction of ministerial positions from 55 to 15.

Although the MDC was a young party, it was bound to give ZANU (PF) a run for their money. MDC could capitalize on people's swelling political discontent and social unrest. While the MDC did not have experienced politicians among its rank and file, the party was capable of causing an election upset judging from what their results when they campaigned for a "No" vote during the referendum on the draft constitution. It must be noted that the party has Young Turks who include lawyers, trade unionists, journalists and other professionals, and that is its source of strength.

That the MDC posed potentially the biggest threat to the ruling party in Zimbabwe's next general elections was without doubt. The vitriolic counter-offensive by ZANU (PF) was expected, but political observers hoped that the ruling party would not fight as dirty as it could; the party has a culture of violence and intimidation against opposition parties. Mugabe has threatened

---

38. *The Zimbabwe Mirror*, 4 February, 2000.
39. Movement for Democratic Change Manifesto, Zimbabwe, August 1999.

people with death. On March 16, 2000, while commissioning the Pungwe Water Project, he was quoted as saying, "Those who try to cause disunity among our people must watch out because death will befall them."[40] A few weeks later he threatened white commercial farmers with "very, very, very severe violence" if they took any action against the mobs of war veterans and ZANU (PF) thugs illegally occupying their farms.

"ZANU (PF) has perfected the art of intimidation and through the structures of the party and the state, it is capable of affecting people's lives in a myriad of ways. This is a pervasive problem and it is extremely difficult to assess its scale," noted the respected London-based human rights watchdog African Rights, in a report entitled "The 2000 Elections, Mankind and Breaking the Rules."

As the Shona say, *"panoda mwoyo gwanzi harisviki"* (if wishes were horses, beggars would ride). The opposition's wish to have a peaceful campaign was marred right from the start. On April 1, 2000, riot police fired teargas in Harare's Central Business District to break up violent clashes when ZANU (PF) supporters descended on about 8,000 demonstrators participating in a peaceful march organized by the NCA. The ZANU (PF) supporters, wielding iron bars and clubs, confronted the NCA marchers along Harare's Union Avenue (now Kwame Nkruma Avenue), between Julius Nyerere Way and First Street. Saturday shoppers were caught in the crossfire as they unwittingly created a buffer zone between the two parties. Eight people, most of them shoppers, were injured. Eyewitnesses and those who saw footage of the attacks on BBC saw that the police merely watched as demonstrators, who were holding nothing but their placards, were beaten up, and some of the members of the NCA were arrested, while those carrying arms were allowed to walk free.

On April 5, 2000, Morgan Tsvangirai, leader of the opposition MDC, told supporters that the violence was threatening landmark parliamentary elections, but said his party had only been involved in self-defense actions. "We have a chronology of violence perpetrated by ZANU (PF) against MDC. This is orchestrated by the government to induce fear and intimidation among voters. It is a strategy of subduing the people of Zimbabwe into submission."[41]

As if to emphasize its appetite for violence, ZANU (PF) gave Zimbabweans a new political vocabulary. The word *jambanja* emerged after the farm invasions and was crowned during the June 2000 Parliamentary Election. This helped

---

40. *The Zimbabwe Standard*, 19 March, 2000.
41. *P.M. News*, Lagos, Nigeria, 6 April, 2000.

Zimbabweans to accept their dismay with an executive order directing the police to ignore crimes classified as "political." *Jambanja* means state-sponsored lawlessness. The police were not expected to intervene or arrest anyone in a *jambanja* scene because those instigating or taking part had prior state blessing and approval. Only war veterans and ZANU (PF) supporters were allowed to engage in a *jambanja*. Hundreds of people, mainly from the opposition and farm workers, were either killed or disabled by *jambanja*. Some lost their homes, while others were swindled out of millions of dollars through company *jambanja*.

The ZANU (PF) primaries exhibit a deep-rooted culture of violence. There was violence between opposing sides in the party. Talking of MDC at an election meeting on April 8, 2000 at Manhenga business center, 15 kilometers out of Bindura, President Mugabe had this to say: "The MDC will never form the government of this country, never, ever, not in my lifetime or even after I die. *Ndingakupikirei ndinomuka chidhoma* (I swear, my ghost will come after you)."[42]

How ironic that the President repeats the notorious "never in a thousand years" declaration made by Ian Smith. The President fails to realize that violence generates fear and that fear breeds hatred, which turns into hostility, leading to counter-violence.

### Growing Discontent

And indeed, violence and death were unleashed against his political opponents — supposedly for rejecting the draft constitution in the February referendum. At least 14 lives had been lost (mostly supporters of the opposition) since the two inflammatory statements made by the President. Many more were injured while property worth millions of dollars was lost or damaged. Tobacco barns went up in smoke. Innocent women were raped in an orgy of primitive savagery. The President, who has boasted of having "degrees in political violence," never said a word to condemn the violence.

Violence, beatings, murders, house burnings and what to do if attacked for wearing an opposition T-shirt became the central themes of civic discourse, ahead of the elections President Mugabe set for June 24-25, 2000. Everyday the independent press brought new reports of atrocities: teachers and nurses attacked, schools closed, opposition activists tortured and opposition parliamentary candidates attacked. Comparisons can be made to the Cultural Revolution in China and the Khmer Rouge (Pol Pot) campaign in Cambodia.

---

42. *The Daily News*, Harare, 10 April, 2000.

The pre-election violence either closed or disrupted schooling in at least 551 schools during March-June 2000. Over 9,000 teachers were forced to flee and many were seeking job transfers to urban areas. The Progressive Teachers Union of Zimbabwe (PTUZ) reported that 2,096 teachers had been assaulted. At least one teacher was killed in Chikomba while 12 cases of teachers or their wives being raped had been reported to the association. The perpetrators had also abducted or raped 25 pupils. A headmaster in the Midlands was reported as having said: "the situation in the schools is as bad, if not worse, than the one prevailing in the commercial farms, yet the extent of media coverage has failed to capture the point. There is no better way of killing the soul of a nation than by destroying its education system."[43] The situation was worse for "O" and "A" level pupils, whose preparations for final examinations had been severely curtailed.

Analysts were convinced that the government was sponsoring the invasion of schools to garner political support in the same way it had supported the seizure of more than 1,000 white-owned farms by the so-called veterans of Zimbabwe's 1970s Chimurenga II (war of liberation). Some teachers and headmasters interviewed charged that the police had in some cases flatly refused to come to their rescue, saying they were ill-equipped to deal with the magnitude of the violence. In one case in Mudzi, a teacher said the police had folded their arms while the mob forced the closure of a hospital and barred nursing staff from treating 15 teachers who had been badly assaulted.[44]

By the end of May, although Mr. Don McKinnon (Secretary General of the Commonwealth) proclaimed after meeting President Mugabe that he believed free and fair elections were still possible in Zimbabwe and that Mr. Mugabe was committed to ending the violence, almost no one outside Cde Mugabe's ZANU (PF) agreed. The sheer magnitude of political violence made it highly doubtful. Amani Trust, a local NGO, compiled a database of violent incidents and offered medical and legal help to victims of violence and torture. By May 14, 2000, it reported 6,120 people affected by violence, including 1,107 reported assaults, nine rapes and 572 house burnings. Twenty-four people had been killed.[45] Nonetheless, much of the violence went unreported because journalists and local human rights monitors became key targets.

More critical than the sheer numbers was the highly public manner in which violence was conducted. Thousands of farm workers and villagers living adjacent to occupied farms were being forced through night-time "re-education"

43. *The Financial Gazette*, 25 May, 2000.
44. *Ibid.*
45. *Independent News*, London, 21 May, 2000.

sessions in which people were ordered to dance, chant and watch as MDC supporters were beaten. The number of people who were traumatized far exceeded the numbers physically harmed.

Despite blanket denials by the government that its supporters had initiated any violence, Amani Trust found that 85% of the perpetrators were ZANU (PF) supporters, 6.6% were government officials or Central Intelligence Organization (CIO) and only 4.3% MDC.[46] In mid-May, 43 villagers, victims of political violence in Mutoko, Murerwa and Uzumba-Maramba-Pfungwe abandoned their homes and fled to Harare. The villagers abandoned their villages after either being attacked or receiving threats of violence from ZANU (PF) supporters and war veterans. There were schoolchildren among them.

Meanwhile, in rural Matabeleland, a large number of villagers were reported to be fleeing their homes to seek refuge in urban centers and rural police stations. Some of the villagers said that ZANU (PF) supporters and war veterans in Insiza, Gwanda South, Plumtree, Lupane and Kezi were beating up people suspected to be supporters of the MDC. Civil servants, especially rural teachers all over Zimbabwe, were not spared. Some of them were forced to go into hiding following accusations that they were supporters of the MDC and that they played a role in the rejection of the government-sponsored draft constitution in February 2000.

A report by another local non-governmental organization, the Zimbabwe Human Rights NGO Forum, implicated high-ranking government officials in the political violence that took place in the Mazowe East constituency.[47] The report, entitled "Who is responsible? A preliminary analysis of pre-election violence in Zimbabwe," gave a detailed account of political violence perpetrated on members of the public. The report was based upon more than 60 detailed statements from survivors of violence. "They named not only individual attackers, but the leading organizers. Their accounts provided compelling evidence that an organized campaign of violence was being sponsored by the ruling ZANU (PF) and high-ranking party members were directly involved," said the report. The report also criticized public institutions such as the state-media, the government and the police for the stance they took against the MDC. "Repeated claims that the leadership of the opposition is engaged in the planning and implementation of violence are unsubstantiated and would seem

---

46. *Ibid.*
47. *The Zimbabwe Standard*, 25 June, 2000.

to be part of an attempt on the part of ZANU (PF) to manufacture a justification for its own actions."[48]

The extent of violence also shocked the initially reticent international election observers who had underestimated the degree of terror. European Union observer group head Pierre Schori said, on June 21, 2000, that his team had never seen such violence. By then at least 33 people had been killed and hundreds injured.

In 1979, Bishop Muzorewa's *Pfumo reVanhu* (a Gestapo-type quasi-military group) terrorized people to vote for the UANC. True, ZANU (PF) also told villagers that if it lost the election it would go back to the bush. At that time, unlike now, many people had confidence in ZANU (PF) as a government-in-waiting. In that year, threats of war, actual intimidation and crude violence actually worked. People voted out of fear rather than through informed choice. However, they have not forgotten that in the 1985 general election, after three years of the Midlands-Matabeleland killings in which some 20,000 people were murdered and thousands more beaten and tortured, every parliamentary seat in Matabeleland North and South went to candidates of the PF–ZAPU party that opposed President Robert Mugabe's ZANU (PF). Thus, Zimbabweans have sometimes turned quiet when threatened to vote for ZANU (PF) but have followed their conscience when voting.

The violence that occurred during April-May 2000 exposed the lie that the chaos on the commercial farms was about land or race. The vicious attacks on black farm workers and the destruction of their property on accusations of being members of the MDC were clear evidence that the violence was nothing more than crude political intimidation. This was part of ZANU (PF)'s election strategy. The party was in grave danger of losing political turf to the opposition. With little to show for 20 years in office, the land invasions were meant to portray President Robert Mugabe and his ruling party as revolutionaries. The attack on whites fed the racial prejudices of the more gullible people. The disorderly land distribution to more than 30,000 unemployed and ruling party supporters on the outskirts of Harare was a clear attempt to purchase political support ahead of the elections.

This chaotic seizure of land around Harare and the actions of the so-called war veterans and ZANU (PF) supporters on commercial farms were likely to have other disastrous ramifications. The threat of a severe bread shortage loomed

---

48. "Who is Responsible? A Preliminary Analysis of Pre-election Violence in Zimbabwe," The Zimbabwe Human Rights NGO Forum, Harare, June 2000.

large on the horizon as the marauders stopped farmers from planting winter wheat. Wheat production fell from 280,000 tonnes in 2001 to 115,000 tonnes in 2002.[49] It was these criminals masquerading as revolutionaries who were sabotaging the economy, not the commercial farmers and the opposition. The full effects on the 2000-2001 agricultural season were massive. Ironically, this is not because blacks had been given land but because people without the skills, capital and financial backing seemed set on damaging Zimbabwe's national heritage.

The case for urgent land reform cannot be disputed and with it the case for an orderly exercise that gives land to deserving blacks who will use it to create wealth for themselves and the rest of the nation. It is not every black person who wants or deserves a piece of land just as it is not every white person who is a good farmer. Mozambique, Uganda and Zambia appreciate the skills that Zimbabwe has on her commercial farms, hence their offer of land at a time when the Zimbabwe government was doing everything possible to incite anarchy in this sector.

The violence and intimidation seriously jeopardized the holding of free and fair elections. Actions of armed ZANU (PF) gangs virtually closed certain areas for campaigning by the opposition. In their interventions on the land, those who operated under the banner of the war veterans effectively cordoned off large sections of the rural areas from the opposition, and staked out a sole claim not only to the land occupied, but also to the constituencies on that land. In the establishment of "re-education centers" and the symbolic displays of renunciation of MDC membership organized by the ruling party, the latter made it clear that national issues could only be discussed in one way — the ZANU (PF) way.

Thus, there was a de facto ban on opposition rallies. Ostensibly to limit campaign-related violence, police invoked the Law and Order (Maintenance) Act to ban the transport of party supporters to rallies and prevent all rallies deemed a threat to law and order. Effectively the ban was applied only to MDC rallies, while the ruling party continued to use government vehicles and vehicles stolen from commercial farmers to facilitate its campaign.

Clearly, the electoral outcome under these circumstances would lack the credibility and broad-based acceptance required for future political stability. This further underscored the need for a return to the rule of law and impartial international monitors to underwrite any election result. This has nothing to do

---

49. *The Zimbabwe Independent*, 4 April, 2003.

113

with Zimbabwe's sovereignty, which is not in dispute, but the need to conduct an election that is free and fair to all competing political interests.

Observers drawn from the world-acclaimed National Democratic Institute for International Affairs based in Washington DC devoted a large part of their report to the violence which had all but killed any prospect for a valid poll. Their report said, "The conditions for credible elections do not exist in Zimbabwe at this time...... The violence has created an atmosphere of anxiety and fear. It has substantially restricted the exercise of freedoms of opinion, expression, association, assembly and movement, as well as the right to be secure from physical harm due to political affiliation. The ability of political parties and many candidates, predominantly from the opposition, to campaign openly and freely do not meet international standards for fair electoral competition."

No wonder government and ZANU (PF) officials were angry about the NDI report, which they claim was biased against them. The opposition said authorities denied it because the situation favored them.

The NDI, which has sent election observers to 50 countries over 16 years, said Zimbabwe's legal framework for the election was badly flawed and contained serious deficiencies. "International experience demonstrates that in countries like Zimbabwe, where violence and fear undermine the potential for credible elections, it is necessary to go beyond the minimum requirements of the election law to build sufficient public confidence in the process," the report said. "Mass media, particularly radio and television, are critical to political parties and candidates providing messages to the voters about manifestos and related positions. As government-controlled media, ZBC should fulfill its obligation to ensure that its media provide accurate and balanced news coverage of all political parties."[50]

The NDI report recommended:
1. improved security for all political parties;
2. impartial administration of the electoral process;
3. tight monitoring of the election;
4. a halt to partisan propaganda on behalf of ZANU (PF) by the state media.

In a stark warning that the balloting itself was at risk, the observers said, "The effects of violence and attempts at political intimidation have undermined trust among Zimbabweans in the secrecy of the ballot and have raised fears of

---

50. *The NDI Report*, National Democratic Institute for International Affairs, Washington, May, 2000.

retribution for voting against the ruling party. Cases of men, women and children being beaten and, in some instances tortured (including eight documented cases of rape) could have far-reaching effects in a society that is not long-removed from the tragedy and suffering of the 1980s Gukurahundi."

MDC secretary-general Professor Welshman Ncube said the current political situation restricted the opposition campaigns. "It is self-evident that the environment is not conducive for a free and fair election....There can be no denying it because even before the NDI compiled its report Zimbabweans knew what was happening."[51] ZUD secretary-general Isaac Manyemba said it was common knowledge the electoral process was fundamentally flawed. "The greatest anomaly in the electoral process is that ZANU (PF) is acting as the judge, jury, prosecutor, and police officer....They are firmly in charge of the process and there is no way they can be impartial when they are desperate to win the election." Manyemba said government refused to establish an independent electoral body because it wanted to retain control of the electoral process: "The legal framework for the election is antiquated and was designed for a one-party state. That's why ZANU (PF) would not want to reform it."[52]

ZIP president Professor Heneri Dzinotyiwei said technical obstacles in the electoral framework were hindering the opposition from making preparations for the poll: delays in publishing the voters' roll for inspection, rushed delimitation of constituencies, and a row over the nomination date affected the opposition. "I foresee a situation where the election would have a lot of discrepancies. It is now generally understood that the election would not be free and fair..... Perhaps we are starting a long-term struggle by not conducting the election properly and people may not respond to a government which wins unfairly," he said.

The opposition was complaining because it did not want to camouflage an electoral fraud which was taking place. There was a bogus voters' registration exercise in which people were registered but not given any form of documentary proof for that. In the event a person's name does not appear on the voters' roll, how would he be able to prove he had registered, in the first place?

During the 2000 general election, the ruling party experienced its first electoral nightmare since ascending to power 20 years ago. The two-day election (June 24-25) turned into a straight contest between ZANU (PF) and the MDC, the labor-backed party launched in September 1999. In the end, ZANU (PF)

---

51. *The Zimbabwe Independent*, 26 May, 2000.
52. *Ibid.*

emerged with a narrow lead — 62 seats out of the 120 contested seats. The MDC collected an impressive victory of 57 seats with ZANU (Ndonga) collecting one seat from its two strong Chipinge constituencies (Chipinge North went to the MDC). The MDC, in existence only for nine months, gave the ruling party a run for its money, leaving many veteran politicians fallen by the wayside.

The resounding defeat of several ZANU (PF) provincial chairmen and senior members of the women's league in the 2000 may have signaled an abrupt end to their political careers and the lifespan of the ruling party. Out of ZANU (PF)'s 10 provincial chairmen, four fell in urban areas. The dominant force on the Zimbabwean political landscape for the past two decades, ZANU (PF) was no longer popular with the urban electorate, especially in Harare and Bulawayo where the party was whitewashed.

The party's chairman for Harare province, Tony Gara (also Deputy Minister of Local Government), was given a good shellacking by MDC's candidate, Tichaona Munyanyi, in the Mbare East constituency. Munyanyi embarrassed Gara by polling 10,754 votes against the latter's 4,265. Masvingo's provincial chairman, Dzikamai Mavhaire, was another ZANU (PF) stalwart who succumbed to the MDC juggernaut after he lost to the labor-backed party's Silas Mangono. He had been pardoned by President Robert Mugabe after the infamous "Willowgate scandal," but Frederick Shava, the ruling party's Midlands chairman, could not be saved by Mugabe this time. Bethel Makwembere of MDC booted him out of the Mkoba constituency. Another party chairman, Bulawayo's Jacob Mudenda, was ousted by Peter Nyoni of the MDC. Nyoni polled 15,271 votes to Mudenda's paltry 3,617.

Members of the ZANU (PF) women's league also suffered defeat. The league's chairperson, Thenjiwe Lesabe (also Minister of National Affairs, Employment Creation and Cooperatives), lost the Mzingwane primaries but was to be imposed on the Gwanda North constituency; she overwhelmingly lost to MDC's election director, Paul Themba Nyathi. Her deputy in the women's league, Oppah Muchinguri (also Minister of State in the President's Office responsible for Gander Affairs), lost to Giles Mutsekwa in the Mutare North constituency by almost 10,000 votes. The women's league legal secretary, Mavis Chidzonga, went the same route and lost her Mhondoro seat to Hilda Mafudze of MDC.

Although the majority of the candidates conceded defeat, they were hoping that President Mugabe would include them in the list of the 20 non-constituency MPs he was entitled to choose under the amended Lancaster House Constitution. Also relying heavily on Mugabe's selection for those 20 slots and, perhaps, the cabinet, were fallen senior party members and ministers such as Dumiso Dabengwa (Home Affairs), Emerson Mnangagwa (Justice, Legal and Parliamentary Affairs), Simon Khaya Moyo (Mines, Environment and Tourism) and Richard Hove (Planning Commissioner). Others to fall were Sithembiso Nyoni (Minister of State), Deputy Minister of Higher Education Sikhanyiso Ndlovu and deputy ministers Cain Mathema and Obert Mpofu, as well as Naison Ndlovu, the ZANU (PF) secretary for production and former Deputy Speaker of Parliament.

Even in some rural constituencies considered safe by ZANU (PF), the MDC turned in an impressive performance. In Marondera East, for example, the Minister of State Security, Cde Sydney Sekeramayi, got a shock when an unknown MDC candidate came within 63 votes of evicting him. In Bindura, Mashonaland Central Governor Cde Border Gezi polled 13,000 against the MDC candidate's 11,000.

The toppling of heavyweights like Dumiso Dabengwa and Emerson Mnangagwa was a real vote of no confidence in the ruling party.

Although the MDC President failed to secure a seat in the Buhera North Constituency, this left him free to concentrate on his bid for the presidency in 2002. ZUD president Margaret Dongo also fell by the wayside as the party lost its only seat in the House. None of the 92 independent candidates won a seat, with most losing their deposits.

ZANU (PF) suffered a heavy defeat in the urban and peri-urban constituencies and won seats mostly in the rural areas. The MDC won overwhelmingly in Harare (all 19 seats), Bulawayo (all 8 seats), Matabeleland North (all 7 seats), Matabeleland South (6 out of 8), Gweru Central, Kwekwe Central and Masvingo Central. In the provinces where ZANU (PF) and war veterans terrorized opposition supporters (resulting in thousands fleeing from their homes), the MDC stood no chance. Most villagers sought refuge in urban areas, and thus were deprived of their vote. Farms, which were occupied by war veterans, were virtually inaccessible to opposition parties. In Mashonaland West, the MDC won only one seat out of 12; in Mashonaland East, also one seat out of 12; in Mashonaland Central, the MDC secured no seat out of a possible 10. In Midlands North, the party secured only 3 out of 11 seats; and Midlands South, 3 out of eight.

Overall, ZANU (PF) polled a total of 1,220,951 votes (48.8%) against MDC's 1,150,793 (47.5%). All other political parties and Independents polled 128,551 votes, bringing the total of opposition votes to 1,279,344, which was more than the votes attributed to ZANU (PF).[53]

This result reflects the fact that ZANU (PF) controls 61.3% of the vote in Parliament.[54] Nevertheless, following the parliamentary poll, the MDC submitted that in 39 of the 62 seats which ZANU (PF) won there had been either gross irregularities in the conduct of the poll or coercion of voters. The MDC challenged these outcomes in the High Court. By the end of October 2003, 13 of those cases had been heard. Of those heard, 7 saw rulings in favor of the MDC. However, ZANU (PF) appealed against these rulings, which had the effect of suspending the judgments. ZANU (PF) MPs, therefore, continued to sit for the seven seats which the High Court found had been secured through improper means. Not a single appeal had been heard; thus ZANU (PF) was still enjoying its booty of apparently stolen seats three years after the poll. It is said that justice delayed is justice denied. Indeed, with the court verdicts so far, MDC was the winner of the 2000 poll.

Another bone of contention is how ZANU (PF) manipulated the imminent impeachment of President Robert Mugabe following the June 2000 election. The MDC presented a motion in the House to have the president impeached. The opposition party introduced overwhelming evidence that included footage on video camera in which the president clearly encouraged and abetted violence against his opponents. Even the newly elected ZANU (PF) had no counter to the evidence. To avoid impeachment, Minister of Justice, Legal and Parliamentary Affairs Cde Patrick Chinamas and the Speaker of Parliament, Cde Emmerson Mnangangwa, suppressed the motion by keeping it off the agenda of parliamentary debate long enough to make it irrelevant; a motion that had been introduced in a previous parliamentary session could not be reintroduced in another session.

The fact that Zimbabweans came out in great numbers to vote in the fifth parliamentary election since the attainment of independence (similar to the 1980 polls) was indicative of a nation seeking change. As mentioned above, the size of the MDC contingent meant that the government had been deprived of the two-thirds majority needed to pass constitutional amendments. While this came too late to prevent sweeping farm confiscations, it did mean President Mugabe would be unable to proceed with plans to introduce through the parliamentary

---

53. *The Daily News*, 4 July, 2000.

54. In other words, in addition to the 62 seats won in the election, President Robert Mugabe has the prerogative to nominate 12 MPs, 8 resident ministers (governors), and the Chiefs' Council 10 seats. With traditional chiefs considered to be allies of the ruling party, ZANU (PF) had a 92-seat majority in the House. This falls short of the two-thirds majority required to pass constitutional legislation. ZANU (PF) had strong opposition in the form of the MDC, which controlled 38% of the vote.

backdoor proposals rejected by voters in the February referendum. This included restoration of the Senate abolished in 1989, which he mooted during the election campaign. In principle, the MDC supported the concept of a second house, but it would veto any format designed to entrench Mugabe's autocracy.

The 76-year-old leader's position was becoming increasingly untenable. The election result was a massive rebuff to his authority. Not only did his message on land distribution and British imperialism fail to find a purchase on the popular imagination, it maybe argued that his strategy of violence and intimidation backfired. While many farm workers were prevented by war veterans from voting or were coerced into voting for ZANU (PF), others clearly voted against their tormentors. What changed most in Zimbabwe since the February referendum was the public mood. From being victims, people appeared to have empowered themselves in order to send a message to Mugabe on his oppressive style of governance and the damage his regime had inflicted on their lives.

In addition to pointing the way forward on economic policies that attract investment and generate employment, MDC MPs would be anxious to expose corruption and misrule by Mugabe's ministers. They were also likely to emphasize that the country's myriad problems stem from his refusal to embrace reform rather than the international conspiracy he had been touting.

After everything has been said and done, the Movement for Democratic Change came close to toppling the ruling party. This is despite reported electoral flaws by international monitors and observers who said it was neither free nor fair. It is no secret that ZANU (PF) abused government machinery, including government vehicles, the police, some units of the Zimbabwe Defense Forces and the CIO to intimidate voters, especially in the rural areas.

Its flaws notwithstanding, results of the 2000 parliamentary election in Zimbabwe emerged with a few lessons: it shows that people do not have to embark on guerrilla warfare to win the hearts and souls of voters; that there is still a chance for the supremacy of the ballot box over the gun; and that even with her debilitating socio-economic problems, Africa is not exactly a "hopeless continent."

Notwithstanding, it looks as though ZANU (PF) is bent on repeating its tactics of terrorizing the electorate each time Zimbabwe has an election. Elected MDC MPs were attacked in their homes and had to seek personal security guards. Every election campaign since independence has been marked by violence, especially with the use of the youth. The seeds of wanton political violence were sown with the Youth Brigade and the Bindura-based people's militia of the mid-80s.

In 2001, even before the presidential election was set for March 9-10, 2002, the governing party had the "foresight" to set up the Border Gezi Training Centre, purportedly to train youth for "national service." When the training program was started (in Bindura) in honor of the late Minister of Youth Development, Gender and Employment Creation, political analysts were skeptical as to the goals and objectives of the training program. In preparation for the presidential election, the monster again unleashed green-fatigued brigades on the populace. Opposition activists who make futile noises against these "Green Bombers" (named after the green flies which swarm over dead animals and human and animal excreta) are paid nocturnal visits that silence them forever. It is estimated that nearly 50,000 youths had already been trained by the end of February 2004.

In March 2003, hundreds of these youth militia were fleeing to South Africa because they say they, too, were being beaten and starved, and were tired of "killing for nothing," as Charlene Smith wrote in South Africa's *Sunday Independent*. She said she interviewed 14 "green bombers" aged from 15–28, "giving the first insight into the terror organization." The stories of the youths interviewed, who come from different areas of Zimbabwe and who did not previously know each other, provide chilling details of the Green Bombers' training and methods. The youths told Smith they went on killing missions after drinking alcohol and smoking *mbanje* (marijuana) provided by their instructors and ZANU (PF) political commissars, because then "you feel nothing for anyone."[55]

The irony of it all is that, win or lose, ZANU (PF) will surely once again dump these political zombies.

Unrelenting political violence continued in all the contested by-elections. Whether in Marondera West, Bindura, Chikomba, Makoni West, Insiza, Kuwadzana, Highfield or Gutu, and in the Zengeza constituency in March 2004, people were beaten, raped and tortured. A teacher was murdered in the Chikomba by-election.

On September 8, 2001, the Amani Trust issued another analysis in which it reported 27,633 affected by violence recorded between July and September, 2001. Many farmers had abandoned their farms in the wake of violent invasions which engulfed the country since early February 2000. Some of the violence during the

---

55. *Sunday Independent*, South Africa, 9 March, 2003.

given period was linked to municipal/mayoral elections and a bi-election in Bulawayo and Chikomba, respectively. In the Chikomba constituency, a headmaster of a school was killed by suspected ZANU (PF) supporters and war veterans. In the three-month period under review, there were 30 deaths from gunshot, burns and beatings, a total of 2,928 beatings, 6 cases of rape, 586 cases of forced detention and 20,853 cases of forced displacement. The other cases of violence were of destruction and theft of property, false accusations, unlawful dismissal from work and barricading of roads and buildings.

Amani Trust's statistics show that 73.3% of the violence was perpetrated by ZANU (PF) supporters, 16% by the police, 4.5% by the army and air force, 2.3% by MDC and less than one per cent by the CIO.[56] The Amani Trust also reported that at least 33.3% of the victims of the reported violence were MDC members and 5.3% ZANU (PF) while the political affiliation of 61.7% of the victims was unknown.

Before the ink had dried in the Amani Trust report, Morgan Tsvangirai, the MDC president, narrowly escaped an assassination attempt on October 12, 2001, and on July 23, his motorcade was attacked by ZANU (PF) youths in Chiveso village in Bindura in the run-up to the Bindura by-election. Again, in Chivu in February 2004, Tsvangirai and his wife Susan escaped from marauding ZANU (PF) youths by a whisker as they traveled to their rural home in Buhera.

It came as no surprise, therefore, when the USA released a report (at the end of March 2003) accusing Zimbabwean security forces of brutality against the opposition and those suspected of harboring anti-ZANU (PF) sentiments. In a damning report, which forms part of the US annual Country Reports on Human Rights Practices, Zimbabwe is grouped with rogue states such as North Korea, Iraq and Cambodia, where political murder is routine. The US State Department said Harare had largely ignored the illegal political killings by its forces. "Security forces committed several extrajudicial killings, and in numerous other cases, army and police units participated or provided transportation and other logistical support to perpetrators of political violence and knowingly permitted their activities," the US report reads, in part. The report contains details of several cases of people who were either abducted, tortured or murdered allegedly by state forces, especially the CIO.

A Zimbabwe Human Rights NGO Forum report revealed that politically-related violence claimed 10 lives in 2003. Of the 10 deaths, six were MDC supporters and two were Zanu PF supporters while the other two could not be

---

56. *The Daily News*, 11 October, 2001.

linked to any party. From 2000 to October 2002, the politically-related death toll had risen to 151. Fifty-eight of the recorded deaths occurred in the year 2002, indicating the impact of violence during the presidential election campaign.

As if the violence caused by the Green Bombers and the so-called war veterans was not enough, Mugabe appeared to encourage Zimbabwe's security agents to sabotage the democratic process in Zimbabwe. On January 9, 2002, the chief of the armed forces of Zimbabwe, General Vitalis Zvinavashe, read a prepared statement at a press conference attended by the heads of all the armed forces, police, CIO and the prison service. The statement declared that the commanders would not "salute any individual who does not possess liberation struggle credentials."

Political analysts, and Zimbabweans who wrote letters in the independent press, expressed horror and disbelief that heads of the armed forces had threatened to overturn the democratic process if military commanders did not agree with the result of the presidential election.

Oppressive bills like the General Laws Amendment Act, the POSA Act and AIPPA were fast-tracked through Parliament at the end of January 2002 as part of an effort to brutalize people and make sure they did not vote for anyone else except the incumbent president. All three laws had as their general theme the protection of the President from criticism and the imposition of massive hurdles in the path of opposition parties and critics of the President and the government to perform their legitimate function of monitoring them. Even Parliament's age-old Standing Rules and Orders, which gave the august House its reputation as the forum of debate, were suspended.

The AIPPA was so ill-prepared and its objectives so nakedly anti-democratic, even members of the ruling party found it repulsive. Of course, this was at a time when any exposure of their unsatisfactory conduct of the country's affairs would reduce the chances of the President's re-election. In addition, this was at a time when the opposition parties could attract far more crowds to its rallies than the ruling party, whose popularity had plummeted because of the use of violence to force people to vote for their candidate.

Under AIPPA, the government-appointed Media and Information Commission was charging high fees (an application fee of Z$20,000 and a registration fee of Z$500,000) as a ploy to close down some private media houses. Journalists had to pay a Z$6,000 registration fee to practice their profession. Thus, journalists and their employers both resolved to register under protest.

It maybe noted that over 70 independent journalists have been arrested and charged with violating AIPPA since the Act was passed in 2002, but none of them had been prosecuted. American journalist Andrew Meldrum was the first to be prosecuted for allegedly publishing false information, in Britain's *Guardian* newspaper. He was acquitted by a Harare magistrate but the government expelled him from the country in May 2003. Meldrum was the fourth journalist to be deported over the past two years, and only a handful of foreign reporters had been granted visas to enter Zimbabwe in the first place.

Meanwhile, violence remained the main presidential campaign instrument for ZANU (PF). It was reported that in 2001 alone, 89 people were murdered, in dark streets and in attacks on houses, and the police never properly investigated. The Human Rights Forum reported 142 cases of torture in January 2002, while 159 cases were reported for the first 16 days of February. By December 2003, even attacks on the clergy had become frequent.

In an attempt to recover ground lost to the MDC in the March 2002 presidential election, the ZANU (PF) government charged Morgan Tsvangirai, the leader of the MDC, with treason, on the basis of a secretly-shot videotape made by Ari Ben-Menashe and his associate, Alex Legault. Aired by Australia's alternative SBS television network in February 2002, the documentary, entitled "Killing Mugabe, The Tsvangirai Conspiracy," alleges that the MDC leader and two other top MDC officials plotted to eliminate President Mugabe. It emerged later that Ben-Menashe's political consultant firm, Dickens and Madison, worked for Mugabe's CIO chief, Nicholas Goche. *The Guardian* of London reported on February 14 that Ben-Menashe had met diplomats in Harare two years earlier and indicated that he had business with Mugabe — long before the video was shot.

*The Guardian* quoted *Time* magazine as saying that Ben-Menashe was "a veteran spinner of stunning-if-true-but yarns." The paper said he had been ruthlessly attacked in the past in *Newsweek*, *The Wall Street Journal* and *New Republic*, all of the USA.

The question remains, to what degree was the 2002 Presidential Election free and fair?

There was violence in all the country's provinces, including Harare and Bulawayo, which the police did not deny. There was evidence that most of those affected by the violence were either supporters of the opposition MDC or those perceived to be opponents of ZANU (PF) and the government. This was manifest in the number of hospitalized victims and in numerous cases of alleged torture, arson, assault and false imprisonment. South African and

Commonwealth observers also fell victim to the violence in Mashonaland Central.

Legislation rammed through Parliament before the election, some of it in circumstances which smacked of official subterfuge, was deliberately designed to sabotage the chances of an opposition victory. Among other restrictive provisions, the General Laws Amendment Act, under which the Electoral Act was amended, banned voter education by anyone other than the government. The POSA made it impossible for the opposition to hold public meetings. MDC meetings were cancelled or interrupted by the police and/or ZANU (PF) supporters. Under that Act the police in Harare banned an MDC meeting with foreign diplomats.

MDC polling agents were abducted. International observers intervened when Mashonaland Central police detained 24 election agents of the MDC who were on their way to Harare to vote. There were reports that in Manicaland 100 polling agents for the MDC were arrested and 29 out of 54 polling stations went without MDC officials, as they were thrown out by ZANU (PF) agents. Free movement of party agents was compromised by acts of intimidation and reported abductions in some provinces, particularly the three Mashonaland provinces (East, West and Central) and the five Gokwe constituencies in the Midlands Province. As a whole the MDC was unable to monitor 52% of polling stations and 9 out of 120 counting stations.[57]

Opposition parties were not allowed to campaign in the three Mashonaland provinces and the five Gokwe constituencies.

There were significant claims of police partisanship and the use of riot police to disperse potential voters in some Harare constituencies raised questions about their impartiality. The police had violently dispersed voters from polling stations, especially in the high-density suburbs.

The voters' roll was released only three days before the election, leaving no time for the electorate to verify its accuracy, and a large number of people failed to vote as a result.

The voters' roll issue was compounded by the preparation and use of a supplementary roll after registration for the 2002 Presidential Election was closed.

The reduction of polling stations in the urban areas had a major impact, especially in Chitungwiza and Harare, where presidential and mayoral and council elections, respectively, were held simultaneously.

---

57. *Ibid.*, 1 April, 2002.

Although voting had been peaceful in many provinces, with more than 50% of the registered voters voting, the major exceptions were the Harare-Chitungwiza constituencies where the voting process was excruciatingly slow, resulting in the extension of both hours and days of voting.

Zimbabwe had no independent electoral supervisory commission, despite recommendations from its Southern Africa Development Community (SADC) partners.

Only ZANU (PF) had access to the public media, which provided slanted coverage.

It should not be forgotten that in addition to the land issue, the demand for "one man — one vote" had been another reason for the liberation war during the 1970s. However, the electoral law currently requires urban dwellers to have proof of house ownership or produce a lodger's card as proof of residence in a given constituency. This change resulted in the disenfranchisement of thousands of voters during the 2002 presidential election.

*Table 11: The overall results of the presidential election were as follows:*

| Name of Candidate | Name of Party | No. of Votes Polled |
|---|---|---|
| Robert Mugabe | ZANU (PF) | 1,685,212 |
| Morgan Tsvangirai | MDC | 1,258,401 |
| Wilson Kumbula | ZANU | 31,358 |
| Shakespeare Maya | NAGG | 11,906 |
| Paul Siwela | Independent (ZAPU) | 11,871 |
| Total No. of Valid Votes | 120 Constituencies | 2,998,748 |

*NAGG - National Alliance for Good Governance*
*Source: The Daily News, March 14, 2002*

About 5.4 million voters were registered for the 2002 presidential election; the voter turnout was a little over 55.5%, considering that there were also spoilt votes. Cde Robert Gabriel Mugabe received 56.2% of the valid votes while Morgan Tsvangirai received 42%.

ZANU (PF) received the bulk of its votes from the provinces where violence was most prevalent — mostly the three Mashonaland provinces and the five Gokwe constituencies in the Midlands. The Mashonaland villages recorded huge turnouts, although observers there saw almost no one queuing to vote at all.

The margin of ZANU (PF) votes as compared to MDC votes was quite large. For example, in the constituency of Uzumba-Maramba-Pfungwe in Mashonaland East Province, ZANU (PF) secured a total of 37,341 votes against

MDC's 3,197. That is about 8.5% of ZANU (PF) vote. When it comes to constituencies in the urban areas like Bulawayo and Harare, where the MDC was popular, the margin between the ruling party and the opposition was narrower. Take, for example, the Harare South constituency. While the MDC registered 13,646 votes, ZANU (PF) scored a whole 6,219 votes. That is about 45.6% of the MDC vote.

Harare alone had 880,000 registered voters, of whom almost 350,000 voters were unable to vote. Their ballots could easily have swung the vote against Mugabe, but the government defied a High Court order to reopen the polling stations at 7 AM on Monday, March 11, the extra day of voting for which the MDC had applied successfully. Although the polling stations were opened late in the day, voters were being arrested as they queued. This effectively disenfranchised thousands. They were accused of attempting to vote twice, although there was no proof that they had already voted. Tellingly, they were all released after the polling stations were closed at 7 PM.

Both Harare and Chitungwiza, with their massive voter populations, are opposition strongholds. ZANU (PF) was frightened at the voter turnout there, and with good reason. As if to confirm the strength of the opposition, the executive mayoral elections in both Harare and Chitungwiza were won by MDC candidates. Elias Mudzuri of the MDC polled 262,275 votes against ZANU (PF)'s Amos Midzi's 56,796. In Chitungwiza MDC's Misheck Shoko beat the incumbent, Joseph Macheka, polling 47,340 votes against Macheka's 16,963.[58]

Thus, when the outcome of the presidential election went in favor of ZANU (PF), some people were inclined to cry foul, especially since the number of voters who actually voted seemed very inflated in those areas where neither the international observers nor the MDC agents had access to scrutinize the voting process and the war veterans and "Green Bombers" were very active. In other words, not only were thousands of Zimbabweans disenfranchised, thousands of ghost voters participated in their stead.

Although the African heads of mission in Zimbabwe endorsed President Mugabe's re-election, the Electoral Commissions Forum of the Southern African Development community countries attacked the process, saying the criterion of fairness was not adequately met. The government had made too many changes to the legal framework governing the election just before the poll. "This state of affairs can only create confusion as to which laws are being applied," the Forum said in a statement. On the political campaign, they said, "The prevailing

---

58. *Ibid.*, 15 March, 2002.

political tension led to such polarization that certain areas were declared no-go areas for other parties. Uneven access to resources, especially the State-owned media, made the playing field uneven for the opposition."

The Commonwealth's 61-member observer mission led by former Nigerian head of state General Abdulsalam Abubakar said that Mugabe's re-election did not reflect the will of the people, had disenfranchised thousands of voters and was conducted in a climate of fear. Joining local observers, the European Union and the US also described the electoral process as "a patently flawed presidential election."

Following this condemnation, Zimbabwe was suspended from the (British) Commonwealth. In mid-February 2002, the EU imposed so-called "smart" sanctions on Zimbabwe after Pierre Schori, the leader of its electoral observer mission, was expelled from the country. The sanctions included an embargo on the sale of arms to Zimbabwe, the suspension of 128 million Euros worth of aid scheduled to be distributed during 2002, and the freezing of assets of 19 Zimbabwean officials, including Mugabe, who were also prohibited from visiting any EU state. The US imposed similar measures several days later, although in December 2001, the US Congress had approved legislation offering aid and economic incentives to Zimbabwe, on condition that its Government act to create an equitable land reform program.

On March 21, at the end of a four-day parliamentary meeting in Cape Town, South Africa, the African Caribbean and Pacific and European Union (ACP-EU) Joint Parliamentary Assembly dealt a heavy blow to President Mugabe when it called for a fresh election within a year. In a resolution, the Assembly stated: "The ACP-EU Joint Parliamentary Assembly calls for new elections to be held within the year under the auspices of the Commonwealth and the International community so as to allow all the people of Zimbabwe the freedom to elect the president of their choice."

The Evangelical Fellowship of Zimbabwe (EFZ), joining other local civic organizations, dismissed declarations by some African observer missions that the March presidential election was free and fair. In a statement on March 21, 2002, the EFZ, which groups several churches and church-related institutions, said: "The idea purported by some African observers that the election was free and fair, in comparison with other elections held in Africa, must be dismissed with the contempt it deserves. Zimbabweans are no less human than people all over the world, and the principles of freedom, justice and fairness that they desire are universal principles to which people all over the world aspire."

The 15-nation European Union (EU), the United States, New Zealand, Canada, Switzerland and Australia imposed sanctions on Mugabe and his top officials over policies which they said had fuelled lawlessness in the country. With the international community's imposition of sanctions, the government and the so-called "war" Cabinet and its cronies began to find they were considered an international shame and, indeed, with Zimbabwe's political and economic crisis worsening, it was possible that government members could eventually find themselves declared international criminals.

The regional SADC, during its annual summit held in the Angolan capital, Luanda, at the end of September 2002, in an unprecedented move barred Mugabe from becoming deputy chairman of the organization. Most analysts say the SADC step not only sent a clear message to Mugabe that the region was unhappy with his policies but also helped stoke pressure against him.

For their part, members of Parliament from Europe, the southern African region and civic organizations in November 2002 passed a resolution calling on Mugabe to step down and hold fresh elections under international supervision. The resolution was passed in Cape Town, South Africa, at a meeting convened to assess the effects of the Zimbabwean crisis on the people of Zimbabwe, civil society and the economy, and its negative impact on the entire southern African region. In a communiqué, the delegates called for an immediate return to the rule of law in Zimbabwe, and an end to politically motivated violence and the selective distribution of emergency food supplies.

Nevertheless, many SADC countries have benefited from Zimbabwe's woes. This is one of the major reasons why they cannot take effective action against human rights violations in the country. For example, while tourism has decreased in Zimbabwe, it has surged elsewhere in the region;[59] investments have dropped drastically in Zimbabwe while they have spread to other parts of the region (the invasion of urban businesses in 2001 contributed to the flight of investment); and skilled labor, including farmers and other professionals like doctors and nurses, have moved from Zimbabwe to neighboring countries. For South Africa, in addition, Zimbabwe is such a strong trading partner that President Thabo Mbeki would not want to rock the boat; and above all, South Africa is enjoying an undisturbed penetration into virtually all regional markets without Zimbabwe, which stood as the only meaningful threat to its expansionary programs.

---

59. Income from tourism fell from US$700 million in 1999 to US$71 million in 2002.

There are other obstacles blocking efforts to bring ZANU (PF) and the MDC to negotiate to find a solution to the country's problems. First, former liberation movements in the region are suspicious about the MDC's intentions when it earlier sought closer ties with South Africa's Democratic Alliance, Renamo in Mozambique, and Congress of Democrats in Namibia. Second, the prospect of a labor-backed MDC government opens anxiety in the ANC tripartite-alliance government, whose strong COSATU ally and its former secretary general are still very much popular with the grassroots. Third, there is resistance to foreign pressure among SADC countries, who fear that there is an attempt at imposing "regime change" in Zimbabwe. The MDC is seen as the proxy of western powers in Zimbabwe, and solving the Zimbabwe situation was made more difficult by the MDC's refusal to recognize Mugabe's "victory" in the 2002 presidential election.

Meanwhile, in September 2002, ZANU (PF) won 700 of the council seats unopposed because MDC candidates in the respective wards had either been denied registration or had fled violence unleashed on the party's leadership. One MDC supporter, Nikoniari Chibvamudeve, was reportedly killed by ZANU (PF) militants while several hundreds were allegedly beaten up and tortured by ruling party militias. The Zimbabwe Human Rights Forum, an umbrella body for the country's major human rights and pro-democracy groups, said 58 people (most of them MDC supporters) had been killed in political violence between January and August 2002. The Catholic Commission for Justice and Peace (CCJP) had, for example, been unable to send observers into the ZANU (PF) stronghold of Mashonaland Central province because it would have been "suicidal" to do so.

In a surprise move, the ZANU (PF) administration approached the United Nations Development Program (UNDP) for financial assistance to organize and run the 2005 general elections. The UNDP resident representative in Zimbabwe, Jose Victor Angelo, confirmed this at the end of August 2003 when he said, "We may have to assist in improving the electoral process in Zimbabwe in order to ensure that nobody challenges the quality of the 2005 elections." The government and the UNDP have enjoyed a tempestuous relationship following the UN agency's flat refusal to bankroll what it considered to be a chaotic land reform program.

In 2005, Zimbabwe will have its sixth general elections and a flawed electoral process could see a flood of electoral petitions, even more than the 2000 elections in which results from about a third of the country's 120 constituencies were contested.

Meanwhile, reports from another well-informed source said that torture of senior officials and the opposition's supporters was being orchestrated by the CIO, Military Intelligence and the police. Between January and November 2002, 1,060 MDC activists were tortured, 227 abducted and beaten, 58 murdered, and 111 unlawfully detained, while 170 were simply picked up in the middle of the night, tortured and later released without being charged.

Opposition legislators, civic leaders, journalists, church leaders and High Court judges were not spared. The arrest and torture of St Mary's MP Job Sikhala and leading human rights lawyer Gabriel Shumba in February 2003 were not isolated events. Reports of the police beating up innocent women and children who line up to buy scarce commodities are abundant. And the arrest of the MDC Harare Executive Mayor Elias Mudzuri and the rise in political crime in both the Kuwadzana and Highfield constituencies ahead of the March 29-30 by-elections negated claims by the presidents of Nigeria and South Africa, Olusegun Obasanjo and Thabo Mbeki, respectively, that Zimbabwe had returned to a state of tranquility following the "successful completion of the land reform exercise." Zimbabweans hoped the South African president must have realized that Zimbabwe was far from "a state of tranquility" when his High Commissioner, Jeremiah Ndou, was illegally held against his will by war veterans in mid-October at Hillpass Farm (previously owned by South African investors). At last, South Africans had no illusions about the nature of lawlessness in Zimbabwe.

By buying into President Mugabe's deceitful assurance that the situation in Zimbabwe has changed significantly from that prevailing in March 2002, the two leaders demonstrated a capacity for self-deception bordering on dishonesty. Any expectation that Nigeria and South Africa will lead Africa's emergence from decades of misrule, that Mbeki's much-touted New Partnership for Africa's Development (NEPAD) initiative can fulfill its promise, loses credibility.

Zimbabweans should not expect the outside world to come and put democratic processes in place for them. It was high time, therefore, that the opposition party was called upon to devise a way to pressurize the independent government to "change its ways." With escalating violence against the opposition and society in general, the MDC called for a two-day strike on March 18 and 19, 2003. Most businesses remained closed during the two days, with many employees staying away from work. This was the first MDC-sponsored mass action, which was described as a "test run." The next phase would depend on responses to demands the opposition party put on the table. These included: the restoration of the rule of law; the release of political prisoners; the depoliticization of the police force and the army; the disbanding of militias known as the Green Bombers; and the repeal of POSA and AIPPA.

When these demands were publicized, there was mayhem in the townships and all over the major cities. Human rights lawyers and Amnesty International reported many people missing (mostly opposition members and journalists from the independent press) and many others being held without being brought to court within 48 hours as required. At one Harare private clinic alone, 250 injured people were treated two days after the stayaway. A doctor at the hospital reported that most of the injuries were broken bones. Several of those treated had had their fingers and toes broken and one man had had both his legs broken.

According to a report released in April 2003 by the Zimbabwe Human Rights NGO Forum (ZHRF), three people were killed and 94 assaulted in politically motivated violence between January and March. The ZHRF said it had also received reports of 11 cases of abduction, 131 of political intimidation and 164 of violation of freedom of expression and movement. About 76 cases of people being displaced from their homes by political violence were also reported, and the report said 159 people were also tortured in March, with cases of torture rising from 16 in January and February. There were 260 cases of unlawful arrest in the period under review, with 103 of them reported in March alone. The report said most of the victims of political violence were supporters of the opposition MDC, with most of the perpetrators said to be ruling ZANU (PF) activists and state security agents.

This is supported by a 26-page report released by the United States Department of State in February 2004, which said: "Security forces committed extra judicial killings. Security forces and government youth militias tortured, beat, raped, and otherwise abused people and some persons died from their injuries....The government continued to restrict freedom of speech and the Press; closing down the only independent daily newspaper, beat, intimidated, arrested and prosecuted journalists who published anti-government articles."[60] The report said the judiciary was not spared, as judges and magistrates have been attacked for handing down judgments against the ruling party while detained persons were not allowed prompt or regular access to their lawyers.

During the June 1–5 2003 demonstrations, several people were injured while two people were said to have died during the mass action. More than 800

---

60. "Country (Zimbabwe) Reports on Human Rights Practices —2003", US Bureau of Democracy, Human Rights and Labor, Washington D.C. February 25, 2004.

MDC officials and activists were arrested in demonstrations dubbed the "final push" to pressure Mugabe to agree to negotiations with the opposition to find a solution to Zimbabwe's deepening crisis. The protest floundered in the face of a heavy-handed response by the military and police forces. Arbitrary arrests, assaults, torture, and general intimidation of the public characterized government's response to the mass action. There were reports from around the country of lawyers who had been abused for representing clients detained during the mass action.

Furthermore, a total of about 200 people were arrested countrywide on October 8, 2003, when police stamped on demonstrations planned by the ZCTU to demand tax cuts and action against spiraling price increases, and what it called "gross violation of human and trade union rights." Hardly a week later, 102 NCA activists were arrested as they prepared to march to Parliament with placards, agitating for a new constitution, and on October 22 some 300 NCA activists (among them the NCA chairman, Lovemore Madhuku) were arrested near Parliament after demonstrating in support of political reforms — riot police used batons and dogs and people were beaten on their backs, hands and under the feet.

The brutality of the Zimbabwe Republic Police was again on display on November 18, when more than 100 Zimbabwean trade unionists and civic leaders were arrested in Harare by armed riot police who broke up peaceful demonstrations against President Robert Mugabe's increasingly autocratic rule. Hundreds of police, many armed with automatic rifles, took up positions across the capital ahead of the lunchtime protest planned by the ZCTU before the government's budget on November 20. The police attacked the demonstrators with batons, dogs and tear-gas. Many demonstrators were beaten. The previous morning, the police had arrested eight union leaders (including the secretary-general, Wellington Chibhebhe, and the president, Lovemore Matombo) in a pre-emptive strike to try to stop the demonstrations. More than 400 labor movement protestors were also arrested in the second biggest city, Bulawayo; the central industrial city, Gweru; the eastern border city, Mutare; the southern town, Gwanda; and the tourist resort of Victoria Falls.

Since its enactment in January 2002, POSA has been used to target opposition supporters, independent media and human rights activities. It restricts their right to criticize the government, and to engage in or organize acts of peaceful civil disobedience. Ever since efforts to stage dialogue to find a solution were initiated after the 2002 presidential election, Mugabe blocked them. Political analysts believe that if Mugabe were out of the equation, there would be greater rapprochement between the opposing parties and a better chance to break the impasse.

Maybe the urban council elections of August 30-31, 2003, where the MDC brought its tally of control to 11 town councils by winning 137 wards against ZANU (PF)'s 87, were a barometer showing that Zimbabweans wanted a change of government. The MDC also won six out of seven mayoral seats, including northern Kariba, where its candidate was set to become Zimbabwe's first post-independence white mayor. This brought the total number of opposition executive mayors throughout the country to 11, against the ruling party's 4 mayors in Kadoma, Kwekwe, Marondera and Bindura. The local elections, which included races for two vacant parliament seats, were beset by low voter turnout and reports of political intimidation by members of the ruling party. The MDC could not field candidates in Marondera, Bindura and Chegutu after ruling party supporters sealed off the nomination courts in the three towns. The poor voter turnout underlined a serious crisis of public confidence in the electoral process.

The Presidential Election (March 2002) Challenge that opened in the High Court on November 3 was likely to put the country's electoral process to its stiffest credibility test ever. The presiding judge, Justice Ben Hlatshwayo, had this to say, "This is not a story about a pound of flesh but a serious matter concerning the heart of the nation." In his preliminary statement, a high-profile South African lawyer representing Tsvangirai said, "The elections were stifled at best because the president (Mugabe), one of the contenders, became the rule maker." The MDC's argument was that many of the laws, regulations, officials and institutions governing the election were not in line with the constitution, and so were invalid. Sections 28, 58 and 113 of the Constitution make it clear that the electoral law governing the conduct of presidential and parliamentary elections must be passed by Parliament. The opposition party also argued that Mugabe's party waged a campaign of violence and intimidation against opposition supporters, bribed voters, reduced polling stations in major cities (where the MDC enjoyed popular support) and monopolized access to state media. Mugabe's regulations "repeatedly and secretly extended the cut-off date for voter registration, thus allowing late registration of voters in areas sympathetic to Mugabe," Tsvangirai argued.

The party focused mainly on issues pertaining to the composition and functions of the Electoral Supervisory Commission and failure by the government to comply with Sections 158 and 149 of the Electoral Act. The main argument by Tsvangirai was that the ESC was not legally constituted and was also not independent of outside influence as required by the Constitution of Zimbabwe. Tsvangirai also argued that Section 158 of the Electoral Act was unconstitutional in that it gave President Mugabe unlimited powers in contravention of the principle of separation of powers.

"By giving the President, a member of the executive branch, the power to amend the Electoral Act, Section 158 goes against the Zimbabwe Constitution that says only Parliament can make electoral laws. Section 158 violates the principle of separation of legislative, executive and judicial powers." The section in question delegates to the President the power to amend the electoral law and this may include power to make deletions from or additions to election laws. Also included in Tsvangirai's heads of arguments was an expert opinion from Jorgen Elklit, a Denmark-based elections expert and professor of Political Science at the University of Aarhus.

MDC attorneys contended that Mugabe became "legislator plenipotentiary and exercised powers to his own advantage in an election in which he was a candidate." Mugabe made numerous changes to the electoral law in the run-up to the poll, in some cases a day before the election, which Tsvangirai alleged were designed to manipulate the outcome. MDC attorneys said one of these modifications overturned a Supreme Court ruling that had declared the General Laws Amendment Act unconstitutional. The law had amended the electoral legislation. Tsvangirai argued that some of the changes disenfranchised a "large number of Zimbabwean citizens who were declared to be 'foreign' citizens," and deprived certain categories of postal voters of their right to cast the ballot. (About two million Zimbabweans live in South Africa and thousands are economic refugees in the UK and the US.)

At the end of the hearing, the judge reserved judgment, thus effectively putting the election challenge into a limbo. The judiciary's delays in handing down judgments that favor the opposition and civic organizations that were fighting against lawlessness and human rights violations were a subtle weapon used by the government. The government also has a history of attacking the judiciary or members of the legal profession each time it is unhappy with judicial decisions. This tended to undermine the credibility and transparency of the judiciary in Zimbabwe.

A stage had been reached in Zimbabwean political history where comparisons with the period of the so-called "dirty war" in Argentina or Augusto Pinochet's Chile could be made. That there is widespread State terrorism in Zimbabwe cannot be hidden or denied. And now, individuals or organizations in Zimbabwe, such as ZimRights, can approach the International

Criminal Court (ICC) seeking the prosecution of those perpetrating atrocities even in countries that have not ratified the Rome Statute. Indeed, in 2002, a group of Zimbabweans sued Mugabe's government in the USA over their relatives who were victims of the orgy of violence and mayhem that swept through the country at the height of the farm invasions and parliamentary elections in 2000.

Nonetheless, from mid-July 2003, there was an unexpected moment of civility between ZANU (PF) and the MDC, which reflected a rare chance to restore some calm to Zimbabwe. Despite this mood, the MDC was still under assault from state security agencies and the party's militia, the Green Bombers. MDC candidates in the August local elections were either being barred from presenting their nomination papers or were being prevented from campaigning. MDC gestures such as attending Mugabe's speech at the first opening of Parliament in three years, and indicating that a swift conclusion to negotiations would be ideal and would render unnecessary its court challenge to the results of the flawed presidential election, were signs of the opposition's willingness to negotiate.

However, ZANU (PF) never tires of distracting attention from the main issues. Analysts have pointed out that a shadowy organization launched in London in mid-November 2003, in a bid to topple President Robert Mugabe's government, could be a ruling ZANU (PF) ploy to distract Zimbabweans from the country's worsening economic crisis. The group, which calls itself the Zimbabwe Freedom Movement (ZFM), is led by a commander and two deputies whose pseudonyms are Charles Black Mamba, Ntukuzo Fezela and Daniel Ingwe.

ZFM is picking up terms such as "illegitimate" and "change," the buzz words associated with the MDC. Observers of the Zimbabwean political scene will recall that shortly after MDC's inception, the ZANU (PF) government alleged that the new party had a military training camp and went on to circulate documents "recovered" at the camp and purportedly originated from the opposition party. The then Minister of Information, Posts and Telecommunications, Chen Chimutengwende, made strenuous attempts to authenticate the documents — with no success. One is also reminded of men in Zimbabwe National Army uniform who went about beating people in nightclubs soon after the 2002 presidential election. They even forced men and women to have sex (and unprotected, at that) in the nightclubs. The government media tried to associate these soldiers with the MDC, saying they were army deserters being paid by the opposition party in order to tarnish the image of the army in the eyes of the public.

It cannot be ruled out that the ZFM could be an extension of the ZANU (PF) strategy, as they are desperate to divide Zimbabweans who yearn for good governance and accountability.

Following the Commonwealth Abuja conference's decision to maintain its suspension until Zimbabwe met key democratic benchmarks, President Mugabe and the ZANU (PF)-dominated Parliament decided on December 11, 2003, to withdraw from membership of the 54-country organization. History has a way of repeating itself. In almost similar circumstances in 1961, apartheid architect Hendrik Verwoerd on his rapturous return from the Commonwealth conference in London tried to spin South Africa's humiliating withdrawal from the club of nations into a national victory.

The opposition appears to be very frustrated and virtually overwhelmed and demobilized by the massive coercive force the government is prepared to use against any expression of discontent. It is ironic that an independent Zimbabwe has come full circle and is now a pariah state, as was the white minority-ruled Rhodesia, whose leaders were also shunned by the international community.

Mugabe's decision to withdraw from the Commonwealth indicates a lack of commitment to democracy and principles of good governance. In keeping Zimbabwe out of multilateral groups that are critical of the regime, Mugabe and his ruling elite are attempting to evade scrutiny and accountability for suppressing their own people. Ironically, almost all the codes of democratic governance Mugabe has been defying were designed as part of the Harare Declaration developed during his tenure as Chairperson of the Commonwealth in 1991.

Zimbabwe needs a homegrown constitution even more urgently than it needs changes in the electoral process (such as the composition and functions of the Electoral Supervisory Commission and the repeal of the Electoral Act, etc.). The talks between ZANU (PF) and the MDC seem only bent on power transference without addressing the fundamentals of good governance and democracy. Of immediate concern should be the setting up of a transitional government, which would be responsible for legislation and adoption of a new constitution. Pro-democracy and human rights advocates like the NCA, the ZCTU, ZimRights, Crisis in Zimbabwe Coalition, The Catholic Commission for Justice and Peace, and civic and church leaders have a role to play in fighting for constitutional change. Once a new constitution is in place, elections can be held with international observers; but Zimbabweans cannot effect regime change without targeting the source of its political authority — the constitution.

### Cracks within the Ruling Party

Leadership and policy failures, as well as mismanagement of the economy and corruption, clearly manifested themselves during the first decade of independence as President Robert Mugabe became preoccupied with power consolidation. The seeds of the current national decay and failure were sown at that time — what historians would see as the political dark ages of the 1980s. Dissent within the ruling party was suppressed and even back then the party relied on coercion.

Despite years of conflict in Matabeleland and part of the Midlands (PF-ZAPU's political bases), ZANU (PF) relentlessly pressed on its Marxist ideology. Negotiations to unite ZANU (PF) and PF-ZAPU went on, despite the open revolt in Matabeleland which took the form of banditry and arms cachement in strategic farms throughout most of Matabeleland, the Midlands and even Mashonaland.

"ZAPU and its leader Dr. Joshua Nkomo are like a cobra in the house. The only way to deal effectively with a snake is to strike and destroy its head," Mugabe urged his supporters in 1983. After his party's victory in 1985, Mugabe called for the liquidation of ZAPU, declaring: "Now take your sticks and beat out the snakes among you."

The deployment of the North Korean-trained Fifth Brigade exacerbated the relationship between the two parties engaged in unity negotiations. However, it was important for the ZANU (PF) leadership that Nkomo should be brought into the fold by hook or by crook. The leadership's "patience" and persistence bore fruit on December 22, 1987, when a unity accord was signed, finally burying the ZANU-ZAPU rivalry that had been going on since August 1963 when ZANU broke away from ZAPU.

However, this unity accord was nothing but cosmetic. President Robert Mugabe called the tune, while Nkomo played a very subservient role. This served the ZANU (PF) leadership very well, but there were signs of dissatisfaction within ZANU (PF) itself. The expulsion of Edgar Tekere, the party's secretary-general and former minister, in late 1988, was the first sign of disagreement in the powerful politburo. Dr. Naomi Nhiwatiwa, another party stalwart and strong leader in the party's women's league, resigned from both the government and the party and went back to her job with the United Nations. Those who dared talk and expound their creative ideas in cabinet were cut down to size. There is the case of the youthful Dr. Simba Makoni, who was sent to head the newly created Southern African Development Coordination Conference in Gaberon as its first secretary general.

Despite having won the 1990 election with an overwhelming majority, ZANU (PF) was divided on the question of a one-party state. A majority of the politburo members was openly against the proposed one-party state and insisted on a referendum, which would almost certainly be lost. In 1992, the government created a ministry to take over from the controversial ministry of Political Affairs. The Ministry of National Affairs, Employment Creation and Cooperatives conveniently swallowed up the former Ministry of Women's Affairs and Cooperatives. However, so controversial was the funding of the ruling party's "political" affairs that the Senior Minister of the newly created ministry, Didymus Mutasa, had a hard time getting his vote passed by Parliament in September 1992. This was so despite the fact that ZANU (PF) held 147 seats of the 150-chamber Parliament.

During the early 1990s, the activities of the opposition parties seemed to have been overshadowed by internal squabbles within ZANU (PF), particularly those in Masvingo and Manicaland provinces. The regions and factions were able to overturn the party structure by demanding local power, autonomy and "democracy," forcing the party hierarchy into continual compromise. The provincial elections held in 1994 saw the party protégés trounced: in the two Matabeleland provinces, for example, challengers who enjoyed Harare's confidence were overwhelmed in key posts by protégés of Home Affairs Minister Dumiso Dabengwa. In Masvingo, the provincial elections were a bruising test of strength between the camps of Politburo Secretary for Legal Affairs Eddison Zvobgo and Harare's man, Provincial Governor Josiah Hungwe. Zvobgo's camp easily carried the province with his protégé, MP Dzikamai Mavhaire, defeating Higher Education Minister Stan Mudenge (now Foreign Affairs Minister), a former technocrat much favored by the President. Appeals for unity after the elections were ignored. Although provincial elections were held, the wrangles still seemed far from being over.

There were several party members who wanted Zvobgo expelled from the party for allegedly decampaigning (i.e., undermining) President Robert Mugabe in the March 2002 presidential election. Added to this scenario, Vice President Simon Muzenda's death at the end of September 2003 re-vitalized power struggles in Masvingo province, where he was the party's provincial godfather. This had tended to accelerate jockeying for President Mugabe's position as it emerged that whoever took over from the late head of state's confidante could be the chosen successor to the political hot seat.

In January 2003, cracks widened in the ZANU (PF) camp in Bulawayo after the party's central committee members in the city passed a vote of no confidence in Jabulani Sibanda, the provincial chairman. The development followed the arrest of provincial political commissar Mazwine Gumpo, for allegedly organizing a demonstration against Vice-President Joseph Msika. Msika, who was in the city, was heckled by a group of ZANU (PF) supporters when he attended a meeting where the ouster of Sibanda was discussed. Sibanda, apparently basking in the support he enjoyed among party supporters, appeared unshaken by the move — which he described as "nonsense." Nevertheless, Sibanda was suspended by the Politburo in March of that year.

Although Sibanda was exonerated of wrong-doing at a central committee meeting in October, party sources said sharp divisions still remained. In mid-November, persistent divisions in the Bulawayo branch forced the party's national commissar, Elliot Manyika, to handpick the provincial executive after feuding camps failed to agree on candidates.

Sibanda was also the Zimbabwe National Liberation War Veterans Association chairman for the province. He was very vocal against the alleged looting of maize grain from the Grain Marketing Board (GMB) by senior ZANU (PF) officials who allegedly re-sold the scarce commodity at exorbitant prices.[61]

Earlier in August, some provincial executive members attending a meeting at the ZANU (PF) provincial HQ in Bulawayo allegedly sought refuge in the toilets when marauding party youths threatened to assault them. Ruling party sources said the youths were seeking the reinstatement of an executive member who was fired. Several ZANU (PF) executive members in Bulawayo have been fired or resigned in the last few months in what party insiders said was part of a leadership wrangle. Provincial party spokesman Sikhumbuzo Ndiweni resigned after he allegedly differed with the party's old guard on his intentions to include youths in the provincial leadership. The sources said riot police were called to the party's offices at Davies' Hall, where they defused the situation.

In Manicaland, ZANU (PF)'s secretary for administration, Didymus Mutasa, battled to unseat the party's pompous provincial party chairman, Kumbirai Kangai. Mutasa played the ethnic card badly by trying to cast Kangai as an outsider in Manicaland (he comes from Buhera). It is doubtful the

---

61. In February 2004, he was elected president of the Zimbabwe National Liberation War Veterans Association at the organization's national congress.

province's population much cared about the ethnic origins of the party chairman. During the primaries for the June 2000 general election and again for the nomination of executive mayor, Mutasa sought to install his own representatives. However, on both counts he found himself in the cold; first when he backed ZANU (PF) candidate, Eddie Musabayana, against the popular "little" Lazarus Nzarayebani, who became the party's official constituency candidate in spite of the Politburo's directives, and then again when he backed the party's official candidate for the executive mayor, John Mvundura, against another party outcast, Lawrence Mudehwe.

Until 1994, the word of President Robert Mugabe and his ruling hierarchy on nominations was virtually law; but increasingly there were signs that this law was being challenged. In mid-January 1995, retired Air Marshal Josiah Tapfumaneyi Tungamirai, the party's Youth Secretary, hotly contested the right to stand for ZANU (PF) primaries in the Gutu North constituency chosen by Vice President Simon Muzenda for the 1995 general election. A Politburo decision endorsed by the Central Committee had ruled that the two Vice Presidents should be entitled to unopposed party nominations wherever they wanted. Mines Minister Eddison Zvobgo (who then was Minister without Portfolio) claimed that the Politburo was merely one of the Central Committee's many sub-committees and could not rule on major policy issues. The Politburo is in theory the servant but in reality was the master of a 100-member Central Committee elected by the party congress. This was a major constitutional challenge to the President, whose appointees form the Politburo, which they regard as paramount. This time the President was drawn into a factional conflict in which he was forced to defend one of the rivals. Tungamirai backed down, though generalized rumblings continued and the dispute simmers on.

The 1995 general election was actually fought during ZANU (PF)'s primaries. A good number of radical candidates, who were critical of corruption within the ruling party, were ousted during the primaries, forcing some to stand as Independents during the subsequent elections. During the election campaign, the party seemed to be debating with itself: the suspended (independent) ZANU (PF) candidates against the party machine. The main focus of interest fell on the suspended Margaret Dongo. Because she felt that she had been "rigged" out of the ZANU (PF) primaries, Dongo decided to fight her own party in the general election.

The ZANU (PF) primaries for the local government elections in October 1995 were also characterized by a split between the ruling hierarchy and the grassroots members. Besides, the primaries exposed the swelling tribal and regional divisions within the party. The split became apparent when the politburo decided, against the wishes of the grassroots members, to impose its own executive mayoral candidates for the urban council elections. Contrary to the directives of the ZANU (PF) leadership, losers of the urban council primaries participated in the council elections as independents. The mayoral polls in Mutare, which were won by Lawrence Mudehwe, an independent, clearly irritated the party hierarchy. Speaking at the ZANU (PF) Women's League National Assembly in Harare on November 3, 1995, Mugabe took a swipe at the independents, saying, "True party cadres do not go against the word of the leadership." There were also contradictory situations in Bulawayo and Masvingo, where Cde Alios Chidoda was overruled by the Politburo.

In an unprecedented challenge to the President's 17-year-old rule, legislators of the ZANU (PF) party in May 1997 refused to authorize a loan of Z$1.2 billion for the new International Airport Terminal. Political analysts reported that Parliament appeared determined to stamp down its authority and to reject the airport project, whose tender was won by Leo Mugabe's Air Harbour Technologies under controversial circumstances. Originally, the project was supposed to be privately funded and the MPs were adamant to stop funding from taxpayers' coffers. For three weeks in a row, parliamentarians stayed away from a crucial party caucus intended to whip them into approving the airport loan.

In September 1997, a feud broke out between two ZANU (PF) camps in Mashonaland West Province. One group was led by the party's provincial chairman, Swithun Mombeshora, who had the tacit support of Ignatius Chombo, Minister of Higher Education, and the other by Nathan Shamuyarira, the then Minister of Industry and Commerce. Chombo's camp was said to have the tacit support of Chegutu's mayor, Willie Muringani, and unreserved backing from Chidarikire, as well as the President's sister, Sabina Mugabe. Shamuyarira, who fell out of favor with Chinhoyi's councilors following the 1997 municipal workers' crisis, was allegedly backed by Charles Ndlovu, the MP for Chegutu West, and by most provincial ZANU (PF) workers.

It was reported that the province was so divided that a number of senior provincial committee members were suspended or expelled from power for reasons described as "frivolous" by political observers. Party cadres were grouped as Zezurus and Super Zezurus, the latter title accorded only to those from Mugabe's rural home in Zvimba and Chombo's home area of Chitomborwizi. Jacobus de Wet, the provincial treasurer, resigned in protest at the "internal power struggle." The MP for Mhondoro constituency, Mavis

Chidzonga was unusually suspended from the provincial leadership because the leadership contended that she did not attend four consecutive meetings of the provincial committee. By September, 9 members of the party leadership were on suspension in a province with 13 MPs. Shamuyarira, who hails from Mahusekwa and is also ZANU (PF) secretary for information and publicity, was described by the party leadership as a "foreigner" in the province, and observers wondered how a black Zimbabwean can be described as a foreigner in his own country of birth.

Infighting within the ruling party is apparently an ongoing affair. The choice of a candidate to represent the party in the August 2003 Makonde parliamentary by-election exposed further divisions, with rival party stalwarts said to be backing their own political allies. Senior politicians from Mashonaland West province made frantic moves to impose candidates on the constituency but faced stiff resistance from the local Chief Nemakonde, who was said to be insisting that his people be allowed to select a candidate of their choice.

According to the sources, Mugabe's sister Sabina was trying to push for her son Leo Mugabe to represent ZANU (PF) in the by-election. Leo is the former chairman of the Zimbabwe Football Association, where he was booted out over alleged misadministration.

Another faction allegedly headed by ZANU (PF)'s information and publicity secretary Nathan Shamuyarira was said to be backing another party activist for the seat ahead of Mugabe's nephew. Local government Minister Ignatius Chombo and Parliament deputy speaker Edna Madzongwe were reportedly canvassing for Lashiwe Murefu, an administrator at the government provincial hospital in Chinhoyi, to stand for the party in the ballot in which the ruling party was battling with the opposition MDC. The ZANU (PF) chairman for Mashonaland West, Phillip Chiyangwa, was meanwhile said to have thrown his weight behind yet another candidate, Artwell Seremani. The outspoken Chiyangwa, who is also the Member of Parliament for Chinhoyi constituency, was said to be close to Seremani.

The seat for Makonde constituency fell vacant following the death in early 2003 of Swithun Mombeshora, who in the run-up to the 2000 Parliamentary elections was imposed on the constituency after the politburo forced journalist Kindness Paradza to step down.

At the ZANU (PF) annual conference held in Mutare in early December 1997, about 5,000 delegates united in a rare display of people power to reject an attempt by the government to impose the war veterans' levy, which had just been rejected in Parliament. President Mugabe, putting on a brave face as the conference appeared to be on the verge of an uproar, simply acknowledged the delegates' firm "*Hatidi!*" (We don't want it!), and immediately ordered Finance Minister Herbert Murerwa to seek other means of raising more than Z$4 billion that was needed to pay off gratuities and pensions to veterans of Zimbabwe's war of liberation. The late Lazarus Nzarayebani, MP for Mutare South, said that it was sometimes necessary for the leadership to learn things the hard way. "We told them from the beginning that the issue of the levy was a non-starter, and true to our predictions, the delegates have shown they do not want it."[62]

Political analysts and conference delegates themselves said the Mutare rebellion was a rude awakening for ZANU (PF)'s leadership, long used to patronage politics and that the event signaled that the party's leaders could no longer bulldoze issues as they had done in the past. The delegates leaped up to embrace each other after the controversial levy was thrown out; several legislators, who themselves had staunchly opposed it days before in Parliament, smiled, laughed and beat their chests, clearly elated that they had been vindicated.

True to tradition, Vice-President Muzenda, speaking ahead of President Mugabe in a speech which analysts saw as testing the waters, had taken a tough line. "Members of Parliament who are elected on the party ticket should be committed to the principles of the party," he rumbled. Then he warned: "We may indeed be forced, as we were forced to do during the liberation struggle, to discard some of our members because they are not committed to the party. They maybe intelligent, they maybe brave, they maybe rich — indeed, they may have many positive qualities, but if they are not loyal to our cause as a party, then they are of little value to the party....True members should adhere strictly not only to the constitution, but also to the regulations and procedures of ZANU (PF). They should do exactly as religious people who adhere strictly to their Bible or Koran and the regulations and procedures of their religion or denomination."[63]

In addition to the war veterans' issue, ZANU (PF) leadership came under sharp criticism over party matters such as why members to its Politburo, the Soviet-styled supreme organ of the once ruling communist party, were not elected — they are appointed by President Mugabe himself. "Comrade President, elections are held at all party structures, from the cell to the province. Why can't the Politburo be elected by the people as well?"[64] asked Mashonaland

---

62. *Afrika News Network*, Copenhagen, 15 December, 1997.

63. *The Financial Gazette*, 11 December, 1997.

64. *Afrika News Network*, Copenhagen, 15 December, 1997.

Central governor the late Border Gezi. He received a standing ovation when he also told the President that it was Politburo members who were seated close to him who had destroyed the party by fanning factionalism. In a rare display of frank talk, he caused quite a stir when he boldly asked why proper audited statements of accounts for ZANU (PF)-run companies were not presented at national conferences for delegates to assess the party's financial position. "It is puzzling to note that the party is always broke yet it has huge investments in a number of companies. Where is the money going? The party has farms, houses, and cattle — what is really happening to these things? I ask again: where is the money going and does anyone care?" No answers were given, although the party owns close to 15 companies, among them ZIDCO Holdings, Jongwe Press and National Blankets.

At this juncture, the national party chairman, Joseph Msika, made attempts to limit the time allocated to Gezi to deliver his speech. This was futile, as delegates shouted him down, with one delegate yelling: "Leave those who tell the truth continue talking. We are tired of thieves and liars in the party!"[65] As one delegate summed it up: "The days when the party's leadership was regarded as demi-gods are over. Issues have to be examined as critically as possible, otherwise we could find ourselves in the political wilderness."[66]

It is no wonder, therefore, that ZANU (PF) failed to pay Z$275 million owed to several local companies, including one of the country's largest advertising agencies, which handled the party's ambitious media campaign in the run-up to the March 2002 presidential election. By the end of 2002, ZANU (PF) failed to service a debt of Z$410 million owed to other suppliers of campaign materials, according to media reports.[67] In desperation, six companies had to file a joint challenge to contest the governing party at the end of September 2003. In a landmark judgment that could provide some relief to several companies that are owed huge sums of money by the ruling party, High Court Judge Charles Hungwe found ZANU (PF) in default of its contractual obligations made with six companies that either printed or distributed its campaign T-shirts. The companies are owed Z$1.8 billion.

Notwithstanding, on December 9, 1997, Minister of Finance tried to adjourn Parliament until the end of January 1998 without resolving the thorny issue of the tax package to finance pensions for liberation war veterans. However, government backbenchers blocked the attempt. The parliamentarians wanted

---

65. *Ibid.*
66. *The Financial Gazette*, 11 December, 1997.
67. *Ibid.*, 27 March 2003.

the Minister to withdraw the Finance (No. 2) Bill, which gave effect to a series of tax hikes, including the introduction of a 5% war veterans' levy. While Murerwa officially withdrew the proposed 5% levy, the increase in sales tax on all goods that attracted 15% to 17.5%, the doubling of sales tax on electricity charges to 10% and the increase in fuel duties of 20 cents a liter remained intact. More than 15 MPs who spoke on the Bill said they did not understand why the Minister was withdrawing only the 5% levy and not the other tax hikes, since it had been agreed at the ZANU (PF) congress the previous week that the whole tax package should be scrapped. Following an impromptu caucus meeting of the ruling ZANU (PF) that lasted over two hours, the government bowed to pressure from the parliamentarians by withdrawing increases in electricity sales tax with immediate effect and the hike in fuel duties from midnight December 31.

Open revolt against President Mugabe would have been unheard of a few years ago. The average Zimbabwean is not happy, and now the President's lieutenants also appear to be unhappy. Zimbabwe's parliamentarians, who had in the past been accused of rubber stamping executive decisions without question, now seemed to be waking up. Several are reported to have openly pointed out that Mugabe was not only out of touch but was now "a liability to the party." Dzikamai Mavhaire, Masvingo Central MP, summed it up when he told Parliament: "We, parliamentarians, seem to be useless. We are just there to give ZANU (PF) the required majority number of seats." Dzikamai Mavhaire, who was quoted in the February 10, 1998 *Hansard* declared, "We believe we are not a monarchy. Honorable members will agree that we must remain a democratic republic.... What I am proposing is that the President must go." Parliamentarians debating a motion to change Zimbabwe's constitution and limit the President to two 5-year terms as opposed to the current unlimited six-year terms expressed similar sentiments. Magwegwe-Pumula MP, Norman Zikhali, said that MPs were not rebelling against the ruling party or executive; they were expressing the sentiments of the people they represented.

While no MP spoke against Mavhaire's contribution to the debate, it left political analysts wondering what was happening. It was not long before serious divisions erupted in the open when the MP for Hwedza, Aeneas Chigwedere, injected tribal sentiments into the debate, accusing one region of having an agenda to use constitutional reforms to unseat President Robert Mugabe. "One region has a secret agenda to achieve through constitutional reform, and all of us are being used as pawns in their game. They are using us as instruments to achieve their goal," he charged. "Mavhaire's master and all the people who are persuading us to make a positive contribution to this motion come from one region. Their aim in reforming the Constitution is very clear — it's to get rid of President Mugabe."[68] The Deputy Speaker of Parliament, Edna Madzongwe, immediately ordered Chigwedere to withdraw his remarks unless he had proof.

Addressing party supporters at a rally at Magunje Growth Point in his home province of Mashonaland West, the President appeared to back Chigwedere's assertions by saying that those who were calling for his resignation were trying to "please their paymasters." The President then took a swipe at ZANU (PF) and government officials who wanted him to quit, describing such officials as misguided elements and traitors who were parroting their masters' voices. "Some people in Parliament are saying Mugabe should go because he has stayed for a long time. We wonder where these ideas, which will destroy the people's wish, are coming from," he asked.

Mavhaire was generally known to belong to a faction led by the Minister without Portfolio and ZANU (PF) national legal affairs secretary, Eddison Zvobgo, which was fighting against another headed by Vice-President Simon Muzenda for the control of Masvingo province. While Zvobgo had made it public that he supports constitutional reforms, he was one of ZANU (PF) leaders who were accused of having ambitions of becoming state president. The situation was not made any better by Zvobgo's apology to the people of Matabeleland for alleged atrocities committed by the Zimbabwe National Army during the dissident era, a statement they said was tantamount to Zvobgo positioning himself for a possible take-over.

Answering questions from pastors at an Evangelical Fellowship of Zimbabwe seminar in Harare in early March 1998, Zvobgo said that it had taken him about a month to read the 260-page report ("Breaking the Silence") on the Fifth Brigade's activities in Matabeleland that was prepared by the Catholic Commission for Justice and Peace and the Legal Resources Foundation. "I did not know and many people did not know — now I am being honest to myself and I want to sleep well — but let me say nobody can be proud about what happened and, for the cleansing of my chest, let me say I am very sorry about what happened." He made sure he stressed that he was speaking for himself, because "I know the implications of this question." Of course, this marked a clear departure from the government's stance. The President had already stated that the dissident era was like any other war situation and should be treated as such.

Zvobgo's apology was considered dubious because it came more than a decade after the atrocities were allegedly committed, and it is the role of the

---

68. *The Hansard*, 3 March, 1998.

President to make such an apology, not a minister without portfolio. This whole episode is covered by the principle of "collective responsibility." After all, it was a cabinet decision to send the Fifth Brigade to Matabeleland. Thus, it seems that Cde Zvobgo may have been concerned about the votes of the people of Matabeleland, more than the losses they had suffered.

In the constitutional-reform debate, there were clear signs that a tribal split was looming. Taking the lead in support of President Mugabe was Mashonaland Central provincial Governor Border Gezi, backed by local MP and Information Minister Chenhamo Chimutengwende, who immediately dissociated their province from statements calling for the President's resignation. The Harare ZANU (PF) provincial executive followed suit, reaffirming its support for the President and denouncing calls for him to step down "before his time is up." An emotionally charged Zimbabwe National Liberation War Veterans' Association chairman, the late Chenjerai Hunzvi, addressing ex-combatants in Matabeleland on March 8, 1998, did not mince his words. While attacking party leaders, including members of the Politburo, for failing to protect the President, he said that he was considering taking over the ZANU (PF) Youth League secretariat — headed by Josiah Tungamirayi from Masvingo — to help revive the party which, he said, was dying. It is ironic that the war veterans were the first to threaten the government when they were pushing for their gratuities and now that they had got them, they were worried that a new government could tamper with the formula. There were many who would have liked to believe the "patriotic" war veteran must have been speaking with tongue in cheek. Moreover, the Chidyausiku Commission looking into the war victims' fund already had implicated Hunzvi in the abuse of the fund and said that he had a case to answer. Observers thought Hunzvi's standing up for Mugabe at a time when even the two vice-presidents, Joshua Nkomo and Simon Muzenda, never raised a finger to defend him was motivated solely by the desire to retain his protection in regard to the war veterans' fund scam.

Amid mounting calls for him to step down, President Robert Mugabe admitted on March 20, 1998 that he faced a rebellion by members of his own ruling ZANU (PF). Speaking before a regular session of the party's central committee, the President spoke of "evil schemers, conspirators and political saboteurs...Let us begin to fish them out and expose them for what they are," he said. "It is indeed a case of arrogant defiance of the party and its leadership. It is a rebellion in itself which such members are engaged in." The central committee was discussing discipline in the party in the wake of Mavhaire's parliamentary speech. Mavhaire's calls were interpreted to mean the President must leave office since he was serving his third term. The Speaker of Parliament, Cde Cyril Ndebele, who had intervened and invoked the Parliamentary Privileges and Immunities provision, which prohibits action against any legislator on issues raised in a parliamentary debate, also came under attack. "Alas, we notice also an even more strange phenomenon. The Speaker, the honorable Speaker, has decided to join in the rebellion against the party as he and those in collusion with him seek to stultify in its political and administrative role to discipline its own members. What rank of madness has gripped some of us?" the President wondered.[69]

Sources close to the 100-member central committee meeting reported that the President's extraordinary display of rage and intolerance turned the bulk of the party against him. Members of the party's central committee were aghast as the President inveighed against "rebellion" by "infidels," saying, "*Mune varoi muno*" (there are witches among us). This remark took everyone by surprise, especially given the Witchcraft Suppression Act provides that whoever accuses any other person of being a witch shall be guilty of an offence. The sources said that it was only members from the President's small province of Mashonaland West and from Harare who railed against Cde Dzikamai Mavhaire, while delegates from the rest of the country maintained a conspicuous silence, refusing to be drawn in. The exception was Robert Marare, who told the President that he was "playing with fire" by ignoring the crisis facing the country.

Nonetheless, in typical Stalinist style, Cde Dzikamai Mavhaire (one of eight provincial chairpersons in the ruling party) was stripped of his position and suspended from the party for two years. A central committee member said delegates were very unhappy with the way the issue had been handled, saying "The whole decision to fire Mavhaire was reached by Mugabe, Msika, Mutasa and Mahachi alone and was imposed on the central committee." The Speaker of Parliament faced unspecified disciplinary action by the party's central committee. While this unprecedented threat of action against the Speaker could spark a constitutional crisis involving the judiciary, it exposed the fragile nature of the 1987 unity accord. ZAPU heavyweights who are now part of the merged ZANU (PF) politburo for the first time took a united stand against President Mugabe and his followers from Mashonaland. Despite the fact that the President had made a public statement attacking the Speaker and was supported by long-time allies Nathan Shamuyarira and Didymus Mutasa (who also publicly insisted that "Ndebele had a case to answer,") the leadership was forced to back

---

69. *AFP*, Harare, 20 March, 1998.

down. The party chairman, Cde Joseph Msika, in an apparent reference to Shamuyarira and Mutasa, said in a televised interview that some party leaders wanted to appear closer to the President than others. This revealed that there was a major deterioration in the cohesion of the ruling elite.

The attack alarmed human rights groups, who said that it was a well-orchestrated attempt to weaken the legislature, to thwart further serious debate on constitutional reforms before the House. Moreover, the ability of members of Parliament to speak freely had been strongly compromised with the possibility of reverting Parliament into a mere rubber stamp of the executive. As if to add insult to injury, General Solomon Mujuru, a member of the politburo attempted to physically assault Zimbabwe's lone independent MP, Margaret Dongo, on the floor of the House on March 25, 1998. Following this, on November 12, 1998, Harare North MP Cde Nyasha Chikwinya was nearly assaulted inside Parliament Building in the Members' Bar. Dzivaresekwa MP Cde Edson Wadyewata accused her of being part of a team plotting the downfall of Harare executive mayor Cde Solomon Tawengwa. She was further accused of masterminding the incident which took place in Hatcliffe, where the mayor was held hostage by angry residents who had gone for days without water, and who were having to buy it by the bucket from a farm five kilometers away. (Hatcliffe was part of Cde Chikwinya's constituency.)

It was obvious the government's majority MPs were bent on using force to suppress the last voices of dissent, even among its own ranks.

However, whatever impression was left, particularly in the "*varoi*-evil-schemers" incident, party sources who requested anonymity for fear of reprisals said the 74-year-old dictator's intolerance to change within the party had left most members opposed to him. After the meeting, there was widespread criticism, privately voiced, of the President's attack and of the meeting's failure to examine any serious issues such as the economic crisis that had triggered unprecedented national strikes and urban unrest.

Earlier, the party managed to rally scarcely 1,000 people (most of them Women's League members and street kids), against the tens of thousands who demonstrated against the government in recent months. The police obligingly escorted the comrades who marched in the streets of Harare to the President's Office, when just two weeks earlier they had clubbed students who were peacefully seeking the same right of access to their president. Addressing the supporters, the President attacked people advocating his removal, saying whites were using them. He bemoaned that it was disheartening that, at a time his government was trying to consolidate the country's hard-won independence through redistribution of land from whites to blacks, "other people are trying to destroy the ruling party and are forming alliances with whites, the very people who oppressed us."

Following the suspension of Dzikamai Mavhaire, the President went to Masvingo province on April 4, 1998. In a clear sign of desperation and defeat, he decided (or, rather, was advised) to go to the rural growth point of Gutu Mupandawana as opposed to Masvingo town, the province's capital. Sources within the party revealed that Gutu was chosen in order to spare the President any inevitable embarrassment, since Masvingo residents were certainly prepared for a show-down; the previous weekend, Zvobgo was forced to intervene to prevent a demonstration in support of Mavhaire. As it turned out, Gutu managed to attract a paltry 5,000 supporters, mostly children who chatted through the speeches.

In another sign of the President's flagging political fortunes, a planned pro-Mugabe rally to counter calls for his resignation flopped in the eastern border town of Mutare when the provincial chairman, Cde Kumbirai Kangai, managed to attract just 48 to 50 supporters. ZIANA reported that the Lands and Agriculture Minister made an attempt to give a speech, trying to take advantage of a crowd which had gathered to greet a group of international volunteers marching across Africa in protest against child labor. Unfortunately, disgruntled liberation war collaborators who chanted songs heckled him and later handed the minister thousands of ZANU (PF) party cards from disaffected members. That Zimbabwe's deepening economic crisis and the President's leadership of the country had much to do with the calls for his departure was not in doubt.

On April 4, 1998, at Kushinga Phikelela College near Marondera, secretary for ZANU (PF)'s Youth Affairs retired Air Marshal Josiah Tungamirai told the seventh session of the party's youth league national assembly, attended by President Mugabe, that all was not well in the ruling party. In an emotional address, he referred to the apathy during the 1995 general election and the 1996 presidential election, which were marked by very low turnouts. He noted that this apathy seemed to have grown into open hostility to ZANU (PF) as reflected in the violent strikes and demonstrations during 1997. "Your Excellency, the party is in crisis and only a fool can claim otherwise," he said. Cde Tungamirai said that in the rural areas *chimbwidos* and *mujibas* (former liberation war collaborators) were working to discredit ZANU (PF), leaving party youths quite uneasy. He noted that it was difficult for the party youth to mobilize when all one could offer was a glorified past and empty promises for the future. "The youth that we target is hungry and angry, for he has no job. The industries are shutting down faster than they were opened. The messages we preach are falling on deaf ears," he said.[70]

At a youth conference in June 1999, young people accused the party of bringing the economy to a crisis point. "Government has failed to manage the basic fundamentals of the economy and is still failing to provide the leadership role assigned it in managing the economy," the party's youth league said. "We find it rather untenable for top government officials to have two or three cars at their disposal when the hospitals are without drugs and the poor peasant is turned away for lack of money.... Where do government's priorities lie in these very difficult circumstances?...We stand by our suggestion to trim cabinet and other posts that appear superfluous."

In a rare show of dissent, some youth delegates walked out in protest over the alleged imposition of leaders in their league and weeks later the women's wing bluntly told Mugabe that women wanted him to deliver on promises to uplift them, saying that although they were faithful, they should not be taken for granted.

The youths and women seemed to echo the sentiments of those MPs whom ZANU (PF) had been trying to victimize, especially in their criticism of the "tired horses" in the presidency and cabinet who did not seem to have any new ideas about the way forward. Victimizing MPs like John Mataure for telling the truth did not solve Zimbabwe's problems and ZANU (PF) soon found itself without a constituency in the under-fifty age group.

Apparently, after the dust had settled on Dzikamai Mavhaire's trial and suspension by the party, Attorney-General Patrick Chinamasa commissioned an in-house inquiry. The ensuing report, prepared by a senior law officer and presented in July 1998, pointed out that no one outside Parliament had the authority to carry out proceedings against a parliamentarian over statements made in Parliament. After analyzing the matter and giving numerous examples of similar cases in other countries, the officer said:

"It is therefore clear that only Parliament can discipline its members on matters pertaining to parliamentary privilege. Not even the chief whip or the party caucus has the power to do so.

"In conclusion, it is my view that freedom of speech and debate provided for in Section Five of the Privileges, Immunities and Powers of Parliament Act is absolute and that it does not only apply to judiciary proceedings in a court of

---

70. Panafrican News Agency, 4 April, 1998.

law.... but to other proceedings, including proceedings initiated by political parties."

According to the report, Ndebele was right and Mavhaire should not have been punished. Whatever the purpose for commissioning the study, it is clear that even the AG, an officer appointed by the President himself, wanted to put the record right for historians.

Even the village party leaders, considered the backbone of President Mugabe's support, openly defied him on December 5, 1998, when they bluntly told him that they could not accept the proposed tax increases. Analysts felt that the disgruntlement was only waiting to explode. When President Mugabe persuaded the late Joshua Nkomo, who was then 81, and Mze (Simon Muzenda, 76) to stay on, he seemed to be saying, "It is not time to go. You want to set a dangerous precedent for me to go." Mze died in September 2003, at the age of 80 and still trying to leave office, but Mugabe had asked him "to wait until a smooth plan is put in place." "Most people in the party and politburo know Muzenda wants to leave office; he has been talking about it for the past year," a reliable source said.

Mugabe wanted to stay on against all odds. In an interview in connection with his 74th birthday, the President said, "I am only a young old man now. When I know I am an old, old man, fine, I will retire."[71]

Addressing ZANU (PF) supporters in Masvingo during his birthday celebrations, President Mugabe had an opportunity to show that turning 74 meant that he had grown wiser and that the public could expect mature and responsible leadership from him. Instead, he descended to the level of the street, casually tossing out insults to those whom he perceived as potential challengers, when he ought to have been offering wise counsel and guidance to the nation. His remarks on the ZCTU leadership were at best unstatesman-like and at worst downright irresponsible and childish. His audience was astonished to hear class-conscious, arrogant remarks from a professed Marxist. He was quoted in the press as saying "[Gibson] Sibanda? To be the president of which country? You have the misplaced belief that you are more powerful than the government. People must weigh themselves and see what they are good at. Some drive trains, some are foremen....People who witnessed the liberation struggle will not accept you (as leaders)."[72]

71. *The Financial Gazette*, 26 February, 1998.
72. *The Mail & Guardian*, Johannesburg, 6 March, 1998.

Four years on, at 78 years of age and with the economy in shambles, Mugabe was no better. Addressing ZANU (PF) supporters at the Harare International Airport upon arrival from a two-week visit to France and Southeast Asia (where he attended the Franco-African and Non-Aligned Movement summits in February 2003), Mugabe attacked Morgan Tsvangirai for "betraying" Zimbabwe and being a British "puppet," saying, "Who the hell are you, anyway, to want to rule this country? *Chikoro hauna, unongovawo chipoko zvako.* (You are not educated, you are just a spook)."[73] Tsvangirai is a leader of the opposition for which more than one million people voted in the March 2002 presidential election. Bringing him to court in leg irons and wearing a skimpy prison uniform in the middle of winter disgraced Zimbabwe in the eyes of the outside world.

His constant outbursts and emphasis on the part he played in the liberation struggle appear specially designed to hide from the nation the President's humble beginnings as a teacher at Hope Fountain, Chalimbana (Zambia) and Ghana. He could not have forgotten that some of his lieutenants also came from humble beginnings, including his two vice-presidents — a carpenter and social worker turned trade-union organizer on the railways. There were many more, of a lesser social standing, who contributed significantly to the political emancipation of Zimbabwe. Some still hold political office. The 21st February movement is supposed to be a youth movement crafted around Mugabe as a role model. His start as a simple teacher was not a stigma and was never held against him, but his lack of respect for other people is.

Once a very popular and charismatic leader, President Mugabe has, over the years, lost the support of the average Zimbabwean, especially the urban voter, because of his handling of national affairs. He has brushed off national problems as petty issues; he ignored the national strike by civil servants in 1996, and went off to the South African Sea resort of Cape Town on a honeymoon with his new bride while the country was almost paralyzed. From Cape Town, he went to attend the SADC summit in Maseru, Lesotho. From Maseru, he flew back home only to lambaste the striking civil servants before taking off for Nairobi to open an agricultural show there. It was only after he realized that the civil servants were not giving in that he bowed to the pressure and awarded them salary increases and bonuses that had not been budgeted for.

When the war veterans took to the streets in 1997, demanding to meet him and air their grievances, he ignored them for months. He only met them when

---

73. *The Daily News*, 8 March, 2003.

there were increasing threats of insurrection. Just as he had done with the civil servants the previous year, he awarded them gratuities and pensions that had not been budgeted for. The same happened with the national protest in December 1997. While Harare was burning, he gave a State of the Nation address which completely ignored the chaos across the road in Africa Unity Square, leaving most Zimbabweans wondering what country he was talking about. During·the food riots in January 1998, although some reports said he was on leave, in a typical example of how "out of touch" he had become, he appeared on national television (and on the front page of the national daily) admiring the tobacco crop of an indigenous farmer. Instead of commenting on the worst riots to rock the country since independence, he dwelt on the land issue which, though that too is very important, was an insult to urban residents (rioters and non-rioters alike) who were bitterly concerned over price increases. Some were heard to say they did not want the land but jobs.

To add insult to injury, people are infuriated by his preference for external affairs and overseas trips. While some argue that he makes blunders because he is misinformed by his lieutenants, others argue that Mugabe (who obtained several degrees through correspondence while in detention and after, and continued to obtain more as head of government) is a well-read person. He is quite aware of what is happening but he ignores it, hoping that it will pass away. Perhaps, he has simply stopped caring. Some believe that one problem is that he is not getting as much support and advice from the current First Lady, Grace, as he got from Sally. Sally, these people argue, was a political force in her own right and was a pillar in his life. As a member of the ruling Politburo, she was so powerful that those who wanted to forge ahead had to bow to her.

Indeed, it is interesting to note that the curtain was finally closing on President Mugabe during the 20th anniversary of independence. On April 18, every year since the end of Rhodesia, Mugabe had filled Rufaro and later the National Sports Stadium with cheering crowds waving red banners. The eastern stand was filled with school children displaying slogans in typical North Korean style, praising the president and what the revolution had achieved. He always made sure that he marched his police and army triumphantly through the stadium and invited all the heads of state in the region to wonder at the air force fly-past above. In 2000, however, the celebrations were cancelled, ostensibly so the money could be spent on victims of cyclone Eline. The President was a lone figure at a wreath-laying ceremony at the vast Heroes' Acre, the North Korean-designed monument west of the capital, just opposite the Chinese-built National Sports Stadium.

Observers of the Zimbabwe political scene believed that a revitalized ZANU (PF) was on the horizon. If party provincial elections held at the end of November 1998 were anything to go by, then one could speak of a revolution within a revolution, because the results of the polls showed that ZANU (PF)'s structures were disintegrating. Most of the new faces were professionals, business leaders, company executives and others who felt the time had come to join, re-join or take an active role in the affairs of a party. The provincial polls, tense in provinces like Manicaland, Masvingo and Mashonaland West because of perennial infighting there, also erased the political hopes of some who had long cherished presidential ambitions, or whose names had been associated with those competing to occupy Zimbabwe House after President Mugabe retires.

The ZANU (PF) primaries for the 2000 general election ended what had almost come to be a lifetime ministerial career for some party heavyweights.

The Manicaland group, who later stood as independents, were joined elsewhere by erstwhile parliamentarians Cdes Richard Shambambeva-Nyandoro, Zebron Chawaipira, Edson Wadyehwata, John Tsimba, Clive Chimbi and Tirivanhu Mudariki. Mvenge and Shambambeva-Nyandoro gained popularity in the House due to their robust stand against excesses of the state. They were also involved in parliamentary investigations of corruption and graft at high levels of government and parastatals.

The 2000 elections witnessed the highest number of independent candidates. The ZANU (PF) Independents opposed the imposition of candidates by the Politburo. Commenting on this imposition of candidates, in an indignant speech at an election rally Cde Simon Muzenda directed people to "vote for baboons" if that was what ZANU (PF) fielded as candidates. This definition of electoral duty perhaps went further than party loyalty required, even if it did provide a candid description of some of the party's high-level scavengers.[74]

This unique "protest" against the Politburo was coupled, as noted above, by the emergence of a formidable opposition party, the Movement for Democratic Change (MDC), a historic first: now, the ZANU (PF) would actually have to fight to make its case.

Some commentators have drawn parallels between the present Zimbabwe and Kenneth Kaunda's last days at the end of 1989. Among the similarities are: the budget crisis, the exchange rate collapse of November 14, 1997, business confidence at a 20-year low, mounting industrial unrest, and food riots in 1999.

---

74. *The Zimbabwe Independent*, 23 June, 2000.

Rumors of an internal "struggle" for power are always rife when it comes to the succession question within ZANU (PF). When Cde Emmerson Mnangagwa lost his seat in the June 2000 general election, Mugabe elevated him to the position of Administrative Secretary at "Jongwe" House (ZANU-PF Headquarters), and then made every effort to ensure he was appointed Speaker of Parliament. It seemed that Mnangagwa was President Mugabe's designated heir. However, in February 2003, rumor from the "inner circle" suggested that there were two factions within ZANU (PF), each trying to position itself for the succession. The stronger was led by the head of the armed forces, General Vitalis Zvinavashe, and Emmerson Mnangagwa. The rival group was centered around the Defense Minister, Sydney Sekeramayi, retired army commander Solomon Mujuru, and politburo member Dumiso Dabengwa.

The death of party loyalist Muzenda seemed to fuel the succession crisis which was unsettling the ruling party and the country at large. The battle for Mugabe's succession had been raging for some time and appeared to be escalating; a committee had been constituted to spearhead the debate (previously held as taboo) in the party, but the committee had become the theater for a battle of wills. Party heavyweights dueled to gain advantage over one another and jockeyed to position themselves for a final assault. The committee caused such rifts among senior members that it had to be disbanded. The political dynamics remained volatile.

Since the attainment of independence from colonial rule in the 1960s, there had been a notion that, once elected, African leaders stayed in power until they died — if they did not suffer the indignity of being ousted. Indeed, there was a spate of military coups across the continent. But Senegal's Leopold Sedar-Senghor, Tanzania's Julius Mwalimu Nyerere and Ahmadou Ahidjo of Cameroon set a precedent in post-independent Africa when they stepped down from their countries' top offices. When Ketumile Masire relinquished power at the end of March 1998, after 18 years at Botswana's helm, he helped show that the continent might be coming of age. President Masire did not leave as a beleaguered leader giving in to mounting pressure, or out of fear of losing an upcoming election; he was simply calling it a day. He left behind a country with a vibrant economy, and that is not just because Botswana was blessed with the discovery of diamonds in the early 1970s. (Quite a few African countries are rich in minerals, but their economies are struggling.) South Africa's President Nelson Mandela continued the salutary pattern by surrendering the helm of the African National Congress to his deputy, Mr. Thabo Mbeki. During the installation of Mbeki as democratic South Africa's second president, in June 1999, Mandela told the press, "I have in a small way done my duty to my country and my people. I welcome the possibility of reveling in obscurity as I am going to do when I step down."

One hopes that Zimbabwe will find a way to change course and follow that trend. For now, it has a leader who not only clings to power, but who is not prepared to accommodate change.

## The Roots of Corruption

A professional and free press, government at every level, parliament, business, the civil service and the judiciary all have roles to play in protecting society from corruption. The lack of transparency and accountability which characterize Zimbabwe's political scene today encourage rising levels of corruption, and intensifying social problems, and can lead to industrial action and disruption in production. Some fundamentals, such as an effective legal system and adherence to the rule of law, have to be put in place. A lack of checks on executive power by the legislature has been identified as the major cause of corruption in the country, and the corruption takes many forms, including kinship and patronage, particularly among civil servants who copy their bosses.

According to reports compiled by the police fraud squad in Zimbabwe, corruption cuts across all sectors of society. A bank manager, for example, may authorize payment of a stolen or forged cheque in return for a "cut." A game officer can be induced to stand by while poachers kill and plunder wildlife. A police officer, after arresting a multi-million dollar fraudster, might be bribed to let him/her go. Magistrates might be paid to pass lighter sentences. Customs officials may allow in imported goods duty free, for a fee. Drivers' licenses can be obtained, even by people who cannot drive at all. Senior government officials and company executives get "commissions" into foreign banking accounts. Others receive gratuitous allocations of shares in companies or can be awarded participation in "joint ventures". Company officials may offer ministry officials a percentage of the contract price should his/her company be awarded the tender — this has become so much the standard that Zimbabweans now call it *chegumi* (10%). The crimes are made easier by economic hardship; low salaries make employees, civil servants and others susceptible to such emoluments.

In white-collar crime, the criminals are known not to pick their target blindly or at random. It takes planning, organization and collaboration. In this category, one sees the involvement of the top echelons of society and learned persons like lawyers, accountants and other professionals. According to reports, the Zimbabwean government and the banking sector lost Z$100 million through white-collar crime in 216 criminal incidents in the first three months of 1999.[75]

Organized crime is on the rise, effected with chilling refinement through syndicates that are willing to part with huge sums of money to achieve their goals. Any stumbling blocks are identified and palms are greased (or physically eliminated). Economic crime involves transfer pricing which could result in millions of dollars being stashed away, tax evasion, smuggling or theft of gold and other precious minerals like emeralds. The perpetrators usually cultivate political and social influence as necessary safeguards for their sustenance by corrupting public figures at relevant tiers of government or, indeed, private organizations. Money laundering, which involves the conversion of illicit proceeds into other assets, the concealment of the true source and ownership of the illegally acquired proceeds, and the creation of a perception of legitimacy of the new source and ownership of the proceeds, has also been on the increase in Zimbabwe. Criminals and syndicates can cross borders and hide their proceeds in neighboring or overseas countries, which makes countries seeking foreign investment an easy target.

If one narrows the field to public procurement of goods and services, one finds that corruption manifests itself in four categories. The simplest is bribery, which is simply the extension of a financial reward in exchange for favorable or preferential treatment. In collusion and bid rigging, competing firms may arrange to structure their bids in such a way that they will jointly provide the service and share the benefits. The third category involves insider dealing, where people in public office award business, directly or by proxy, to someone who will make sure they also ultimately benefit. The fourth category is post-award corruption, which takes place after the award of the tender. Here, the winner seeks to recoup expenses incurred in the bribery either by over-invoicing, or lowering the quality of goods/services supplied, or extending the life of the contract.

Despite attempts by leaders to clean up corruption in Africa, graft remains the order of the day in many countries. Business people seeking government contracts can routinely expect to pay through the nose in Nigeria and Kenya, for instance. The demands will be made perfectly clear, usually in the form of a "service fee" or a percentage of the contract. The squeeze may also be put on them in Uganda and Tanzania, despite promises of better administration. However, it is likely to be rather subtler and less demanding.

---

75. *The Insider*, Harare, 21 June, 1999.

Halting corruption should be regarded as a development imperative because it impedes economic growth and limits the ability of countries to reduce poverty. Since much public corruption can be traced to government intervention in the economy, policies aimed at liberalization, stabilization, deregulation, and privatization can sharply reduce the opportunities for corrupt behavior. One must emphasize the term "sharply reduce," because the assumption that corruption cannot thrive in an environment of competition, transparency and accountability which usually follows privatization and deregulation is fast being proven wrong. A study by Barbara Harris-White and Gordon White of the Institute of Development Studies at Sussex University argues that corruption is being privatized, with politicians and a new economic elite replacing state officials as the prime agents of corruption. At the same time, it is being made easier by the growing use of tax havens and offshore financial centers that facilitate the covert laundering of illegal gains.

There is also a persistent notion that if one pays bribes, work moves faster. This is particularly so where government regulations are pervasive and government officials have discretion in applying them. Individuals are often willing to offer bribes to officials to circumvent the rules and officials are occasionally tempted to accept these bribes. However, whatever the shortcomings of African administration, it is generally true that it takes two to tango. According to Transparency International, West European companies — led by those from Belgium and Luxembourg — contribute most to corruption in international business. By comparison, according to the organization, United States business people lose out on contracts, as they are less willing to pay.

The problem is not just restricted to developing or transitional economies. Revelations in Japan, Italy and the United Kingdom have demonstrated that corruption is also entrenched in highly industrialized democratic societies. Multinational corporations from Europe, the Indian sub-continent and Japan, for example, find it easier to pay bribes, as there are no laws in their countries forbidding these practices. Partly because of its reputation as a highly corrupt continent, Africa has just about a share of just about 4% of world trade.

As Zimbabwe's economy sinks deeper into the quagmire, corruption is infiltrating ever more deeply into the system. What was once confined to the elite is creeping into other areas of the government. However, as in so much of Africa, it is a matter of survival for those at the bottom of the pyramid, as well as padding for the leadership's already fat bank accounts and a source of political patronage. In order to instill some sense of transparency and accountability and, thus, to bring down the level of corruption, it is significant to identify the roots of the evil.

### One-party political systems

Contemporary events and experience have shown that Marxist-Leninist dictatorships or one-party systems of government brought about by *de facto* one-party "democracies" are highly prone to corrupt activities. A joke used to make the rounds in Kiev and Moscow: Brezhnev was showing off all his magnificent vacation retreats, from the outskirts of Moscow to the Black Sea resorts. His mother was so impressed by the properties that she couldn't stop herself from asking, "But, son, what will happen when the Reds come back?"

Like Brezhnev's mother, some African nationalist leaders were given impressive tours of certain of these "socialist" states, and they clearly liked what they saw. When they overthrew the colonial systems in their respective countries, they were determined to imitate not the "classless" society that was being touted but the tight grip on power and privileges for those at the top. They introduced Marxism-Leninism as it was practiced, not as it was described in philosophy books. While they preached socialism, they also emphasized that multi-party systems ran contrary to African values as reflected in the dynastic states of the past.

Where there is a one-party system of government, there are no forces to counter negative policies or legislation. With its overwhelming majority in the Zimbabwean Parliament, ZANU (PF) could do absolutely anything it wanted — it held 147 seats out of a possible 150. ZANU (PF) is a broad movement, as opposed to a party, with a political agenda which it had built on its success in the liberation struggle, and drew its staying power from patronage. It was able to stifle any opposition, and the political system was marked by an absence of transparency and accountability.

A classic example is the pay-off of people for liberating their own country. When Zimbabweans took up arms, they were inspired by something grander than financial gain. But later, when the "war veterans" pressured the government for compensation, the President promised them all sorts of things, without consulting anyone. The constitution says that Parliament has the sole power to authorize public expenditure. Even when the question was finally brought before Parliament, in December 1997, the Minister of Finance tried to side-step parliamentary procedure by fast-tracking the Finance (No. 2) Bill and the Appropriation (Supplement: 1997-98) Bill. Together, they sought to raise nearly Z\$5 billion in unbudgeted costs for the ex-combatants. The MPs approved this "fast-track" legislative approach which deprived them of a chance to scrutinize the contents of the bill; equally incomprehensible is that although the MPs had unanimously opposed the Bill, after a bit of arm-twisting they went along with it.

And there was no apparent need for urgency, at all, to justify such a departure from normal procedure.

Choking under these payoffs to war veterans, the Government spent another Z$66 million, at the end of January 1998, buying 50 new Mercedes Benz 230Es to beef up its VIP fleet. This purchase, the third in the past three years, came at a time when thousands of Zimbabweans were taking to the streets in violent protests against the food price increases imposed at the beginning of the New Year.

In November 1997, the Government had purchased 20 Cherokee four-wheel drive vehicles worth Z$7 million, from an American company, for use by ministers and provincial governors. This meant ministers and governors each had two vehicles allocated to them "as a measure to prolong the lifespan of the ministerial Mercedes Benz vehicles." The Government had already purchased 48 230E Mercedes Benz, in September 1996, for use during the World Solar Summit in Harare. Information from the Central Mechanical Equipment Department (CMED) — a government department responsible for maintaining government vehicles — had it that the Government then sold the other Mercedes Benz 230E to ministers for between US$6,000 and US$10,000 each (instead of the market value, which was US$25,000). The Government lost about US$700,000 in the process. Some senior ministers who had known about the chicanery in advance are said to have taken their old Mercedes Benzes to the CMED for (free) major repairs and engine overhauls just weeks before they bought them outright, further prejudicing public coffers. The public outcry fell on deaf ears.

All government executive officers down to the level of Deputy Secretary are officially issued government cars. It has been estimated that there are about 31 officers at Permanent Secretary and equivalent level, and 1,030 government officers at Deputy Secretary and equivalent level.[76] Moreover, they do not pay tax for the use of the vehicles, as their counterparts in the private sector have to do. It is known that, on retirement, government officials at these levels are allowed to take the vehicles with them at book value.

Figures from the Ministry of Transport and Energy show that CMED spends an average of Z$16 million a month on fuel — Z$9 million on petrol and Z$7 million on diesel. One MP even joked that the CMED must do something about the misuse of cars, because at times a minister travels some 60km to buy groceries.

Perhaps Zimbabwe's Government should take a leaf from Botswana, where government ministers use government vehicles for official business only. In

---

76. *The Zimbabwe Standard*, Harare, 5 Octrober, 1997.

Zimbabwe, ministers use government vehicles and drivers for their private business — their fuel bills are unlimited. In December 1998, the Deputy Minister for Transport and Energy reported to Parliament that the CMED was owed a total of Z\$239.7 million.[77]

The Presidential cabinet is another area where waste and unaccountability are rife. In the July 1997 cabinet reshuffle, Zimbabweans were told that the President had "trimmed" the government by merging some ministries; they were not told that the number of ministerial positions had been increased from 50 to 52, excluding the Speaker (who is ranked as a senior minister) and his deputy. Observers have become so cynical as to call such events a cabinet recycling. Some cabinet ministers were demoted, but not disgraced as they were tacked in the President and vice-presidents' offices. There are seven ministers of state in the president's office and two ministers without portfolio — which seems hard to justify. In all, there were two ministers in the Planning Commission (Cdes Richard Hove and Swithun Mombeshora); two Ministers without Portfolio (Cdes Edson Zvobgo and Joseph Msika); and five Ministers of State (Cdes Witness Mangwende, Cephas Msipa, Oppah Rushesha-Muchinguri, Sithembiso Nyoni and Tsungirirai Hungwe). In the latest reshuffle, at the end of 2002, a new position of Minister for Special Affairs in the President's Office was created. And, of course, there was that geriatric duo of vice-presidents who cost the taxpayer a fortune in salaries and allowances and will continue to do so with their hefty pensions when they finally leave their sinecures.

These cabinet re-shufflings do not appear to be driven by the need for efficient administration. The commendable job of merging eight ministries into four was overshadowed by the creation of new jobs for various individuals. While a planning commission was indeed needed, it could have been headed by a civil servant rather than two ministers with all their perks. A government department could handle indigenization, and war veterans' affairs, and "gender affairs." There were already associations catering for the interests of indigenous (black) entrepreneurs and war veterans. In trying to justify these appointments, President Robert Mugabe said, "These ministers have projects that need to be supervised....They will also follow up progress, if it is not being made, they will look at why, visit sites — they are kind of inspectors, because there is slow performance by ministries."

One might think that if slow performance by ministries is the problem, more ministers is the wrong solution. Maybe the Russian president got it right when he fired the entire government on March 23, 1998, because "the old

---

77. *The Insider*, Harare, 28 January, 1999.

government had not succeeded in resolving a series of key problems and of late has lacked dynamism, initiative and fresh ideas."[78] Listening to President Boris Yeltsin's TV broadcast, Zimbabweans could not help but associate his words with their own 18-year-old "dead wood" government.

In February 2004, President Mugabe again expanded his cabinet. Most curious was the anti-corruption and anti-monopolies post. The anti-corruption portfolio logically should have been accommodated within the jurisdiction of the Ministry of Home Affairs, while the anti-monopolies one would have been better served under the Ministry of Industry. The appointment of Witness Mangwende and Cain Mathema as governors for Harare and Bulawayo, respectively, was another unjustified waste of resources because all urban areas are already under the Minister of Local Government. After all, the Urban Councils Act makes no mention of governors. Cities are run by elected Executive Mayors. It remains to be seen what responsibilities the new governors would assume.

As if all this were not extravagant enough, monthly salaries for staff of Zimbabwe's foreign missions were exceptionally high.

*Table 12: Monthly Salaries for Staff at Zimbabwe's Foreign Missions*

| Position/Grade | As of July 1996 | As of January 1998 | |
|---|---|---|---|
| | (Z$) | (Z$) | (US$) |
| UN Ambassador | 910,000 | 240,000 | 15,112 |
| Ambassadors in a special grade* | 640,000 | 240,000 | 15,112 |
| Ambassadors in D2** | 400,000 | 208,000 | 13,464 |
| Officers in Grade D1*** | 250,000-300,000 | 166,000 | 11,872 |
| Grade P5**** | 200,000-230,000 | 160,000 | 10,109 |
| Principal administrative officers | 155,000-230,000 | 102,000 | 6,978 |
| Senior admin. officers, executive officers and private secretaries (Grade I) | 151,000-200,000 | 96,000 | 5,663 |
| Administrative officers, executive officers and private secretaries (Grade II) | 80,000 | 64,000 | 4,421 |

*Source: The Financial Gazette, 5 March 1998.*
*\*Mostly international organizations at the UN seat in Geneva, the European Union, in Brussels, the United Kingdom, the United States and several European countries.*
*\*\*Equivalent to permanent secretary at home.*
*\*\*\*Equivalent to deputy secretary.*
*\*\*\*\*Includes senior trade and commerce promotion officers.*

In addition, ambassadors and high commissioners receive an entertainment allowance of US$2,159 (Z$32,000) a month and the same amount for food and clothing. All embassy staff receive free accommodations, electricity and water.

---

78. *Metro*, Stockholm, 24 March, 1998.

Members of Parliament have expressed concern over the extravagant salaries and the large number of missions (38) that Zimbabwe maintains abroad, suggesting that some of the embassies, especially those in countries with which Zimbabwe does not have meaningful trade, be closed and others merged to cut costs.

In its tenth report to Parliament on October 7, 1998, the Public Accounts Committee noted that the Ministry of Foreign Affairs overshot its budget by Z$48.5 million during the 1993/94 financial year and by Z$60.7 million during the 1994/95 financial year, in contravention of section 102(1)(b) of the Constitution of Zimbabwe.[79] In response, the Secretary for Foreign Affairs, Cde Andrew Mtetwa, acknowledged that the country had too many foreign missions, but just stopped short of saying that several of them were serving no useful purpose whatsoever. He particularly attributed over-expenditure to an increase in airfares, especially for the children of officers serving abroad, and freight charges for the luggage of returning officers — there was no limit on goods these returning officers could bring back.

Specifically, Parliament's Departmental Committee on Service Ministries discovered, for example, that during the 1997-98 financial year, Z$15 million had been allocated for freight, port and agency fees for property acquired abroad by officers returning home,[80] while extra costs were also incurred for the storage of diplomats' household goods back home. One official said, "In some cases, we found out that while the government was paying the rates for the diplomats' houses in Zimbabwe, these houses were actually being rented out."[81] In addition, Z$18.8 million was paid in school fees for the officers' children studying abroad. For those children who remained at home, at boarding schools, airfare for visits to their parents during school holidays, plus airfares for the officers traveling back and forth on duty, cost Z$11.5 million. The officers were even treated at government expense, because their personal insurance as civil servants was not enough to cover consultation fees. At the time of the investigation, Z$3.9 million had already been spent on medical expenses.

It is no wonder that the Ministry of Foreign Affairs exhausted its allocation of Z$391 million only three months into the 1999 financial year.[82] Zimbabwe's mission in Washington said it was threatened with having its power and telephone service cut off. The ministry was said to be so broke that it could

---

79. *The Zimbabwe Standard*, 11 October, 1998.

80. *The Insider*, Harare, 28 January, 1999.

81. *The Financial Gazette*, 13 May, 1999.

82. *The Herald*, 21 April, 1999.

hardly even buy stationery. In April 1999, Cde Mudenge, who himself spent Z$21,000 in one night at a Harare restaurant entertaining his counterpart from the DRC, defended his ministry's expenditure and blamed its financial crisis on the dollar's crash. There is no doubt that the depreciation of the zimdollar against the major currencies, which occurred in late 1998, was a contributory factor since the greater part of the ministry's expenses was in foreign currency. Once again, this was proof that the government needed to cut down on its spending in order to stabilize the zimdollar.

This extravagancy has continued to create problems for the foreign missions. In January 2003, diplomats complained that the payment of salaries at diplomatic missions had been erratic since September, because of Zimbabwe's severe foreign currency shortages, which have forced the government to spend most of its meager hard cash inflows on crucial imports of food, electricity and fuel. The diplomats said most of their colleagues were finding it difficult to meet personal expenses and some of their spouses had been forced to take on paid part-time work, violating diplomatic regulations. Spouses of diplomats posted overseas are not allowed to work in paid employment because their living expenses are covered by a monthly stipend provided by the state.

The permanent secretary in the Ministry of Foreign Affairs, Willard Chiwewe, confirmed that the government was having "hiccups and difficulties like everyone else nationally in finding foreign currency to pay our diplomats abroad, and as such, we have been late in paying them."[83] The country's shortage of hard cash has hampered imports of food, electricity and liquid fuel.

In one of the more bizarre episodes in Zimbabwe's tragic economic history, the shortage of foreign currency became so critical that the government issued a directive on June 18, 2003, through the Reserve Bank, instructing commercial banks to pay the overdue salaries at Zimbabwe's foreign missions. Sources said Interfin was spared because it had already provided US$2 million towards the payment of external government commitments.

Meanwhile, the average taxpayer was unable to pay school fees and children were having to leave school. Students who had been sent abroad on state scholarships were sent home, too: it was reported in February 1998 that South African universities were sending students back, apparently fed up with the Zimbabwe government's continued failure to pay fees. In September 2003, disgruntled students at Fort Hare, who were beneficiaries of a scholarship fund set up by President Robert Mugabe, (himself a former Fort Hare student) said

---

83. *The Financial Gazette*, 23 January, 2003.

they risked having their allocation of food cut off soon if the government failed to once again honor its financial obligation in time.

Health services were in appalling condition. Public funds were being diverted for the upkeep of the Executive Presidency and Cabinet Ministers, relatives and friends. Furthermore, hardly a month passed when President Robert Mugabe did not travel abroad. Zimbabweans have nicknamed him Vasco da Gama, after the first explorer to go around the world. At numerous meetings that might be attended by only two or three presidents out of the invited ten or so, Mugabe was usually one of those two or three. Others may have sent their representatives, and representatives rarely travel by chartered plane. Such cost factors did not inhibit Mugabe.

Mugabe's frequent travel, with his huge entourage of security and other personnel, can be illustrated by his trips at the end of October 1997 when he was in Edinburgh, Scotland, for the Commonwealth Heads of Government Meeting. After that, he stayed home for just a day before proceeding to Malaysia for an economic meeting. Then, after two days at home, he left for Libreville, in Gabon, for another economic meeting. By November 17, he had also been to Dar es Salaam in Tanzania and Gaborone in Botswana. Besides his wife, he traveled with delegations averaging 30 people on all the trips. He was even present at Dr. Kamuzu Banda's funeral, despite the fact that when Banda died, in November 1997, he was no longer head of state. In 1997 alone, the President made 22 foreign trips.[84]

It was a well-known secret that senior officials accompanying the President helped themselves to Z$12,500 a day, while ministers were given Z$15,000 so they could "sleep and eat decently." When in Jamaica for the G-15 Summit in February 1999, President Mugabe's 41-member delegation ran through Z$3.5 million (US$90,000) in expenses in ten days.[85] On his 15-day Grand Tour of the Orient and the Middle East in May 1999, a senior official would have collected a total of Z$187,500 in allowances, it was disclosed.

Thus, the plundering began in relatively innocent ways. It was not uncommon for an Air Zimbabwe flight to or from Europe to be cancelled at short notice so that Mugabe family members and their cronies could use the Boeing 767 for a private shopping trip to London or Paris.

Ironically, the Cabinet itself had set up a committee in September 1996, supposedly to scrutinize or even veto delegates who go on foreign trips. This set

84. *Star Tribune*, Minneapolis, Minnesota, USA, 15 February, 1998.
85. *The Zimbabwe Independent*, 21 May, 1999.

up came as a result of revelation by the Treasury that it had disbursed an extra Z$25 million, over the previous two years, to finance impromptu foreign trips by government officials and civil servants. The Government's 20 fully-fledged ministries, the Office of the President, Parliament and a host of other public departments spent an average of Z$60.5 million each financial year on air travel, hotel accommodation and subsistence for public officials on foreign trips and state visits.[86]

This disclosure came at a time when there were increasing calls by government officials and MPs for stricter controls on the number of public officials and civil servants who should indulge in foreign forays.

Mugabe's hastily arranged trip to the UN's World Summit on the Information Society in Geneva, in December 2003 cost the beleaguered Zimbabwean economy an estimated Z$2 billion in accommodation and expenses for the president and his entourage (including expenses during their five-day stay in Ethiopia). He took a delegation of 20 government officials and state security agents who were paid US$400 daily for nine days in allowances. On the way back from Geneva he stopped in Addis Ababa, Ethiopia, where he attended the Sino-Africa summit.

The ailing national carrier, Air Zimbabwe, is affected by these trips. For example, on this occasion cancelled tickets that had already been booked on scheduled flights cost an estimated Z$3 billion. It was estimated that the trip cost a total of Z$450 million on fuel alone. To replace the Boeing 767-200, Air Zimbabwe was forced to hire a plane for US$1 million (about Z$600 million). Official sources said Mugabe spent about US$66,971 (Z$402 million) in hotel accommodation in Switzerland for his entourage attending the three-day summit.

Like the late Kim Il Sung of North Korea, President Mugabe is the supreme ruler presiding over a vanquished tribe. He can order up a helicopter for elections and purchase dozens of cars when the nation is starving. His annual expenses on overseas trips are never computed.

In a *de facto* one-party democracy, policies are often drafted on an *ad hoc* basis and in ways that serve party members and their constituencies. Even subjects such as indigenization and land reform (where implemented) have played into the hands of the political elite. In the absence of an effective opposition or a strong parliament, corruption would remain widespread, alienating foreign investors.

---

86. *Financial Gazette*, Harare, 19 September, 1996.

In Zimbabwe, popular frustration with the government was mounting as living standards continued to decline rapidly. The new-found expression in massive civil-service strikes and the national protest against the war veterans' levy at the end of 1997 was a sign of a bitter confrontation.

## Allocation of Resources to the Less-privileged

Having come into power with ambitions to set up a socialist state, it was inevitable the independence government would set up institutions and funds to help those who were less privileged. The socio-economic system Zimbabwe inherited at independence was biased against the African population. But to redistribute resources equitably is a tricky business. When such resources are controlled by officers chosen on the basis of their political royalty rather than professional background, there is bound to be a lack of transparency and accountability. Here was an opening for political activists to reward themselves for the "pain" suffered during the liberation of Zimbabwe.

Right from the day the Demobilization Fund was set up in 1982, there were signs of trouble. First, the officers in charge had difficulty in distinguishing genuine ex-combatants from impostors. It is not clear why some form of cooperation and communication with the Army Headquarters and the British Training Team could not clear that up. After all, when both ZANLA and ZIPRA guerrillas went to assembly points, a register was compiled. Secondly, the people appointed to administer the fund had questionable financial control credibility; they were appointed on the basis of having worked for the party in one of the African or European capitals. The result was that many who had not earned demobilization funds were rewarded for having participated in the war of liberation and those in the corridors of power, especially the ones with "brains," had unfettered access to demobilization money.

In 1994, the European Union (EU) donated Z$15 million to the Zimbabwe National Army, following the government's announcement that it was going to reduce the size of the army from 50,000 to 40,000. A fund was set up to enable soldiers who had voluntarily retired to go for further education so that they could easily enter into civilian life. However, the fund was looted in a racket, which is said to involve three private colleges in Harare, another three in Bulawayo and one each in Gweru and Masvingo. The retired soldiers are said to have connived with the private colleges to raise fake requisitions to pay for courses after which the college and the "student" divided the spoils.

In a bid to beat the housing shortage afflicting most Zimbabwe's cities, a National Housing Fund and a Housing Guarantee Fund were established in 1995. Prospective homeowners were contributing part of their hard-earned wages into the funds. The idea was that the Government would top up the funds with taxpayers' money to help build houses for those who had contributed towards the funds and they were expected to repay the money over an agreed period of time. The envisaged average cost of the houses was about Z$200,000. However, instead of benefiting the middle income group which had been contributing money towards the funds, funds were diverted to an illegal VIP housing scheme to build luxury houses for a host of top government officials as well as the First Lady, whose house cost Z$5.89 million to build.[87] Among the "illegal" beneficiaries were also the Commissioner of Police, who built a house for Z$1.1 million and a High Court judge whose house cost Z$1.07 million to build.[88] It is understood that some of the "illegal" beneficiaries actually got cash loans from the funds, with which they used to make improvements on their houses, farms and businesses.

The funds are said to have been looted of over Z$200 million,[89] resulting in the suspension of several construction projects around the country including low-cost housing schemes and homes for civil servants who subscribed to the funds. The VIP housing scandal was blamed on one senior officer in the then Ministry of Public Construction and National Housing, now the Ministry of Local Government and National Housing. It is reported that this officer ran his own construction company, through which he diverted resources to himself and his friends, including girlfriends. There are also details of how the officer gave contracts to "briefcase" companies to supply equipment and ordered that these companies be paid immediately.

In April 1997, Justice George Smith, sitting in the High Court, recommended that the Public Service Commission investigate the illegal VIP housing scandal and that corrupt and incompetent officials who abused the illegal VIP scheme be weeded out. However, contrary to assurances by the government that the scandal was under investigation, there was never any sign of it.

Immediately after independence in 1981, the government created the District Development Fund by an act of Parliament. The main objective of the

---

87. The mansion was sold to the Libyans for Z$35 million (*The Zimbabwe Independent*, 27 July, 2001)

88. *i'Africa News Network*, Copenhagen, Denmark, 16 July, 1997.

89. *The Financial Gazette*, 5 February, 1998.

DDF water division was to provide rural people with community-owned boreholes. The DDF Act (1981) states that the objects to which the fund maybe applied shall be for the development of communal lands and resettlement areas. The Act did not cover any senior government officials and yet, between August 1995 and August 1998, about Z$4.7 million[90] was spent drilling boreholes for politicians and other private persons with political connections.

Interestingly, the identities of the high-ranking government officials involved in the looting of the DDF had been concealed in the Comptroller and Auditor-General's report presented to Parliament in December 1998. However, independent media investigations showed that the Comptroller and Auditor-General himself had a borehole drilled, at a cost of Z$18,812, at his Borrowdale residence in Harare.[91] In an interview, the Auditor-General stated that "It was not in the public interest to include the names."

Notwithstanding, the original report compiled by auditors included such VIPs as the controversial business tycoon the late Roger Boka, who had seven boreholes drilled between August 1995 and March 1998 on his homestead and at his Boka mine, at a cost of Z$165,672 which was believed to be still outstanding. The Minister of Higher Education and his wife had five boreholes drilled on their farm in Makonde, and Littleton farm in Chegutu, between June 1996 and January 1997, at a total drilling cost of something in the vicinity of Z$115,240. The Minister of Rural Resources and Water Development had a borehole drilled on her homestead in Harare at a cost of Z$31,647. Also appearing in the report was the Deputy Minister of Industry and Commerce, who had a borehole drilled on his homestead in June 1997 at a cost of Z$26,768. The Resident Minister and Provincial Governor of Masvingo had two boreholes drilled, at a cost of Z$34,861. ZANU (PF) Secretary for Administration and member of the Politburo had a borehole drilled, at a cost of Z$22,292. The report did not mention the name of a high-ranking government official who leases Hatcliffe Farm in Harare and owed the DDF a staggering Z$451,807 for an unspecified number of boreholes drilled on his farm. The government's chief of protocol had a borehole drilled at a cost of Z$18,269. A government official had a borehole drilled in Chegutu, in July 1996, at a cost of Z$24,504. The Secretary for Information, Posts and Telecommunications, on unspecified dates, had several boreholes drilled on his Chipoli farm in Shamva at a cost of Z$451,807.

---

90. *The Zimbabwe Independent*, 25 December, 1998.
91. *Ibid.*

The DDF water program began when it was established that about 60% of communal and resettlement people were drawing water from unprotected water sources.[92] The auditors' report shows that the exercise of drilling boreholes for politicians deprived some 52,250 communal and resettlement farmers of water facilities.

Tabling the Auditor-General's report before Parliament in December 1998, Finance Minister Cde Herbert Murerwa recommended immediate steps be taken to recover the amounts owed by government officials who benefited at the expense of villagers. The High Court Judge Justice Smith strongly recommended an inquiry into the DDF.

Signaling a change of times, *The Herald*, for once, described this type of corruption with revulsion. Its editorial of January 16, 1999, said:

> "The looting of public resources has become so frequent and widespread that people have come to accept it as if it is the norm. In fact, a scheme which is not abused is now more surprising than a looted one. That is how much corruption has become entrenched in this country.
>
> Because of the deep-seated nature of corruption and the networks involved, from those in the top echelons of authority to the shop floor, be it in the public and private sectors, the abuse and looting appear extremely difficult to detect. By the time it is exposed the coffers will be empty and the poor continue to suffer as a result....Corrupt individuals in this country have been treated with kid gloves for a long time. It is time to put in place measures and mechanisms, which make people accountable."[93]

> "The stories we write... show that the worm of corruption is boring through the entirety of our society, from central Government to local Government and down to non-governmental organizations, from big private and public companies to small indigenous outfits.
>
> "If higher officials are involved in corrupt activities, they cannot stop their juniors....It is this perception among people that those in high office, who should be setting the moral example, are corrupt, which has made corruption spread and permeate the whole society."[94]

Indeed, emulating their higher-ups, senior employees at DDF headquarters were alleged to have swindled more than Z$12 million worth of material and plant equipment in 1998.[95]

---

92. *Zimbabwe: The Rise to Nationhood*, pp30-31, Minerva Press, London, 1998.
93. *The Herald*, 16 January, 1999.
94. *Ibid.*, 3 August, 1999.
95. *Ibid.*, 10 April, 1999.

It would have been surprising if the Social Welfare's Social Dimension Fund had escaped the wave of fraudulent activities which were characteristic of Zimbabwe during the 1980s and 1990s. When the Economic Structural Adjustment Programme (ESAP) began in 1991, the government set up the Social Dimension Fund to provide financial assistance to train retrenched or retired workers in business management. It emerged at the end of February 1999 that the fund was prejudiced of over Z$10 million in fraudulent deals involving senior personnel in its disbursement department. Officials within the department were allegedly conniving with outsiders to make fraudulent claims over a six-year period. Well-placed sources in the Ministry of Public Service and Social Welfare indicated that thousands of intended beneficiaries had been unable to access the money to finance their educational needs. It was understood that false death certificates and claims for school fees were delivered to the assessment committee vetting the deserving cases.

The National Social Security Authority (NSSA) was no exception. In March 1999, a benefits officer was facing allegations of siphoning well over Z$3 million from the authority through a well-orchestrated fraudulent scheme. NSSA was established for the purpose of collecting money from every employee on a monthly basis to finance a national social security scheme. The officer was suspected to have operated seven Post Office Savings Bank (POSB) accounts into which he deposited moneys and then re-deposited the moneys into one of his. The matter came into open after the computerization exercise at NSSA.

Upon independence, a War Victims' Compensation Fund was set up to benefit veterans who sustained injuries caused directly or indirectly by the war during the period between January 1960 and February 29, 1980, and the dependants of deceased war veterans. Between independence (1980) and April 1997, Z$1.5 billion had already been paid out.[96] The equivalent of US$40.9 million (Z$450 million) was disbursed under the Act during the 1996/97 financial year alone.

However, by early 1997, there were stories of persons who were not entitled to compensation receiving large sums of money. Notable among the beneficiaries were high-ranking government officials making claims on grounds of "mental stress" caused by the war situation. Reports also abound of high-ranking government officials recommending friends and relatives to be compensated for injuries not sustained during the war. In addition, there were reports that civil servants administering the fund were acting in concert with

---

96. *The Financial Gazette*, 22 July, 1999.

middlemen siphoning off thousands of dollars in bribes for the expeditious processing of files.

After a public outcry for the executive to intervene, President Mugabe was forced to suspend payment of compensation in March 1997 to facilitate investigations. A commission of inquiry, the Chidyausiku Commission, was set up in July 1997. Apparently, all along the ex-combatants had been watching. Perhaps the only reason they kept quiet was that they continually expected to be given their share; when they realized that the gravy train was stopping at every junction but theirs, they lost patience. They went to the ZANU (PF) headquarters and assaulted senior party officials and ransacked the building. The ZANU (PF) leadership did not take the hint. Right at Heroes' Acre, in the midst of Mugabe's monologue in commemoration of the dead heroes and, naturally, those still alive, the war veterans broke into revolutionary songs and drowned him out. At first, the President made an effort to ignore the outburst, but to his bewilderment they continued.

During its investigations, the commission discovered that looters of the fund included high-ranking politicians and officials of the ruling ZANU (PF) party, members of the law enforcement agencies and defense forces and senior government officials. It was reported that 79 prominent citizens received a whopping total of Z$23 million from the fund.[97] However, not all of these big fish were summoned to appear before the Commission. Of the 52,407 people who claimed compensation between 1980 and March 1997, the Commission managed to interview only 112. In a process in which the government spent another Z$1.4 billion, a much greater population could have been summoned for investigation.

Further subverting the process, as the Chidyausiku Commission dragged its feet, there was growing concern that bona fide beneficiaries of the fund would further be prejudiced since it was not likely that disbursements of the commutations would resume before the inquiry was over. Moreover, by November 1997 it began to look like the commission was out to embarrass the ex-combatants while protecting some top government officials and politicians. One observer described the commission as a game of "political expedience," saying its terms of reference had already been overtaken by events, since the President had already agreed with the former fighters on one-off gratuities of Z$50,000 each plus a Z$2,000 monthly pension each from January 1998.

---

97. *The Herald*, 10 August, 1998.

Notwithstanding, the commission of inquiry had already uncovered a good number of government officials, and relatives of those with political connections, in its hearings. Suddenly, when some of them threatened to tell the whole story, there were demonstrations at the High Court. Oddly, it was none other than the war veterans themselves who led these demonstrations. In contempt of court, they sang and danced in the courtroom where proceedings were in progress. After disrupting the commission's work, they spilled into Samora Machel and disrupted traffic; the police did nothing to bring them to order.

Once the war veterans had received their rewards, it remained to be seen what action would be taken against those who had been found to have falsified compensation claims. Although both Justice Chidyausiku and Chief Secretary to the President and Cabinet Dr. Charles Utete refused to divulge the contents of the report presented to the President in June 1998, reports filtering from top government officials indicated that recommendations submitted to the government were inconclusive and surprisingly watered down. The commissioners did not offer any clear solution on how to deal with the looters, but left it to the Attorney-General's Office and a task force that would launch detailed investigations.

Such an approach would absolve the government from taking any direct action to punish those caught, especially if the culprits were political cronies or business associates. It could be implied that people were washing their hands of the matter. Clearly, such a move contrasted sharply with the recommendations of the Justice Sandura Commission, which were decisive and actionable, and indeed several cabinet ministers were sacked. Instead, the Chidyausiku Commission recommended that the AG's Office draws up amendments to the War Victims' Compensation Act and tighten the process of disbursement of money under the Act. Promulgated in 1980, the Act replaced the repealed Victims of Terrorism (Compensation) Act, which came into effect on August 10, 1973. The 11-member commission said in its report that if a number of the stringent requirements in the Rhodesian 1973 Act were incorporated in the new Act, the current problems might have been avoided. Ironically, by dwelling on weaknesses of the new Act, the commission seemed to equip those who had abused the fund with defensive material to justify their behavior.

It came as a big disappointment when the government abandoned the official probe into the looting of the War Victims' Compensation Fund, at the end of April 2000. "There will be no further investigations because no one in the political establishment is keen to do so. The probe has reached a dead end," a high-ranking government official was reported to have revealed.[98]

The creation of commissions of enquiries each time a scandal surfaces has the disadvantage that the commissioners are hand-picked by the President and, in most cases, are bound to protect the "interests" of politicians. It maybe recalled that the findings of the Chihambakwe Commission (appointed in June 1982 and completed its work in early 1993) on the dissident activities and the atrocities that followed in Matabeleland and parts of the Midlands were never published. Then there were the Dumbutshena Commission on the disturbances at Entumbane and the Land Tenure Commission which never saw the light of day, but instead have (hopefully) been tossed into the archives. In the case of the report of the Dumbutshena Commission, it is no surprise that the Minister of Legal and Parliamentary Affairs was reported in March 2000 that "the report had disappeared."

A permanent independent judicial commission would be far more effective. Optimally, it would be comprised of persons of undoubted integrity and impeccable repute, and would be vested with three overriding powers:

(1) the power of subpoena, which would enable the commission to collect evidence to ensure that any person called upon would be obliged to give evidence under oath. This would deter those who would be contemptuous to the judiciary's proceedings (one woman called before Justice Chidyausiku had actually shouted that he had no right to question her, since the judge had been in the service of Zimbabwe-Rhodesia, i.e. the Muzorewa government);

(2) the power of amnesty, which would enable the commission to seek a compromise with small-scale offenders in order to expose the big fish. Today, every time commissions conclude their findings, it is clear that only the small fish are caught; and

(3) the power of prosecution, which would ensure that justice prevails, law and order are restored, and that a real deterrent prevails against the pursuit of self-enriching, corrupt indulgences.

From the Demobilization Fund to the Paweni case, on to the Willowvale scandal and the latter-day VIP housing scandal and the War Victims Compensation Fund — in every case the same people, especially the politicians, not only condone but may have been involved in Zimbabwe's corrupt activities. The judicial commission should be unrestricted as to its operations, in that it must be able to proceed against any persons, no matter their status and political authority. Such an anti-corruption crusade has succeeded elsewhere, one recent

---

98. *The Financial Gazette*, 27 April, 2000.

example being the United Kingdom, where the "Sleazy Affair" was exposed and partly led to the downfall of the John Major Conservative Government in 1997.

The fascinating case of the missing AIDS levies produces a perfect example how the ZANU (PF) government has let down every segment of the public. The AIDS Levy was introduced at the end of 1999 and deductions from the salaries of the already over-taxed worker started in January 2000. Yet, right in the middle of the bitterest election campaign Zimbabwe has ever seen, someone somewhere decided to deep his hand into the till again.

It was revealed at the end of April 2000 that there was no money in the National Aids Council Trust Fund bank account. Responding to the public reaction, the Minister of Finance, Cde Herbert Murerwa, suddenly produced a total sum of Z$117 million. However, as people understood that something in the region of Z$400 million had been collected, the Minister's comment that he hoped "this clarifies any doubts about our commitment to the fund" constituted hypocrisy of the highest order. Indeed, any lingering doubts were certainly clarified. Still, the Zimbabwe National Network for People with HIV/AIDS (ZNNP) did have some questions to ask. "We want the Minister to verify his calculations and also explain where the money was being kept before it was deposited into the account," the ZNNP president Mr. Frank Guni demanded. "We want to know the amount of interest that accrued from the levy, if it was being kept in a bank."[99]

At the outset, the Community Working Group on Health, which is a partner to the ZNNP, had expressed concerns that the government would divert funds from the levy to other courses. In January 2000, a group comprising labor and civil society submitted a document to the Ministries of Health and Finance calling for the suspension of the levy until several issues had been addressed. The group demanded a binding and transparent mechanism for the disposal of the levy funds. They also demanded that there should be an agreed plan of priority areas for its use and a mechanism for identifying beneficiaries and ensuring those poor communities, their support groups and organizations were sufficiently catered for.

Tobacco farming presents another example. The alleged misappropriation of the 20% tobacco export retention scheme administered by the Tobacco Growers Trust (TGT) took center stage at the 43rd annual congress of the Zimbabwe Tobacco Association, held in June 2003. The TGT scheme was introduced by government in 2001 to help farmers obtain hard cash for inputs

---

99. *The Zimbabwe Standard* Online, 30 April 2000.

after growers complained that they were being charged rates for hard currency on the parallel market. Under the scheme, jointly administered by the country's six tobacco associations, growers were supposed to receive 20% of foreign currency earned from tobacco sales during the previous marketing season.

However, small-scale tobacco growers were unhappy at the TGT's failure to allocate them funds to procure inputs for the 2003 crop. They accused TGT officials of diverting funds and tractors, bought under the mechanization program and meant to assist growers, for their own benefit. In early 2003, the TGT acquired about 200 tractors but it was alleged that other non-tobacco-growing farmers, including "resettled" senior government officials, had benefited from the tractors ahead of the intended beneficiaries. Other growers accused the TGT of diverting funds to different crop ventures. Furthermore, tractors purchased from Asia in August under the 20% foreign currency retention facility, went to about 45 high-ranking ZANU (PF) officials and prominent business people ahead of ordinary indigenous farmers who had no access to finance in the face of surging input costs which were putting a squeeze on their operations.

Meanwhile, the shortage of maize-meal since April 2002 opened another door for the exploitation of the less-privileged by those above them. In February 2003, a Gweru city councilor was arrested after residents had accused their councilors and senior ZANU (PF) officials of diverting maize-meal for resale on the black market. Earlier, in September 2002, angry residents had stormed the home of another ZANU (PF) councilor to protest against the chaotic distribution of maize-meal in the suburbs, particularly segregating against those suspected to be MDC supporters.

The provision of food is a basic human right. The International Covenant on Economic, Social and Cultural Rights reaches further than basic rights benchmarking to outline specific provisions about the right to food. Zimbabwe acceded to the Covenant in 1991, and is thus bound to recognize everybody's right to adequate food, to act to ensure that this right is realized fairly and as widely as possible, and to cooperate with the international community to ease domestic hunger. It is incumbent upon the government to provide food for all its subjects irrespective of their political, religious or other affiliation; yet there is overwhelming evidence that the ZANU (PF) government has provided food aid to supporters while denying it to perceived adversaries.[100]

---

100. *Not Eligible: The Politicization of Food in Zimbabwe*, Human Rights Watch, New York, 24 October, 2003.

The use of food as a political tool is morally abhorrent and violates international law. The government should impress upon the leadership of all political parties that it is prohibited for politicians and party supporters either to use food to influence or reward constituents and voters, or to withhold access to food as a reprisal for perceived political opposition.

Meanwhile, in Masvingo, the District Administrator and a senior manager with the GMB appeared in court charged with corruption involving 15 tonnes of maize grain delivered to the Deputy Minister of Gender, Youth Development and Employment Creation on February 5, 2003. They were charged with contravening Section 4 (b) of the Prevention of Corruption Act.

The Zimbabwe National Vulnerability Assessment Committee (ZNVAC) reported that at least 200,000 tonnes of maize earmarked for starving Zimbabweans was unaccounted for, with no indication whether it reached intended recipients. The ZNVAC is a task force of non-governmental organizations working in collaboration with the ministries of Agriculture and Finance as well as the Civil Protection Unit, the World Food Program (WFP) and the Food and Agriculture Organization. The committee undertakes surveys to assess Zimbabwe's food supply and security situation.

In its report on Zimbabwe's food security situation, the ZNVAC said there was a glaring discrepancy between the amount of food distributed to starving people by GMB between April and December 2002 and the quantity of maize imported into the country over the same period. The ZNVAC said in its report: "Distribution of GMB imports at the community level is inconsistent with reported imports at the national level. For the period April 1, 2002 to December 1, 2002, total maize available from domestic availability, GMB imports and food aid was 1.3 million metric tonnes. The requirement for this period was 1.1 million metric tonnes, indicating a surplus of 200,000 metric tonnes at the national level."[101]

The ZNVAC, which advises the government and aid groups on the food supply situation, recommended that the discrepancy between levels of food imports and availability at the community level be investigated. There were also widespread (but unconfirmed) reports that some of the food imported to feed hungry people has been illegally siphoned out of Zimbabwe.

The consequences of the abuse of resources allocated to the less-privileged will haunt the next generation.

---

101. *Zimbabwe National Vulnerability Assessment Committee Report*, Harare, January 2003.

### Aid Programs

There is ample evidence that international aid programs are liable to widespread corruption. This happens in countries as diverse as Nigeria, Kenya, Mozambique and Russia — billions of dollars meant for the establishment of a market economy ends up in the hands of those who formerly had been the staunchest opponents of capitalism, etc. In Africa, the IMF and World Bank type of economic reform goes hand in hand with increased corruption. This undermines development.

The World Bank lends about US$20 billion annually to support development projects in the areas of health, education, the environment and infrastructure, mainly in developing countries. For example, in July 1998 the World Bank and the government of Zimbabwe concluded negotiations for a multimillion-dollar rehabilitation project for the country's national parks. After five years of negotiations, the government got Z$1.2 billion (about US$67 million) for the improvement of roads, electrification, staff capacity building, the provision of housing and construction of various facilities like interpretation centers.

In May 1998, the World Bank instituted an external investigation of its expenditures following the uncovering of information about possible kickbacks and embezzlement. The Bank set up a special internal fraud team and hired the accounting firm of PricewaterhouseCoopers and two other fraud specialists to look into possible cases. Earlier, another phase of the investigation had already led to a civil lawsuit against a former bank official who was alleged to have taken tens of thousands of dollars in kickbacks from a contractor on a water project in Algeria.[102]

In September 1998, the World Bank reported that some 37% of all African assets were held abroad, far higher than any other region. The United Nations Conference on Trade and Development (UNCTAD) 1998 annual report said that much of this wealth "appears to have originated from the illicit diversion of public funds."[103] Writing in Canada's *Southern Press*, Jonathan Manthorpe says, "Monsters like Mugabe, the former Zairian leader Mobutu Sese Seko, deposed president Suharto of Indonesia and others are in many ways the creations of benevolence from the West." Manthorpe is convinced that the actual amount siphoned off was at least double the figure mentioned by the World Bank. He cites the example of a Canadian high commissioner to Zimbabwe some years

---

102. Panafrican News Agency, 17 July, 1998.
103. *UNCTAD Annual Report*, New York, September 1998.

ago, who, on going through the accounts, "noticed that much of an annual R4 million discretionary fund had been going to President Mugabe's wife, Sally — ostensibly for a women's project she claimed to be running. She provided no evidence that even one poor woman benefited from the donations," Manthorpe noted. "The woolly-minded, guilt-driven passion in the West to throw money at underdeveloped countries all too often results in sustaining petty despots....Far from alleviating the people's plight, foreign aid frequently prolonged and entrenched their poverty and oppression."[104]

In September 1998, the EU Commission revealed that a sum of 4.5 million Swedish Crowns (2.4 million ECU) of aid to Bosnia and Rwanda was suspected to have been swindled. However, an internal report from the EU Commission's fraud squad, UCLAF, set the estimated figure at SEK15 million.[105] The affair originated from four contracts to the tune of SEK21.6 million between the EU Commission and a consultancy firm from Luxembourg in 1993 and 1994. After the revelation of the swindle, one head of department within the EU Commission was suspended while investigations were being carried out by police in Luxembourg. By the end of that year, the extent of corruption revealed within the Commission was so wide and deep-rooted that there was a lively debate in the European Parliament. It came as no surprise, therefore, that Jacques Santer and his entire Commission were forced to resign on March 15, 1999.

A survey of 54 countries in 1996 by the international corruption watchdog, Transparency International, revealed that the 20 most corrupt countries were all developing nations. Nevertheless, TI also noted that, "Much of the corruption in the developing countries is the direct result of corrupt multinational corporations and tax laws in the industrial countries. Most of the bribes on international contracts are paid by executives of corporations in the most advanced countries and it remains an outrage that the governments of these countries have not legislated to curb international corrupt practices."

Authorities in Harare must have felt alarmed by TI's report, in mid-September 1998, showing that Zimbabwe was on its way to becoming a top member of the corrupt league. The Berlin-based global watchdog compiles an annual index of 85 countries, ranking them between 0 and 10 — the 0 ranking indicating a "highly corrupt" country and a ranking of 10 indicating that it is perceived as "highly clean." The index records the degree of corruption as seen by

---

104. *Southern Press*, Canada, March - April 9, 1999.
105. *Metro*, Stockholm, 23 September, 1998 and Riksdag & Department, Nr 27, 9 October, 1998..

businesspeople, risk analysts and the general public. Zimbabwe, which scored 4.2 points, was ranked number 43 on the world's corruption stakes, alongside South Korea. In sub-Saharan Africa, Zimbabwe was number 11. The notorious honors for the top 10 most corrupt countries in sub-Saharan Africa went to Cameroon, Tanzania, Nigeria, Kenya, Uganda, Ivory Coast, Senegal, Ghana, Zambia and Malawi, in that order. Zimbabwe's trading partner Mauritius was ranked number 12, South Africa 13, Namibia 14 and Botswana the least corrupt sub-Saharan nation at number 15.[106]

TI's Corruption Perceptions Index for 2003 ranks the country at a dismal 106 out of 133 countries surveyed. Zimbabwe joins Angola, ranked 124th, at the bottom of the ladder. "Clearly, the negative perception has been reinforced by the apparent lack of urgent action designed to deal with a very real problem as well as the negative perception. The perception that there has been corruption even in the process of the land distribution simply reinforces broader problematic perceptions in respect of economic and political corruption," TI said. The two major factors for the country's increasing corruption record were corrupt investment tender systems and policies that were benefiting a few individuals while the rest of the country's population bore the brunt of the economic woes.

An effort is underway in Zimbabwe to indigenize the economy and the target for financial aid from the international community is small- and middle-scale business concerns. When funds are secured on the international market place, they are channeled through the government. By June 1994, for example, Z$550 million was earmarked for disbursement to the indigenous business sector. The World Bank was providing Z$150 million and the government had secured Z$400 million from undisclosed sources. At the end of July 1996, a Z$600 million World Bank facility to help small-scale indigenous businesses became operational. This money is used to import capital goods needed to start or expand business activities.

The leadership in the Indigenous Business Development Centre (IBDC) must, as a matter of principle, toe the party line if they want to have access to this international aid. At one time, the politburo had demanded that even civil servants were expected to carry ZANU (PF) membership cards. This was received with public disgust. Some executive members of the IBDC resigned their positions because they could not stand the party's intrusion in the running of the organization.

---

106. *The Financial Gazette*, 24 September, 1998.

Interestingly, although the IBDC later fragmented amidst much rivalry, the majority of the founding members are now successful entrepreneurs running billion-dollar empires including banks, transport firms, telecommunications concerns, as well as exporting entities.

What happens when NGOs do not toe the party line? The Private Voluntary Organizations Amendment Act presents an example. Some members of the executive of women's business organizations, like Women In Business (WIB) and the Indigenous Business Women's Organization (IBWO), were forced to resign their positions under pressure from ZANU (PF). The IBWO launched a trust fund in 1995 to make sure the organization does not depend on party handouts. But, IBWO's ambitious plans to establish a commercial (OMA)[107] bank from which the organization's 25,000 members would borrow money for capital projects at concessionary rates was reported to have floundered in June 2003.

Aid, being fungible, may ultimately help support unproductive and wasteful government expenditures. Perhaps as a result, many donor countries have focused on issues of good governance, transparency and accountability, and in cases where governance is judged to be especially poor, some donors have scaled back their assistance.

Money gained as a result of corrupt practices finds its way into financial safe havens in developed countries, where it is difficult to trace or recover due to the sophistication of the laws and regulations governing the international banking system. The war against corrupt activities connected with aid programs might be fought more effectively with the help of the international donor organizations themselves. They should consider introduction of anti-bribery clauses in public procurement contracts and a requirement that chief executives of companies bidding for such contracts undertake not to pay bribes, and punish those employees found guilty of corruption. Furthermore, African governments themselves should take strong punitive measures against those that take or solicit bribes, while the donors who fund the procurement should impose stringent penalties against companies found guilty of corrupt practices.

It is encouraging that some multinational institutions like the World Bank have launched a concerted campaign to crack down on corruption in development programs receiving their aid. Billions of dollars are leaking away. The United States, for example, decided not to contribute to the World Bank's 1997-99 program for assistance to the poorest countries, mainly in Africa,

---

107. OMA is an acronym that represents the Ndebele and Shona words for women.

because the funds have only lined the pockets of the ruling elite. However, some observers argue that corruption is an excuse employed by donors to help address domestic budgetary problems by cutting their own aid budgets. They argue that the concern now being shown by multinational institutions and northern governments about corruption in the southern hemisphere smacks of hypocrisy. The self-righteous attitude now emerging seems out of place, when the same organizations often turned a blind eye to aid abuse by some regimes (e.g. Mobutu's regime in Zaire) during the Cold War years.

### Centralized Allocation of Assets and Projects

Local businesses as well as foreign investor communities, including donor agencies, have urged the government of Zimbabwe to exercise more transparency in business dealings. The level of fraud, dishonesty and corruption practiced within government institutions not only do they have a negative impact on the economy and efficiency of government, but they can endanger the security of the government and the nation as a whole. The Zimbabwean government was, in the first six months of 1992, prejudiced of more than Z$17 million, while in 1991, 26 people were prosecuted for receiving more than Z$321 million in bribes.[108]

Then there was the alleged sale of a 51% stake (Z$6 billion majority shares) in the Hwange Thermal Power Project to YTL International of Malaysia at a well below market price. In September 1996, President Robert Mugabe vigorously defended the government's decision to award the Malaysian Corporation a tender for the privatization and expansion project of Zimbabwe's largest thermal plant. The privatization and expansion project had originally been put out to tender, but the outcome of tender submissions was pre-empted and prominent American and European power companies were shut out. When the board of the Zimbabwe Electricity Supply Authority (ZESA) protested, its members were promptly fired. Critics of the agreement described it as "back-door privatization" and decried the rather extreme "lack of transparency."

Earlier in October 1995, the award of a tender for the international airport took a twist. After a long period of assessment of tenders put forward, the contract was won by Air Harbour Technologies. However, two facilitators linked to the deal were reportedly awarded US$1 million (Z$9 million) for the role they played in influencing the Cabinet's decision. It appears tender procedures were ignored. The Air Harbour Technologies design was Z$300

---

108. *Panafrican News Agency*, Dakar, 1 December, 1997.

million more expensive than that of any other participant, and offered less space, with prohibitive repayment considerations. It is understood that the Government Tender Board had voted against the Air Harbour Technologies design. Furthermore, the company was associated with the president's nephew, Leo Mugabe.

A story on the Harare International Airport tender broke in *The Daily News* in November 2000. The paper had leaked a letter, written by Hani Yamani (son of Sheikh Yamani of OPEC fame), which implicated President Mugabe; his nephew; the Speaker of Parliament, Cde Emmerson Mnangagwa; senior government ministers, past and present, including the Minister of Finance, Cde Hebert Murerwa; Kofi Annan's son; the Palestinian ambassador to Zimbabwe; and many others, in a major bribery scandal around the tender process for the construction of Harare's new International Airport. The original letter was written to President Mugabe himself. Yamani details the total of US$3 million which he says he paid to Mugabe, various ministers, and government officials in order to ensure that his company, Air Harbour Technologies, was awarded the contract to build the new airport, in the process overturning the decision of the Government Tender Board to give the contract to a French company, Air de Paris. Bemoaning an apparent reduction of his influence with Mugabe, and feeling cut off from the President's circle, Yamani complains that a sum of US$1 million, which he had set aside to build the President a new house, had not been fully disbursed for that project because some of it had been siphoned off by ministers, officials, and confidants of the President and his wife along the way. He further accused these same people of diverting as much as US$250 million of other funds involved in the construction project into their private accounts.[109]

The "house" in question is a unique mansion built on 10 hectares. Architects who have seen it say it is as large as a medium-sized hotel, covering three acres of accommodation mostly on three floors, including two-storey reception rooms, an office suite and up to 25 bedrooms with adjoining bathrooms and spas. There are two lakes built on the southern boundary of the property. The Chinese-style roof is clad with midnight-blue glazed tiles from Shanghai, with the ceilings being decorated by Arab artisans from Libya known for their artistry and craftsmanship on ceilings and wall decorations. And to top it off, there is a helicopter pad to facilitate the commute to the international airport for all those foreign trips.[110]

---

109. *The Times UK*, 6 April, 2001.
110. *The Daily News* on Sunday, Harare, 31 August 2003.

Corruption scandals have surfaced regularly over the two decades plus of President Mugabe's rule. However, this is only the second occasion in which anyone has managed to personally link Mugabe with financial wrongdoing. The first time was during hearings in the US Senate into the collapse of the Bank of Credit and Commerce International (BCCI) in 1992. Testimony given during those hearings alleged that BCCI had secured preferential banking rights in Zimbabwe by bribing Mugabe and the late Vice-President Joshua Nkomo with a bag full of cash, and then a payment of US$500,000 from the BCCI branch in Park Lane in London.

In the case of the PTC Cellular Telephone and the ZBC tenders, the Government Tender Board also was overruled. Politicians wanted the contract awarded to Ericsson International AB of Sweden, but the Tender Board found the bid too pricey and suspected the politicians had a particular interest there; when Tender Board members said, the "PTC adjudication was clearly manipulated," they were suspended at the end of March 1996.

In another case, involving the setting up of a second cellular telephone network, Net Two, it was obvious that the company that won the tender did so because of its connections with political bigwigs. It was in April 1997 that Strive Masiyiwa's Enhanced Communications Network (Econet) lost this second tender to Telecel. Apparently, a foreign company and a Zimbabwean consortium that included the husband of the Minister of Information, Posts and Telecommunications and the President's nephew jointly owned Telecel. According to sources, the Government Tender Board had concluded that the best submissions came from Econet and Telecel. In a compromise decision, the board recommended that both Econet and Telecel should be jointly licensed under a 50/50 shareholding. However, a decision was taken outside the tender board to exclude Econet, there by creating a rift between the Information Minister and the Government Tender Board.

Econet decided to fight this decision all the way through the courts. It made two applications to the court seeking a license on the grounds that the Minister of Information, Posts and Telecommunications at the time, Cde Joyce Teurairopa Mujuru, had failed to comply with the procedures laid down by the Supreme Court and asked that the license given to Telecel be canceled. Meanwhile, in May 1997, President Mugabe asked Attorney-General Patrick Chinamasa to advise all losing Net Two bidders to form a consortium so they could be granted a third license, a move analysts said then was a ploy by the Government to kill Econet's court bid. Nevertheless, in December, the High Court ruled that Econet (an indigenous company) be granted the license to operate the nation's second mobile telephone network. The Ministry of Information, Posts and Telecommunications (which was a party to the case) said it accepted the ruling and would proceed to implement the High Court order. In the ruling, Judge President Justice Wilson Sandura also declared null and void the license awarded in March of that year to Telecel to operate the network. At the same time, Sandura ordered the Posts and Telecommunications Corporation to conclude an interconnection agreement with Econet and implement the agreement forthwith. In addition, he ordered that the costs of the application be paid by the Minister of Information and Telecel who were among the five respondents in the case.

While Strive Masiyiwa, Econet chief executive, was battling for a cellular telephone network license at home, he had been awarded the Z$500 million tender to provide a service in neighboring Botswana, beating local and international competition. This was like a slap in the face for the government. What Masiyiwa could only say after the award of the Botswana tender was, "The Lord opens doors no man can shut. Glory to God." Sure enough, The Lord opened the doors for Econet not only in Botswana and later in Nigeria and Kenya but at home as well. To boost Econet's Net Two project, a consortium of local and international banks, in a joint-venture with Standard Bank of London, structured a Z$740 million financial package in March 1998.[111]

Unfortunately, this was not the end of the mobile telephone saga. On February 17, 1998, President Robert Mugabe's Cabinet, already notorious for its propensity to discard transparency and to abandon its own policies to serve its political expediency, circumvented the judicial process by granting a third operating license to Telecel after this had been flatly rejected by the courts. The Cabinet felt that it had come to a "compromise" to accommodate as many indigenous players as possible. While the government now trumpeted a desire to see more indigenous players in the mobile phone business, questions over its earlier decisions remained. Why did the government not accommodate Econet a year before, it initially awarded Telecel a second license? Secondly, was it not strange that the government suddenly granted a third license to Telecel, without even going to tender? Had it not been for political considerations, the government could simply have granted Econet the third license in the first place and avoided the costly court battle that ensued after Econet had been shut out. The cash-strapped government spent up to Z$18 million to fight Econet in the courts. It seems that government, in general, and the Ministry of Information in

---

111. *The Zimbabwe Independent*, 6 March, 1998.

particular, will keep on moving the goal posts until the chosen few are in a position to line their pockets.

The company survived an attempt by the government to shut down its profitable operation in early February 2004 on the grounds that it was "subversive." Ignoring the legislation governing the telecommunications industry, acting Minister of Transport and Communications Jonathan Moyo ordered Econet to switch off its earth station that connects its 160,000 international business subscribers to the rest of the world. Justice Omerjee declared Moyo's regulations "null and void and of no effect."

In his ruling against the regulations, Omerjee said: "The world, including most African countries, has moved away from monopolistic policies and they are adopting a system that gives consumers maximum access. There is no reason Zimbabwe should be dragged back to the dark ages."

*Potential investors are bound to be put off by such shenanigans.*

Municipalities around the country are no exception. For example, the mayor's residence, initially estimated to cost about Z$5 million, but said to have soared to Z$55 million by November 1998, was built without going to tender. In addition, the Harare City Council awarded a contract worth over Z$200,000 (Z$243,880)[112] for the interior decor and design of the guest wing of the multi-million-dollar executive mayor's Gunhill suburb official residence (popularly referred to as Harare House) to a Harare company without going to tender. Sources close to the deal said the contract was awarded to Interior Design Centre, a company owned by the wife of Councilor Israel Magwenzi, a member of the council's executive committee, in contravention of the Urban Councils Act which demands that all jobs worth over Z$200,000 should go to tender. This fiasco came at a time when Harare's streetlights were out of function and the roads were full of potholes.

The list goes on. It came as no surprise, therefore, when Local Government Minister Cde John Nkomo suspended both the Executive Mayor and the entire Harare council in February 1999. Sighting Section 54, subsection 2(a) and Section 114 of the Urban Councils Act, the minister said this was to halt a further deterioration of the situation in the city and facilitate a probe into the running of the council. He said that the council in 1998 failed to provide its residents with water and had also failed to pay its workers. The Harare City Council had also failed to remove refuse from residential areas. Cde Nkomo said out of the 90

---

112. *The Financial Gazette*, 2 April, 1998.

council trucks, only seven were on the road while seven out of 56 tractors were operational.

The ministerial report on the operations of the Harare City mentioned that Harare's former executive mayor allegedly allocated 100 residential stands irregularly and distributed them to Cabinet ministers including Cdes Eddison Zvobgo, Oppah Muchinguri, Peter Chanetsa and Ignatius Chombo; High Court judges — Chatikobo, Chidyausiku and Chinhengo and other people. It was also discovered that Cde Tawengwa had allocated various commercial stands to his own company, Solta (Pvt) Ltd., trading as Somvech.[113]

It was difficult not to draw a direct connection between the chaos in the capital city and the ruling party's misgovernance. The Thompson Report saw the connection quite clearly and concluded: "The developments at Harare City Council clearly demonstrate the weakness of a system that emphasizes the importance of party politics and allegiance over and above the obligations imposed by the civic electoral mandate. It appears that a party system of establishing local governments is therefore inappropriate for Zimbabwe. The present arrangements require review."[114]

The corruption in the Harare city council was deep-rooted and chronic. When a new MDC council introduced a culture of accountability, it became an enemy of the ZANU (PF) government. It was quite obvious that the arbitrary suspension of the Executive Mayor, Elias Mudzuri, at the end of April 2003 was politically motivated in an effort to perpetuate the corrupt allocation of residential stands, and tenders for lucrative jobs. Mudzuri was elected in March 2002, taking over the administration of the capital city and seeking to pull it from the mess that it had sunk to since 1980. ZANU (PF) stage managed at least two demonstrations at Town House in an attempt to unseat Mudzuri and his team.

The government's refusal to allow the council to borrow money, apart from frustrating the council's development strategy, seriously undermined its ability to provide adequate and efficient service to Harare residents. In the case of the last ZANU (PF) mayor, Solomon Tawengwa, the ruling party had bent over backwards to defend him yet he had failed to deliver. The ZANU (PF)-appointed Chanakira Commission created more controversy than good governance.

---

113. *The Herald*, 18 June, 1999 and *The Zimbabwe Independent*, 2 July, 1999.
114. The Thompson Report on the City of Harare, June 1999.

Meanwhile, in February 1998, the executive mayor of Bulawayo, the late Abel Siwela, granted himself a council-owned site in Gwabalanda to put up a filling station; George Mlilo, the city's Director of Engineering Services, acquired another plot. In Mutare, the engagement of Knobspear Security to guard the local authority's premises and the hiring of Bitcon (Pvt) Ltd, which got a multi-million dollar contract to resurface all roads in the city, were both done without going to tender.

This goes on and on, despite the leadership code adopted at the ZANU (PF) Congress, held in August 1984 and attended by 6,000 delegates. The new leadership code was designed to reduce corruption among party leaders by limiting the amount of property that they were permitted to own.

In the light of difficulties and conditions imposed by banks on indigenous business people who wanted to borrow money for payment of duty on capital goods, the government hatched a special scheme. The Duty Deferment Facility allowed indigenous business people to spread duty payments on imported capital goods over a period of 12 months plus a three-month grace period. Under the terms of the facility, a beneficiary was required to deposit a down payment of 10% of the total duty costs upon collection of the goods from customs. A bond, equivalent to the outstanding duty, was required as security. The DDF attracted a 15% interest rate, far below the 35% cost of borrowing money on the local market in 1998.

In February 1998, the facility was terminated amid charges it was being abused by non-deserving individuals, including government officials and politicians who used it to import personal goods. Reports by the officials from the Department of Customs and Excise and the Ministry of Finance (the parent ministry) said the state was owed millions of dollars in unpaid duty by leaders in government, top politicians and a handful of indigenous business people who had illegally used the scheme. Some individuals breached the stipulated procedures by failing to pay the duty within 12 months. Others succeeded in being granted preferential treatment after seeking ministerial intervention. One case was reported in which the Department of Customs was forced to reverse its earlier decision to seek full payment from a client who had failed to pay the necessary duty in time.

Another notable case involved a revolving fund set up in the 2003 Budget. The government set aside a Z$2 billion revolving fund to cater for distressed companies, but because of rampant corruption some government officials wanted bribes for processing loan applications. The interest rate was fixed at 25% per annum, while the loan was payable over 36 months with a three-months grace period on capital. By December 2003, only 17 companies had benefited from the revolving fund.

These revelations came at a time when the government was attempting to improve its revenue collection mechanisms and was taking a high public posture against corruption. It has become a trend within ruling circles to create special funds which are not made public but are made known to those who have the right connections. Know-how is very much outpaced by "know-who."

The major cases of corruption involve huge government contracts in which influential persons, including Cabinet ministers, have been accused of enriching themselves through *chegumi* (the "10%" phenomenon), or simply a "cut" or "push." Although "cuts/pushes" tied to big government contracts are difficult to prove, an increasing number of cases of corruption were being heard in the courts by 1998, with Home Affairs Minister Cde Dumiso Dabengwa acknowledging that at least 80 cases of fraud were reported throughout Zimbabwe every week.[115]

A senior police officer observed that of the 94 cases of corruption which were investigated by the police fraud squad in 1998, about 75% involved tendering and contracts. Ninety per cent occurred in the public sector and involved Z$1 million and above. According to the Zimbabwe Congress of Trade Unions, the government had lost Z$30 billion between 1997 and 1998 through corruption; Z$17 billion through state-owned companies. A snap survey conducted by Transparency International Zimbabwe at a workshop on corruption it held in Nyanga in May 1999, at which a senior police officer was a guest speaker, revealed that politicians topped the list of the most corrupt people, followed by customs officials, indigenous business people and police officers. Foreign businesspersons and councilors also ranked very high and so did civil servants. Men were generally more corrupt than women, while teachers were said to be the least corrupt.

In 1998, parliamentarians were agitating for the establishment of a parliamentary committee on transparency and corruption. The National Economic Consultative Forum, a think-tank which hammers out policies that can help turn the economy around, also called for an anti-corruption body to deal with the growing problem. Unfortunately, the anti-corruption task force set up in 2001 has also remained largely ineffective, due to the inadequate resources and expertise.

Analysts say Mugabe's regime has never been keen on combating corruption, as its reluctance to ratify international treaties like the SADC

---

115. *The Financial Gazette*, 13 May, 1999.

Protocol Against Corruption shows. The Protocol seeks, among other things, to promote and strengthen mechanisms to eradicate corruption in the region. Only four countries — Botswana, Malawi, Mauritius and South Africa — have ratified the SADC protocol, which can be operational if it is ratified by at least two-thirds of the members.

Parliamentarians struggle to address these issues, but to no avail. The extra-parliamentary legislation effectively denies participation by its members and members of the public in the legislative process, and opens the way for large-scale corruption. And then, the media is constrained by certain colonial and draconian laws, which make it almost impossible for journalists to investigate and expose high level corruption.

## Commodity Shortages and National Disasters

Whenever there are shortages and disasters on a national scale, governments all over the world tend to shoulder the burden of alleviating the suffering by creating funds and distribution centers. Very often, this provides new opportunities to defraud the government.

During the drought period of the 1980s, haulage business became popular. The government had to feed millions of people in the communal lands. A haulage company owned by the late Mashata Paweni was one that was caught cheating, but the extent of the fraud was never documented. It is known that Paweni's company was overcharging for every kilometer covered, with the knowledge of high-placed government officials who were willing to share the profits. It was said, but never proven, some ministers were directly involved.

Late 1988 and early 1989 were dominated by accusations of corruption against members of the government. In October, Edgar Tekere, a former Secretary-General of ZANU (PF), was expelled from the party; he had persistently made such accusations, in addition to criticizing the government's plan to introduce a one-party state. Earlier in September 1988, students demonstrated at the University of Zimbabwe and the Harare Polytechnic over reports that some government officials, including ministers, were involved in the illegal buying and reselling of motor vehicles. In January 1989, President Mugabe appointed a joint commission to investigate reports of illegal transactions involving several senior ZANU (PF) officials. As a result of the Sandura Commission's findings, five Cabinet Ministers and one Provincial Governor resigned from their posts in March and April. One of the ministers was sentenced to jail, but was given a Presidential pardon the very next day. After a period in the wilderness, some of these men again have been rewarded with top jobs. In civilized countries, a person standing for public office first has to be cleared of any criminal activities.

It has been the tendency of the Executive to respond to public anger and demands by establishing commissions of inquiry in order to postpone taking painful decisions. But Zimbabwe has an effective and professional police force, whose duty it is to investigate and prosecute all offenders without fear or favor.

Fuel shortages that started in early 2000 resulted in a fuel import racket in mid-2001. Zimbabwe needed 60 million liters of fuel a month, or 720 million liters annually. Official sources said cabinet ministers and ZANU (PF)-aligned businessmen holding direct fuel import licenses issued by the National Oil Company of Zimbabwe (Noczim) were abusing the permits for self-enrichment. It was revealed that government pals were using the licenses, issued to import fuel for personal or company use, to buy the product for resale. The racket was particularly strong in Harare and Bulawayo, raking in millions for those involved.

The illicit trade in fuel came to light as National Railways of Zimbabwe (NRZ) sources complained that one of the Vice-Presidents was using most of the railway utility's storage facilities for private profit. A source claimed that the Vice-President, who owns Chehesai Transport (Pvt) Ltd, was importing fuel through Botswana and paying nothing for fuel storage at NRZ facilities in Gweru and Chivhu. He was said to be banking approximately Z$1.5 million every three days from the fuel.[116]

Noczim sources said that as of June 2001 there were 246 high-profile individuals who held direct fuel import licenses. The number of permits had since increased dramatically because of a huge black market. Fuel industry sources said that at least Z$3 million was needed to get a fuel license. However, there were individuals who bought licenses from racketeers and others who got them through connections. The liberalization of the fuel market saw a glut of players, especially individuals, in the market. Most of the licensees had permits to import fuel for family or company use. The government rewarded corruption and graft at Noczim (and other public-owned companies) with exit packages for the blue-eyed offenders and punished the public with staggering fuel prices. One company that came under the spotlight was Comoil, a company belonging to the younger brother of Saviour Kasukuwere, a ZANU (PF) MP. It was reportedly selling petrol at Z$1,800 per liter, compared with the government-controlled

---

116. *The Zimbabwe Independent*, 20 July, 2001.

price of Z$450 per liter; diesel was being sold at Z$1,700 a liter instead of Z$200. In August 2003, the police impounded 20,000 liters of petrol and 15,000 of diesel and accused the company of contravening price controls.

At the beginning of October 2002, senior members of staff at Noczim were accused of colluding with drivers of private oil firms to siphon scarce fuel from Noczim depots for resale, mostly in Harare, in a racket that was costing the state firm millions of dollars. High-level oil industry officials said more than two million liters of fuel, mostly diesel, worth over $140 million at current pump prices, had been diverted to illegal selling points in the past year through a well-coordinated scheme. Reliable sources said that the drivers acted as middlemen; most of the fuel was from the Mabvuku and Msasa depots in Harare, where senior officials would authorize the drivers to have additional fuel pumped into their tankers, which they would then take to these outlets.

Meanwhile, in September 2003, senior management officials at the oil company were under police investigation for leaking fuel onto the parallel market and selling the commodity above the prices gazetted by government. Sources within the Ministry of Energy and Power Development said Noczim was in turmoil with reports that the Chief Executive Officer, Webster Muriritirwa, abruptly resigned at the end of August under unclear circumstances. He is reported to have taken a job with Tamoil in Libya. Sources say the probe at Noczim was aimed at curbing corruption and improving fuel supplies to public transport and government departments.

While the Zimbabwe Republic Police were closing in on the Noczim officials, it became clear that ruling party and government officials were also implicated in the scam. Thus, Noczim affair became too hot for the police. "There are several high-ranking government officials who have been looting Noczim fuel for resale on the parallel market," as a Noczim source said. Fuel supplied by government for its departments was also being abused, with reports of widespread corruption along the delivery chain.

It is possible to identify other policy-related sources of corruption; one that comes to mind is the existence of multiple exchange rate practices and the *foreign exchange allocation* scheme. Some countries have several exchange rates; one for importers, one for tourists, one for investors, etc. Differentials among these rates can lead to attempts to obtain the most advantageous rate, although this rate might not apply to the intended use of the exchange. Multiple exchange rate systems are often associated with anti-competitive banking systems in which a key bank with government connections can make huge profits by arbitraging between markets. Countries that have little foreign currency distribute what they have through various schemes, with varying degrees of transparency. If, for example, state-owned commercial banks ration scarce foreign exchange by allocating it according to priorities established by government officials, interested parties may be willing to bribe these officials to obtain more than their share.

During the UDI period, the Smith regime introduced foreign currency allocations and during the 1980s the independence government carried on with the allocation system. The difference was that those with no connections with people in high places could not lay their hands on it, never mind how many times they applied for it. A greater portion of the foreign currency was allocated to those with "know-who," and they were using it to travel abroad and to import luxury goods. The extraordinary access to foreign exchange allocation given to the relatives of those in power was quite conspicuous. Others, who may have wanted foreign currency in order to be able to educate their children outside Zimbabwe, had no alternative but to go into self-imposed exile.

Most of Zimbabwe's foreign exchange transactions are conducted on the black market because of the severe hard cash crisis and because the government refuses to devalue the Zimbabwe dollar from Z$55 against the United States dollar. They did allow devaluation of the zimdollar on nine other occasions to meet the interests of specific sectors. In September 2002, the US dollar was trading at up to Z$900, the rand was over Z$80 and the pound was about Z$1,200 on the parallel market (black market). Foreign currency dealers said that rates on the parallel market were likely to devalue further because of increased capital flight and because more speculators were likely to invest in the foreign currency market, further putting upward pressure on the cost of living. They said an increasing number of Zimbabweans were leaving the country, selling their assets and converting them into foreign exchange, while some foreign companies uncertain about their future in Zimbabwe were also doing the same.

A rising number of workers were also using their earnings and other assets to invest in foreign exchange. The closure of currency exchange offices (owned by those with connections) at the end of 2002, purportedly to stamp out dealings on the black market, further aggravated the country's worsening foreign currency squeeze. Those at the top already had what they needed, anyway. The ban drove the parallel market deeper into a real black market, where the greenback at one time was fetching as much as Z$6,000. James Makamba, a former ZANU (PF) MP and central committee member who is also a founding member and chairman of Telecel Zimbabwe, was brought before the courts under the anti-graft crusade.

The prominent entrepreneur was arrested on February 9, 2004 on allegations of externalizing billions of dollars in foreign currency. Arrested during the same month and for the same allegations was Jane Mutasa of the ZANU (PF)-aligned IBWO. The country lost an estimated US$350 million due to the externalization of foreign currency in 2003 alone[117] (at Z$ 4,500 to US$1 according to the auction system introduced in January 2004).

Economic refugees are said to be sending at least £20 million into Zimbabwe every month and thus driving up asset prices, compounding the crisis.

Local companies have also been hard hit by the foreign exchange crisis, which has left them unable to import the raw materials, spare parts and machinery necessary for them to remain viable. Among those hardest hit are manufacturers, most of whose equipment is imported, and transport operators, many of whom have been forced to ground their vehicles because spare parts are unavailable.

Economic analysts estimated that the state was receiving about US$2 million each day through the Reserve Bank during the months leading to August 2003. The government was not, apparently, utilizing this money; what were they doing with it? Observers could only assume that they were exporting it, perhaps in preparation for a life in exile should things in Zimbabwe get out of hand. Corruption seemed to be driving economic policy: influential government officials could access foreign exchange even at the old official rate of Z$55 to US$1, and sell it for a fortune on the parallel market or through importing luxury goods for resale.

*Price controls* are a common tool that governments may employ when goods are in short supply and prices shoot up. Price controls are intended to lower the price of the given commodities below their market value (very often for social or political reasons); but these controls create incentives for individuals or groups to bribe officials to maintain the flow of such goods or to acquire an unfair share at the artificially low price. Price controls also often lead to hoarding of essential commodities. In Zimbabwe, at the height of price controls in the mid-1980s and again in October 2001, there were bound to be shortages of such commodities as bread, cooking oil and rice. While the general public experienced hardships, some retail outlets could obtain the commodities under the counter, only to force customers into "conditional" buying. Some retailers were reprimanded for hoarding.

---

117. *The Financial Gazette*, 26 February, 2004.

Indeed, the hasty decision to re-introduce price controls in October 2001 on a wide range of consumer goods from maize meal to sugar, cooking oil, fresh milk, flour, bread, margarine, salt, meat and soap was a political move by the government to please the electorate as Zimbabwe neared the 2002 presidential poll. The excuse that it had introduced controls because consumers could no longer afford these basic commodities was not watertight. In fact, the government failed to address the root causes of the problem, in other words farm invasions and so-called war veterans.

One of the effects of price controls is a rise in inflation. Zimbabwe's year-on-year inflation rose to a record high of 300.1% in May 2003. However, analysts fear that this is not a true reflection of conditions on the ground, where price controls and food shortages were pushing up the cost of basic commodities. Price controls do not, in practice, stabilize prices and minimize inflation. What they achieve is the creation of shortages, as manufacturers discontinue or progressively reduce production as rising costs destroy operational viability.

The only way prices can be stabilized or reduced is by the elimination of shortages, and the stimulation of competition. The law of supply and demand states that the price of an economic good is determined by the interaction of supply and demand. If supply is greater than demand at any one time, the surplus will generate a downward pressure upon price. And conversely, if demand is greater than supply, the scarcity will force prices up. According to this model, it follows that there must be a price at which the amount offered equals the amount required. By contrast, State-imposed price controls and food shortages caused by drought and the government's controversial land reforms spawn a thriving black market in basic foodstuffs, which lifted the prices of these by more than three times in 2003 alone.

To bring the rampant inflation under control, the government must curb its own expenditure, by containing corruption, by achieving exchange rate stability and by encouraging the growth of productivity of labor and enhanced production efficiencies.

*Trade restrictions* can be a prime example of government-induced source of corruption. If importing a certain commodity is subject to quantitative restriction (e.g. only so many vehicles can be imported each year), the necessary import licenses become very valuable and importers will consider bribing the officials who control their issue.

*Natural resource endowment* (emeralds, gold, exotic lumber) can constitute a source of corrupt activities, since they typically can be sold at a price that far exceeds their cost of extraction and their sale is usually subject to stringent government regulation, to which officials can turn a blind eye.

During the 1980s, an illegal trade in emeralds was centered at Sandawana in Mberengwa. None of the ringleaders was caught but some of those who traveled the length and breadth of the country to obtain the emeralds were. The businessmen provided a ready market, but they were basically safe. Black businessmen were not the only people involved in this racket.

In 2002, allegations of plunder and looting of diamonds in the Congo were made — and by no less credible organizations than the United Nations, which named Zimbabwe in Resolution 1457 on the "Illegal Exploitation of Natural Resources and Other Forms of Wealth in the DRC."[118]

At the end of November 2003, it was reported that ZANU (PF) *chefs* were among directors of nine companies whose 14 gold-buying licenses were cancelled by the government due to allegations of illegal trade in the precious mineral. The firms, which were licensed in March, were required to surrender 150 kg of gold a month to the Reserve Bank's Fidelity Printers and Refineries; but they were believed to have delivered only 39.2 kg in the seven months from April to October. On a monthly remittance of 150 kg, they should have delivered 1 050 kg by the time the licenses were cancelled.

Senior officials in the Mines and Minerals Development Department said there were many politicians involved in the "game," hence the difficulties in controlling it. The President of the Zimbabwe Miners' Federation, Nixon Misi, told a local daily that the banned concessionaires were fuelling the parallel market. The country was said to be losing 70% of its gold to smugglers.

While the government publicly accuses illegal gold panners of smuggling, reports were rife that senior government officials were the real culprits.[119] Senior government officials involved in mining confirm the allegations, saying, "These culprits are very influential. So how then do you make decisions to eliminate the trade when you are involved in it.... It is about those organizing the *makorokozas* (gold panners)."

Indigenous woodlands with economic potential are concentrated in the dry region of Matabeleland North Province, where Zimbabwean teak and other native hardwoods are profitably exploited. Zimbabwe has almost exhausted its

---

118. Interim Report of the Panel of Experts on the Illegal Exploitation of Natural Resources and Other Forms of Wealth of the Democratic Republic of the Congo, UN Security Council, S/2002/565, 22 May 2002.

119. These include identified ministers and deputy ministers; a retired army general and a recently retired provincial governor; and other army and police officers.

reserves of good quality hardwood. Furniture manufacturers and other users of hardwood are importing quality hardwood from Botswana, while others are trying to source it from Mozambique to maintain the standard of their products. The situation is not likely to return to normal soon because it takes up to 130 years for hardwood to reach the harvest stage.

Meanwhile, in November 1996, a Malaysian company secured logging rights in Zimbabwe's pristine forest reserves. The deal signed between Hasedat Corporation and the late Vice President Joshua Nkomo's Development Trust of Zimbabwe (DTZ) set alarm bells ringing in Harare. The logging concessions involved mahogany, mopani, mukwa, and teak. The multi-tentacled DTZ had considerable leverage with rural district councils which control local woodlands in Matabeleland.

*Low wages in the civil service* as compared to the private sector are also a stimulant for corruption. When civil service pay is too low, personnel may feel obliged, or at least justified, in using their positions to collect bribes in order to boost their income — particularly when the expected cost of being caught is low.

In September 1997, the Department of Customs and Excise was investigating a series of cases of corruption when it was reported that it had lost more than Z$10 million in a period of one year. A well-orchestrated racket was revealed between an indigenous shipping company and some customs officials. Confirming the racket, an official in the Ministry of Finance, under which the customs department falls, said this had happened on more than ten occasions. Alarm bells rang, as it became clear that this was not an isolated problem. It is fair to suggest that one of the ways to reduce this type of corruption would be to strengthen the civil service as an institution based on merit and appropriate salary scales that pay a living wage. This measure alone could reduce the economic incentive for public officials to indulge in corruption.

In November 2003, rampant corruption was revealed at the Zimbabwe Revenue Authority (Zimra), where the State was being deprived of millions of dollars on a daily basis as workers under-receipted cash received and pocketed the difference. The alleged fraud only came to light when a customer who had paid duty for his car lost the receipt and went back to the authority's offices to look for a copy. He was shocked to discover that the copy of the receipt showed that he had paid duty of only Z$5 when in actual fact he had paid Z$5 million. Although preliminary investigations revealed that Zimra might have been prejudiced of Z$29.2 million, sources said that more than Z$100 million could have been lost in the widespread scam, which seems to have been going on for years. "Besides changing figures on the office receipts," said a source in the parastatal; "the customer's account was also altered to remove any suspicion."

*Bureaucracy and red tape* may force people who are trying to obtain certain services to resort to bribing public officers, thereby facilitating corruption. An example which comes to mind is the disbursement of the War Victims Compensation Fund suspended by President Mugabe in March 1997. As the Chidyausiku Commission found out, civil servants administering the fund were acting in concert with middle-men to deprive beneficiaries of thousands of dollars in bribes, in exchange for expeditious processing of files. In July 1998, the Auditor-General, Mr. Eric Harid, bemoaned the fact that despite numerous measures put in place by the government to curb corruption (such as the Prevention of Corruption Act, the Misconduct Statutory Instruments and the powers given to the Auditor-General to deal with corrupt officials), the country's environment remained mired in bureaucracy that only encouraged the scourge.

When red tape creates long delays in obtaining certain documents or services, corruption is encouraged. It takes about six months to obtain an ID (the metal national identity card, which is required before one can enter into contractual agreements, for example), and another six months or more to receive a Zimbabwean passport. People in a hurry have to find a way to expedite the process. In April 2003, some officials at the passport offices were found to be running a racket with prices ranging from Z$15,000 to Z$30,000.

In September 2002, a scam was revealed in which hospital clerks and government registry officers solicited thousands of dollars from people waiting for birth confirmation records that they needed in order to acquire a travel document. Two policemen in Bulawayo were among those arrested.

Those wishing to live and work in Zimbabwe also have to pay, as senior officials at the Department of Immigration are said to be soliciting bribes for residence permits.

The Vehicle Inspection Depot (VID) is another center of abuse. In July 2002 alone, six vehicle inspectors based at the Masvingo depot faced corruption charges for issuing more than 500 drivers' licenses in return for cash payments.[120] Meanwhile, VID inspectors were asking for amounts varying from Z$200 to Z$1,000 in order to issue certificates of fitness for commuter omnibuses.

---

120. *The Daily News*, 1 Nov., 2002.

Car loans for civil servants are scarce, and this prompts employees to bribe the administrators of the loan funds in order to beat the three-year waiting period.

Customs officials at ports of entry are another fertile field, as is the Deeds Office where those wanting to invest in the country are supposed to get encouragement. It takes no less than six months to register a company at Electric House. Even obtaining a sales tax number requires a bribe in Zimbabwe.

Since this type of corruption involves an element of mutual obligation and benefit, it is difficult to expose and usually come to light only when one of the parties fails to honor his part of the deal.

*Government expenditure* and its effect on economic growth is an interesting question to consider. How does corruption affect it? Most economists think that the level and type of spending undertaken by governments affect economic performance. Fairly robust evidence suggests, for example, that high rates of health-delivery systems and enrolment in schools are related to superior economic growth. The impressive economic growth of the "tiger states" of South Korea, Singapore, Malaysia and others rides on the back of a sound program of technological development supported by a strong educational system. However, when it comes to the composition of government expenditure, corruption may tempt government officials to choose expenditures less on the basis of public welfare than on the opportunity they provide for extorting bribes. For example, large projects whose exact value is difficult to monitor may present lucrative opportunities. One might expect that it is easier to collect substantial bribes on large infrastructure projects or high-technology defense systems than on textbooks or teachers' salaries. Furthermore, highly discretionary authority and off-budget expenditure and revenues that are not accounted for lend themselves to corruption; ghost workers and even ghost departments are manifestations of this.

According to the Comptroller and Auditor-General, Eric Harid, the Ministry of Defense was defrauded of Z$1.2 million in the 1995/96 financial year. In December 1999, the Minister of Defense, the late Cde Moven Mahachi, was finding it difficult to contain alleged corruption by senior army officers that prejudiced his ministry of millions of dollars through purchases of unsanctioned military hardware. *The Mirror Online* reported the Minister as saying, "We have lost several millions of dollars in the way some of our major contracts involving huge purchases were executed, but we are in the process of tightening procurement procedures."[121]

By December 1999, about Z$1 billion radar equipment had been lying idle for years at Suri-Suri Air Base in Chegutu because it could not be used. The equipment had been acquired from China under unclear circumstances. In addition, the Zimbabwe Defense Forces was involved in a legal battle in 1997 with a Spanish car firm which supplied defective Santana vehicles worth more than Z$200 million.

Investigations were also underway over possible fraud to the tune of Z$9.5 million in the Department of Social Welfare; and the Ministry of Home Affairs lost Z$1.4 million to an employee of the SSB (Salaries Service Bureau) who manipulated records.[122] An audit report also highlighted instances of government officials receiving expense money for trips that were, in fact, canceled.

At the end of September 2002, Auditor and Comptroller-General Eric Harid issued a damning report showing that Treasury was owed more than Z$575 million by civil servants, including more than $380 million by the President's Office, in outstanding travel allowances and other advances. The report, which also highlighted gross negligence in the administration of the fiscus and covered the financial year ended December 31, 1999, revealed that most government ministries and departments ignored Treasury instructions with impunity and exceeded their allocations for advances on travel allowances.

Some of the advances to the public servants had been outstanding since 1991; by now, the individuals involved may have left the civil service or died. President Robert Mugabe's office, which was the main culprit, exceeded its advances limit for all the 12 months during the period under review by an average Z$20 million a month, against a budget of only Z$8 million.[123]

Other culprits included the ministries of public service, education, local government and home affairs, which accounted for a combined Z$150 million. Harid noted in his report that the advances were either not cleared immediately after the trip or were not accounted at all. "This would make it appear that advances were being used as soft loans... In some cases, officers were being given advances before clearing previous ones, contrary to laid down Treasury instructions."

In a political system where a dictatorial regime intends to hold onto power at all costs, large sums of money are spent on security agencies. In Zimbabwe, for example, in July 1997 the government allocated a whopping Z$570 million to the

---

121. *The Mirror Online*, 20 Dec., 1999.
122. Electronic Mail & Guardian, 6 May, 1998.
123. *The Financial Gazette*, 3 October 2002.

state secret service arm, the Central Intelligence Organization (CIO), which accounted for more than half the Z$926 million allocated to the Office of the President and Cabinet.[124] Political analysts point out that much CIO expenditure, such as construction and equipment, is covered under the votes of other ministries. For instance, the CIO was allocated various amounts in 1996 for construction projects under the former Ministry of Public Construction and National Housing's vote and other costs such as the acquisition of presidential helicopters were paid for under the Ministry of Defense's vote. Economic analysts called the CIO allocation, categorized as "special services," an "obscene gesture" to the people of Zimbabwe at a time when other essential ministries like Health and Child Welfare, Environment and Tourism and Mines were having to run on a shoestring.

The more corruption, the less is spent on health and education. Spending on health and education as a ratio to GDP is significantly lower than other expenditure items. Other components of government expenditure, most notably transfer payments such as social insurance and welfare payments, are also negatively and significantly associated with corruption, but health and education turn out to be the only components of public spending that remain significantly associated with corruption when the level of per capita income is used as an additional explanatory variable.

In December 1997, Justice Smith officially opened a three-day workshop on national integrity against corruption sponsored by Transparent International. Proponents for firm action to counter corruption cite not only moral issues, but the recognition that corruption erodes and destroys economies. Corruption is a significant cause of inflation, and the misuse and misappropriation of assets increases production and operational costs, consequently dragging down consumers' living standards. Estimates suggest that corruption's direct impact upon the inflation rate is at least two percentage points, let alone the direct repercussions upon inflation of the state's budget deficit. Corruption contributes an estimated Z$1–4 billion per annum to the national budget deficit, a deficit Zimbabwe is supposedly striving to contain. Research by the African Development Bank in early 2003 shows that corruption can cause up to 50% of taxes to be lost, while adding up to 100% to the cost of government goods and services.

*Tax evasion* or claiming tax exemptions brings about loss of tax revenue to the government, thus hurting the budget. It may also cause monetary problems if

---

124. *The Zimbabwe Standard*, 1 August, 1997.

it takes the form of improper lending by public financial institutions at below-market interest rates.

The allocation of public procurement contracts through a corrupt system may lower quality of infrastructure and public services.

Among the many disagreeable aspects of corruption is evidence that it slows economic growth through a wide range of channels. In the presence of corruption, businessmen are often made aware that an up-front bribe is required before an enterprise can be started and that afterwards corrupt officials may lay claim to part of the proceeds from the investment. Businessmen, therefore, interpret corruption as a species of tax — though of a particularly pernicious nature, given the need for secrecy and the uncertainty that the bribe-taker will fulfill his part of the bargain; that diminishes the incentive to invest. Empirical evidence suggests that corruption lowers investment and retards economic growth to a significant extent.

Prospects of quickly eradicating corruption look bleak. Most of the anti-corruption laws and regulations are not worth the paper they are written on without the political impetus to make them effective. The ZANU (PF) leadership code of the 1980s is a typical example. To have any real impact, the fight against corruption needs to be much more high profile, demanding the concerted action of governments, international agencies, business and civil society organizations.

It is refreshing to read reports from Zimbabwe's House of Parliament that indicate legislators in May 1998 had started a campaign for the establishment of a parliamentary committee on transparency and corruption, a committee that would act as a transparency watchdog on all local and international transactions undertaken by the government and parastatals. The idea was that whenever there were queries raised in government transactions, the committee would move in and investigate; and any such deals would not be ratified by Parliament until the committee's investigations were complete. Parliamentarians have over the past couple of years refused to ratify certain government contracts citing lack of transparency, although they were in the end forced to endorse them. The most notable included the Z$1.2 billion tender to build the new Harare International Airport and the Z$250 million tender to supply equipment for the PTC's mobile phone service Net One. Even the government-controlled daily, *The Herald,* did not mince words. In an editorial on January 15, 2004, the paper noted: "Never before or since has Zimbabwe been up against cases of corruption that depict the total lack of conscience, patriotism or the sheer greed of some people..." After years of serving as a rubber-stamping institution, parliamentarians were battling to assert their authority vis-à-vis the executive and demanding some respect for the legislature.

The saying that "power tends to corrupt, and absolute power corrupts absolutely" has its roots implanted in Zimbabwe. Once regarded as a "clean" leader who even tried to introduce a leadership code through which all political leaders had to register their assets (although the results of the exercise were never published), Mugabe has lost credibility because of the way he has dealt with those believed to be corrupt and those close to him who have been awarded tenders in a manner that is not very transparent. Most of the government leaders involved in the Willowgate car scandal have now been taken back. Nothing has happened to those allegedly involved in the VIP housing scandal. The same applies to those who "looted" the War Victims Compensation Fund where the biggest beneficiary was his brother-in-law Reward Marufu. His nephew, Leo Mugabe, is "everywhere." He won the tender to construct the new Harare International Airport amid a storm of controversy, which resulted in some countries even withdrawing their aid. He was also involved in the cellular phone saga, as a shareholder in Telecel. No matter how hard President Mugabe tries to distance himself and make it look as though his nephew is in business on his own, that is very difficult to swallow. He is too young and "came from nowhere." Besides, some have even argued, Leo is not so powerful that parliamentarians who had refused to approve a loan for the airport would change their minds for him. The only person who commands that kind of loyalty is the President, Robert Mugabe, himself.

# PART II. ECONOMIC EMPOWERMENT

## CHAPTER 4. THE INDIGENIZATION POLICY

### Prerequisites for Indigenous Investment

A competitive and self-sustaining domestic private sector is the driving force for economic growth and industrial development. It is crucial for the industrialization of the economy, and for the creation of tangible wealth and employment. There are many things that Zimbabwe must do to promote indigenization of the economy.

The harsh realities of colonialism are revealed in a new light once a country attains independence. The fact that the BSAC built railway lines, roads and bridges, schools and hospitals (using Zimbabwe's own mineral, agricultural and labor resources) is good, in itself. However, the scale of land deprivation and economic backwardness within the African communities were so horrendous that it will take a long time for the African population to attain economic independence. The fact that a few blacks have amassed wealth while the majority still live in dire poverty does not in any way mean economic independence. Only when the general populace has access to decent housing, health facilities and education, a plate of *sadza nenyama* (maize meal and meat), and some disposable income, we can sit back and smile.

Experience has shown that indigenization of the economy can succeed in an environment characterized by economic growth and spearheaded by a vibrant domestic private sector. In order to bring about macro-economic balance, a two-to three-year ceiling on government consumption should be accompanied by fiscal incentives to stimulate productive investment, privatization of state enterprises through employee stock ownership schemes, strategic partnerships and indigenous institutions, as well as commercialization of state enterprises. These measures would help reduce the budget deficit. At the same time, resources in the public sector, the private sector and the community at large should be mobilized and channeled towards the achievement of economic empowerment.

*Economic growth* and economic expansion can be powered by the engine of a sound industrial base, i.e. the establishment of new industrial enterprises and related economic activities. At independence, Zimbabwe already had a strong industrial base, as reflected in her import-substitution created to deal with a decade of economic sanctions during the UDI period. The challenge now is to establish an incentive and institutional structure that directs investment towards industries that are productive and can be competitive in the future. Attention must be paid to costs and to growth in productivity from the beginning. Because of the importance of economies of scale, it also means that many import-substitution industries should be set up with a view to become exporters.

The creation of Export Processing Zones was a positive development in this regard. On the basis of this industrial development, economic expansion should result in employment creation and poverty eradication, expansion of the domestic market and widening of the tax base. The widening of the tax base would lead to the reduction of the budget deficit, which stood at Z$1.019 billion during the 1991/92 financial year (US$1 = Z$2.270) and during 1997/98 had increased to Z$11.654 billion (US$1 = Z$55), i.e. almost double its target of 7.5% of GDP. By the financial year ending December 2000, the deficit had risen to Z$81.818 billion (US$1 = Z$55).[125]

*Private investment* must be increased, in conjunction with industrial development. This would be achieved through the encouragement of tangible incentives to those with viable projects. The door should be open to people with ideas irrespective of their political affiliation. The government has been willing to back individuals and consortiums with financial guarantees, but the process is rife with nepotism and tribalism. It is possible to establish new indigenous enterprises and new joint ventures that promote the transfer of technology; by buying shares in existing non-indigenous companies by indigenous people; by privatization of state enterprises; take-overs; employee stock ownership schemes; subcontracting and outsourcing.

Transparency is essential in order to encourage investors to direct their resources to Zimbabwe. Through the establishment of new enterprises, an environment could be created to foster an increase of indigenous private investment in the economy. And increasing indigenous private investment in the Zimbabwe economy would lead to economic expansion, creation of employment and more wealth, leading toward the eradication of poverty.

*Mobilization of financial resources*, particularly medium- to long-term finance, would be crucial for increasing indigenous private investment in the economy and for economic expansion. In order to create an enabling environment for the mobilization of financial resources, the government should further reduce its

---

125. Europa World Year Book, Vol. II, 2002.

consumption expenditure and accelerate the commercialization and privatization processes so as to reduce the budget deficit. The reduction of the budget deficit fosters macro-economic stability, which is conducive for productive investment and mobilization of financial resources. Furthermore, educational campaigns for the promotion of domestic savings should include themes like savings against drought, savings for poverty reduction and investments on the Zimbabwe Stock Exchange through trust funds. Joint ventures and linkages between foreign and indigenous companies should also be encouraged as a way of mobilizing foreign capital and investment. Reducing corporate taxes would help. In Japan, for example, several financial institutions that assist business start-ups are exempted from paying taxes. In order to mobilize medium- to long-term finance, it would also be necessary to promote the establishment of leasing and venture capital companies. These would help solve the problem of collateral.

*Review of the tender system* which governs the operations of the different sectors of the economy should be undertaken, to make sure it does not have a constraining effect on the indigenization process. Government Tender Board (GTB) procedures should be designed to foster indigenization of the economy through preferences and stipulations that favor indigenization openly and transparently. Quasi-government organizations, parastatal corporations and local authorities should also be subject to directives on preferential procurement from indigenous enterprises. Tenders won by non-indigenous companies should be subject to sub-contracting requirements to indigenous companies. In addition, sub-contracting arrangements between large companies and small- and medium-scale indigenous enterprises should be encouraged through an incentive scheme. A procurement directive should call upon government agencies, parastatals, state owned companies and organizations to set aside certain areas of procurement of goods and services for participation only by indigenous owned enterprises. Such procurement should follow normal competitive procurement procedures to ensure the program did not come into disrepute. The public sector should review its procurement procedures in consultancy services to promote activities of indigenous professionals.

It must be understood that such a deliberate bias in favor of indigenous (black) entrepreneurs maybe controversial in certain cases. A typical example is the white-dominated security industry. When, in May 1998, the government-owned Cold Storage Company (CSC) awarded a country-wide multi-million dollar security service contract to two well-established and white-owned companies, there was a barrage of protests from indigenous (black) security companies who felt the contract should have been awarded to indigenous companies in line with the government's declared indigenization policy. Guard Alert and Securitas emerged the winners of the CSC tender, beating 27 other bidders. Naturally, the CSC dismissed the protests, saying it could not deviate from laid down procedures to accommodate companies whose services were not up to standard. The Zimbabwe Indigenous Security Association felt it was an egregious example of protecting a white-dominated security industry.

Although an attempt was made to provide preferential treatment, particularly in the construction sector where tenders worth Z$10 million and below were awarded to indigenous constructors, the margins were not enough and the whole tendering business was clouded with corruption. In many instances, both in the public and private sector, information relating to the examination, clarification, comparison of bids and recommendations for the award of a contract was being disclosed to bidders and other persons not officially concerned with such process. Bidders influenced the process, and bids were won even by candidates who could not conform to all the terms, conditions and specifications of the bidding documents.

Indigenous firms can be helped to compete in various ways. One is to use plain language in writing contracts and the laws governing contracts, to help such firms to interpret them correctly.

Another approach is to require that tenders above a certain size consider bids from several potential suppliers. That is not as simple as it sounds, however. Given the declining value of the zimdollar against major currencies, Treasury Circular No. 2 of October 1990 was issued advising that the value limits of the various classes of tenders for both the government and parastatals would be reviewed; but then it imposed stringent value limits: all tenders below Z$150,000 required quotations from between five and seven eligible suppliers; tenders between Z$150,000 and Z$500,000 required the general manager or head of a parastatal to establish a transparent system of tender receipt, security, opening and adjudication consistent with the good procurement practices, and those worth over Z$500,000 should be finalized at the GTB. These limits were quickly and severely eroded by inflation. After the November 1997 crash of the zimdollar, even very small jobs required going to tender. Tenders were piling up faster than they could be processed. The thresholds had to be reviewed again.

*A change in the duty structure* must also be implemented. Right now, if goods imported by air freight from Europe, the Americas or Asia arrive in Harare but are destined to an EPZ (an Export Processing Zone, that is, land on which certain factories and businesses are built) elsewhere in the country, they must be processed through the Department of Customs in Harare, and then be reprocessed upon arrival at their ultimate destination. That is a costly exercise for importers and causes endless delays.

Although the purpose of such a system is to generate revenue for the state, it should do so in a way that promotes investment instead of serving as an obstacle to economic growth and a hindrance to effective corporate operations. When the government announced that all importers had to clear their goods at the initial port of entry, in 1998, many importers, particularly those far away from the initial ports of entry, lost business and had to pass the increases in costs on to their clients. The result of the Customs Department ruling was to slow down investment in the EPZs at a time when city authorities and private companies had ploughed in enormous amounts of funds to develop stands.

The concept of the export processing zone is promoted on assurances of minimal regulation and an absence of customs duty liability; the government's continuing failure to align the Customs Duties Act with the Export Processing Zones Act severely undermines the drive to establish EPZ enterprises. Furthermore, while the legislation provides that many capital goods are exempt from duty, that exemption only applies to one importation of such capital items in any five-year period. That is hardly consistent with the stated goal of encouraging investment, business development and the transfer of technology.

*Low and stable inflation and interest rates* would help companies to invest in new ventures and expand their existing concerns. However, the budget deficit has pushed up inflation, which stood at 52.3% as of May 1999 and nudged 622.8% in January 2004. Interest rates, which were pegged between 35 and 40% as of June 1998, were both a product of and a tool for combating this problem. However, both inflation and the high interest rates placed tremendous demands on the average individual as well as businesses and further compounded the difficulties of marginalized blacks seeking loans. To add to this, government continually placed further demands on company and individual earnings through onerous direct and indirect taxes in order to support its extravagance.

*A commercial-farm settlement scheme* must be designed to promote the development of indigenous commercial agriculture, and the government should introduce a long-term lease scheme (with option to buy after a period of, say, ten years). Preferably, these two schemes should favor those who have qualifications in agricultural science. The principle of one-person, one-farm should be enforced. The prohibition of land ownership by foreigners and companies (except in special circumstances) should be adhered to. Last but not least, a limit on farm size and a land tax for under-utilized land in general and agricultural land in particular should be introduced. The imposition of a land tax would encourage the release of surplus land onto the market, and would provide the government with funds for promoting indigenous commercial agriculture.

*Skill development* is crucial for economic development. Zimbabwe particularly requires entrepreneurial skills, technological know-how and economic development management skills. Technological know-how is needed for research and development as well as for the manufacture and marketing of products in the newly established enterprises. Skilled manpower is needed for developing a strong indigenous technological base for industrialization. Economic development management skills are needed for designing of appropriate policies that will promote indigenization of the economy as well as economic growth and development. Financial management skills like planning, buying, costing, pricing, stock control, record-keeping, cash flow projections and marketing are essential for success in any business venture. Skills in public management and economics can contribute to the much-needed increase in efficiency of resource use. However, Zimbabwe runs the risk of pricing itself out of the market for professional people if it does not reduce its income tax levels and improve conditions of work.

*Good governance* is an important part of an environment conducive to the attraction of investment. As far as the investor is concerned, good governance encourages investment and the transfer of technology. It is quite apparent that economic growth and national development cannot be sustained if there is no effective transparency and accountability. Investors are willing to invest in countries where not only the infrastructure is developed, but where the game is played straight.

Hand-in-hand with this is the need for greater participation of the people in their governance. Whatever the form of government that exists in the country, appropriate mechanisms must link rulers to ruled, and vice versa. Reforms to bring more genuine democracy should overcome the *de facto* one-party system, end legal and material constraints to forming and running political parties, and end state repression of the opposition.

Therefore, the unification of the people of Zimbabwe as a nation, the entrenchment of political stability, the elimination of poverty, and the dictates of justice and equality necessitate an acceleration of the process of indigenization. In July 1998, the government issued a policy framework for indigenization of the economy. Government policy was founded upon five objectives:

1) To give indigenous Zimbabweans economic empowerment by increasing, mainly through economic expansion, their productive investment in

the economy so as to create more wealth and eradicate poverty. Whereas previously the government had advocated for "wealth redistribution," it now emphasized wealth creation.

2) To create conditions that will allow the hitherto disadvantaged Zimbabweans to participate in the economic development of their country and earn self-respect and dignity.

3) To democratize the ownership of the economy so as to eliminate racial differences arising from economic disparities.

4) To develop a broad-based competitive domestic private sector to spearhead economic growth and development.

5) To develop a self-sustaining economic structure.

To achieve these objectives, the government formulated a variety of specific and broad-based strategies, the first of which was the declared intent to reduce the budget deficit by reducing government consumption expenditure and by improving its revenue collection system, with a view to reducing inflation and high interest rates, thereby creating a stable macroeconomic environment. In addition, the government was to establish provincial committees to ensure that the indigenization policy was implemented throughout the country. Furthermore, in declaring an intention to work closely with the indigenous business community and with non-indigenous business organizations which articulate the objectives of indigenization of the economy, and through the use of incentives, the government hoped to motivate joint-ventures between indigenous and foreign companies as well as between local non-indigenous and indigenous companies.

In 1998, the government proposed to encourage the establishment of more venture capital and leasing companies, and to stimulate savings for employment creation, poverty eradication and economic indigenization through tax-free interest arrangements. In addition, the government stated that it intended to introduce measures to protect strategic infant industries. The intention was to institute a study to identify industrial sub-sectors or industries in which Zimbabwe has a comparative advantage. Furthermore, it would use incentives to encourage sub-contracting arrangements between large companies and small- and medium-scale indigenous enterprises. Quasi-government organizations, parastatals and local authorities would also be subject to directives on preferential procurement from indigenous enterprises. Tenders from non-indigenous companies would be subject to subcontracting requirements to indigenous companies (by the winning non-indigenous tenders).

If taken too far, these measures would, unfortunately, be disincentives to further non-indigenous and foreign investment. Encouragement of the indigenous population ought not to mean that tenders would be awarded with little or no consideration of merit, price, quality and reliability. The future of the economy requires that all enterprises be treated fairly on common criteria.

The strategies drafted also envisaged that employee stock ownership schemes would be encouraged in the private sector and in those state enterprises as were to be privatized. The government also intended to commission a study to identify all laws that inhibit the development of indigenous enterprises so that they could be changed. It had identified an array of sub-strategies to address and reverse the prevailing lack of entrepreneurship. Also identified were technical skills among the indigenous people, including a curriculum review at vocational and technical training institutions, entry into tripartite arrangements involving indigenous entrepreneurs, vocational training institutes and non-indigenous entrepreneurs for development of training programs.

Not much has come of these fine intentions, as the government lacks the will to move forward. Like previous economic revival programs (Zimcord, the Five-year Transitional National Development Plan, Esap, Zimprest, the Millennium Economic Recovery Plan and the National Economic Revival Programmme announced in March 2003), the indigenous investment policy has turned out to be a glorified wish list founded more on rhetoric than reality.

Employee stock ownership schemes have not materialized.

No study has been carried out to identify laws that inhibit the development of indigenous enterprises.

Preferential procurement by government departments from indigenous enterprises has largely benefited the ZANU (PF) elite and cronies.

The privatization of state enterprises has been abandoned.

As shown below, the economic empowerment lobby has been hijacked by ZANU (PF) insiders.

The government tender system is in shambles because of increasing violation of prescribed procedures, and tenders have been awarded in such a way that they benefit a few chosen individuals.)

Programs for rapid, effective and viable economic indigenization must be supported by all elements of both the public and private sectors, reinforced by the international community.

### The Economic Empowerment Lobby

Before independence in April 1980, the majority of African entrepreneurs were involved in retail business with small shops in the high-density areas (townships) and in the communal lands. Those who were able to establish such business concerns went through extremely trying start-up conditions, and needed talent and wits to get the necessary resources. Many of them began by selling vegetables, by bicycle, in the low-density areas (European-only areas — *kumayadhi*). They could not borrow money from financial institutions, first and foremost because they did not have collateral. Even if they had had collateral, and financial skills, this generation of businessmen had to contend with institutionalized discrimination as banks would not have dreamed of granting loans to blacks in any case.

These same black businessmen survived the sanctions imposed on Rhodesia after UDI. They helped nationalist organizations and donated to the freedom fighters in the then Tribal Trust Lands, both in money and in kind. On the insistence of the nationalists, they refused to pay income taxes to the Smith regime. However, after independence, the same nationalists demanded that these businessmen pay all the income taxes backdated to the days of the illegal Rhodesian regime. Despite the large amounts involved, they have survived and went forward with the establishment of "super markets" in the high-density areas.

Some were involved in commercial farming, the majority of them in the purchase areas. In the communal lands, there were farmers who branched into commercial crops like cotton, sunflower and tobacco. Immediately after independence, others went into coffee growing.

Besides these, some enterprising businessmen went into manufacturing — against all odds. Their determination to prove themselves made them succeed. Most of them had moderate educational qualifications with a Form Two (two years secondary school) or Form Four (four years secondary school — American junior high school) background. After independence, some of them were lucky enough to get the backing of those in key positions to influence the awarding of contracts and bank loans. During the early independence period — the period of "protectionist socialist governance" — a third generation of businessmen emerged. They were engaged in transportation and other hospitality services. Many members of this generation lived in exile, mostly across the Zambezi in Zambia.

The fourth generation is made up of people who found their way into the mining sector, especially the mining of emeralds and gold. Most of these were "socialists" in high government departments, whose ideology was overwhelmed by the allures of the capitalist way of life. Overnight, they amassed so much wealth that they became "small rulers" in the areas of their birth. The code of conduct introduced by the party was ignored as the party hierarchy embarked on the road to capitalism. Black capitalists popped up overnight like mushrooms. This class of capitalists, pushing hard for the implementation of economic empowerment, seems to be made up of people who acquired wealth during the mid- to late-80s. They tend to be ostentatious. In recent years, black businessmen have been involved in multimillion dollar tenders, and not without scandal. Some politicians retired on huge pensions, while others are reported to have had astonishing access to the demobilization funds for ex-combatants.

A fifth class of black entrepreneurs would be those people who took over from the generation of the 1940s and 1950s. Whereas that generation of black entrepreneurs lacked formal education and access to capital, this generation has both, and is putting them to good use. They have worked for years in large conglomerates and in banks. They took advantage of the liberalization of the financial sector during the first phase of economic reforms — Esap. Most of them made their money on the money market; therefore their origins in the world of business are public knowledge. They seem to be finding that it may be possible to begin a business and succeed without the help of underhanded deals or political connections.

It is clear that, after independence, the government managed to foster national cohesion — the necessary harmony that enabled the cross fertilization of ideas for building winning strategies in the free market. One of the key ingredients was the government's decision to invest heavily in science and technology education. This investment in education developed the nation's human resources, so that the emergent black entrepreneurs were able to recognize the opportunities offered by free market reforms in the 1990s and were able to invest in areas and resources that would propel economy forward. By investing in financial institutions, and industrial and mining concerns, the black entrepreneurs gained the flexibility that enabled them to create businesses with the capacity to produce goods that had both a national and regional demand. Within a period of ten years, many African businesses had transformed their economies from satellite patterns of growth — where the bulk of their agro-based exports went to their former colonial master — to fully-fledged regional traders, competing with and even surpassing many of the first regional trading companies.

Black entrepreneurs have found the vital ingredient necessary for economic independence and have made giant strides in shifting the balance of forces in national trade. However, the unwillingness of the ruling ZANU (PF) party to transform its political culture has become a hindrance.

In spite of the rapid industrialization and modernization that is taking place in the Southern African Development Community, politically the government has opted to retain the usual African traits of heavy dependence on undemocratic practices. Political patronage has remained a major vehicle for transacting businesses, in both the public and private sectors, and is a stumbling block to the creation of a truly prosperous, open and free market. Intolerance of dissenting views and repression of opposition has remained a major feature of national political life. The ZANU (PF) leadership claims that it can adopt the Western free enterprise culture minus the political freedoms that normally go with it. On this issue, President Robert Mugabe is most vocal, often accusing the Western nations of attempting to impose their own brand of democracy upon people whose political culture is incompatible with Western democracy.

Mugabe has publicly declared that it would be better to be dominated by another South-South partner (Mahatir Mohammed's Malaysia) than to remain under Western or South African domination. One wonders whether this argument is inspired by personal considerations more than by economic sense. Eager to demonstrate his political muscle at home, and his loyalty and commitment to his friendship with Mohammed and to the idea of South-South colonization (the so-called "smart partnership"), Mugabe, at the end of 1996, proceeded, without consulting any of his colleagues or the country's Parliament, to award a contract to develop the Hwange power station to Malaysia's YTL, a company which was said to have links with members of Malaysia's president. In an era where calls for transparency in business transactions and good governance are growing louder by the day, this deal met with heavy media and public censure.

Following the collapse of communism, there are very few free and democratically-governed countries with which Zimbabwe can claim to enjoy cordial relations, both within the continent and outside. Malaysia has come to the rescue, but it hardly can replace the IMF. Within government circles, Malaysia is now recognized as a very special friend and is seen as a blueprint for Zimbabwe's future economic development. Aspects of Malaysia's Vision 2020 have been cited as guidelines which Zimbabwe could use for the future economic prosperity and sovereignty.

Zimbabwe's adopted strategy vis-à-vis indigenization, in the absence of a policy document, has to a large extent conformed to the East Asian governments' strategies. Their interventions have taken many forms, some of which are already being practiced in Zimbabwe; these include functional interventions in the shape of resource allocations designed to affect the general mechanisms of production. In Zimbabwe's case, interventions are mostly selective, designed to meet the different needs of specific industries and firms. Many a time initiatives to sell a firm or a private company on the open market have been thwarted on the basis of non-participation of specific black entrepreneurs. The government has been interfering in the marketplace, from the awarding of tenders of multimillion-dollar projects to the buying and selling of private companies.

In August 1997, the government created Africa Resources Investment (ARI), as a vehicle, an investment arm, to warehouse shares in companies whose acquisition would be government-facilitated; in other words, ARI was to negotiate for and acquire shares in Zimbabwe-based multi-national corporations and state parastatals as part of the country's indigenization policy. The warehoused shares would then be disposed to consortiums of indigenous entrepreneurs and enterprises at a later date, according to the government. This arrangement brought about many questions by both government and private-sector executives over the state's ability to conduct transparent transactions in the hot issue of indigenization. There were quiet allegations that some senior ruling ZANU (PF) officials and top members of the government were using the warehousing of shares to buy time so they and their partners could set up shell companies and consortiums that eventually would bid for the assets.

President Mugabe strenuously denied that ARI could be used by politicians as a platform to enrich themselves, as ARI committee members were not allowed to negotiate for shares in their individual capacity. "ARI is now a government committee, negotiating for the government," the President said. "We cannot be seen to be negotiating for ourselves.... otherwise people will accuse us of doing things for ourselves."[126] ARI was led by a five-member committee of Justice Minister Emmerson Mnangagwa, Planning Commissioner Richard Hove, Minister of State for Security Sydney Sekeramayi, the Minister for Gender Issues in the President's Office Oppah Rushesha-Muchinguri, and Home Affairs Minister Dumiso Dabengwa. Prior to August 1997, the indigenization

---

126. *The Financial Gazette*, 16 October, 1997.

committee had operated as a two-member outfit with only Mnangagwa and Hove, plus Mawere (a former officer with the Washington-based International Finance Corporation, now based in South Africa) as its advisor. This prompted charges that it was nothing but a "Midlands committee doing things for just one section of the Zimbabwean community." It looks the President conceded as much when he expanded the committee's membership, saying that in making the new appointments he had taken into account the issue of regional balance.

Problems beset the new committee as soon as it embarked on assignments. Amid questions of a possible conflict of interest, the chairman of Africa Resources Ltd (ARL, a mining, manufacturing and financial services group), Mutumwa Mawere, was under pressure to give up his advisory role in ARI or step down as chairman of ARL. However, the new ARI committee had been divided into two camps, and one camp was insisting he should stay on. As an advisor to ARI, Mawere would no doubt have had access to inside information on share purchase negotiations between the government and the multi-nationals. This would obviously give Africa Resources Ltd an added competitive in projected acquisitions. Furthermore, there were also reports of disagreements over the state of the committee's financial books, with some committee members insisting that an external auditor be called in to audit the books before further work could be carried out, another source said. Meetings of the five-member committee took place under a tense atmosphere.

The stakes were high. International conglomerates Lonrho and Anglo American Corporation (AAC) had publicly been identified as targets for share negotiations and eventual acquisition by ARI, among other locally-based multi-nationals. The South Africa-based mining group AAC, had already agreed to sell 21% of its stake in Bindura Nickel Corporation and talks eventually led to the formal acquisition of shares worth nearly Z$146 million in December 1997.[127] In addition, ARI had already successfully negotiated a joint partnership with AAC to run Unki (platinum) Mine in Shurugwi, in the Midlands.

According to the government, the acquired shares would eventually be off-loaded to identified indigenous individuals and groups. ARI was also expected to take over the final negotiations for the acquisition of a controlling interest in the Zimbabwe Mining and Smelting Company (ZIMASCO), based near the Midlands town of Kwekwe.

Meanwhile, in November 1998, there was mounting confusion among some cabinet ministers and ZANU (PF) Politburo members over what had been

---

127. *Ibid.*, 18 December, 1997.

achieved in the purchase and warehousing of shares in multinational corporations and parastatals as part of the economic indigenization drive. Some senior government officials were quite unaware of how many shares had been warehoused so far, or their total value. A senior member of both the government and the all-powerful Politburo said, "There is scarce information on what has been done so far and how much progress has been made." He said the ruling party would seek a comprehensive appraisal from the party's finance secretary Cde Emmerson Mnangagwa, who was the Minister of Justice, Legal and Parliamentary Affairs. Another high-ranking party official added: "We want an audited report of shares bought and transactions which have been successfully negotiated before the new board appointed for ARI embarks on new initiatives. Many senior party members are in the dark about what is happening."[128]

In September 1997, the government had ordered that pension funds with more than Z$25 billion worth of assets should invest at least 10% of their portfolio with ARI. (Population estimates vary, because the Registrar-General manipulates figures for elections purposes; but 12.4 million blacks against 120,000 whites have been touted on several occasions.) This provoked an outcry from the pension industry and from economic commentators, who argued that the government was bent on propping up what was then believed to be black entrepreneur Mutumwa Mawere's collapsing business empire. The confusion was aggravated by the fact that Mawere had been involved in both ARI and his mining and industrial conglomerate, ARL. Most observers held the view that ARI duplicated the National Investment Trust, which was also created to warehouse shares for black Zimbabweans as the government's divestiture program picked up momentum. (Only the names were changed.) In the 18-months' budget (June 1997-December 1998), the Minister of Finance Herbert Murerwa allocated Z$200 million to the NIT (although funds never made it to the trust). However, the air seemed to have been cleared when Emmerson Mnangagwa, who headed the Cabinet's indigenization committee, explained that ARI would complement the NIT.

Notwithstanding, by October 1998 NIT was failing to raise money to buy shares reserved in three privatized companies after its funds were diverted by the State to pay war veterans gratuities. The NIT had shares in Dairyboard Zimbabwe Limited (DZL), the Cotton Company of Zimbabwe and the Commercial Bank of Zimbabwe (CBZ). It also had a shareholding in Zimbabwe Reinsurance Corporation, which was being privatized in October 1998. In both

---

128. *Ibid.*, 5 November, 1998.

DZL and Cottco, the trust had a 10% stake and a further 26% in CBZ. However, it was understood that Dairyboard was planning to offload its shares onto the market after the trust failed to meet the June 1998 deadline by which it was supposed to have taken up the offer.

Against this background, the news broke that the emerging financial giant, Transnational Holdings Ltd., had an ambitious plan to buy the NSSA's 43% stake in Financial Holdings (Finhold). This did not come as a surprise to many observers in the indigenization field. Transnational Holdings was owned by a group of local business persons who include Nicholas Vingirayi, Gibson Muringai, Freeman Kembo and Michael Mahachi. The share-warehousing concept has always been suspected as a door behind which arcane deals might be concluded. Negotiations to dispose of NSSA's stake in Finhold in March 1999 coincided with allegations of insider trading (involving the financial institution, the Cotton Company of Zimbabwe and Southampton Life Assurance Society of Zimbabwe) by the indigenization task force of the National Economic Consultative Forum (NECF). The three companies were said to have a capitalization of about Z$13 billion.[129]

The chairman of the NECF indigenization task force, Philip Chiyangwa, sent a letter to Justice, Legal and Parliamentary Affairs Minister Cde Emmerson Mnangagwa, strongly suggesting he institute investigations. Since Albert Nhau was known to have been associated in the negotiations that ensued in the acquisition of a controlling shareholding in Southampton and since he was also current chairman of Finhold, it was hard not to conclude that there was a continuing relationship that would give Transnational Holdings access to beneficial information about the Finhold Group.

Indeed, when Transnational (in conjunction with an unnamed consortium of Zimbabwean investors headed by Nhau) acquired the 49% held by the South Africa-based Southern Life as well as the 3% held by Southampton Employee Share Trust, institutional investors and a group of individuals interested in the acquisition cried foul.

To consolidate its resolve for indigenization, in December 1997 the government appointed a board to head ARI. The board cut across the race divide, and was to be chaired by banker James Mushore of National Merchant Bank of Zimbabwe. Conspicuous by their absence from the board were members of the Affirmative Action Group, a vocal pressure group which, at the end of 1997, had ruffled a few feathers including those of government officials with its

---

129. *The Herald*, 24 March, 1999.

empowerment rhetoric, as well as the Indigenous Business Development Centre, the country's first black economic empowerment group.

Parallel to this development, the government appointed a consortium of three banks as its financial advisers in running the Africa Resources Investment Trust. The three banks, Trust Merchant Bank of Zimbabwe, Commercial Bank of Zimbabwe and Kingdom Bank, were selected by a panel of judges who considered presentations from 13 financial institutions. James Mushore, the trust chairman, said the financial advisors' brief would be to raise appropriate funding to enable the trust to purchase assets approved by the government-appointed empowerment committee. (Nothing materialized. As noted in Footnote 133, Mushore was reported to have fled to the UK.)

To consolidate its position on the indigenization process, the government set up the National Investment Trust of Zimbabwe (NITZ) in 1998. Its objective was, among other things, to increase and facilitate the involvement of economically disadvantaged Zimbabweans in the national economy and to promote savings among indigenous people. According to the Notarial Deed of Trust for the establishment of the NITZ, eleven trustees — Zimbabweans of "high professional" standing — are appointed by the Minister of Finance after consultation with the President. The main task of the trustees would be to formulate policies to ensure the participation of indigenous people in the privatization of parastatals.

The list of trustees did not please Zimbabwe's indigenous economic empowerment pressure groups, which included the Indigenous Business Development Centre, the Affirmative Action Group and the Indigenous Business Women's Organization. The black-led pressure groups lodged their complaints to Vice-President Simon Muzenda, stating that, "The torch bearers of empowerment should be people who have distinguished themselves either professionally or otherwise on the complex task of transformation. Our view of the nominees for the NITZ board leaves us with the inescapable conclusion that we are not going anywhere. While we would not like to comment on the credentials of each of the members in their individual capacities, we can safely say that the entire board is completely silent on the day-to-day struggle for black economic empowerment."[130] Some of the trustees were said to be quasi-government employees or to run companies involved in the same business the NITZ was set up to do: which was seen by the petitioners as a conflict of interest.

---

130. *The Financial Gazette*, 20 May, 1999.

With such high stakes, it is inevitable that many organizations were competing for control of the Zimbabwean economy. Since long before, there had been calls for the indigenization of the economy coming from several quarters. About a decade after independence, these calls culminated in the formation of the IBDC, led by bus operator Ben Mucheche. After independence, the government had put emphasis on direct controls to promote large-scale import substitution, a policy which discriminated heavily against local enterprises. However, the situation radically changed with the formation of the IBDC. It was felt that most Africans were involved in retail not because they lacked imagination, but because the cost of entry into manufacturing was prohibitive. In November 1992, the IBDC embarked on a massive factory construction exercise intended to provide low-cost workshop facilities that would enable skilled indigenous craftsmen to enter the manufacturing sector.

An organization was founded in 1994 to help women entrepreneurs establish themselves in business. Women in Business (WIB) sought to foster an entrepreneurial spirit among professional women and even rural women who had always followed strictly peasant roles or concentrated on basketry, sewing, pottery, and crotchet work. With WIB well established, the Indigenous Business Women's Organization (IBWO) followed; it launched a trust fund in 1995. IBWO was expected to establish a commercial bank from which the organization's members would borrow money for capital projects at concessionary rates but, as of now, that is still a pipe dream. WIB and IBWO proved popular with emergent rural and urban businesswomen; they actively promoted the entry of women into commerce and industry as equal players. The enterprises ranged from labor-intensive soap manufacturing, general dealers, retailers, and industrialists to consultants.

Adding to these activities was the Zambuko Hillary Clinton Centre in Harare. Zambuko Trust is an NGO whose main aim is to provide finance to small businesses through its micro-credit facility. Between 1997 and 1998, it had granted loans worth Z$28.5 million to women, representing 80% of the total portfolio of the Z$36.8 million. It had already provided loans worth Z$91 million to women and other small businesses since 1992.

As part of measures to promote indigenization of the economy, the Zimbabwean government gazetted a list of sectors reserved for local investors through Statutory Instrument 108 of 1994. Foreign investors are allowed to take up only 25% of equity in companies undertaking projects in the reserved sector list, which includes armaments manufacture and marketing, public water provision for domestic and industrial purposes, agriculture, forestry, transportation and retail and wholesale trade.

In 1994, the IBDC was rocked by a power struggle. The radical Affirmative Action Group (AAG) was formed, with Philip Chiyangwa at its head. The AAG's agitation brought indigenization firmly onto the national agenda. Unfortunately, it soon became clear that this was a club of personalities jostling for their personal interests. Some members resented the fact that the organization was dominated by the Mashonaland province leadership. After the death of Peter Pamire in a mysterious car accident in June 1997, Saviour Kasukuwere was appointed vice president while the Matabeleland-based transport operator Matson Hlalo was co-opted as national vice president, mainly by the will of the Mashonaland province-dominated leadership.

In February 1998, Chiyangwa unilaterally dismissed Kasukuwere, accusing him of being "sponsored by big multinationals to confuse the empowerment agenda." Kasukuwere had attended a meeting of business leaders on February 6, convened by Anglo-American chief executive Philip Baum on behalf of the Harvard Institute. Much mudslinging followed. In an effort to discredit Kasukuwere, Chiyangwa said, "I cannot ride or carry people with fake skin, regardless of what they think is their position in the AAG. Kasukuwere is too much in love with whites, and I worry when I am associated with such a person." However, observers thought Chiyangwa was unhappy that he had not been able to gain the respect that Kasukuwere had earned from the public and the corporate world. Despite his remarks, he was keen to get close to Anglo American to take advantage of their unbundling. While accusing Kasukuwere of fraternizing with whites, he surprised many observers by appointing Jonee Blanchfield, Eric Bloch and Don Fergurson to the board of Zeco, his Bulawayo-based acquisition.

Members from other regions that included Manicaland, the Midlands and Masvingo became disgruntled with the AAG's constitution, which vested overriding powers in the founding chief Philip Chiyangwa, including the power to appoint vice presidents and to fire them with no recourse. Kasukuwere's dismissal was short-lived, though; Chiyangwa soon reinstated him, apparently influenced by the immediate backlash by representatives of the AAG's five regions, who went public to oppose the dismissal.

A consequence of these quarrels was the resignation of vice president Saviour Kasukuwere and his Mutare region senior members who were championing the formation of a breakaway group. The rival group planned to comprise indigenous professionals like accountants, lawyers, doctors and related associates from the commercial and industrial sectors; the breakaway group sought to be apolitical and to broaden its membership; they apparently had the support of other members from the AAG's five regions, who were also disgruntled with the AAG's constitution.

As if these problems were not enough, there was an increasingly gaping conflict on the question of unaudited financial books. Since its inception in 1994, the AAG had not presented any audited accounts, as required by the organization's constitution.

Before the dust could settle, another black empowerment lobby group emerged, in April 1998. The Zimbabwe Indigenous Economic Empowerment Organization (ZIEECO) had Mr. Paddington Japa Japa, an indigenous businessman, as its interim president. This brought to five the number of organizations advocating black economic empowerment, the other two being the IBDC and IBWO. Some of the members of ZIEECO's interim executive were reported to be ZINATHA president Professor Gordon Chavunduka and Professor Welshman Ncube of the University of Zimbabwe. Japa Japa described the AAG as a "self-enhancement" group, claiming his organization would strive to uplift the lives of most blacks, who were finding it difficult to survive under the current harsh economic environment. He said that ZIEECO would assist blacks in approaching banks with project proposals, as well as help in negotiations with the government on any crisis. One of the organization's objectives was to act as a watchdog on reports of racism at workplaces, schools, sporting associations, hospitals and anywhere else in Zimbabwe.

However, black empowerment groups would continue to have no impact on the economy until they buried their differences and formed a strong united organization. At least, the Zimbabwe National Chamber of Commerce (ZNCC) and the Confederation of Zimbabwe Industries (CZI) boasted concrete empowerment programs, which included business and management training, sub-contracting and linkages, franchising and micro-business entrepreneurship, which were gradually nurturing small enterprises to attain competitive levels. For example, in July 1996 the ZNCC launched the Micro Business Development Corporation to develop secured incubator work sites which enable informal sector workers to expand their economic activities to a level where they could move into the formal sector.

The CZI, for its part, runs the Zimbabwe Enterprise Development Programme (ZEDP), which specializes in linkages and sub-contracting projects. Introduced in 1995 to integrate the small-to-medium-scale enterprise (SME) sector into the mainstream economy, the program had succeeded in creating multi-million dollar businesses for the country's small firms and had helped create hundreds of jobs while facilitating the transfer of vital technology. By July 1998, there had been linkages and subcontracting projects worth some Z$45 million, which had created some 852 jobs.[131]

Just when large local firms were trying to reduce costs because of Zimbabwe's harsh macroeconomic climate, the linkage program proved beneficial to large corporations. The plan had created more than 200 business linkages across the country, valued at more than Z$300 million, while more than 3,500 new jobs in all sectors of the economy had also been created by May 1999.[132] While the program is spearheaded by the CZI, it is funded by the United States Agency for International Development (USAID) and the Norwegian Agency for International Development (NORAD). Under the ZEDP scheme, which provided business opportunities for thousands of Zimbabweans retrenched by both the private and public sectors, large corporations shed their non-core businesses and subcontract these to small-medium enterprises (SMEs), whose company profiles are kept in a national data base administered by the CZI, which links the partners.

The economic indigenization campaign gathers momentum, although local economists are of the view that as long as the split among the country's empowerment pressure groups remained, donors and other financiers find it difficult to deal with them. Black economic empowerment pressure groups feel that the government should consider offering "free" shares to employees as it divests its assets in parastatals, if blacks are to make meaningful inroads into the economy. Otherwise, those who are already rich will continue to benefit, as only they have the finances to buy shares, and the disadvantaged black majority who were supposed to be the primary beneficiaries of the indigenization thrust will still be left empty-handed. A formula could be devised, in the case of privatized parastatals, whereby employees could be given shares and pay for them later, through dividends. It is a fact that blacks most did not and do not have cash to pay for these shares. As whites own more than 90% of the country's wealth, it is argued that a deliberate positive bias towards blacks is necessary in order to change Zimbabwe's economic landscape.

A typical scenario that illustrated the dilemma faced by black Zimbabweans was that, due to lack of capital, shares meant for workers in privatized parastatals were still being held by the underwriters. The government

---

131. *The Herald*, 16 July, 1998.
132. *The Financial Gazette*, 10 June, 1999.

had already privatized four parastatals, namely Dairyboard Zimbabwe Limited, Cotton Company, Commercial Bank of Zimbabwe and Cold Storage Company. There were more parastatals such as Air Zimbabwe, Posts and Telecommunications Corporation and ZIANA lined up for commercialization and privatization, but there was no way the average workers at these parastatals could raise the money to acquire allocated shares.

Another frustrating scenario was the increasing number of company liquidations. Admittedly, many of these were a result of economic hardships since the introduction of economic reforms in 1990. However, some of them had been through mismanagement and sometimes, economic sabotage. In these cases, workers were not being provided for nor enabled to take over the companies concerned. In other words, these liquidations could have been contained, if all the stakeholders were serious about improving the economy and the general living standards of the people. Furthermore, it is likely that productivity would go up where employees acquired meaningful stakes of ownership, for example by channeling pension funds into take-over bids in the event of a company being liquidated. However, the prevailing Pensions and Provident Act did not allow for such initiatives. By failing to introduce such enabling legislation, the government was failing to bring indigenous people into the mainstream economy.

Zimbabwe's financial institutions, for years accused by black business people of bias, could not escape the blame for failing to support the drive for black economic empowerment. In July 1997, a row over stiff lending conditions erupted between black economic empowerment pressure groups and financial institutions appointed to disburse the Z$800 million (US$72.7 million) World Bank facility. The loan had been negotiated between the government and the World Bank arm, the International Development Association (IDA), to support and promote rapid growth of private sector enterprises.

The IBDC in particular argued that its members could not meet these requirements because of historical disadvantages. It also preferred an 18-month grace period as opposed to the proposed three months, a five-year repayment schedule and that all sectors ranging from agriculture and transport be allowed to access the money.

Nevertheless, the Small Enterprises Development Corporation, which was one of the disbursing institutions, contended that the conditions and terms were fair and competitive and most serious business people seemed to be able to meet them. Financial institutions, which claimed commitment to black economic empowerment, pointed out that applicants lacked detailed project proposals. It was also a common trend that most prospective black entrepreneurs were not innovative enough, as they only ventured into traditional areas like bottle stores and general dealer shops. Besides, statistics showed that up to 90% of start-up projects failed to get off the ground and banks needed to be strict. Banks also accused indigenous business people of signing checks they could not cover, and of spending borrowed money on luxuries instead of the projects.

Although the black economic empowerment lobby voiced concern over the terms of the facility, there were encouraging levels of enquiry and the rates of approval registered. For example, the Zimbabwe Development Bank, one of the disbursing institutions, approved about Z$12 million (US$1.09 million) to clients from Harare, Bulawayo and Mutare during the first 30 days of approvals in June 1997. In addition, as the facility was available to Zimbabwe for the next 40 years, it meant that many businesses should be able to access the funds several times over the period.

On October 31, 2002, the Minister of Industry and International Trade told delegates at a National Economic Consultative Forum meeting in Gweru that the government had set aside a Z$2 billion facility to assist distressed indigenous-owned companies facing collapse and to further empower indigenous business people, at an interest rate of between 15 and 25%.[133]

Meanwhile, because the government encourages joint-venture projects, numerous joint-venture small- and medium-size businesses have sprouted in the country. One foreign organization that has also taken a keen interest in establishing ties with Zimbabwean venture capital firms is the Canadian Alliance for Business in Southern Africa (CABSA). Operating in Zimbabwe since September 1996, CABSA assists organizations that have a capital base of over US$250,000 (Z$4 million) to upgrade their technologies and gain external expertise through Canadian companies. There are not many indigenous businesses which possess this type of capital base. Therefore CABSA, which is sponsored by the private sector Alliance of Manufacturers and Exporters of Canada, decided to establish links with local venture capital funds in order to assist Zimbabwean small businesses to establish themselves and become ready for CABSA to source technical partners. (Zimbabwe has more than five venture capital firms which enable local enterprises to secure financing.)

Basically, the CABSA program enables local enterprises to use Canadian companies to upgrade their technologies and gain external markets for their products or establish agencies and distributorships in Zimbabwe for Canadian

---

133. *The Daily News*, 1 Oct. 2002.

companies. By March 1998, CABSA had reviewed over 230 projects, with five local companies in the construction, textiles, mining, education and training sectors being linked with Canadian counterparts with a view to establishing joint ventures. In April 1998, at least six new export-oriented Zimbabwe-Canada joint ventures worth over Z$40 million were being considered and were expected to create a large number of jobs. In 1997, Zimbabwe was among the top group of countries which conducted business with Canada with exports of different goods in excess of 16.6 million Canadian dollars (about US$24.1 million).[134]

Included in the race to provide finance for SMEs is the UNDP, which in 1998 provided over Z$14 million. Through Empretec Zimbabwe, the UNDP also supported informal sector entrepreneurs in graduating to small- and medium-scale enterprises. There were about 900,000 micro-, small- and medium-sized businesses in Zimbabwe in 1995, compared with over one million by the middle of 1998. Empretec Zimbabwe (in cooperation with ZimTrade, CZI, Business Extension and Advisory Services and Franchising Association of Zimbabwe) provides services to the small- and medium-scale enterprises.

Another significant international player in the development of SMEs is the Commonwealth Africa Investment Fund (COMAFIN), initiated by heads of government in July 1996 to jump-start new and existing projects that contributed to economic development and job creation. With an initial capital of US$63.5 million, the Harare-based COMAFIN had already used about US$50 million by June 1998 in assisting more than 12 projects dotted around Africa, with Zimbabwe drawing more than US$1.3 million for a fish-rearing project in Lake Kariba.[135]

At a time when the government was under fire for the failure of its indigenization program, in 1991, the Venture Capital Company of Zimbabwe (VCCZ) announced it had invested over Z$222 million in 60 new small- and medium-size indigenous businesses over the past six years to April 1998 and created more than 1,500 jobs. VCCZ had provided start-up capital, through equity funding, amounting to Z$34 million to four new production ventures in Harare over the first four months of 1998 alone. The VCCZ was established with capital from local and international shareholders, including banks, insurance companies and private sector companies. Operations began in 1992 and 28% of

---

134. Panafrican News Agency, 20 May, 1998.
135. *The Financial Gazette*, 18 June, 1998.

the money invested by April 1998 had already been repaid and no company funded by the venture firm had collapsed.

The advantage with venture capital funding is that it did not attract interest, leaving the entrepreneur free from the burden of current punitively high interest rates of more than 40%. The ideal level of equity financing from the VCCZ ranged from a minimum of Z$250,000 to a maximum of Z$5 million and that no collateral was required. The VCCZ could also enter into co-financed projects if funding requirements of a project exceeded its equity ceiling. Its equity in the current projects ranged from 21% to 49%.

The economic empowerment lobby is neither confined to the independence government nor empowerment pressure groups; influential individuals have also taken center stage. A typical example is the saga over the indigenization of the giant high-carbon ferro-chrome mining firm, ZIMASCO. ZIMASCO is a very strategic mining concern, employing more than 4,000 workers and earning the country about Z$1.4 billion in hard currency annually. It was owned by white former Rhodesians through an offshore company registered in Mauritius. For years, the government had been negotiating to buy the firm so the state could later pass on its shares to as many blacks as possible.

Former commander of the Zimbabwe National Army, the retired general Solomon Mujuru, defied an order by President Mugabe to back out of a multi-million dollar deal he concluded in May 1997 with Union Carbide. General Mujuru bought 27% in ZIMASCO, a subsidiary of Union Carbide; the President argued that the shares should be bought by a group of black businessmen and not by an individual. The General held firm — a move widely seen as a direct challenge to Mugabe's authority. Mujuru, an ex-combatant who still enjoyed wide support among the military, and who was retired by Mugabe before reaching 50, indicated that the only place he would consider selling some of his shares would be to groups with a broad-based indigenous thrust. Backed by a coalition of powerful politicians and businessmen, Mujuru clinched the deal to localize about half the shares of the Kwekwe-based mine. Mujuru acquired the 27% stake through Nyika Investments, a consortium of businessmen, at a heavily discounted rate. He was understood to have paid about Z$40 million for the shares.[136] He bought into ZIMASCO, which had an asset base of close to Z$1 billion, with financial help from Trust Merchant Bank, a local bank owned mostly by blacks.

---

136. *Ibid.*, 19 February, 1998.

In 1996, the country's sole asbestos fiber producer, African Associated Mines, was taken over by an indigenous ownership. The former owners, British-based Turner and Newell, dismissed criticism of the take-over, saying, "the deal was a straightforward, arms length business deal...." The Z$600 million take-over attracted considerable criticism from some indigenous pressure groups, who were convinced that the country's majority would not benefit from Mr. Mutumwa Mawere's deal with the British company.

Meanwhile, in January 1998, Anglo American Corporation Zimbabwe Limited concluded a multi-million dollar deal under which it would dispose of its majority shareholding in its Bulawayo-based subsidiary Clay Products to management. Some four Clay Products officials, led by the general manager Killian Mudzimu, formed a company, Walton Investments (Pvt) Ltd., to effect the take-over.

The Clay Products story was just one of the cases where Zimbabwe's emerging indigenous entrepreneurs, battling to be part of the country's mainstream economy, were increasingly resorting to management buy-outs (MBOs) of established and flourishing companies instead of starting from scratch. Unfortunately, some of the acquisitions ended up collapsing, leaving the new owners under a heavy debt burden and exposed to a growing perception that indigenous entrepreneurs are poor managers. Economic and financial experts pointed out that the attractive buy-outs did not seem to achieve the intended objectives of broadening control of the economy, creating additional employment and transferring wealth to previously disadvantaged groups. Instead, they reversed the entire economic empowerment process, which the government had encouraged as part of its economic reforms.

Many companies were selling off because future market trends showed that competition from cheaper imports would create a less favorable environment. The new indigenous owners often had not thoroughly analyzed such economic indicators. They based their acquisitions on the company's past and present performance, rather than future projections. Because of Zimbabwe's closed economy during the 15 years of sanctions, during UDI, most of the manufacturing industries catered only for a Zimbabwean (Rhodesian) market with no competition from outside manufacturers. With the introduction of economic structural reforms, the situation radically changed.

Notwithstanding, in early July 1998, Beehive Management Services, a consortium of five indigenous entrepreneurs, bought tire maker Dunlop's Z$6 million manufacturing company, which enjoyed a 90% monopoly of the local market. The company even exported to three of 14 SADC countries in direct competition with South African tile manufacturers. Several similar MBOs have taken place since 1995, the most notable being those of indigenization crusader Philip Chiyangwa's Native Africa Investments' multi-million dollar acquisition of the Tirzah Group of companies and ZECO, and Leo Mugabe's acquisition of Industrial Steel and Pipe; what happened afterward is a mixed story. In Bulawayo, previously high-performers like bicycle manufacturer Zimbabwe Cycle, television distributor Supreme Sales and Hire and Tony's Panel Beaters disappeared from the industrial landscape a few years after changing hands.

There were those who felt that the collapse of the indigenous businesses had little to do with the lack of markets or competition. "It is all about poor management and lack of creativity among some of our people. Running a business is not child's play," said Minister of State in the President's Office in charge of Indigenization, Cde Cephas Msipa. His ministry encouraged the MBOs of existing firms because they already had premises, assets and a ready market instead of indigenous businessmen having to start from scratch. Msipa said that the majority of indigenous Zimbabweans did not have the money for capital goods and machinery. Financial institutions often find it easier to lend money to a business that is operating than to an entirely new venture. However, it should not be forgotten that much of the machinery used by such local companies was outdated and could not meet the standards and quality of imported goods. And since Zimbabwe opened the economy to international competition in 1991 after years of being a closed market, and since the end of the apartheid era in South Africa in 1994, there was a flood of cheap imports which had saturated the local market.

The companies that collapsed were illustrations of poor assessment of the constantly changing economic environment. The costly bank loans (prevailing interest rates were over 40%) killed many of the acquisitions that were facilitated through the banks, in the first place. The majority of emerging indigenous entrepreneurs lacked financial and marketing skills; ordinarily, before acquiring a business, one would hire experts to research the company's market, state of the machinery and capacity to meet future requirements. Another major weakness of indigenous entrepreneurs was the wholesale replacement of experienced staff with friends and relatives as a cost-saving measure but one which inevitably led to poor management. And then, some who are new to business get carried away by the size and stature of a company and are influenced more by ego than by reality.

As foreign investors bailed out of Zimbabwe's floundering economy, black entrepreneurs speedily took over abandoned businesses. Some saw this as promoting black empowerment. However, it signaled massive foreign disinvestment from the country and was not creating crucial new enterprises. By the end of 2002, indigenous businesspersons were approaching banks to craft deals to give them the financial muscle to snap up companies previously owned by white Zimbabweans or foreign firms. Anti-white rhetoric has prompted many white Zimbabweans to abandon their businesses and leave the country, to invest in neighboring SADC countries.

Indigenous consortiums are now in control of major companies such as Lobels Bread (Pvt) Ltd, Zimbabwe Sun Hotels and seed supplier Seed Co. A group of black entrepreneurs bid for the control of United Tours Companies, a leading tour operator and car hire service provider, while indigenous players were said to be positioning themselves to take over the assets of multinational oil companies.

The emergence of indigenous consortia leading take-overs of firms in vital sectors of the economy took the high-performing Zimbabwe Stock Exchange (ZSE) by storm in mid-2003. Financial behemoth Old Mutual Plc's stranglehold on the local economy through ownership of significant stakes in listed companies was progressively whittled down by the emergence of aggressive indigenous acquisition barons since the beginning of 2001. During this period, a number of significant take-overs took place.

Economic commentators note that while black entrepreneurs benefited from the flight of foreign investors and local white businesspersons by snapping up established companies (sometimes at discount rates), the country nevertheless needs the financial resources and technical assistance that multinational firms have at their disposal. Continued foreign disinvestment would give the wrong signals to potential international investors, discouraging further foreign participation in existing operations or their investment in new enterprises. Black entrepreneurs face the serious challenge of maintaining the businesses they have taken over and expanding them under a harsh operating environment characterized by high inflation (400%) and a severe foreign currency crisis that has led to fuel and raw material shortages. Inflation was forecast to reach 800% by the end of 2003 and hard cash inflows continue to decline, adversely affecting a large number of companies already in distress. Indigenous businesspersons face the same crippling problems that forced their predecessors to sell in the first place and that have led to the closure of at least 500 companies in the past few years.

Economists also warn that the cause of black empowerment would not be served merely by the take-over of existing white-owned firms. The real test is whether black entrepreneurs will have access to adequate financial support to launch new enterprises that can create more wealth and employment. There is a tendency for such access to be limited to those who already have a proven business track record or, less justifiably, to politically connected individuals.

Cabinet ministers and other top ZANU (PF) functionaries entered the agro-processing sector, through the acquisition of shares in quoted counters Natfoods and Innscor in mid-2003. State Security minister Nicholas Goche, Youth, Gender and Employment Creation minister Elliot Manyika, the party's Mashonaland East chairman Ray Kaukonde, and businessmen Antony Mandiwanza and Kenneth Musanhi formed a consortium (Takepart Investments) to acquire stakes in large agro-processing firms. Records at the Companies Registry show that the businessmen are all directors of Takepart.[137]

A number of veterans of the 1970s war that brought Zimbabwe's independence from Britain in 1980 have "turned their guns into plough shares." Retired air marshal Josiah Tungamirai made news by breaking ground in the entertainment industry, joining forces with gospel musician Elias Musakwa of Ngavavongwe Records and Michael Chidziva, chairman of Tanaka Power to acquire a controlling stake in Gramma Records and the Zimbabwe Music Corporation (ZMC). In the telecommunications sector, Daniel Shumba, a former military man and ZANU (PF) Masvingo Province chairman, was awarded the first license to operate a fixed telephone network, TeleAccess Communications, in 2002. Shumba also owns one of the largest information technology companies in Zimbabwe, Systems Technology, and the low profile Kings Haven Hotel in Avondale. And as mentioned earlier, the former ZANLA commander, retired army general Solomon Mujuru, has become a major player in the mining industry through his shares in ZIMASCO.

As has been mentioned, such acquisitions are part of ZANU (PF)'s strategy to muscle its way into key sectors of the economy. Members of the consortium have also benefited from the fast-track land reform exercise and are seeking to consolidate their wealth by creating synergies between farming and agro-processing.

The doyen of the acquisition culture, Mutumwa Mawere, who presides over an empire, only seems to have whetted his appetite with the watershed take-over of the Associated African Mines of Zimbabwe in the mid-1990s. Through his African Resources Limited (ARL) or its associate, Ukubambana Kubatana Investments (UKI), he maneuvered to take shareholdings in Turnall

---

137. *The Zimbabwe Independent*, 4 July, 2003.

Fibre Cement, General Beltings, Steelnet, ZimRe Holdings group and its associates, Nicoz Diamond and Fidelity Life Assurance Company. ARL also splashed Z$5 billion to wrestle a strategic 21.9% stake in First Banking Corporation from other shareholders.

Furthermore, a number of deals have been done in the past few years in which the same consortiums and people benefited from the sale of government shares in companies listed on the Zimbabwe Stock Exchange. Privatization Agency of Zimbabwe (Paz) admitted that the ZSE was a conduit for indigenous economic empowerment during the disposal of government's shares in listed companies. Paz was established in 1999 to lead, advice and manage the sale of government shareholding in over 40 institutions in line with the government's policy of parastatal privatization.

In some cases, it is not the individuals' business acumen but their political relationships that have thrust them into company ownership. Some will argue that evidence to this is as yet sparse and anecdotal, but a cursory glance at the company take-over syndicates suggests otherwise. Most of these syndicates have, albeit as silent partners, politicians who are known for their penchant for influence peddling. These groupings are formed to wrestle companies from their owners, under the façade of black economic empowerment. In effect, Zimbabwe is merely dispossessing the few whites and replacing them with a privileged black clique.

Even the banks seem to have been drawn into this mess. They are channeling funds to well-connected businesspeople who tie up capital and run up large debts in questionable acquisitions. In the meantime, aspiring businesspeople without top access are left outside, their business plans resting in their desk drawers, overshadowed by this new breed of corporate predators.

Openings still existed for indigenous participation in the mining sector, which was slowly emerging from a three-year slump, thanks to platinum and firming bullion prices on the international metals market. South African mogul Mzi Khumalo took Mthuli Ncube, John Mkushi and Albert Nduna on board at Metallon.

Up to 40 locals were believed to be jostling for a 15 per cent stake worth about US$40 million in Australian-listed Zimbabwe Platinum Mines (Zimplats), which was originally earmarked for the National Investment Trust, a government initiated empowerment trust that, however, failed to raise the required funds.

Analysts have lauded the increased participation of indigenous businesspeople in the domestic economy, saying it was a shift towards ensuring a stable economy driven by people with a long-term commitment to the country. However, some analysts question whether what Zimbabwe is going through is genuine indigenization or the creation of one mammoth cartel. Indeed, there have been accusations that the emergent class of entrepreneurs is fronting either for powerful politicians or foreign interests.

It is not a crime for cash-rich individuals to move in whenever an opportunity arises, but it can be counter-productive if the objective is to enable small entrepreneurs to venture into business and eke out a living. Since the introduction of indigenization, political heavyweights have wrestled away various projects from small entrepreneurs.

In the main, it appears the concept of economic empowerment has been narrowed to the transfer of businesses owned by whites into indigenous (black) hands. Franchising may be an exception. This had always been an exclusively white domain in Zimbabwe. However, with the creation of the Franchise Association of Zimbabwe (FAZ) in 1996, many indigenous entrepreneurs saw this as an opportunity for them to enter into business. One farmer, Tobias Musariri, now holds the local Bedford vehicle franchise. Franchising is not capital intensive and does not require collateral.

Indeed, disadvantaged by colonialism, Zimbabweans need more than share ownership to grow into a meaningful level of economic empowerment. Socio-economic processes impact job creation; attention must be paid to the granting of finance, the transfer of skills such as financial control and marketing, and education on business ethics. The common weakness among indigenous entrepreneurs is their reluctance to spend money on training in financial management and marketing of products.

Notwithstanding, the private-sector arm of the World Bank, the International Finance Corporation (IFC) in November 1998 set up what it calls the Enterprise Services for Southern Africa (ESSA), based in Harare. This is a consultancy to assist small- to medium-size enterprises in Zimbabwe and the SADC region to solve technical and management problems that constrain the growth and expansion of indigenous businesses.[138] Since the clients were expected to contribute half of the fees towards their training, it was hoped that the indigenous entrepreneurs would bite the bullet and invest in their own future. (In the unstable investment climate created by the lawlessness

---

138. It was envisaged to run courses that would include strategic management and business planning, management information systems, productivity and quality control, improvement of financial planning and management, marketing and other subjects determined by the client needs.

accompanying the farm and company invasions, this promising project, like many others, has evaporated.)

*Political Patronage*

The government and the ruling party are moving resolutely towards economic empowerment of the majority in Zimbabwe. There is no doubt that the economy, long dominated by the minority white Zimbabweans and foreign multinational corporations, is in the process of structural change. Quite a number of black entrepreneurs have appeared on the scene over the decade since the introduction of Esap. There is no economic sector where a black Zimbabwean has not established himself. This alone speaks volumes for the creative and imaginative potential in a people long deprived of a chance to show what they can do. The old generation businessman proved that he could make it despite lack of resources, financial and marketing skills. The new generation, despite having financial and marketing skills, lacked the required land, premises, capital goods and financial resources to start a business venture. This is where the independence government stepped in to make sure that the abundant resources Zimbabwe possesses are distributed equitably.

Since the opening up of the economy to free market forces, international financial and development agencies have shown a willingness to back Zimbabwe's indigenization efforts. Although conditions laid down by these institutions have sometimes been too stringent for those with new project proposals, some small- and medium-size entrepreneurs have managed to get approval for their expansion projects. However, when the loans provided by international organizations are approved by Parliament, it is logical that the government must be involved in the screening of recipients; and Zimbabwe's experience has shown that the screening process is likely to favor those well known in the ruling party. Even when the World Bank loan agreement was ratified in Parliament, backbenchers expressed concern based on the way previous credit facilities had been disbursed: instead of helping needy people in the rural areas, i.e. the growth points, the money was largely restricted to the capital, Harare. This time around, the government promised that US$2 million was being set aside for each of the country's ten provinces. However, that seemed doubtful since this loan was supposed to create a revolving fund, and of the Z$400 million that was previously granted, nothing had "revolved."

To prevent abuses, the World Bank itself included safeguards. According to the deputy resident representative, Mr. Kapil Kapoor, the bank would periodically bring in external auditors to "make sure the procedures are being followed....This will ensure that powerful people with connections in government do not get access to these funds. Usually these people have larger companies than what we are looking at."[139]

The previous Z$400 million credit facility had been disbursed through the Credit Guarantee Facility, an arm of the Reserve Bank. This time round, it was planned that the US$75 million facility would be distributed among five financial institutions for disbursal to contribute towards reducing the economic imbalances left over from the days when the country was ruled by the white minority.

Unfortunately, the economic empowerment pressure groups have very much been invaded by the ruling ZANU (PF). Some former founders and presidents of the IBDC, for example, left the organization because of political interference. "There were a lot of political agendas beginning to creep in.... Daily, it appeared we were being sucked into a political role," commented one founding member. A former IBDC president agreed, saying, "When I was in the IBDC, certain politicians saw the organization as a perfect platform to push for their interests. That is still the main problem. People with the right connections are getting (state) tenders ahead of those without."

One maybe forgiven for thinking that both the aggressive Affirmative Action Group led by Philip Chiyangwa and its geriatric brother, the Indigenous Business Development Centre, led by Ben Mucheche and Enock Kamushinda, were ZANU (PF) appended structures like the Women's League or the Youth League led by Air Marshal Josiah Tungamirai. In their public statements, the leaders of these groups unfailingly promoted government policy and thinking towards the indigenization of the economy. It appeared as if the party had secretly hired them as hit men in its confrontation with white big business, which they blamed for all the country's economic ills.

In contrast, there are some indigenous businessmen who were never what people would describe as "blue-eyed boys" of the ruling ZANU (PF) party. One such prominent entrepreneur is Sam Gozo. He started his lone struggle for economic emancipation in the early days of independence. At the height of the campaign for a socialist economic system during the 1980s, the businessman appeared on the TV program "The Road to Socialism," where he blasted ZANU (PF)'s socialist theories. Later, in a 1994 magazine interview, Gozo complained that ZANU (PF) had initially marginalized black entrepreneurs like himself by

---

139. *Sapa-IPS*, Harare, 17 March, 1997.

barring them from party leadership at any level. It was only in 1993, he said, that the party leader, Mugabe, had directed that prosperous business-people were eligible for election to party posts. Until then, they were treated like "revisionists" and lackeys of the capitalists. Gozo recalled that in the 1980s, when foreign exchange was as rare as good jobs were in the 1990s, he was among the indigenous entrepreneurs who could not secure any foreign currency no matter how many times they applied for it. "Most of us could not help noticing the excessive foreign exchange allocation given to the relatives of those in power," he lamented.

During these hard times of economic structural adjustment, many other black business people who built up their enterprises so painstakingly in those early years, both before and after independence, are helplessly going under. The main reason is the government's inability or unwillingness to settle its accounts with them. (The government accuses them, in turn, of failing to complete projects on time, or at all.)

Political affiliations and tribalism have for a long time held sway in important business matters. A classic example is an attempt to award a license for the operation of Zimbabwe's second mobile telephone system (known as Net Two) to Telecel, despite the fact that Econet had also been recommended by the GTB. Telecel was made up of a company from the Democratic Republic of Congo and a consortium of local business-people which included James Makamba, Philip Chiyangwa, Leo Mugabe and other indigenous groups. At one time, the government ordered Strive Masiyiwa, Econet's chief executive, to sell his Z$100 million cellular telecom equipment to Telecel or surrender it to the government for no compensation.

This issue was so heated that a conflict became public between the Vice President Dr. Joshua Nkomo and the then minister of Information, Posts and Telecommunications, Cde Joyce Teurairopa Mujuru. Dr. Nkomo, who was at that time acting president while President Mugabe was in London on one of his overseas trips, was reported to have threatened to resign from Government unless Econet was awarded the license. Minister Mujuru disregarded Nkomo's order, describing him as "senile" and thus preferring to give the license to Telecel. It was understood that "Umdala" threatened to resign, not only over the Net Two license, but over the wave of corruption where only those close to Mugabe were being awarded all the lucrative business contracts.

Strive Masiyiwa's persecution by the government was considered one of the ugliest examples of how an insensitive and arrogant institution set about trying to grind into submission its citizens. Enhanced Communications

Network, now known as Econet Wireless (Pvt) Ltd., had been fighting the government over the issue of cellular phones for four years. Masiyiwa categorically refused to bankroll any of the politicians. That episode, in which the chief villain appeared to have been Joyce Mujuru, also spotlighted the government's ambivalence about indigenization. The government, with the exception of the late Vice President Joshua Nkomo, would have preferred other black entrepreneurs rather than the assertive and litigious Strive Masiyiwa to operate the second cellular network. Masiyiwa's subsequent victory ought to have been celebrated by all advocates of genuine rather than cosmetic indigenization. He had fought and won a bruising battle against Goliath. Yet not many of his fellow business-people seemed to want to be seen to be publicly sharing his moment of glory.

Meanwhile, the face of political patronage is seen in Roger Boka. In contrast to the ostracism of Strive Masiyiwa, Boka was the "chosen" one. Standard procedures were clearly bypassed, in his case, right from the word go. Who awarded him a license to start the United Merchant Bank (UMB) in 1995? It is clear that the UMB's "capacity" to grow and bring in other players was in part due to the political patronage it enjoyed. Few apparently questioned its credentials because the public posture its founder adopted enjoyed the support of the President and his leading ministers, while its lack of adequate capitalization was ignored by the Registrar of Banks and Financial Institutions, equally overawed by intimations of political support. It is no wonder some ministers took a casual attitude towards the collapse of the UMB. The Minister in the President's Office responsible for indigenization, for example, simply observed: "Banks collapse everywhere. It happens." And addressing Zimbabwe's embassy staff in Cairo, President Mugabe had the audacity to proclaim that Roger Boka had "demonstrated remarkable initiative as a businessman.... The demise of his bank could have occurred because Boka was not aware of the problems early enough." The banking sector was plunged into turmoil as a result of Boka's "remarkable initiative," which included forged CSC bills amounting to a cool Z$1.2 billion. An official report prepared by RBZ governor Leonard Tsumba and released in September 1998 revealed that the late Roger Boka had transferred nearly US$21 million (over Z$600 million) of suspected clients' money to his personal foreign bank accounts without following normal exchange control rules, i.e. he had circumvented the bank's foreign exchange department. He was also reported to have siphoned more than Z$500 million from his UMB to finance his other companies. The report stated that, "Documentation examined indicates that at least US$20.9 million could have been externalized.... There is no evidence that Boka paid the local currency equivalent relating to these transfers. It is therefore highly probable that depositors' funds were used for this purpose."

Thus, an unaccountable political elite bypassed laid-down banking procedures to advance the career of a favored son, and it ended in tears, for many. Dr. Tsumba's report blamed the laxity of supervisory and licensing regulations in Zimbabwe, which he said were ineffective. The victims, of course, were the ordinary depositors, many of them taken in by the evidence of political endorsement.

Roger Boka himself was quite a controversial economic empowerment proponent. In a series of full-page advertisements in the press, he charged that Zimbabwe's minority white community sought to keep blacks out of the country's mainstream economy. With the help of connections in high political circles, Boka systematically broke into critical sectors hitherto dominated by multinational corporations and all-white commercial outfits, most notably those of mining and tobacco marketing. He built the "largest tobacco auction floors" in the world. While viciously attacking Zimbabwe's minority whites, Boka found no irony in employing some "good enough whites" in his expanding mining and tobacco empire and in doing business with other whites; he must have realized that he would have to deal with them, because of the complexities of economic globalization.

In many ways, Roger Boka was a paradoxical figure. Although prone to manipulation by powerful political forces, he perhaps lived by example as a champion of black advancement. His meteoric ascendancy on a self-made corporate ladder created a conglomerate that soon rivaled long-established white-owned corporations, giving some hope to thousands of blacks he employed in a country choking on frighteningly high unemployment. His UMB, before it collapsed, helped many indigenous businesspersons access loans to start their ventures without collateral (as required by other banks) in an attempt to speed up indigenization. Indeed, most of those who borrowed from the bank never did manage to service their loans, and that contributed to the downfall of the financial house. Unfortunately, the banking crisis his actions triggered has tended to eclipse his good deeds. At his death at the end of February 1999, IBWO said that Boka was "deeply concerned with the economic empowerment of women and he did not hesitate to assist women in Zimbabwe." IBDC mourned the death of Roger Boka, describing him as a role model and man of action: "All the indigenous people of this country were following in his footsteps."

239

Ironically, Boka's vision to rescue Zimbabweans from poverty left most of the people and organizations to whom he lent money, and those who bought shares, uncovered for inspection by liquidators. Individuals had spent tens of thousands of zimdollars acquiring shares in the Boka Tobacco Auction Floors (BTAF). The IBWO was one of the organizations which bought thousands of shares from BTAF in the hope of profiting from the crop, which is considered Zimbabwe's "cash cow." There is no doubt that Boka's maverick lending practices to black-owned companies and individuals (especially influential people in government and ZANU (PF)) were intended to promote the indigenization crusade. However, as inevitably happens in such instances of political patronage, those at the top managed to get away, while the small fry who had borrowed money from the now defunct bank were asked to repay as a matter of urgency. The published list of debtors included names of well-known entrepreneurs, whose flourishing businesses would be at risk if they were required to repay the loans immediately. So much for helping indigenous people gain a stake in the mainstream economic infrastructure.

This was followed by two other major financial scandals involving the First National Building Society and the ENG Asset Management. Unfortunately, it is now an open secret that some locally-owned banks and asset management firms are used as conduits for money-laundering activities and speculative investments. Even the new governor of the RBZ, Gideon Gono, bemoaned that, "The underground nature of some asset management companies is evidenced by the fact they do not even have physical addresses or working contact phone numbers; which makes it all the more difficult to gather information about them."

Zimbabwe's banking sector has expanded from about 10 banks and asset management firms to more than 30 in just 12 years, and despite threatening insolvency they still manage to pump loans to the politically-connected.

Billions of dollars have gone into the creation of loss-making parastatals, which appear to have been set up as convenient factories for the creation of jobs for the party's favorite children, never mind their gross lack of expertise in the corporations' particular fields of operation. To this day, the huge budget deficit (against which the World Bank, the IMF, the European Union and all the other potential rescuers of Zimbabwe's tottering economy have railed), is partly due to the extravagant consumption habits of the parastatals. A typical example is the National Oil Company of Zimbabwe. Even Cde Chikoore, the Minister responsible for the parastatal, agreed in an interview in July 1998 that there was rampant corruption and yet chose not to take any action to put the house in order.

Many Zimbabweans wonder how, on the grossly inadequate remuneration packages of the public service, so many civil servants, members of parliament, ministers and their deputies and permanent secretaries have been able to acquire farms and large herds of cattle, diverse investments and business interests, and luxurious up-market residential properties for themselves and all their relatives. The government turns a blind eye to these signs of political patronage and corruption. In a speech delivered in July 1999 at a reception to mark the opening of Parliament, President Mugabe publicly acknowledged his awareness that some of his ministers were corrupt. He did so in a dismissive, almost jocular manner and apparently his audience found his comments a cause of great hilarity.

A few parastatals have been privatized or have had their government feeding tube narrowed somewhat. In essence, however, most of them operate under the aegis of a cabinet minister, whose own political agenda may be totally divorced from the company's performance. Most of these parastatals were and are quite often still being run by inept and corrupt party favorites, and in recent years they have acquired the new practice of firing executives and re-hiring them as "consultants." At the PTC, some of the top executives who were given hefty packages in October 1998 were re-hired as consultants; Jacob Makina was even appointed chairman of the board running the newly created ZimPost. Perhaps this practice can be traced back to 1995, after the late Dr. Bernard Chidzero had resigned his cabinet position as Senior Minister of Finance when Mugabe announced his appointment as consultant to the Ministry of Finance.

The government of Zimbabwe, both politically and administratively, operates on a well-oiled and well-rehearsed patronage system. Even the choice of private-company indigenous chief executives has less to do with the candidate's respective qualifications for the job and more to do with fulfilling political or personal promises, or laying the groundwork for a smooth patronage system. Once an appointment has been made, loyalty and obligation have been established and reciprocation must follow. The commercial and industrial landscape is littered with the legacies of black entrepreneurs who would have survived if the government had let them operate freely without demanding "pay-back" and fealty.

The appointees are, in many (if not most) cases, of low caliber. These people cannot excel in their functions and so are particularly beholden to the people who appointed them. They, in turn, make appointments based on the same criteria, partly to establish obligations to themselves and partly to conceal their own misdeeds by having leverage over their subordinates. Appointments in excess of the organization's requirements are also made by creating new positions, with titles like "minister of state."

At the very lowest echelons of power there is generally a pool of underpaid, dispirited and unmotivated administrative officers and employees who lack the connections to move up the ladder, and the resources and facilities to do their jobs properly. Some emulate their superiors and indulge in petty graft and corruption. It is not uncommon to find officers and employees selling eggs and chickens in their offices during working hours. Others battle on in impossible conditions or depart for the private sector. The universal guilt in itself prevents accountability, to a large extent, because even if a case of corruption is exposed, prosecution is rare. Witnesses are hard to come by, and in the event an official is prosecuted, the presidential pardon stifles justice.

Political patronage is also reflected in the upper structures of the army. The government poured out billions of dollars in October 2003 on fancy cars for top army generals and other officers, as well as on a fleet of trucks for ordinary soldiers — at a time when millions of Zimbabweans were facing starvation. The government's purchase of expensive 4x4 Pajeros for army officers and trucks to carry soldiers only, while the majority live in poverty and squalor, was widely criticized. Many Zimbabwean roads are in a poor state, and there are serious public transport problems in almost all of Zimbabwe's high-density suburbs, while other key services, such as State hospitals and clinics, and State colleges, have collapsed due to lack of funding.

The appointment of judges is also done on a patronage basis, which included the award of land leases and farms that were occupied during the land invasions — a move that was widely seen as compromising judicial independence. If the reputation of the judiciary has been tarnished, it could be because there is a growing perception that some judges are beholden to the executive; that they refuse to uphold rights to which applicants are constitutionally entitled; that they drag their heels in hearing cases where applicants expect early redress; and that they lean over backwards to accommodate the claims of the state, even when the state has difficulty making its case.

A typical example is in the (March 2002) presidential election challenge brought by the MDC leader, Morgan Tsvangirai against Mugabe. Before the case was due to be heard in the High Court on November 3, 2003, a High Court judge approved a petition by two senior government officials that allowed them to remove themselves from the case. (The Registrar-General, Tobaiwa Mudede, had been cited in his capacity as head of the body that conducts elections; the Minister of Justice, Patrick Chinamasa, was responsible for preparing Statutory Instruments and other orders under the Presidential Powers [Temporary Measures] Act that tilted the elections in the president's favor).

The net result of political patronization is corruption, massive devaluation of the currency, economic stagnation and high inflation. Pot-holed roads, a useless telephone service, power cuts and water cuts affect the efficient and smooth functioning of business, not to mention a rapidly escalating crime rate and the growth of armed and violent robberies which stem from ineffective policing and the desperation of the unemployed millions. Official lawlessness and contempt for the law by the public-sector management is filtering down to the general populace. The antics of Zimbabwe's commuter omnibus drivers probably originate here.

Worse, the race to influence the indigenization of the economy has assumed tribal connotations. It is understood there are factions within the government actively lobbying to create an informal hierarchy of the Zezuru clique. Obviously, this is unacceptable in a country as diverse as Zimbabwe.

Meanwhile, by the late 1990s the ruling ZANU (PF) party's leadership came under mounting pressure from members and its parliamentarians to produce audited statements of its finances — for the first time since independence. The party's balance sheet and investment portfolio were apparently privy to few individuals. In addition to taxpayer "contributions," ZANU (PF) receives donations from private companies anxious to have good relations with the ruling party. For example, during the 1996 presidential election campaign the party's legal secretary received Z$14 million from the late business tycoon Tiny Rowland.[140] Since the introduction of the controversial Political Parties (Finance) Act in 1992, up to the financial year ending December 1999, the party had received a total of Z$500 million in direct funding from taxpayers. Besides this direct funding from the state, ZANU (PF) has several investments through its holding company M&S Syndicate, which has business controlling vehicle sales, property investment, importation and distribution of industrial machinery, lamp bulbs, asbestos mining, water pumps and steel and building materials. Some of its firms have supply contracts with government departments such as the army, air force and central stores, and one supplies textbooks to schools and colleges throughout Zimbabwe.

---

140. *The Financial Gazette*, 21 May, 1998.

Sources within the Tax Department said, at the end of May 1998, that officials there were having difficulties in prosecuting some ZANU (PF) companies found to be defaulting in their tax payments. This department apparently conducted investigations into the tax affairs of some of these firms in 1997, but faced political interference when it tried to investigate companies owned by the ruling party.

Most Zimbabweans underestimate the negative effects of political patronage on the economy, choosing to ride the bandwagon — "if you can't beat them, join them." There seems to be a parallel with Indonesia, where friends and relatives of President Suharto secured special favors from state commissions and regulatory bodies on the pretext of putting ownership in local hands. National survival depends on keeping ownership and management of key economic sectors under domestic control, but it also depends on keeping corruption at a manageable level.

The murky agenda of groups such as the AAG and IBDC seems far more oriented to "grabbing" rather than building. It is difficult to perceive how share ownership in parastatals and quoted companies will help build black business, or how the color of the shareholders will affect the efficiency of their operation. What Zimbabwe desperately needs is the emergence of small- and medium-sized businesses, which prosper and grow under astute and honest management. Needed as well is education as to how businesses function, the dangers and benefits of loans (and the necessity of their repayment) and the discipline necessary to succeed. Too often, the end product of success is seen and not the hard work needed to get there. For the country to prosper and grow, an ever-increasing participation by indigenous entrepreneurs providing real goods and services is vital, together with the understanding that people earn money or make money, in contrast to the idea that people "get" money.

## CHAPTER 5. ECONOMIC REFORMS

### The Land-Reform Program

The economy of Zimbabwe is very much dependent on agricultural production, which contributes an annual average of about 15% of the country's gross domestic product (GDP) and is an important provider of raw materials for the industrial sector. Between 1965 and 1975, agricultural output rose by 75%, while its value more than doubled. Maize, tea, groundnuts (peanuts), potatoes, cotton and sugar were the main crops apart from tobacco, which was severely affected by UN sanctions, and there was much stock-raising. In 1974 primary products accounted for over 80% of exported revenue.

In 1980, two-thirds of the labor force were involved in agriculture (including forestry and fishing), which contributed 14% of GDP. Open trading on the world tobacco markets was resumed in early 1980 after its interruption by UN sanctions. Following disappointing prices for a low quality crop of 122,000 metric tons in 1980, a strict limit on production of 70,000 tons was introduced for 1981 and the high quality crop made tobacco Zimbabwe's largest foreign exchange earner that year. By 1984, agriculture contributed 11.4% of GDP with about 70% of the labor force engaged in the sector in 1985. However, its contribution declined to 12.9% of GDP in 1990, and employed 68% of the labor force.

Agriculture contributed 28% of GDP in 1998 and employed about 63.8% of the labor force in that year. In 1999, 60% of wage-earners were engaged in agriculture. During 1990-2000 agricultural GDP increased by an annual average of 3.8% while it grew by 4.9% in 1998, by 6.6% in 1999 and by 5.0% in 2000.[141]

Therefore, it is easy to understand why land, as a commodity, has been at the center of Zimbabwe's struggle since the First Chimurenga, during the 1890s. Beginning with BSAC (British South Africa Company) occupation of the country, land was being confiscated and sold to settlers and private companies according to special interests.

After the conclusion of the Ndebele War in 1894, a land commission was formed to investigate the problem of relocating the Ndebele people. In 1898, a British Order-in-Council reiterated the principle of assigning land to Africans. More than a hundred separate reserves of vastly different sizes were designated throughout the country by 1913.

The basic pattern of land allocation was firmly set by the early 1920s. The 1923 Constitution formalized the existing reserves. To "legalize" these activities, the Land Apportionment Act was passed in October 1930. This introduced the principle of racial segregation into land allocation throughout the country. Prior to this Act, the only racial element of official land allocation had been the creation of Native Reserves restricted to communal African occupation. The Land Apportionment Act defined six separate categories of land. The most important categories were Native Reserves, accounting for 22.4% of the whole country; Native Purchase Areas — 7.7%; European Areas — 50.8% (comprising virtually all high veldt land surrounding the railway lines and all major urban

---

141. *Europa World Year Book*, 2002, vol. II, London.

centers); and the "unassigned" areas, comprising 18.4%. (Zimbabwe's total land area is 390,582 km².)

In 1969, the Smith regime passed the Land Tenure Act, which replaced the Land Apportionment Act. Despite the fact that most European-owned farms were clearly under-utilized, the Rhodesian Front government sought a solution to the European "agricultural problem" by expanding the amount of land available to white farmers while more rigidly segregating African and European areas. The resulting Land Tenure Act converted most existing "unassigned land" into European areas, but otherwise made only minor changes in designated boundaries. The Act divided the country into three basic categories of land: European, African and "national" — the last comprising most of the national parks and game reserves. European and African areas were equalized, each with 46.6% of the total country. Forest, park and game reserve lands were also included in parts of the European and African areas, leaving 40% of the country available to European farms and settlements; 41.4% to Tribal Trust Lands; and 3.8% to Purchase Areas (a special category of land ownership reserved for black commercial farmers; the Shona term for "Purchase Area" is Kumatenganyika).

Thus, under the Land Tenure Act, about half of the country was reserved for Europeans and although the Act was repealed in 1979, this made little difference to the distribution of land. Communal lands comprised 41% (16,299,328ha) of the total land and supported over 80% of the total population. Commercial farming areas, on the other hand, comprised over 40% (15,194,456ha)[142] of the total land — owned by a mere 6,700 white farmers.

The land question (along with the electoral franchise) was one of the central issues which sparked and successfully concluded the war of liberation during the 1970s. Over-population, erosion and the results of the war only made the land hunger more acute. Land redistribution in the communal areas was a pressing need; but it had to be done without reducing the overall production of the commercial farms. Ironically, only 40% at most of the arable land on such farms was under cultivation. Some of this land was originally owned by black farmers, but was taken over for white use as recently as the 1960s.

In 1983, the independence government amended the constitution to change the term "Tribal Trust Lands" to "Communal Lands," but leaving the legal pattern of land distribution intact.[143] However, a major feature of the government's socio-economic program since independence had been land

---

142. Agricultural, Technical and Extension Services, Harare.
143. Constitution of Zimbabwe Amendment Act (No. 3).

resettlement. Under the terms of the Lancaster House Agreement, this required the purchase of land on a willing seller/willing buyer basis. Despite initial plans to resettle 162,000 families in three years and the development plan's aim to resettle 75,000 families in five years, a ministerial statement in 1988 admitted that only 40,000 families had been resettled since independence. Promises of accelerated land redistribution were a feature of the 1990 election campaign, based on the expiry of the Lancaster House Agreement in April 1990. It is known that Britain gave more than £47 million for land reform in the period 1980-96 — but few of the farms that were acquired found their way to the deserving poor. Most ended up in the hands of Mugabe's cronies.

Although the number of white farmers dropped to about 4,500, there was only limited African penetration of the commercial farming sector. In order to acquire 6 million of the 11 million hectares owned by the commercial sector, the government amended the constitution[144] to allow the government to fix its own price for compensating owners of commercial farms without right of appeal to the courts. And to permit the compulsory acquisition of land, Parliament enacted the Land Acquisition Act in March 1992.

To speed up resettlement, the Ministry of Agriculture, Lands and Water Development appointed a five-member Derelict Land Board in October 1992, to help in identifying derelict land and recommend it for resettlement or other purposes. Maximum use of derelict land had been one of the calls of both commercial and small-scale farmers, who argued that the government should not rush to take away land from farmers in production while there were large tracts of land not being used. Land belonging to absentee owners had already been identified for resettlement and more land belonging to deregistered cooperatives had been designated for resettlement in September 1992. Some of it had already resorted to State-land and had been earmarked for resettlement. In February 1993, a Masvingo provincial land committee identified ten farms which it said were under-utilized. Six of the farms were said to be owned by government ministers.

In 1994, it emerged that acquired land-leases for large state-owned farms were being given to political insiders instead of the landless peasants; in reaction to local and external pressure for accountability, the government canceled land-leases for large state-owned farms that had been given to 98 ZANU (PF) associates. Parliamentary pressure resulted in publication of the full list of 345

---

144. Constitution of Zimbabwe Amendment (No.11) Bill, passed by Parliament on December 12, 1990.

white and black tenant farmers involved in the program. These state farms were being leased for as little as Z$5,000, compared to the commercial rate of Z$100,000 per annum for a tobacco farm.[145]

In October 1997, President Mugabe announced that the hitherto slow pace of the land resettlement program would be accelerated, declaring that the constitutional right of white commercial farmers to receive full and fair compensation for confiscated land would not be honored and challenging the British, in their role as former colonial power, to take responsibility for assisting them. A list of 1,503 properties to be reallocated was published in November.

Between 1984 and 1997, villagers from Chihwiti, Nyamatsitu and Mhondoro communal lands repeatedly invaded properties that the state had leased to white commercial farmers. In each instance, the government evicted these landless villagers by force. In June 1998, the Svosve people of the Marondera and Wedza districts undertook a series of illegal farm occupations. In August, ZANU (PF) introduced the second phase of the program to resettle 150,000 families on one million hectares of land each year for the next seven years, and at the "Land Conference" in Harare in September the country launched an international appeal for Western donors to support its land reform. But when the UNDP decided, after the Harare donors' conference, that the land redistribution was chaotic, donors felt they could no longer justify funding a program that lacked transparency, failed to address poverty alleviation, and undermined self-sufficiency in food production.

Under pressure, the government agreed to reduce its plans, and was restricted to using 118 farms which it had already been offered. In November, nonetheless, 841 white-owned farms were ordered to be confiscated by the state. Compensation was to be deferred.

Pressure exerted by the IMF in light of a forthcoming release of aid brought an assurance from President Mugabe that his administration would not break agreements for a gradual land-reform program. Yet, despite the public's and Western financial institutions' call for transparency in the land-reform program (which involved about 1,500 farms designated in December 1998), insiders continued to snap up acreage in the rich Mashonaland West province, thereby depriving thousands of congested communal farmers of arable land. This came against a background of farm invasions in nearby Mhondoro by disgruntled peasants who had lost confidence in the government's land redistribution drive.

---

145. *New African*, London, Sept. 1994.

At the center of the controversy was Coburn Estates, bought from Rob Patterson in 1997. The farmer used to have 3,500 acres under summer crops and 1,500 acres of winter crops. With a 300-strong workforce, he used to produce some 130,000 bags of maize a year and could produce more food than all the Mhondoro/Ngezi communal lands put together.[146] The prominent settlers at the farm were said to include the deputy Speaker of Parliament and MP for Chegutu East, an assistant commissioner of police, TA Holdings former chief executive, a director in the Ministry of Environment and Tourism, a provincial veterinary officer in the Ministry of Agriculture, two businessmen, a chief security officer with the Harare city council and two government officials.

Other farms in the area include Buttercombe Farm, where a Harare City councilor's lease was challenged by neighboring peasants. There were strong suspicions that the councilor was in a joint venture with a top government official. A Higher Education Minister was known to lease nearby Littleton Farm, which neighboring peasants also threatened to invade. Then there was the Stanhope Estate, which was lying under-utilized after having been allocated to some businessmen. It was split into four parts and allocated to four tenants, of whom two were prominent Harare bankers.

At the end of March 1999, the President contravened the agreement for an orderly distribution of land when he announced a new plan to acquire a further 529 white-owned farms. He accused the USA and the UK of "destabilizing" Zimbabwe through their control over the IMF, which was delaying financial assistance to the country. Mugabe then threatened that Zimbabwe would sever its relations with the IMF and the World Bank, although the Minister of Finance continued to hope that further aid would be released shortly. In May 1999, the government agreed a plan which aimed to resettle 77,700 families on one million hectares by 2001. The plan was to be partially funded by the World Bank, and was broadly accepted by the Commercial Farmers' Union (CFU).

In late February 2000, the "war veterans" (many of whom were too young to have participated in the liberation war) began to occupy white-owned farms. Suddenly, the implementation of land reform became urgent. It is quite clear that this urgency was artificially created by the government. It had shelved an important national agenda for over two decades. The spontaneous land invasions by the Svosve people in 1998 were a stark revelation, but instead of seizing on the initiative of the Svosve people, the government's reaction was to crush the revolt. Thus, the 2000 land invasions can be seen as a ploy to regain

---

146. *The Zimbabwe Independent*, 31 December, 1998.

support after the humiliating defeat in the constitutional referendum and before the general election due later that year.

The police refused to act against the occupiers, declaring that the "political issue" lay outside their jurisdiction. A ruling by the High Court in mid-March in favor of the white farmers was ignored by the war veterans, and the police failed to take steps to evict the "protesters." The President repeatedly denied that his administration was behind the occupations but made no secret of his support for them. The invasion became increasingly violent, and two farmers were killed in April. A few days before, Mugabe had threatened violence against farmers who refused to give up their land voluntarily, and following the violence he declared that they were "enemies of the state." The international community condemned this increasingly militant stance, which also extended to the treatment of the opposition, in particular the MDC, which was subjected to a campaign of intimidation and aggression.

A constitutional amendment approved in April 2000, shortly before the dissolution of Parliament to prepare for elections, stated that white farmers dispossessed of their land would have to apply to the "former colonial power' for compensation. Many farmers were aggrieved, as their land had been purchased under Zimbabwean law. Chaos reigned.

In mid-May, Mugabe met with war veterans and the CFU and announced the creation of a land commission to redistribute farmland. Shortly afterwards, however, he signed a law allowing the seizure of 841 white-owned farms without compensation. In early June, a list was published of 804 farms to be confiscated. Farmers were to be granted approximately one month to contest the list. Later in June, Mugabe also threatened to seize foreign-owned companies and to nationalize mines.

Shortly after the June 24-25 general election, Mugabe announced that some 500 additional white-owned farms would be appropriated for resettlement. In December 2000, a court ruling upheld previous opinions that declared the appropriation of white-owned farms without compensation payments to be unlawful, and urged the government to produce a feasible land-reform program by June 2001. However, the President announced that he would not accept court-imposed impediments to any further land-reform measures.

Zimbabwe's Chief Justice, Antony Gubbay, came under pressure for his ruling in the Supreme Court. He announced in February 2001 that he would retire some months ahead of schedule, in June, following allegations of government intimidation. He shortly rescinded his decision, but there was intensive negotiations for him to retire with immediate effect in March. His agreement was reportedly secured in exchange for a promise by the government not to seek reprisals against other judges who had opposed its actions. Gubbay was succeeded by Godfrey Chidyausiku, who was a former Deputy Minister in the Ministry of Justice, Legal and Parliamentary Affairs, and was believed to be a close ally of Mugabe.

The new land acquisition laws introduced after the land invasions of early 2000 brought with them problems of accountability and transparency. In December 2001, uncertainty gripped the commercial farming sector following the announcement by the government that about 800 commercial farms would be acquired, with just three months' time to vacate. According to the amendments to the Land Acquisition Act, farmers served with acquisition orders could remain on the farm but were confined to their houses, which they would vacate within three months. A CFU spokesperson said: "Farmers have invested billions of dollars on the crops planted this season and will make serious losses if they leave the crops on the farms."[147] About 700 commercial farmers were issued with farm acquisition orders countrywide, as the government fast-tracked the land reform program.

Top government officials who were demanding the immediate eviction of the farm owners were grabbing some farms, themselves. The intended beneficiaries of the land reform program, especially farm workers, were not being resettled. Even the chairman of the National Land Committee and Minister of Local Government and National Housing, were reportedly embroiled in a wrangle over Erewhon and Nswala farms in the Lomagundi district. A provisional High Court order protecting Jean Simpson's farming operations did not help.

The allocation of land occupied by the so-called war veterans continued in September 2002, with ministers, ZANU (PF)-aligned chiefs, public servants and police officers receiving farms.

Some of the beneficiaries of land handouts under the A2 commercial farming scheme are relatives of top government officials, Cabinet ministers and Members of Parliament. The VIP land allocations list belied the official line that the land resettlement program was transparent and designed for the benefit of the landless. One of the Vice-Presidents was reported to have taken over part of Umguza Block owned by the financially troubled Cold Storage Company, while the other one was taking over Chindito and Endama farms in Gutu. The farm

---

147. *The Daily News*, Harare, 29 Dec. 2001.

belonged to Mr. Chris Nel Smit, who was reported to be negotiating for a compensation of about Z$15 million for the farm's assets.[148]

Thousands of people who registered for land and whose names appeared in the press just before the Presidential Election as having been allocated land were still waiting for it. Hundreds of land-hungry peasants, most of them unconnected to top government officials, had meanwhile been ordered to vacate the farms they had invaded after March 31, 2001.

The stated goals of the fast-track land reform program were to resettle people from densely populated communal rural areas to newly acquired farmland, and to "achieve optimal utilization of land and natural resources and to promote equitable access to land to all Zimbabweans." However, despite Mugabe's statement in July 2002 that decongestion of communal areas had been achieved, rural areas are still densely populated. For instance, in Chiweshe, people are still packed together like jailbirds. Chiweshe District, in the sprawling Mashonaland Province, is a region renowned for its rich soil, but Chiweshe, with a population of more than 100,000, had less than 1,000 people resettled. A government minister acknowledged that no resettlement had occurred in Chiweshe from the early 1980s, when the government began land redistribution. The area was also overlooked during the second resettlement phase, in the 1990s. A similar scenario can be found in the other provinces: Manicaland, Masvingo and the Midlands.

Professor Sam Moyo, a land expert, said that there was considerable lack of decongestion in some areas. "Some farmers under the commercial farming A2 model have excessive pieces of land, with some of them owning two to three farms each. This obviously tends to limit decongestion," Moyo said. The main culprits were apparently provincial governors, provincial administrators and district administrators as well as the land committees tasked with the processing of applications and the allocation of land. Disgruntled would-be beneficiaries have complained that the government officials ask for bribes and other favors in return for a recommendation of their applications. In other cases, it has been alleged that they favored friends and relatives or supporters of the ruling ZANU (PF) party. Also worrying are the revelations that the Libyans had acquired vast tracts of prime land, whose location the ZANU (PF) government was keeping secret. As if that were not enough, they also secured hunting concessions and then service stations and hotels; and there was talk of giving them the Mutare-to-Harare oil pipeline and the Msasa fuel storage facilities.[149]

---

148. *Ibid.*, Harare, 23 May, 2002.

Mashonaland Central's Mount Darwin District also voiced her concern about the lack of resettlement in the area. The province, which is also blessed with fertile soils, is home to more than a million people. However, Elliot Manyika, the governor of the province and Minister of Gender, Youth and Employment Creation, admitted that only about 15,000 people from the province had been resettled.

In Mashonaland West's Banket area, concern was raised that ZANU (PF) loyalists were using their political influence to obtain farming plots for their children (some of whom were still going to school) under the communal or A1 resettlement program. John Mautsa, the director of the Indigenous Commercial Farmers' Union, said: "We are aware of families being involved in the multi-ownership scandal. However, the problem is difficult to stem because some of the culprits use different names."

In mid-August 2003, 1,000 settlers at Little England Farm (under Burney Investments) in Zvimba (Mashonaland West) were stunned when they were ordered to vacate the property to make way for the widow of President Mugabe's late nephew, Innocent Mugabe, along with 68 State House officials and 21 "selected settlers." Barely a day later, some 5,000 settlers from Chief Nyavira's area in the same Zvimba district were ordered to vacate farms that the government had allowed them to occupy in 2000.

One thousand homes belonging to villagers resettled by the government at Windcrest Farm (near Masvingo City) were burned down; this must have brought back to many Zimbabweans painful memories of the British South African Police (BSAP), who had ransacked and burnt villages to make way for the new white land owners. Now, on August 25, 2003, the police destroyed homes and property worth an estimated Z$100 million at the farm — all in a bid to force the resettled peasant families to make way for a government insider who wanted the farm for himself and his family.

When the fast-track program started, the government said it intended to resettle more than a million people over a three-year period. However, it appeared the program had been hijacked by those with political connections. Still, the Minister of State for the Land Reform Programme, Flora Buka, played down allegations of corruption in the land redistribution exercise saying, "Concerning allegations of corruption in the provincial land committees, I do not have evidence. I can't act on the basis of speculation."[150]

---

149. The Libyans want to acquire the fuel pipeline, storage facilities, service stations and rail loading facilities at Feruka to make Zimbabwe their distribution centre in southern Africa, currently dominated by Iranians, Saudis and Kuwaitis.

No sooner had the Minister uttered these words than her ministry produced a damning report. Dated January 2003, their land audit highlights the systematic looting of prime farms by senior government officials and ZANU (PF) cronies. A reliable source said, "The report authenticates reports that government officials and ZANU (PF) cronies have corruptly awarded themselves more than one farm in various provinces. Names of several top government officials, army, police and CIO officers and many others are appearing in several provinces. In short, the report paints a classic picture of looting that has characterized the affairs of the party over the years."[151]

Thus, it came as no surprise on July 30, 2003, when none other than President Mugabe ordered top officials with multiple farms to surrender them within a fortnight. Mugabe was reacting to a preliminary report by the Presidential Land Review Committee, led by Charles Utete, the former Cabinet Secretary. Without mentioning any names (touted by President Mugabe as the committee's primary focus), the committee accused top ruling party officials of being "proud owners of several farms." Politicians had acquired several farms and registered them in the names of their children, mothers, sisters, and brothers.

Indeed, before the ink was even dry on the Utete Committee report, there was already a whiff of panic within the ranks of politicians and civil servants — some of whom should have known better, as they were the architects of the government policy of "one man, one farm." Matabeleland North Provincial Administrator Livingstone Mashengele, who doubled up as the chairman of the Joint Operations Committee on land, confirmed that there were more than 50 multiple-farm owners in the province:

> I have been told that ministers, politburo and central committee members with more than one farm in the province and other provinces have to report to the President when surrendering their extra farms. So I cannot comment on these people, it is not my area of jurisdiction. What I can tell you is that my committee is going to interview more than 50 people who appear on a list that we have prepared. It is at this meeting that they will decide which farm to keep or let go.[152]

By taking a scythe to illegal multiple-farm ownership, the government was trying to shore up the credibility of the controversial land reform and endear

---

150. *The Daily News*, Harare, 23 May 2002

151. *New Zealand Herald*, 29 March, 2003.

152. *The Financial Gazette*, 11 September, 2003.

itself to a skeptical public that has long dismissed the reform as a sham. It remained to be seen whether the government would expose all the multiple-farm owners irrespective of their positions in government and the ruling party.

The audit by the Joint Operation Committee on Land, which comprised the police, army, Lands and Resettlement and local government officials, was the third such audit following that made by the Presidential Land Review Committee and the Ministry of State for the Land Reform Programme before it.

After the euphoria that accompanied the initial wave of violent farm seizures that signaled the onset of this political storm, the mood, especially among the landless who were meant to be the beneficiaries, had now lapsed into skepticism. ZANU (PF) insiders were accused of acquiring several farms per individual, and the allegations provoked strong reactions even among the government's longstanding sympathizers and supporters. Officials tried to explain this away by saying that "the law of the unintended" took hold when senior politicians in ZANU (PF) helped themselves. It was, however, widely believed that the authorities' deafening silence over allegations of corruption in the land reform process suggested a tacit approval. It was only in the second quarter of 2003 that President Mugabe, probably realizing that the scandal was too large to be swept under the carpet, belatedly appointed former senior civil servant Charles Utete to head the Presidential Land Review Committee to investigate cases of multiple-farm ownership.

As of mid-January-2003, the government claimed to have resettled over 300,000 families under the A1 model scheme as well as about 51,000 others under the A2 model scheme.[153] However, in April, Agriculture Minister Joseph Made revised the figures down to 210,000 settlers under the A1 scheme and 14,880 under A2.[154] This discrepancy raised questions as to how well the scheme was being monitored. (The Presidential Land Review Committee gives 127,192 under A1 and 7,260 under A2.)

In Matabeleland South, only 117 A2 farmers had moved onto their allocated plots (out of a possible 2,259). In Mashonaland West province, which used to produce an estimated 40% of the country's major crops such as maize, tobacco and wheat, plots were lying idle with no production or land preparation having been done. Manicaland had the highest uptake at about 60%, with Mashonaland East province registering less than 40%. Agriculture Minister Joseph Made said that the government had so far acquired 11 million hectares of land as the fast-

---

153. *The Zimbabwe Standard*, 19 January, 2003.
154. *The Sunday Mail*, 20 April, 2003.

track land-reform program purportedly came to an end. He said that a total of 2,670 farms measuring 5,069,782ha had been acquired under the A1 model and 2,209 farms measuring 4,934,892ha acquired for the A2 model.[155] (The Presidential Land Review Committee gives 2,652 farms measuring 4,231,080ha under A1 and 1,672 farms measuring 2,198,814ha under A2.) By the end of September 2003, white farmers owned 1,377 farms,[156] or roughly 1.2 million hectares (3% of the whole country).

The poor land uptake resulted in more than 60% of land that is normally put under crop lying idle. It became increasingly clear that the newly-resettled farmers would not, in the near future, produce enough food for the country. The government was estimating a maize production of 570,000 tonnes from the season's planted hectares. The output constituted less than a third of what the country requires to bridge two marketing seasons. [157]

The wheat crop is also severely affected by changes in the land tenure system. Zimbabwe consumes some 400,000 tonnes of wheat annually, most of it local. In 2002, less than 150,000 tonnes of wheat were produced, down from 360,000 tonnes in 2001; this resulted in severe bread shortages. The cropping area also fell to less than 40,000 hectares. Normally, about 50,000 tonnes are imported as gristling wheat.

The 2002-03 agricultural season was generally poor, and then the often chaotic land-reform program resulted in the displacement of over 3,000 highly-mechanized commercial farmers, reducing by 45% the area under cultivation (compared to any other year including 2001-02 season, the peak of farm invasions).

In January 2004, President Mugabe appointed yet another committee (a 5-member national committee), known as the Presidential Land Resettlement Committee, to beef up the Land Review Taskforce led by Special Affairs Minister John Nkomo. However, given the policy contradictions and blunders, not even the amendments to the Land Acquisition Act,[158] committees of inquiry,

---

155. *The Zimbabwe Independent*, 14 February, 2003.

156. JAG said the situation on the ground indicated that between 500 to 600 farmers were still on their properties while less than 200 of them were still involved in production.

157. Zimbabwe requires 1.8 million tonnes, excluding 500,000 tonnes strategic grain reserves every year. Government estimated a deficit of 1.09 million tonnes for the 2003/04 marketing year.

158.The government began to confiscate farms on the basis of a presidential decree in 2000, followed by the Land Acquisition (Amendment) Bill in November 2000, with further amendments to facilitate the forcible eviction of defiant farmers passed in September 2002 and November 2003. Another presidential decree in December gave government powers to compulsorily acquire farming equipment that dispossessed farmers were holding in warehouses. Thus the government sought to resolve the shortage of tillage implements and other on-farm infrastructure.

and the purging of the judiciary could improve production. Farming requires proper financing and planning, which were conspicuously absent since the farm invasions in 2000. The tinkering with the legislation has failed to address the fundamental issue of security of tenure, which is crucial to securing funding. Without the title deeds, which are still held by their white owners, black farmers cannot obtain bank loans.

Zimbabwe exacerbated the situation by failing to provide the much-needed inputs to the resettled farmers, including draught power to till the virgin land and seed for those whose land was tilled. The nation required 80,000 tonnes each of basal and top dressing fertilizer, but as of December, the government had managed to deliver only 59% and 33% respectively.

The displaced commercial farmers used to contribute 90% of the country's seed requirement; now, the demand for maize seed increased from 32,000 metric tonnes to 87,000 metric tonnes. However, there had not been a matching increase in production. It cost the country US$2,000 (Z$1.65 million) to import a metric tonne of maize seed, which put the total bill at about US$110 million (Z$90.6 billion). The 2003-04 agricultural season was in doubt as the 37,000 metric tonnes of maize seed in store could not meet the national requirement. There was no foreign currency to secure imports needed to cover the deficit, estimated at 50,000 metric tonnes.

The Tripartite Negotiating Forum in its deliberations acknowledged that the land was being under-utilized because of unrealistic and unavailable producer prices. "Farmers need to be assured of viable producer prices through a system of pre-planting and post-harvest price announcement," the TNF said.[159]

Meanwhile, Justice for Agriculture estimated that about 750,000 people who lived and worked on Zimbabwe's formerly white-owned farms were now destitute. The end of commercial agriculture had produced a massive humanitarian crisis. It is hard to arrive at solid statistics, but with only about 600 white farmers remaining on their land, more than 4,000 other white-run farms were closed down and their work forces dispersed.

Before President Mugabe began seizing white-owned farms at the beginning of 2000, about two million farm workers and their families were supported. Commercial farmers employed about 300,000 workers, with an annual wage of Z$15.1 billion. The closure of 90% of the farming sector resulted in a loss of Z$13.6 billion in wages for the farm workers, most of whom had been

---

159. TNF is a tripartite grouping established in 1998 and comprising representatives from the government, employers and labor.

left out of the land redistribution program.[160] Statistics released by the government showed that only about 10% of former farm workers were beneficiaries of the land reform program.

According to the February 2003 report of the United States-based Famine Early Warning Systems Network, the number of farm workers and their dependants affected by the fast-track resettlement program rose sharply, from 488,000 in August 2002 to one million in December of the same year. Almost all the farm workers lost their jobs and their homes as farm invasions and work stoppages were ordered by the ruling ZANU (PF) Party. Many primary schools in the commercial farming areas, which had been supported by the farmers, closed down. Most of the farmers who were forced to abandon their properties without compensation fully paid off their workforce. However, needless to say, most of the benefits paid to the workers quickly ran out (as two non-governmental organizations have estimated). The General Plantation and Allied Workers Union of Zimbabwe (GPAWUZ) said few of the dispossessed farm workers were likely ever to work again.

Agricultural experts had warned the government that Zimbabwe would face serious food shortages in 2002 if it embarked on the "haphazard" land reform program. The chaos triggered Zimbabwe's worst food crisis, which left more than seven million people (more than half the population) in need of imported emergency food aid. Notwithstanding Mugabe's public outbursts against Western donors, government had been approaching them behind the scenes. In July 2003, the government, through the finance ministry, implored the WFP to provide food relief and drugs. Harare submitted requests for 600,000 tonnes of food aid, a large consignment of medicines, and Z$885 billion for the revival of the agricultural sector. The donor community, predominantly made up of Western countries, was reportedly reluctant to bail out Harare due to the political stalemate. Mugabe also turned to the Far East for help, but there was nothing to show for his forays to Hong Kong, Malaysia, Thailand and Vietnam.

Furthermore, stock-feed producers like Agrifoods reported that they were affected by the impact of drought and the controversial government land-reform program that led to the shortage of major inputs such as wheat, maize and cotton. By April 2003, Agrifoods was meeting less than 50% of farmers' demand for stock-feed. Output of beef stock-feed, for example, declined from 1,500 tonnes to 250 tonnes a week in March 2003, forcing Agrifoods to import raw materials in a bid to boost production. The shortages contributed to milk

---

160. *The Financial Gazette*, 10 October, 2002.

shortages, while production of pork products had declined as the number of slaughtered pigs fell from the normal 250,000 a year to 95,000 in 2002. Farmers said some livestock producers had been forced to slaughter their animals because they could not feed them.

The commercial beef herd was reported to have fallen from 1.4 million in 2000 to about 125,000 head of cattle in December 2003.[161] (The Cattle Producers' Association estimated that in Masvingo only about 1,000 beef cattle had survived out of the 54,000 in the province.) Poultry output had fallen by 60%, leading to a drop in the export of day-old chicks and frozen chickens to Mozambique, Botswana, Malawi, Uganda, Ivory Coast and the DRC.

Agricultural research stations, key components of the country's agro-industry, were collapsing owing to the farm evictions, prompting donors to hold back funding, it was reported in August 2003. Zimbabwe had some of the most advanced research institutes on the continent, especially in grain seed development, improvement of cattle breeds, and skills training. The research stations in all the country's provinces were funded by commercial farmers through levies while international donors provided equipment and expatriate expertise. Government-sponsored research stations were almost defunct because of budgetary constrains due to lack of funding from donors. Officials at the Agricultural Research Trust Farm said they had stopped all off-station trials for the new seed varieties since the farmers who used to grow the seeds had been evicted. As a result, the new varieties were no longer being tested in the different regional climatic conditions in the country.

The seizure of commercial farms by government officials ran counter to the Abuja Agreement signed by Zimbabwe on September 6, 2001, which called for a transparent land reform program. Commercial agriculture earnings in real terms were down by 8.4% in 1999-2000 and fell by another 7.9% in 2000-01 due to the disturbances (Hondo yeMinda). Commercial farms produced between 40 and 50% of the total maize crop under normal circumstances while CFU members produced 80% of the flue-cured tobacco crop. Tobacco contributed about 40% to the country's foreign currency earnings.

Only about 600 white commercial farmers were left out of a total of 4,500 farming in Zimbabwe. CFU deputy director Gerry Grant said 98% of the farmers had been evicted from their properties by the government since the start of the often violent reforms in February 2000. The commercial farmers lost close to

---

161. The national herd is said to have dwindled from 5.1 million in 1998 to 125,000 in 2003 due to drought, foot-and-mouth disease, shortages of stock feeds and destocking by most farmers due to the land reform programme.

Z$50 billion in movable assets and property. As of February 2003, the government had managed to compensate 126 farmers out of over 3,500 displaced at the height of the land seizures. It was reported that even those 126 farmers did not get full compensation.

According to farming industry officials, over 400 farmers left Zimbabwe permanently and more than 3,200 had migrated into towns and cities. Growing numbers of white farmers settled in Zambia, bringing more than US$100 million in investments with them. It was estimated that Zimbabwean investments would raise tobacco production there from 4 million kilograms a year to 20 million kilograms within five years. In March 2003, the Zambia Investment Centre said it had received 125 applications from Zimbabwe farmers seeking to settle in Zambia. The white farmers also fled to other nearby countries, notably Mozambique, and helped shore up their rural economies. The Nigerian state of Kwara was offering commercial farmers from Zimbabwe and South Africa, mostly of British origin, land to invest and resettle, and some expelled farmers are growing cotton in Kigumba sub-county in the Masindi district of Uganda.

Court orders barring some farmers from being evicted from their properties were ignored by those overseeing the allocation of land to newly resettled black farmers. This was also despite a High Court interim ruling in Bulawayo on October 4, 2002, by Judge Misheck Cheda ordering police in Matabeleland provinces to stop evicting any farmers until the administrative court had confirmed the government's acquisition of farms and the evictions had been served properly. The order also stated that any farmer being unlawfully evicted from his farm should be permitted to stay on the property.

Despite Agriculture Ministry claims to the contrary, compulsory land acquisition continued even after August 2003. At the end of November, the government gazetted (decreed) an amending legislation, the Land Acquisition Bill, which sought to amend the principal Act. This would empower the government to acquire plantations and farms engaged in large-scale production of tea, coffee, timber, citrus fruit and sugar cane, on a compulsory basis. It would also empower the government to acquire land which has Export Processing Zone status or agro-businesses with Zimbabwe Investment Centre certificates.

Another decree allows the government to confiscate millions of dollars worth of agricultural equipment owned by former farmers who have already been dispossessed of their land and homes. The equipment includes combine harvesters, tractors, irrigation equipment, cultivators and harrows, and materials such as fertilizers and chemicals. The Bill states:

> The total hectarage of land required for resettlement purposes specified in the land reform programme is indicative only of the minimum hectarage of such land; accordingly, the acquiring authority is not prevented by that programme from acquiring land in excess of the hectarage so specified... For public information, it is declared that the state intends to acquire not less than 11 million hectares of agricultural land for resettlement purposes in terms of the land reform programme.

The proposed legislation would also repeal the Hippo Valley Agreement Act of 1964. The Act facilitated and protected massive investments in crop production and processing by Anglo American Corporation in the Lowveld.

If the Bill were passed into law in its current form, it would be a major threat to the huge sugar and citrus projects pioneered by Sir Raymond Stockil in the 1950s and 1960s in the Lowveld. Already, sugar estates in Mkwasine and Triangle have been occupied and partitioned for resettlement. The Bill contrasts sharply with recommendations of the Utete Land Review Committee which said land under exotic forests should not be resettled.

"Given the high level of vertical integration, the long gestation period and the contribution to the national economy of the exotic plantation forestry industry, it is recommended that land in this category should be maintained in the current state without any fragmentation," the Committee recommended.

These controversial policies are reflected in the decrease in agricultural production.

Out of the 11.02 million hectares under commercial farming prior to the advent of the fast-track land reform exercise, only 220,400 hectares remain unlisted for compulsory acquisition: just 2% of what used to be Zimbabwe's commercial farmland. According to the CFU, the remaining area would produce not more than 5% of national requirements.

Zimbabwe's commercial farm production was valued at Z\$69 billion, representing 14% of the country's GDP. Commercial agriculture contributed US\$765 million in exports in 2001, or 38% of Zimbabwe's total exports. Already the seizure of white-owned farms had slashed output from the sector by more than 50% in 2002, affecting local companies that rely on farmers for raw materials and markets. It was predicted that the decline in agricultural output by about 60% in 2003 would lead to a steady contraction of industry as the decline in commercial farming feeds through to the rest of the economy.

Soya bean production from the commercial sector in the 2003 season was projected at 60,000 tonnes, down from 170,000 tonnes. The output of tobacco, the single biggest earner of critically-short foreign exchange, dropped to 80.2

million kilograms in 2003, from 166 million kilograms in 2002 (216 million in 2001 and 236 million kilograms in 2000); tobacco netted US$179 million in 2003 compared to US$372 million in 2002. The Zimbabwe Tobacco Association membership, dominated by large-scale commercial farmers, dropped from a little more than 1,000 to about 350, as many farmers were evicted.

There were fears that production would hit record-low levels during the 2003-04 agricultural season due to ever-increasing prices of inputs. (The ZTA was forecasting a crop of 60 million kilograms.) Prices of basic inputs such as fertilizers, chemicals, seeds and fuel for draught power had increased by at least 300% over the past three months to August 2003. A bag of ammonium nitrate fertilizer cost Z$45,000, up from Z$18,000. Another stumbling block was that the retail outlets and private tillage providers were not accepting personal nor travelers cheques, forcing most farmers to reduce the land under crop to very small pieces.

Maize output, which fell by 60% partly as a result of drought, was seen collapsing further because the new black farmers did not have farm inputs. The wildlife industry, another foreign currency earner (through the sale of animal products as well as hunting and photographic safaris), lost more than Z$6 billion worth of animals between 2000 and 2002 because of rampant poaching during the land seizures. And Zimbabwe was denied permission to sell ivory stocks accumulated over the last five years to 2002 by the United Nations Convention on International Trade in Endangered Species.

Officials with Wildlife and Environment Zimbabwe said statistics collected by one of the country's largest conservancies, Bubiana, indicated that local game ranches were battling a serious crisis. At least 70% of wildlife had been lost to poaching since the end of 2002. Bubiana conservancy alone, an intensive breeding area for the endangered black rhino, lost 362 animals between 2000 and 2002. Environmentalists said it would take several years for the industry to regain resources lost through poaching and as a result of the land invasions, which led to the clearing of vegetation and tree felling by villagers and war veterans as they built their homesteads. This resulted in habitat loss and was expected to cause soil erosion in some areas and other environmental problems that will cost the country dearly to repair.

Official government statistics show that more than 300,000 families have been resettled on over 2,900 farms acquired from the whites. The new farmers require schools, clinics and roads. More than Z$160 billion is needed to complete the agrarian reforms, with at least 60% of the amount going towards infrastructure development.[162] With the rain season at its peak in January 2003, most of the land the government had confiscated was lying idle; the resettled people had no resources to work it. The government's efforts to raise Z$64 billion through an Agri-bond failed dismally as only Z$10 billion was raised. And Western donors, led by the IMF and the World Bank, severed economic ties with Harare in 1999 in retaliation for Mugabe's decision to expropriate white-owned farms to resettle landless blacks.

In sum, the rapacious land grabbing by senior government officials and their cronies has rendered the entire program suspect, and their revolutionary credentials as well.

### Economic Liberalization

After a decade of socialist experimentation with economic development in Zimbabwe, the government finally realized that the policy of centralized planning was not working. Initially, people were given to believe that the Economic Structural Adjustment Programme (ESAP), introduced in 1991, was Dr. Bernard Chidzero's brain-child. Since he was the Senior Minister of Finance and Economic Development and had previously worked in the United Nations, it was his duty to put the crippled socialist economy back on its feet. However, economic analysts would like to believe that this was the IMF's economic therapy as exposed in many countries in Africa, Asia and Latin America. Ghana and Tanzania had been through it all before.

For almost two decades, African states have been implementing economic structural adjustment programs that are promoted as being aimed at establishing a foundation for sustained economic growth. However, even in countries which have been regarded as good examples in implementing those policy prescriptions, economic take-off has been elusive. Since the mid-80s, most sub-Saharan countries have embraced the Western prescriptions, some of which were political liberalization and correcting past macroeconomic mistakes. Those African countries that have followed agreed policy have done well, in terms of loans; lending to Africa increased by nearly two-thirds in 1997 to US$2.9 billion.

However, African countries should start seeing and realizing sustainable solutions to their economic problems in themselves, otherwise they will become nations of foreign aid junkies. Although Africa can welcome financial aid from the IMF and other Western donor countries, it must be with the knowledge that foreign assistance will not move the continent out of its economic quagmire.

---

162. *The Financial Gazette*, 3 October, 2002.

Foreign aid without an underlying commitment to transform the way business is done is simply money down the drain.

To start with, export competitiveness is the key to a sustainable build-up of foreign exchange reserves, even if it means giving export and tax incentives to local industrialists reeling from the prevailing macroeconomic instability. Industrialists should continue to lobby governments for export incentives and a better economic environment.

With financial "donations" from the IMF and the West, most of the countries on the African continent had attained or were on the way to achieving macroeconomic stability by 1995. They adopted realistic exchange rates, removed price controls, freed interest rates and allowed trade liberalization. Loss-making parastatals were not just reformed, some were sold to private owners — a process that is still gathering momentum in Zimbabwe.

Despite these measures, however, there was no sign that the continent was about to experience a firm economic upturn. Experience has shown that even in Latin America and Asia, structural programs have not achieved the desired goals. Thus, the commitment and sincerity of the IMF and World Bank in promoting genuine economic development is highly doubtful. History shows that, in the whole development of the capitalist system (to which the two financial institutions belong), capitalist individuals and organizations are known for seeking greater profit even from the poorest of the poor countries. It is in this context that some scholars are beginning to ask the real motive behind the IMF-World Bank activities in underdeveloped countries.

When talking about free competition and free markets, it must be noted that in reality capitalists do not whole-heartedly want competition. Economic history shows the emergence of cartels and joint-stock companies. The ultimate objective is for the capitalist corporations to create captive markets both at home and abroad.

While in the West, governments retain ownership of quite a sizeable number of strategic industries, in Zimbabwe the government is being stampeded into selling all its industries to the private sector. Economic researchers will agree that many government-owned companies are a burden to the country's fiscus. However, it should be observed that were it for the prevalence of patronization, quite a majority of these companies would be able to make a profit. A typical example is Zimbabwe Newspapers (Pvt) Ltd., a parastatal that had been making losses — until the former secretary general of SADC, Simba Makoni, was appointed as chief executive in 1994. Many Zimbabwean economists see the international financial institutions' insistence that the government "get rid" of its companies as a subtle way of perpetuating the weakness and dependence of underdeveloped countries.

In the industrialized West, the role of the state has been vital in facilitating and sustaining the impetus of the industrial revolution. This revolution saw the manufacturing sector become the engine for dynamic economic growth, which it remains up to the present day. The British government was both the facilitator and the major employer in the steel industry, shipbuilding, railway and automotive industry. By extension, had it not been for the active role of the state in other Western countries like Germany, France and the USA, and in Japan, these countries would have remained exporters of cheap raw materials and importers of expensive manufactured goods.

The Bretton Woods institutions insist on another pre-condition for financial support — the removal of subsidies — whereas the benefactors' economies provide subsidies to their own primary industries and insist on quotas for any foreign imports. French farmers, for example, are among the most vociferous opponents of the removal of subsidies. About SEK8.8 billion (US$1.04 billion) of European taxpayers' money is spent in subsidizing tobacco farmers every year.[163] The USA has very strict quotas on cotton and sugar, which keeps prices up at home and deprives developing countries of a market.

The most worrying macroeconomic impact of Esap has been the closing down of local industries in the manufacturing sector and the corresponding emergence of various multinational food outlets. This can be seen as symbolic of the IMF programs, which have turned Zimbabwe from a semi-manufacturing nation to a net consumer of finished goods. The IMF's emphasis on free competition between local industries and well-established Western corporations is clear testimony to their aim of de-industrializing the local economy.

In an effort to divert attention from the crumbling manufacturing sector, the IMF has constantly advocated the development of Zimbabwe's tertiary sector to create employment and the much-needed foreign currency. However, experience shows that the service industry can never be the engine for permanent and worthwhile economic growth. For instance, no matter how much money the tourism industry will generate, Zimbabwe will never be said to be industrially developed. The economic structural programs have not succeeded in diversifying Africa's productive base and promote exports. Looked at from another angle, if the governments of the USA, Germany, France, Japan

---

163. *Metro*, Stockholm, 10 September 2003.

and the former Soviet Union had not protected their infant industries from the already established industries from the British Isles in the nineteenth century, they could not have survived the competition. Zimbabwe, too, needs the state to protect its industries and to regulate the economy.

Zimbabwe's economic reform program had two components, namely fiscal adjustment and economic liberalization. Of the two components, the IMF reported that fiscal adjustment seriously missed its targets, and not simply due to the successive droughts that occurred in 1991-92 and 1993-94 as is commonly claimed, but because the goals were unrealistic. At the launch of the reform program in 1991, the budget deficit (considered the national ulcer) was projected at 5% of GDP by the end of the first phase of the shift to market mechanisms. However, government profligacy saw the deficit remaining above 10% of GDP and it was largely financed by domestic borrowing. This state of affairs culminated in the interruption of the program in 1995 when the IMF suspended balance of payments support to the country.

In 1992, the IMF had envisaged an 18% growth of GDP between 1991 and 1995, but the growth actually achieved during that period was one per cent. This gross forecasting miscalculation obviously had the effect of making the fiscal adjustment appear more feasible than was actually the case. During the same period, manufacturing, which accounted for about a quarter of the country's GDP, declined by 14% and it was unlikely that other components would offset this decline in the short run. The GDP per capita decline was 9%. Neither the government nor the IMF had made allowance for these short-term effects of liberalization. This meant that the macroeconomic decline compounded the fiscal problem. The government entered into a debt-trap due to the failure to fully address fiscal adjustment. Since the real interest rate considerably exceeded the growth rate, the ratio of debt to GDP rose rapidly.

It was not surprising, then, that in March 1999 a senior World Bank official admitted that economic structural adjustment programs had failed to achieve the intended results. He blames this failure on "the donors' administrative glitches." Robert Calderisi, the bank's external affairs manager for Africa region, said the programs failed to yield results because recipient countries were not fully told of their long-term side effects. "If I were an African myself I could have been angry with the World Bank and other donor agencies for the SAPs because not enough information was given about what to expect in the first place. It took too long for the benefits of the SAPs to be understood on the continent."[164] He

---

164. Panafrican News Agency, March 30, 1999.

explained that the whole essence of SAPs was to shift economic activities from the urban to rural areas, but overall growth rates on the continent had not been strong enough to reduce poverty.

Notwithstanding, the government continued its economic reform program in 1994, with the announcement of a series of measures which included the flotation of the Zimbabwe dollar and the devaluation of the currency by 17%, the introduction of a two-tier exchange rate system and the easing of controls on the availability of foreign exchange. The five-year development plan (1991-95), including a three-year structural adjustment program supported by the IMF, sought to restrict government expenditure by reducing the number of public-sector employees, and to relax government controls on prices, imports and investment. However, in September 1995 the IMF announced a six-month suspension of assistance to Zimbabwe in protest at the government's failure to impose sufficient restrains on public expenditure. The payment of salaries to civil servants consumed more than 30% of central government revenue in the mid-1990s.

In April 1998, the government launched the second phase of its long-term development initiative, designated the Zimbabwe Programme for Economic and Social Transformation (ZIMPREST). While ZIMPREST turned out to be a glorified wish list, the Millennium Recovery Plan, after it, seemed to be a confused and confusing policy document founded more on rhetoric than reality.

It must be observed that although the pursuit of Esap inflicted much severe hardship upon the country, it also did much that was beneficial to the medium- and long-term well-being of Zimbabwe and its population. A significant consequence of Esap was that progressively between 1991 and 1996 the country enhanced its international image as a desirable and positive investment environment. Economic liberalization and trade deregulation policies were well received by the international investment community, as was the more welcoming attitude, as demonstrated by the investment facilitation extended by the Zimbabwe Investment Centre and a reduction in bureaucracy.

Prospective investors witnessed an economy that was recovering from a state of trauma and decline, with increasing determination to combat the high inflation which had existed for a very prolonged period. The inordinately high taxation levels, which had characterized fiscal policies for over two decades, remained untenable, but were nevertheless slowly falling. Stringent exchange controls were being relaxed, with foreign investors assured of profit remittability and capital externalization, and constraints upon imports had become virtually non-existent. Most important, the country appeared to be politically stable and determined to operate in democracy. Gradually, the country's international image improved, with an ever more favorable perception in the media and highly receptive audiences at investment conferences promoted in London, Hamburg and elsewhere. Substantial inflows into the ZSE allowed share prices to soar, with developed countries' pension and investment funds expressing the desire to participate in one of the world's most rapidly growing emergent markets. Large capital injections boosted mining, manufacturing, tourism and other economic sectors such as construction and transport.

Unfortunately, as prospects of economic growth increased, so did the government become more and more complacent, autocratic, arrogant and disdainful of the prevailing economic needs, steadily reversing all its achievements in the economic field over the preceding years. One factor after another eroded the positive investment profile. By early 1998, the international press reflected nothing but negative images of Zimbabwe. Even local communal periodicals in countries like Sweden portrayed Zimbabwe as a Stalinist dictatorship where land is being "nationalized."

The government's blatant disregard for accepted ethical commercial practice was indicative of rampant autocracy, nepotism and corruption. For some considerable time, recognition had been growing that corruption had become endemic in Zimbabwe; that tenders were not necessarily awarded on merit but in pursuit of hidden agendas; and that many of those in authority were becoming ever-wealthier whilst the majority of the population was finding it continuously more difficult to survive. This awareness peaked with the award of the contract for the partial privatization of the Hwange Power Station. Ignoring established tender procedures and the considered and authoritative opinions of the ZESA directors, government concluded an agreement of intent which markedly conflicted with the tender specifications.

Investor skepticism was then reinforced by the government's grossly biased handling of the cell-phone saga. Numerous other examples were cited by the media, the private sector and the investment community as the government interfered more and more in the commercial sector. However, it was in the last few months of 1997 and early 1998 that the country really devastated its image. Beginning with the vitriol that formed the basis of almost every political statement on the emotional issue of land redistribution, the fundamental issue of the need for a just and equitable policy was wholly submerged by a resurgence of racist antagonism, compounded by fears of injustice, by economic destruction founded upon the collapse of agriculture, and by expectations that asset expropriation in all economic sectors would become the order of the day. Instead of the government taking measures to allay national and international concerns, it resorted to ever-greater confrontational rhetoric, backed by threats.

The government itself succumbed to pressures, precipitously yielding to demands of the country's ex-combatants, with blissful disregard for the repercussions upon the fiscus and the economy. Wide-ranging sympathy for the plight of the war veterans was alienated by the magnitude of the debt burden imposed upon the taxpayer and the extent to which not only the deserving but also thousands of others were to benefit from the panic-driven agreement concluded by the government (the President) without even normal democratic consultation with Parliament. Its ill-considered actions then forced the government to scrabble anxiously to raise the necessary funding and, as it had done all too often in the past, it sought what had always been as the easiest way out: the imposition of additional taxes, irrespective of the severe hardships that would impose upon the population. Again disregarding democratic process, the government tried to bulldoze the tax-enabling legislation through the legislature, and was stunned when the usually submissive Parliament declined to comply.

On November 14, 1997, fuelled by the rash of negative economic development, the Zimbabwean dollar crashed, introducing still greater fragility into the economy and causing a rapid surge in inflation. While the dollar had been overvalued, and its decline in value was inevitable, the extent and rapidity of the fall was extreme, stimulated by nationwide economic despondency, reaction to rumors, and failure of the authorities to respond assertively to the crisis. The combination of the threatened increased taxes and rising inflation was the catalyst to the ZCTU-led mass national protest action on December 9, 1997, the bloody price-rise riots of January 19-20, 1998, and the great stay-away of March 3-4, 1998, which, although peaceful, resulted in a direct rebuff of government threats against both the workers who stayed away and industrialists who closed their factories.

This did not go down well with potential investors and the IMF. The new reform program, ZIMPREST, appeared to be bogged down largely because of the fiscal indiscipline with the government. In January 1998, the cash-strapped government, already under siege from a restive population protesting against high food prices and flawed state policies, negotiated a stand-by credit facility from the IMF worth up to Z$3.2 billion (US$175 million at current exchange rates). With Zimbabwe entitled to a quota of SDR261 million (Special Drawing Rights) in the IMF, this would amount to SDR131 million.[165] The funds, to be provided under the IMF's Enhanced Structural Adjustment Facility (ESAF), would be disbursed in quarterly tranches starting with the end of March, and then at the end of June, September and December. This facility would support measures to be implemented in 1998 under the second leg of Zimbabwe's economic reforms that were started in 1991 and ended in 1995. It should be noted that repayments of some US$60 million on IMF loans made under the first leg of Esap were also due in 1998.

Stand-by arrangements are aimed at providing short-term (one to two years) balance-of-payments support for deficits of a temporary or critical nature. Being a short-term program, the focus is on macroeconomic policies rather than on structural policies. Under the arrangement, the member country is required to observe certain economic performance criteria and the program is reviewed periodically. These performance criteria, in Zimbabwe's case, include: containing the budget deficit to a certain percentage of GDP (5% by the turn of the century) through a combination of expenditure and revenue measures; a tight policy to lower inflation to 4.5% by the year 2000; the central bank was required to maintain a minimum level of net foreign exchange reserves of four months import cover (estimated by some analysts at around two months' imports); ceilings on government borrowing from the banking sector (it was estimated government borrowing at that stage had amounted to Z$24 billion or 14% of GDP and had exceeded the target by 118%); avoidance of external payments arrears; avoidance of restrictions on the importation of goods and services; avoidance of price controls and government subsidies. The IMF brought in the land issue as a criterion, and received written assurance from the government that it would implement the land reform program in accordance with the law.

Thus, on June 1, 1998, the IMF provided the first disbursement of US$53 million, in view of the reduced budgetary deficit achieved in the 1996-97 financial year. Although this was peanuts in comparison to IMF funds injected into other sickly economies of Asia, economic analysts thought the mere release of the hard currency into the RBZ was enough to prevent a major run on the Zimbabwe dollar (which was then trading in the Z$17.50-18.00 range against the US dollar). Besides, bodies such as the World Bank, the European Union and its investment bank, the European Investment Bank, the African Development Bank, PTA Bank and many other international financial institutions are influenced in their assessments of Zimbabwe by the country's standing with the

---

165. SDRs are allocated to member countries in proportion to their IMF quotas. Its value is based on a basket of key international currencies.

IMF. Thus, the benefits of the receipt of IMF support of foreign exchange receipts are massive. Exchange rate stability would accompany improved levels of foreign exchange reserves. Although exporters may generate lesser incomes in terms of domestic currency (and may forfeit some export market competitiveness), importers would benefit significantly. The cost of imports would decline, and as a result Zimbabwe would cease to suffer the hyperinflation which was exacerbating poverty.

It is essential that Zimbabwe participates in international financial institutions that provide aid for economic development. NEPAD is one such institution. Spearheaded by President Thabo Mbeki of South Africa, Nigerian President Olusegun Obasanjo, Senegalese President Abdoulaye Wade and Abdelaziz Bouteflika, President of Algeria, NEPAD seeks to increase aid to Africa from the West in return for good governance, respect for human rights and the rule of law. However, incensed by the "good governance" and "rule of law" clauses, the ZANU (PF) government attacked NEPAD as a foreign concept devised to further destabilize Africa.

Notwithstanding, the IMF board made it clear that credit to Zimbabwe would be disbursed in tranches on the basis of the government meeting agreed fiscal and monetary targets. The institution was particularly keen to see how the government would improve the worsening balance-of-payments position and also implement a collection of revenue-enhancing measures without imposing additional taxes on the overburdened and combative Zimbabwean population. Furthermore, the IMF expected the government to reduce its total foreign and domestic debt, estimated at over Z$60 billion and attracting Z$1 billion a month in interest payments,[166] to enable the RBZ to tighten domestic credit and at the same time build up foreign currency reserves. Sources said the IMF was also keen that the government cut its non-productive spending to concentrate more resources on crumbling social services such as the health and education sectors.

In November 1998, the World Bank, for its part, proposed converting the country's Z$32.8 billion domestic debt into an off-shore facility to free resources for the productive sector long crowded-out by the government's insatiable appetite for money. One way of externalizing the domestic debt was for the World Bank to release funds for the government to retire treasury bills that were currently in issue. Such a move would mean that domestic investors holding treasury bills would have extra liquidity, which could be used to purchase shares in state-owned enterprises, thus enabling the government to accelerate the

---

166. Panafrican News Agency, 30 July, 1998.

stalled privatization exercise. The World Bank loans would be made available at attractive concessionary rates. However, sources within the donor community were quick to point out that the World Bank proposal would only be implemented if the IMF, which had shown the government a red flag, resumed balance of payments support for Zimbabwe.

Over the years, public sector borrowing in Zimbabwe has been accommodated by the banking system, which the RBZ has since warned would fuel money supply growth. The governor of the Reserve Bank, Leonard Tsumba, said at the end of November 1998, "Total domestic debt has seen the interest bill rising rapidly, emphasizing crowding out as the real danger to economic activity as it not only negatively impacts on money supply growth but also has an added effect of pushing up borrowing rates as well, thus starving the productive sector of essential financing."[167] Economic analysts reckoned that the government was paying an annual interest bill of Z$10 billion on the domestic debt, which accounted for 40% of GDP.

Economic observers were under no illusion about the tough challenges facing the government, particularly at a time when all economic fundamentals were pointing in the wrong direction, while a restive population was squirming under the burden of food prices and taxes. Inflation rose from 19% in 1997 to an all-time record high 53% in March 1999 (the IMF expected it to be brought down to 18% by December 1998). The ZANU (PF) government was known for its habit of bringing in unbudgeted outlays (such as almost Z$5 billion spent on gratuity and pension payments for ex-combatants in December 1997 and an estimated Z$1.8 billion bail-out to holders of fraudulent Cold Storage Company bills issued by the collapsed United Merchant Bank). Equally threatening to the deficit target was the decision to award public servants a 21% pay hike, which cost the Treasury over Z$1 billion.

Real economic growth in 1998 was forecast at only 3%, with 3.7% in 1997, while the country's major export earners were not expected to recover much from the low international commodity prices. Inflows from tobacco, the single largest export earner, were projected at some Z$10 billion, while local exporters of such minerals as gold, ferro-chrome and nickel were twiddling their thumbs, hoping for a major revival of prices which had plummeted on the back of an over-supply on world markets. Against this background, the IMF package was received with guarded enthusiasm by the private sector.

---

167. *The Zimbabwe Independent*, 4 Dec., 1998.

The key to achieving sustainable growth and meeting targets agreed with the IMF was the need for the cash-strapped government to push ahead with its privatization program, which was expected to have raised more than Z$1.6 billion for state coffers in the 1998 fiscal year. Other measures needed to make good use of the IMF funds and other bilateral donor aid from the West were drastic cuts in the indirect taxes that affect costs and prices. If sales taxes and duties on industrial materials and equipment were to be halved, one could expect inflation to be reduced and production volumes and demand to begin to improve. Furthermore, by allowing prevailing interest rates to be brought down, the lower costs of production would further stimulate this trend and promote a more rapid recovery in many of the industrial and commercial sectors that were struggling. To minimize the initial negative impact caused by such cuts on taxes and duties, the government would have to curb its profligacy (the gaping government deficit has averaged 10% of GDP in the past decade), cut down on the size of the government (the Cabinet in particular), and stick to its budgeted expenditure — something it failed to do in 24 years of independence.

Unfortunately, things did not turn out as planned and thus the IMF was forced to suspend disbursement of the US$20 million second tranche until the outcome of the land conference in September 1998. This second tranche was originally scheduled for early July 1998. A combination of factors that included the collapse in tobacco prices saw the disbursement date pushed further to mid-August. The second tranche was largely dependent on the June fiscal, monetary, foreign exchange and divestiture targets being met. In August, the IMF expressed its satisfaction with all these targets but sounded a word of caution over price controls and the pace of divestiture.

It appears the Congo War, and the government's policy over land and price controls, might have cost the country additional financial support from the IMF, for the institution decided to suspend the balance-of-payments support for December 1998 as well. That would not have solved all the country's economic problems, but it would have helped inject confidence and underpin financial stability.

The delay in the release of these funds was expected to have severe consequences for Zimbabwe, which was projected to have a balance-of-payments deficit of US$346 million (Z$13.3 billion) by the end of 1998. The postponement of US$53 million (Z$2.0 billion) was largely due to the IMF's concern about the government's military spending in the Democratic Republic of Congo (DRC). The funding of the civil war was estimated to be costing Z$70 million a month in May 1999. After Zimbabwe's intervention in August 1998, the

Zimbabwe dollar lost an average 20.7% of its value to the US dollar. Economic analysts reported that the central bank did not have adequate reserves to ease the foreign exchange shortages, with suggestions that its reserves were down to between three and four weeks' import cover. The intervention could not have come at a worse time. The country was reportedly owed more than Z$2 billion for arms, food and uniforms supplied to Laurent Kabila, but military sources said when the final cost of a prolonged intervention in the DRC is worked out, the country will end up having spent more. By mid-May 1999, the country had spent at least Z$500 million of the unbudgeted public funds on the war. The Defense Minister, the late Cde Moven Mahachi, asked the Cabinet to urgently authorize a Z$1.2 billion supplementary budget, part of which would help finance the war in the Great Lakes region. The government was also using more resources to buy military hardware for use in the war. The Ministry of Defense's budget for the 1999 financial year was Z$5.4 billion.[168]

The government's steps to seize 841 commercial farms in contradiction to the agreement reached at the land conference in September and the high cost of Zimbabwe's civil service wage bill were other factors which prompted the IMF to delay the release of funds. Moreover, the government had already missed some of the targets set out in the second generation of market reforms, particularly on the privatization and commercialization of ailing state enterprises. Apart from the disposal of government shares in local blue-chip Delta Corporation, which was completed in May 1998, the Finance Ministry had still to meet its target of either privatizing or disposing of state shares in such diverse corporations as Astra Holdings, Zimbabwe Development Bank, Zimbabwe Reinsurance Corporation and the Cold Storage Company.

As mentioned earlier, most foreign aid donors and investors usually follow the fund's lead when dealing with developing economies. Organizations such as the EU and its investment arm, the European Investment Bank, the African Development Bank, PTA Bank and other important financial and aid institutions work in collaboration with the IMF. For example, Zimbabwe receives about £12 million (£1 = Z$61.802 as of November 1998) worth of aid from Britain annually. The aid covers projects for water irrigation, health, sanitation and work in various government departments. In 1997, the Swedish International Development Cooperation Agency (SIDA) provided Zimbabwe with aid to the tune of 148 million SEK (1 SEK = Z$3.25).

---

168. *The Financial Gazette*, 13 May, 1999.

According to USAid officials, a total of US$132.8 million was earmarked for release in tranches in 1999 for various projects in Zimbabwe. For the first quarter of the 1999 fiscal year, Washington had already quadrupled aid for Zimbabwe from US$2 million to about US$8 million.[169] USAid had over the last 18 years provided the country with over Z$25 billion for agriculture/food security, education, family planning, HIV/AIDS prevention, small-scale private sector development, low-income housing, emergency food aid, financing of technical assistance for land reforms and Communal Areas Management Programme for Indigenous Resources (Campfire).

USAid stopped funding of all Campfire projects in Zimbabwe amidst allegations that the decision was politically motivated. The USAid withdrawal was one of many by international donors from Zimbabwe in protest against the deteriorating human-rights situation. The suspension of the funding was likely to lead to the collapse of projects run by rural communities in over 50 rural district councils throughout the country. USAid had spent over US$8 million on Campfire projects over a period of 13 years to the time of the suspension in September 2003 (US$28 million in overall aid). Projects funded by USAid included community-fishing, eco-tourism, hunting concessions, photographic safaris and clinics and schools, among others.

Another donor still waiting for the IMF's green light is the European Commission. The EC had over the years supported the government of Zimbabwe in various projects in education, health, agriculture and mining and was in the process of approving other health projects. Although EC staff would not give figures, it was reliably understood that about US$200 million (Z$7.6 billion) were earmarked for the country once the IMF had released the balance of payments support.

By April 1999, authorities in Harare were becoming jittery because of IMF's prevarication. While the Finance Minister was busy negotiating with the IMF to release funds, the Politburo was threatening to cut off links with both the IMF and the World Bank. Jongwe (President Mugabe) himself attacked the IMF. "Let that monstrous creature get out of our way…. Unless I am prevailed upon to see things otherwise, not just by the way of arguments but by something concrete that the IMF is doing, I will lead my government in the direction where we dismiss the IMF as an institution that we can relate to — and this is coming very soon," he warned. The Zimbabwean government appeared to be increasingly turning east as the nation's crises deepened.[170]

---

169. *Ibid.*, 15 April, 1999.

Most Zimbabwean businesses, suffocating from galloping interest rates and inflation, worsened by the local dollar's crash plus sharply rising input costs, had also looked to the IMF's aid to improve the local macroeconomic climate. America, Britain, France, Germany and Japan are the major contributors to the IMF, which gives loans to poor countries to revive their ailing economies. If Zimbabwe had received the US$176 million facility as envisaged in 1998, the country would have qualified for a three-year enhanced structural adjustment facility which would have replaced the standby facility on expiry. This would have provided Zimbabwe with a larger access to IMF resources on concessional terms.

Although the first phase of the economic structural adjustment program was supposed to reduce the budget deficit to a sustainable level of about 5% of GDP by 1995, the deficit escalated to more than 10%, resulting in a poor macroeconomic climate marked by high interest and inflation rates. Interest rates (which were standing at more than 40%) made the cost of borrowing money too costly for local companies seeking to expand operations and create jobs. While the World Bank released Z$4.8 billion (US$300 million) between 1991 and 1997, it had provided Z$24 billion (US$1.5 billion) worth of assistance to the country since independence in 1980.[171]

At the end of October 2002, the IMF expert on Zimbabwe, Gerry Johnson, said that the country was on the brink of an economic crisis and that government mismanagement could soon plunge the nation into a hyperinflationary spiral that would bring the economy to its knees. "One does wonder how much longer can the economy be allowed to collapse. I don't know at what point people in government start to realize that something has to happen."[172]

Zimbabwe's problem was basically three-pronged, namely declining production in all sectors, artificially low interest rates, and a fictitious fixed foreign exchange rate. The Zimbabwe dollar was trading at Z$1,400 to the United States dollar on the parallel market at the end of October 2002 and Z$5,600 at the end of October 2003. Zimbabwe rejected the IMF's prescriptions

---

170. In a study, The Heritage Foundation and *The Wall Street Journal* rated Zimbabwe as the least free and most restricted economy in sub-Saharan Africa. Neighboring South Africa, on the other hand, was named in the survey as "the third most liberal economy in sub-Saharan Africa and one of the most unrestricted economies in the world."

171. Panafrican News Agency, 9 April, 1998.

172. *The Daily News*, 6 Nov.. 2002.

for economic recovery and refused to service its debt. It recently had its voting rights suspended by the world financial body, one step short of being expelled.

An accelerating crisis would force companies to shut down nationwide, with prices doubling on a monthly basis — just as the nation struggles with a catastrophic famine. Workers' already shriveling salaries would be rendered worthless overnight and the Zimbabwean dollar would collapse even further. Short of restoring the rule of law, the best hope to restore some semblance of economic sanity would be to raise interest rates. That would bring down inflation, which was now 622.8%, to manageable levels and give Zimbabweans some incentive to save or invest Zimbabwean dollars instead of spending them or bidding for foreign currency.

Economists see little hope that the country can escape an economic meltdown unless it secures new assistance from the international lending agencies. President Mugabe would have to reverse the international pariah status he has earned by years of farm seizures, the stolen presidential election and broken promises to ease political repression. As of 2004, the governor of the Reserve Bank of Zimbabwe was trying to woo the IMF and EU countries to reconsider their positions. Unemployment was reported at 80% and the minimum wage of Z$98,000 was lower than the relevant Poverty Datum Line (PDL) of Z$325,450.53. The ZCTU was looking to have the PDL re-set to a figure above Z$500,000.

### Parastatal Privatization

After April 18, 1980, the independence government embarked on the creation of parastatals in an effort to create jobs for the pool of Zimbabwean intellectuals both returning from exile and those already in Zimbabwe. The discredited Smith regime's policy of segregation had precluded the creation of such positions. By the late-80s, almost every ministry had a couple of parastatals under its roof. A typical example is the Ministry of Transport and Energy, which has under its aegis  Air Zimbabwe, Noczim, National Railways of Zimbabwe, ZESA and Zimbabwe Iron and Steel Company (ZISCO). The majority of the parastatals, like Noczim, were non-profit making concerns and were referred to as strategic concerns created to empower Zimbabweans and to control strategic sectors in the economy. Many economic analysts believed that they should be off-loaded in order to mobilize funds needed to service the snowballing domestic debt.

Although privatizing the country's loss-making behemoths would be a positive development, one would need to ensure that no monopoly powers accumulated in private hands where they could be abused. Prior to privatization, regulatory arrangements would have to be put in place.

No country has used only a single method of privatization. Citizens may be encouraged to invest directly in privatized companies (this method can promote quick privatization, since it avoids problems of enterprise re-structuring or corporate governance); and competitive bidding, direct sales to consortia of investors, and selling by public offerings can also be effective. Competitive bidding increases the selling price and ensures a transparent process because of the need for clear rules. Direct sales to consortia of investors, on the other hand, are simple and inexpensive to arrange; while selling by public offering leads to broad share distribution and reduces criticism that public assets are being transferred to a tiny elite.

Financial re-structuring is often essential before a company is privatized. For example, writing off a parastatal's debt maybe the only feasible way to unload a company whose liabilities are much greater than its asset value. Furthermore, cutting "fat" out of organizations soon to be privatized generally makes them more saleable. Many parastatals, such as the NRZ, Air Zimbabwe or Noczim, are known to be grossly over-staffed. In these organizations the best policy would be to downsize prior to the sale to ensure that workers get fair compensation and because investors shy away from buying into immediate labor disputes. Besides having an excess of unskilled and semi-skilled labor, many public sector organizations are handicapped by old plant, and often their most senior managers lack experience of running a company on business lines. And yet, the performance of such organizations is capable of being transformed.

Zimbabwe's privatization initiative was first mooted during the first phase of economic reforms introduced in 1991, though much of the little privatization that has been done to date occurred after the lapsing of that phase of market reforms. The problem was that it was never clear who exactly was responsible for the process of privatization — the Minister of State responsible for parastatal reform and indigenization, the Planning Commissioner, the President's Office, the Ministry of Finance or the line ministries responsible for the different parastatals?

In 1998, after an unexplained, and probably unjustifiable, delay, government released the details of the successor program to Esap, called the Millennium Economic Recovery Programme. Key elements were predominantly the same as in Esap, including intents of disposal of state assets and privatization of public enterprises, but, except for the establishment of the Privatization Agency of Zimbabwe ("Paz"), there was no evident sense of urgency on the part of the government, or of any real acceleration of disinvestment.

The role to be played by Paz had its own political overtones within members of the Cabinet. The old guard wanted the Cabinet to approve and monitor every step of the privatization process while reform-inclined members preferred that the government only laid down policies and procedures and then leave Paz to handle the actual privatization. The government set up Paz in September 1999 to sell its shareholding in the roughly 50 companies it either partly or wholly owned. The Paz director, Andrew Bvumbe, said his agency's role was to give technically sound advise to the Cabinet and that only the government had the final say on what should be disposed of and how that should be done. However, the director pointed out that there was a need for an Act of Parliament to clearly stipulate the terms of reference for Paz. This was the case in other countries, like Zambia, where an Act of Parliament defines the terms of reference of the agency and clearly spells out where government comes in and where its role ends. There was also a need to create an autonomous privatization body as in Zambia, but the Zimbabwe government decided to house Paz under the President's Office.

Paz's manual on privatization says the government's domestic debt stood at Z$146 billion (or 67.7% of GDP) as of June 1999.[173] The manual also says that the interest bill on the government's debt was expected to shoot up to Z$21.6 billion against an initial estimate of Z$10 billion in 1999.

As of June 1999, major public enterprises such as Noczim, ZESA, the PTC, GMB and ZISCO had combined total losses of Z$14.8 billion.[174] The losses were contributing to the government's widening fiscal deficit, which averaged 10% of GDP in the past decade — one of the highest such rates in Africa. In December 2003, domestic debt had ballooned to Z$607.11 billion, as government borrowed heavily from the private sector to prop up ailing parastatals and finance subsidies on grain and fuel.[175] The deficit in turn was being financed by heavy borrowing from the private sector through the issue of state-guaranteed grain bills, agrobonds and petrofin bills. On November 4, 2003, the government went to the market for Z$10 billion to finance fuel procurement for the national oil company, which ran out of stocks in mid-October. In a move to sustain the

---

173. *The Financial Gazette*, Harare, 6 April, 2000.
174. *Ibid.*
175. *Business Day*, Johannesburg, 5 November, 2003.

controversial land reform program, the government was subsidizing the price of fuel to resettled farmers as well as grain and wheat purchases from them, through the GMB, thus incurring a heavy deficit.

Despite the 2004 budget's lack of imagination, it marked a U-turn in government's populist policies, ushering in a new era where parastatals that had benefited from subsidies for decades would now charge break-even prices. The new pricing policy was intended to enable perennial loss-making parastatals such as Noczim, Air Zimbabwe and NRZ (whose fortunes had nose dived due to uneconomic prices) break even and pay their own way. The state-owned companies that have been privatized, after initially being commercialized, have, to a large extent, turned around from being low profit-making or outright loss-making entities to important contributors to the fiscus. Parastatals that have been privatized include the Dairy Marketing Board (Dairyboard Zimbabwe Limited — DZL); the Cotton Marketing Board (Cotton Company of Zimbabwe — Cottco); the Commercial Bank of Zimbabwe (CBZ), The Rainbow Tourism Group Ltd. and The Agricultural Bank of Zimbabwe Limited.

The Zimbabwe Reinsurance Corporation (ZimRe), which was 100% owned by the government, had an initial disinvestment of 48% of its equity through a public issue. Eighteen per cent of the shares were sold through a public offering, while 10% preferential share allocations went to pension and provident funds. Another 10% went to the National Investment Trust, 5% to insurance companies and another 5% to ZimRe employees.

The disposed shares in State-owned companies were to be offered to both local and foreign investors (who would be allowed only a 40% stake in any of the parastatals). By allowing foreign investors to participate in the privatization process, the government hoped to benefit two-fold, as it would get much needed foreign currency as well as funds for the domestic financing of its budget. One example is the strategic alliance deal between the Rainbow Tourism Group and Groupe Accor of France; Groupe Accor released US$5.9 million (Z$220 million) to pay for a 35% equity stake in RTG.[176]

Initially, the privatization of the Dairy Marketing Board, the Cotton Marketing Board and the Commercial Bank of Zimbabwe made the Treasury richer by Z$4 billion.[177] In other words, these companies' financial performance has improved significantly after privatization, confirming the need to privatize quickly the remaining parastatals. Instead of providing huge amounts of public

---

176. *The Zimbabwe Mirror*, 17 March, 2000.
177. *The Zimbabwe Independent*, 3 April, 1998.

funds to parastatals, the government is now receiving substantial sums from privatized companies. With the international financial institutions and donors reluctant to release aid to Zimbabwe, it is apparent that the government could raise funds from parastatals to get the economy back on track.

Other candidates for either commercialization or privatization and the disposal of shares were Astra Holdings, the Tobacco Research Board, Finhold, NRZ, Air Zimbabwe (Airzim), the Cold Storage Company, the Forestry Commission, the PTC, ZESA and Olivine Industries. Two of the worst loss-making parastatals, Noczim and the Grain Marketing Board, had not been listed for privatization as yet, as they were still regarded as "strategic" entities. The State still clings to Air Zimbabwe, although it had been reduced from a fleet of 18 planes at independence to three in 2003.

Many Zimbabweans (including ZANU-PF MPs) felt that commercialization *cum* privatization was hijacked by the ruling elite in the name of indigenization. Generally, the people heading the commercialized parastatals were the same people who had been responsible for their dismal performance earlier; they were merely shuffled from one parastatal to another like cards in a poker game. The taxpayers' money is used during the whole process of privatization, thereby increasing the budget even further. Speaking in Parliament at the end of May 1999 (before the June 2000 election), Hwange West MP Allan Elliot likened state coffers to a garden, saying: "We grow rows of lettuce and we put rabbits there to manage them and when there is nothing left, we grow another lettuce and we put the same rabbits there. We keep on doing that...." He went on to say that the indigenization process apparently "turns individual black businessmen into overnight millionaires when they sell onto the private sector. I would, therefore, caution: let us not hide behind any of these slogans."[178]

Pumula-Magwegwe MP Norman Zikhali said that commercialization in Zimbabwe had only managed to establish "a very small clique of people establishing themselves as an elite in the African community; all is done in the name of indigenization." For his part, Masvingo Central MP Dzikamai Mavhaire had this to say: "When we fail to do certain things we think miracles will come out in commercializing or privatizing a parastatal." Citing Noczim, he said it had become a norm for ministers to appoint the same people who had failed to lead commercialized entities in other sectors. "When we commercialize, we have seen that mostly the same people who have been there, who have not been able

---

178. *The Daily News*, Harare, 25 May, 1999.

to run the company time and again are the same people overnight who will become revolutionaries of the commercialization."

Parastatals have gobbled up huge sums of public resources. In 1998 alone, they cost the government more than Z$11 billion in subsidies, contributing to a ballooning budget deficit which has, over the years, remained one of the sticky areas in Zimbabwe's negotiations with the IMF. The country's budget deficit shot up to Z$8.3 billion during the first five months of 1999, far higher than the target of Z$6.4 billion set by the Treasury at the beginning of the year.[179] Such resources could have gone to more critical investments like the construction of dams and roads and the installation of electricity in rural areas. Thus, the main objective for commercialization is to make parastatals self-sustaining and profitable, thereby reducing the government deficit. This would in turn strengthen the Zimbabwean currency and act as a catalyst for domestic saving once the government stopped crowding the private sector by reducing its domestic borrowing.

The low level of domestic savings has long been identified as the underlying obstacle to attaining sustainable socio-economic development; it is a major reason for the meager investment levels of 18% of GDP. For the country to attain at least a 5% growth rate per annum, investment as a percentage of GDP should oscillate around 25%.

This problem of low domestic savings is not peculiar to Zimbabwe alone in the sub-region; other countries are also grappling with the agenda of capital formation. Given the considerable capital investment needs in the provision of infrastructure, education, health and social amenities, capital formation cannot be over-emphasized.

One thing that emerged from the flotation of DZL, Cottco and CBZ is that the privatization initiative being championed by the government, albeit at a painstakingly slow pace, can influence economic growth through its effect on domestic savings and the efficient allocation of capital among competing entities.

In general, it has been well-chronicled that capital markets encourage private savings by the wide portfolio of assets with different risks, yields and liquidity they provide. At the same time, competition among the end-users of these savings will encourage efficient use of capital by investors in the private and public sectors, which should result in a direct impact on Zimbabwe's economic growth.

---

179. *The Financial Gazette*, 11 August, 1999.

Given Zimbabwe's current predicament — an economy about to crash as the international community freezes aid and grants — it is important to revisit the privatization program in an endeavor to expedite it so as to curtail the current hemorrhaging of the fiscus. In December 1998, the Reserve Bank of Zimbabwe reported that the country's major state-owned enterprises recorded a staggering Z$31 billion overall operating loss for the 12 months ending December 31, 1997. Unfortunately, there is no prize for guessing that Noczim posted the highest loss of Z$1.7 billion — its debt peaked at a staggering $22 billion in 2000. In 2002, GMB recorded a deficit of Z$14.4bn, which was equivalent to 1.4% of GDP, reported to be Z$1,200bn. ZISCO also posted a loss of Z$9.5bn while ZESA, NRZ and meat processor CSC incurred losses of Z$1.1bn, Z$2.1bn and Z$3.2bn, respectively.[180] The GMB and ZISCO have been a perennial drain on the national fiscus, despite repeated attempts by the government to rescue the firms from collapse. Notwithstanding, Finance Minister Herbert Murerwa indicated in June 2003 that privatization of loss-making parastatals was not a priority for the government because it was not in the national interest.

Of course, neither is bankruptcy in the national interest. The now privatized state-owned enterprises contributed over Z$1.5 billion to the fiscus during the year 2000.

Most of the state-owned firms have been hit hard by foreign currency shortages and can no longer import spare parts or replace obsolete machinery. The fact that Zimbabwe had lost its international credit rating means that its parastatals can no longer secure international loans critical for their operations.

The virtual collapse of some of these state companies meant that they were no longer effectively serving the nation (only political interests). The fact that GMB had no strategic food reserves to feed the nation in times of drought was a clear failure as a strategic state entity. Not only was GMB failing to stimulate grain production, it was failing to efficiently distribute farming inputs at a time when more than 7 million Zimbabweans were in desperate need of emergency food aid. Another example is Wankie Colliery, which provides coal for the cement, sugar, tobacco and steel industries, among others. It was operating at 50% of capacity in February 2003, because it had no foreign exchange to import spare parts for its dilapidated machinery. In April 2003, the parastatal had yet again postponed the repayment of a £6 million debt (about Z$550 million) to CDC Capital and WestLb of Britain, loans secured with the European institutions ten years ago to build and rehabilitate coke oven gas plants. WCC

---

180. IMF Report of July 2003.

bears a number of other obligations locally and regionally, and none of the outstanding liabilities has been serviced consistently.[181]

Nonetheless, ZESA (Zimbabwe Electricity Supply Authority), one of the country's seven major parastatals, posted an operating surplus of Z$1.1 billion and a net surplus of Z$105 million. This was a result of an increase in the number of customers and consumption per customer, and an average tariff adjustment of 18%. In addition, one of the few blue-chip parastatals that is still government-dominated, the Industrial Development Corporation of Zimbabwe Limited (IDC), has continued to chalk up billion-dollar profits annually.

The stock market has always allowed for the wholesome participation in acquiring shares of privatized companies — though there were the ongoing investigations of insider trading on the local bourse. This has been made abundantly clear in the case of Cottco, DZL, and CBZ and, of late, ZimRe. The Zimbabwe Stock Exchange allows competition between various instruments of a bank-based financial system and the non-bank financial intermediaries. In addition, the stock market allows risk sharing on an individual basis without the need for government guarantees, offers instruments, which do not suffer from cash flow mismatch, and facilitates the development of other markets such as derivatives. This is the time for the government to seriously expedite the privatization program so as to alleviate the fiscal burden from the households and private business. These companies are not natural loss-makers, but the environment in which they do business guarantees a continuation of loss making.

In practice, the extent of the state's disposal of assets and disinvestment from public enterprises (parastatals) during the five years of Esap was insignificant and since then has accelerated marginally, but nevertheless remains minimal. The disinvestment and disposals were below the expectations provoked by Esap and were insufficient to make any significant contribution to Zimbabwean economic recovery. The state's approach to privatization was, at best, half-hearted. In most instances it was only prepared to effect a partial sell-off, although there was no credible reason for retention of equity participation. The entities divested from cannot be considered to be of national strategic importance, no matter how substantive their actual economic contributions or potentials were. There could not, therefore, be a strategic justification for government retaining some of the shares in the enterprises. It is not government's role to be an investor or a speculator, and its parlous financial

---

181. *The Daily News*, 18 April, 2003.

circumstances, which are tantamount to those of insolvency, render it unlikely that investment or speculation motivated the state to remain a shareholder in the various "privatized" entities. In all probability, the misguided perception of those in authority was that those retained shareholdings could, together with indirectly exercised influence upon bodies such as the National Investment Trust and NSSA, enable a continuing use, or abuse, of control over the ventures.

At the same time, the government was clearly reluctant to pursue a concerted program of asset disposal and, more pronouncedly, of public enterprise disinvestment, because of the widespread perception that doing so would disinherit Zimbabwe of its national heritage. At the very least, it was felt that privatization must be targeted towards indigenization.

However, few of the indigenous population had the resources necessary to invest meaningfully into the enterprises and hence, undoubtedly, the farce of the establishment of the National Investment Trust. The Trust could only invest with funding provided by the government — to all intents and purposes, money was merely moved from one pocket to the other; and, the warehousing of shares with financial institutions was equally farcical, as no likelihood exists of transferal to the indigenous within a reasonable time period.

Neither tactic achieved any effectual economic empowerment of the indigenous population. Meanwhile, the concept of indigenization also deterred the government from permitting any major investment by non-residents of Zimbabwe, which could at least have generated very considerable foreign exchange inflows, and a one-time profit for the government, with possibly the benefits of strategic partnerships, the introduction of new technologies and, in relevant instances, access to export markets and import inputs.

There seems to be little choice, however desirable it may be to protect Zimbabwe's economic sovereignty. Quicker privatization of loss-making parastatals seems to be the only option on the horizon for stemming the flow of government's external debt.

Government sources mentioned that Finance Minister Simba Makoni, who sought a speedy privatization process both to raise badly needed cash and to placate the IMF, wanted to limit the role of the Cabinet to policy-making and supervision. Makoni feared that if the Cabinet were to monitor and approve every case, it would lead to a long-drawn out process that would fail to bring the cash and the IMF stamp of approval.

The government was forced to adopt a fast-track program to dispose of its enterprises after international donors blacklisted it. More than Z$5 billion was expected to be raised in the year 2000 alone through the sale of some of the government enterprises, but only five state firms had been sold since 1998. The government intention was to retain 25% of the total shares; 10-15% would fall under the Economic Empowerment and indigenization Department, while between 5-10% would be set aside for employee ownership of the parastatals.

The ailing parastatals were a burden to the government, resulting in a budget deficit of more than 10% of GDP. Dismal performance of public enterprises was a result of not only exchange depreciation and inadequate pricing policies, but inappropriate investments, political interference, high incidence of corruption, mismanagement and inefficiency. This resulted in the government subsidies, leading to a high budget deficit and ultimately to the current macro-economic instability. In both private and public enterprises, transparency and public scrutiny can expose many problems, which can then be dealt with rapidly and effectively. It is far better to pay fewer people higher salaries in the quest for efficiency.

Admittedly, every government has a duty to develop the infrastructure of the country. While this responsibility cannot be shirked by palming it off on the private sector, this does not mean that private competition cannot be allowed in them at all. Sectors falling under this infrastructure would be represented by ZESA, NRZ, PTC, and Zimbabwe Broadcasting Corporation (ZBC), and would include roads, national water supply, education, health, defense and the police.

The process of privatization continued, with the PTC, Noczim, NRZ and ZESA at the top list. Sources within the telecommunication field said that the unbundling of the PTC into three entities, namely TelOne, ZimPost and Net*One, had seen top government officials and some cabinet ministers scurrying for the assets, "making a killing before privatization."

During the period June 2000 to June 2001, parastatal (government) property was disposed at knockdown prices to party functionaries and shares in state-owned companies were sold to foreign interests under conditions of secrecy. In June, it came to light that top government officials, including some cabinet ministers, were lobbying for local businessmen linked to ZANU (PF) to be granted licenses to operate fixed networks by the Postal and Telecommunications Regulatory Authority of Zimbabwe (PTRAZ). PTRAZ was launched at the beginning of 2001 as the only legitimate board to issue any license. Here, politicians realized that despite the telecoms sector being capital-intensive, the returns were exceptionally good and could be accrued within a short space of time.

Meanwhile, the Office of the President and Cabinet was the winning bidder for assets disposed in March 2001 by Noczim. Highly placed government sources said the assets, which included Noczim's Chirundu warehouse, the company's Mutare depot and transport fleet, were acquired by the Central Intelligence Organization for about Z$100 million. The assets also included a 76% stake held by Noczim in Oil Blending (Pvt) Ltd. Senior government sources close to the deal said the President's Office wanted the outcome of the asset disposal program to remain a secret because of fears it would expose the whole government asset disposal exercise for the farce it was.

The Noczim asset disposal program was part of a restructuring exercise started by the government in order to transform the state-run fuel procurement agency into a regulatory body for Zimbabwe's oil industry. Under the restructuring, the debt-ridden Noczim would oversee the activities of private oil companies, which would take over the role of importing fuel into the country.[182]

The privatization program, expected to raise money to bail the government out of its financial woes, had only managed to raise Z$7.1 billion: just 32.3% of the budgeted Z$22 billion, in the period ending December 31, 2001. This amount was raised through the divesture of government stakes in Noczim, the Cotton Company of Zimbabwe Limited, the Zimbabwe Reinsurance Company Limited, Dairyboard Zimbabwe Limited, WS Craster and Zimbabwe Development Corporation. Total external arrears payments, on the other hand, continued to build up, reaching US$762.7 million (Z$41,948 billion) by the end of the same period.[183]

In 2002, Paz abandoned its plans to raise Z$40.9 billion through the disposal of loss-making entities, with only Z$462 million being realized from the disposal of government shareholdings in some entities by September of that year. That Z$462 million was raised from the disposal of stakes in CAPS Holdings Limited, the Zimbabwe Reinsurance Company, Zimchem Refineries and Munyathi Mining Limited.

By mid-2002, parastatals were on the verge of collapse and thousands of workers were staring unemployment in the face; the country was on the brink of economic collapse. Several parastatals were about to cease operation because of corruption and misadministration.

The CSC, smitten by a Z$230 million debt, was one government-run company that was operating under severe financial stress and was on the brink of collapse. Despite the company earning the country more than Z$2 billion in

---

182. As at the end of January 2004, Noczim owed international suppliers US$171 million.

183. Of this amount, parastatals' arrears amounted to US$220.6 million (Z$12,133 billion). Other culprits were the government, which owed US$497.2 million, and the private sector, with a debt of US$45 million. *The Daily News*, 17 May, 2002.

foreign currency every year from beef exports to the EU, the problems affecting the company continued to mount. Some of its assets were put under the hammer due to the mounting debt.

The Zimbabwe United Passenger Company (ZUPCO), a State transport enterprise, was another serious contender for the scrap heap. Running an ageing fleet of buses, the company was operating on a shoestring budget and was losing ground daily. Most of ZUPCO's problems could be attributed to the ruling ZANU (PF), which disrupts its services when it commandeers buses for political or State occasions. There were also allegations that the ruling party did not pay on time for the public transport's services. And then ZUPCO, together with NRZ, another beleaguered parastatal, are involved in the money-sapping "Freedom Train" project[184] which has almost brought both to their knees.

Privatization of the Road Motor Services (the road haulage department of NRZ) set a precedent for how the commercialization of parastatals would end. The company, after two years privatization, went into liquidation after it became bankrupt.

Government efforts to privatize the parastatals through Paz bore little fruit. By 2004, Paz had failed to come up with proper mechanisms to speed up the privatization of the loss-making parastatals. Meanwhile, hundreds of jobs were being lost as companies crumbled because of the harsh economic climate. Zimbabwe's isolation by the international community and the IMF and the World Bank ensured that parastatals could only survive through domestic funding. There is no new investment flowing in when a country is classified as a high-risk investment destination.

*Industry and Export Promotion*

Industrial development is an essential pillar to a national economy. It can provide a base for the export of manufactured products; it is one of the best training grounds for skills development; it is an important source of structural change and diversification; and it can increase the flexibility of the economy and reduce dependence on external forces. Industrialization also provides employment and domestic savings.

During 1965-1977, sanctions created the incentive for import substitution, particularly in the case of commodities imported from the European

---

184. The "Freedom Train" is a subsidized train service to ferry workers to and from town during peak hours. These trains were introduced in Harare and Bulawayo in 2000 as a way of buying votes for ZANU (PF).

Community. There was a growth in employment and income and these in turn generated more demand and saved foreign currency. This demand-induced growth and import substitution accounted for a major share of the growth during this period. In 1975, the upward trend in the manufacturing sector growth stopped; and by 1978, the GDP in real terms fell by 12.1% and in per capita terms the decline was over 20%.[185] This was largely because of the liberation war and the effect of the prolonged sanctions on imports of intermediate inputs and the resultant increase in production costs.

Import substitution was a sound policy in Zimbabwe. A substantial number of manufacturers started to export to other COMESA (Common Market for Eastern and Southern Africa) states, SADC, Asia and Europe. About 50% of all regional trade is in manufactured goods. However, the majority of investment opportunities with an acceptable rate of return are found in production for the local market. The challenge is to establish an incentive and institutional structure that directs investment towards industries that are productive and can be competitive in the future.

Industry (including mining, manufacturing, construction and power) contributed 40% of GDP in 1990. From 1980 to 1991, industrial production had increased by an annual average of 2.1%. In 1992, its contribution was 35% of GDP, an increase of 3% over 1991.

In 1999, industry contributed 23.8% of GDP and engaged 11.7% of the employed labor force. During 1990-2000, industrial GDP increased by an annual average of 1.5%. Industrial GDP declined by 1.9% in 1999, but increased by 7.4% in 2000.[186]

The energy that drives Zimbabwe's industry is derived principally from hydroelectric power and coal. Imports of energy products comprised 11.9% of the value of total imports in 1995. In 1998, the country purchased 40% of its energy from neighboring countries. In 1998, a new project was introduced to supply electricity to communal lands by solar energy systems, funded by Italy. The Italian Government cancelled the project the following September, owing to Zimbabwe's political and economic difficulties.

The mining industry produced revenues that increased between 1969 and 1978, despite sanctions, and after 1979 exploitation of mineral reserves increased. The USA imported more than R$30 million worth of "strategic and critical commodities," particularly nickel and chromium, in 1973; and despite sanctions,

---

185. *Southern African Economist*, Harare, May 1990.
186. The *Europa World Year Book*, Vol. II, 2002, London.

1975 was a record year for the mining industry, with output valued at R$169.8 million.[187] Nickel emerged as a major export, and there were four principal nickel mines operating. In 1980, an estimated 6% of the working population was employed in mining, which contributed 8% of GDP. Gold and nickel were the major mineral exports. Mining and agriculture provide about 70% of foreign exchange earnings. By 1984, mining contributed 5.6% of GDP, a decrease of 2.4% in comparison to 1980, and had 5% of the labor force employed in the sector. Gold, asbestos and nickel were the major mineral exports. In that year, gold exports were worth about Z$160 million.

In 1990, mining contributed 8.2% of GDP. In 1991, it contributed 6.1% of GDP, a drop of 2.1% in comparison to the 1990 figure. In 1992, it went on to contribute just 4.7% of GDP. By the end of 1998, the sector was experiencing one of its worst years, providing lower levels of both employment and foreign currency earnings. In 1999, it engaged 4.5% of the employed labor force. Mining GDP, in real terms, declined by 3.0% in 1999 and by 11.0% in 2000. From 2002 to June 2003, the mining sector declined by 7.1%, with gold production suffering a significant fall of 18%.

The mining sector was going through a severe crisis on the international scene as prices continued to remain depressed. Most commodity prices in 1997 nose-dived, with gold leading the pack when it went through the US$285-an-ounce mark (US$387 an ounce was the lowest price recorded in 1996). The price of copper, which at the end of 1996 was US$2,260 a tonne, slipped to below US$2,000 a tonne by the end of 1997, and nickel prices, at US$6,891 a tonne in 1997, were much lower than the 1996 nickel world prices.

Besides the depressed international commodity prices and high interest rates (40.5%), mining companies were reeling from the expensive administration of import tariffs — despite the adoption of a harmonized tariff description system — and the hikes in electricity tariffs.

The situation was boosted by the announcement of the discovery of significant diamond deposits in October 1999; and in December 2000, the development of the site of one such deposit, at Murewa, was announced. Unfortunately, in June 1999 the Hartley Platinum Project (begun in March 1996) was abandoned owing to viability questions and geological problems. However, in March 2001, it was announced that a share in the Hartley venture had been sold to a South African company and that the site's viability was under review.

---

187. *Ibid.*, 1977.

During the UDI period, manufacturing surpassed mining in importance, particularly food processing, metals (mainly ferro-chrome and steel), engineering, chemicals and textiles. In 1980, manufacturing employed about 15% of the labor force and contributed 24% of GDP. Between 1965 and 1974, widespread breaking of UN sanctions produced a fall in unemployment and a real increase in GDP of 83%. However, real GDP declined by one per cent in 1975, 3.4% in 1976, 6.9% in 1977 and 2.5% in 1978. Exchange rate stability was maintained for 25 years until the strained balance of payments position led to devaluation of the Rhodesian dollar in September 1975, October 1977 and again in April 1978, a cumulative depreciation of about 15% against the US dollar.

Re-investment, stimulated by rising domestic and foreign demand, reversed the downward trend at the end of 1985, when growth in industrial output reached 30%. Growth in 1986, however, fell to less than one per cent, as a result of a reduction, in real terms, of import inputs into the sector. In early 1987, a number of foreign companies sold their investments in the country, reflecting a loss of confidence in the economy, and output in the manufacturing sector fell by 5% in that year. Persistent sabotage of the railway and pipeline between Mutare and the Mozambican port of Beira led to recurrent fuel shortages.

In 1990, manufacturing contributed 26.4% of GDP, and employed about 16% of the labor force in 1985. The sector contributed 26% of GDP in 1991 and 30% 1992. The most important sectors, measured by gross value of output, were food processing, metals (mainly ferro-chrome and steel), chemicals and textiles. In 1993, the sector's contribution to the GDP was the same as the previous year's. However, the sector contributed 26.4% of GDP, so that overall during the period 1985-95 the sector's GDP increased by an annual average of 2.4%. An increase of 17.9% was recorded in 1996.

The sector, whose share of GDP was estimated to have fallen to below 15% in 1998 from around 25% in 1997, continued to suffer from cash flow difficulties, high interest rates, antiquated machinery and a generally weak domestic and export demand for goods and services. The largest slowdown was in the chemicals and petroleum products group, where production plummeted 6.4% when compared to 1997.[188] To make the situation worse, production in the textiles sector was reeling from the loss of the domestic market to cheap imports from the Far East.

In 1999, manufacturing contributed 16.4% of GDP, and engaged 8.1% of the employed force in that year. During 1990-2000, manufacturing GDP increased by

---

188. *Quarterly Digest of Statistics*, December 1998, Central Statistical Office, Harare.

an annual average of 1.6%. However, manufacturing GDP declined by 7.0% in 1999 and by 10.5% in 2000; 11.5% in 2001; and by 17.2% in 2002. Industrial output fell by 13% in 2002, analysts said, and was expected to plunge further in 2003.

Zimbabwe's economic growth in 1998 was officially reported to be 1.6%, compared with the initial forecasts of 3.7%.[189] Growth was subdued through most of the economy, including the large services sectors, and the growth rate during 1998 fell below the regional average of between 1and 2% to 0.8%. The decline in the country's growth rate was largely blamed on the depressed commodity prices on the international market, particularly those for tobacco and major minerals, the sharp depreciation of the local currency against the currencies of Zimbabwe's major trading partners, high inflation, the financial sector crisis experienced earlier in the year and the contagion effects of the financial crisis in south-east Asia that was spreading to various parts of the world.

The country's export earnings were down 16% in 1998 alone, despite the depreciation of the Zimbabwean dollar against a basket of major currencies. Exports plunged from US$3 billion in 1996 to US$1.7 billion in 2002.

Zimbabwe's long-awaited industrial policy framework was finally launched at the end of March 1999, by Industry and Commerce Minister Cde Nathan Shamuyarira. The policy, initially expected to be published in 1996, was prepared by the industrial task force of the National Economic Consultative Forum. It envisaged a greater participation by indigenous people in the national economy and proposed that the industrial sector would outpace both agriculture and mining in terms of growth and contribution to the GDP over the next ten years. The blueprint was designed to advance economic performance and achieve annual growth of at least five per cent within ten years and placed greater emphasis on developing the export potential of Zimbabwean firms to arrest the decline in export receipts experienced since the introduction of economic reforms in 1991.

The document outlined the different responsibilities that the government, the private sector and labor had to undertake to ensure smooth implementation of the industrial program. The public sector would be required to create an enabling environment through enactment and implementation of appropriate legislation, removing obstacles to competitive production, streamlining obstructive bureaucratic procedures and speeding up privatization. The

---

189. And that was much lower than the 3.2% registered in 1997, never mind the robust 7.9% in 1996.

government would also be expected to offer incentives for private sector participation in industrial development. For its part, the private sector was expected to focus on improving productivity through modernization of production processes, skills development, creating an environment that recognized and respected the contribution of labor, as well as provide rewards that were commensurate with performance. It was also expected to emphasize competitiveness by producing goods that met international standards. To support this industrialization process, labor was expected to strive to increase productivity and to participate in strategic planning and the setting of goals.

The government made a range of concessions that included the automatic right to employment for expatriates linked to investment projects, the elimination of the reserved sector list and removal of investment approval requirements. There was no doubt that increased investment in industry would create more jobs and a better quality of life for workers, and, not least, it was reasonable to anticipate the government which would see improved flows to the fiscus.

Corporate and business leaders hailed the industrial policy framework as a good strategy for a country whose historical industrialization was founded on a policy of protectionism and sanction-busting measures introduced during the UDI period in the mid-60s. Nevertheless, other business leaders thought that good fiscal management and the creation of a conducive economic environment should complement the launch of the policy. Some commentators blamed the decline of industrial production on poor economic policies by the government, as well as its bad management of the economy.

One may recall that the liberalization of the economy under Esap led to the removal of protectionism, resulting in viability problems for the country's manufacturing sector. Economic growth was erratic during the decade to 2000, with the period 1991-95 (the first phase of the economic reforms) being one of the worst. Zimbabwe's industries, burdened by a deteriorating macroeconomic climate marked by runaway input costs, were increasingly being forced out of business, as evidenced by the number of closures over the past few years. The country had already seen at least 12 mines being closed or sold over the past two years to 1999, throwing more than 2,000 people from their jobs, largely because of free-falling commodity prices.

Economic analysts were predicting tougher times for many companies during the new millennium unless the macroeconomic environment stabilized. Most forecasted that growth would falter further before improving, probably by the end of 1999. Thus, it was incumbent upon the government to provide a congenial macroeconomic environment. The industrial policy framework depended on fundamentals that government, not industrialists, had control over: the high inflation rate and the high nominal interest rates, etc.

To recapitulate, trade between the UK and Rhodesia ceased with UDI in November 1965, and trade with many other countries was restricted. The country responded by considerably diversifying the economy and by searching for new outlets. There was widespread breaking of sanctions, with Rhodesia's agricultural, mining and manufacturing sectors improving and real GDP growing at an annual average rate of 7.2%. Much of Rhodesian merchandise was shipped from South Africa and Mozambique as exports from those countries. However, Rhodesia's closure of the border with Zambia and Zambia's refusal to re-open it curtailed Rhodesia's trade with the Democratic Republic of Congo and Zambia, and caused considerable loss to Rhodesia Railways.

The Rhodesian dollar was introduced in February 1970, replacing the Rhodesian pound at the rate of R£1 = R$1.720.[190] In 1973, gross national product (GNP) rose by 6.5% in real terms. Owing to increased guerrilla activity, defense spending was increased and taxation raised in the 1974-75 budget; and the Rhodesian economy was hard hit by the Arab oil embargo in 1974, particularly as it extended to Portugal and South Africa (on whom Rhodesia relied for supplies). Petrol rationing was re-introduced in February 1974. The economy began to feel the effects of international recession in 1975, leading to low demand for primary exports, declining export prices, decreasing industrial output and a strained balance of payments position.

The high cost of Chimurenga was exacerbated in 1976. The closure of the Mozambican border left Rhodesia totally dependent on South Africa for its trade. Extended periods of military service reduced the skilled labor force and white emigration exceeded immigration by over 6,000 in 1976. The spread of the guerrilla campaign throughout most of the country hampered communications and reduced the numbers of tourists by over 35%. Defense expenditure accounted for 23% of the record 1976-77 budget, which saw a deficit of R$59.7 million.

---

190. From September 1949, the value of the Rhodesian pound was US$2.80, so the initial value of the Rhodesian dollar was US$1.40 (US$1 = 71.43 Rhodesian cents). This valuation remained in effect until August 1971. Between December 1971 and February 1973, the Rhodesian dollar was valued at US$1.52 (US$1 = 65.79 Rhodesian cents). Since February 1973, the Rhodesian dollar was US$1.689 (US$1 = 59.21 Rhodesian cents). In terms of sterling, the exchange rate between February 1970 and June 1972 was R$1 = 11s 8d. or 58.33p (£1 = R$1.714).

Legal independence provided a stimulus to all aspects of the economy. The UN Security Council lifted trade sanctions at the end of 1979 and this, combined with the easing of transport and trade restrictions caused by the war, enabled Zimbabwe to participate fully in international trade. Exports increased by 28% and imports by 45% in 1980, creating balance of payments difficulties for the country. The GDP growth rate was 14% in 1980, the first improvement in real terms for five years, but fell to 8% in 1981 without the once-only benefits which followed the ending of Chimurenga. Problems which threatened continued growth included transport difficulties and the departure of Europeans whose skills could not yet be filled by qualified Africans. As much as 40% of the adult labor force, lacking those skills, could have been unemployed. Plans to expand the economy also depended on the procuring of sufficient finance, particularly from foreign governments. A three-year economic plan, aiming for average annual growth of 8%, was announced in February 1981, but relied heavily on external financing. In March 1982, the Zimbabwe Conference on Reconstruction and Development (ZIMCORD) received pledges of about US$800 million, but the flow of funds was disappointing.

In 1982, the Government published its first post-independence development plan. The Transitional National Development Plan postulated a GDP growth rate of 8% per annum, with production of goods rising faster than services and a 3% annual growth in wage employment. The plan's GDP growth targets were not achieved.

Production in the non-material sectors grew 4.2% per annum and material production grew at 1.4%. Employment generation was not achieved in spite of administrative interventions aimed at stabilization. The failure to achieve plan targets was caused by drought over most of the period, which affected production, demand and domestic resource mobilization. In addition, the internal security problem caused by dissidents operating in Matabeleland made foreign investors nervous, and the world recession had an adverse impact on the availability of the external resources from the country's own exports to sustain the plan.

The second post-independence plan, the 1986-90 five-year Transitional National Development Plan, aimed at an average GDP rate of growth of 5.2% and the creation of 28,000 jobs a year. In the event, GDP grew by 0.2% in 1986. Patchy rainfall and foreign exchange shortages[191] played a role. In 1987, GDP

---

191. Foreign exchange was limited, despite improvements in export earnings, due to relatively high debt obligations and low levels of capital inflows.

registered a -0.7% growth in a context of poor rains, foreign exchange cuts and slow world economic growth. The World Bank attributed the slow growth rate to a sharp decline of investment in the productive sectors, weak export growth, and a poor incentive environment for economic restructuring and internal macroeconomic imbalances that involved a large transfer of private savings into public debt.

The situation looked brighter in 1988; GDP grew by 5.3%, which translated into an increase of 23% in per capita income. The good performance was attributable to increases in import allocations from the Export Revolving Fund, barter arrangements and programs, export promotion programs and supplementary allocations to export orientated industries. In 1989, the economic growth stood at 3.5%.

*Table 13: Government Budget (R$/Z$ '000)*

| YEAR | REVENUE | EXPENDITURE | SURPLUS/ DEFICIT |
|---|---|---|---|
| 1966-67 | 156,654 | 147,658 | 8,996 |
| 1971-72 | 242,102 | 234,718 | 7,384 |
| 1976-77 | 530,870 | 590,637 | -59,767 |
| 1981-82 | 1,482,400 | 2,006,500 | -524,100 |
| 1986-87 | 3,056,456 | 3,822,106 | -765,650 |
| 1991-92 | 7,925,392 | 8,944,717 | -1,019,325 |
| 1996-97 | 22,858,400 | 30,303,700 | -7,445,300 |
| 1999 | 58,564,000 | 77,908,000 | -23,836,000 |
| 2000 | 87,825,000 | 155,346,000 | -81,818,000 |

Source: Europa World Year Book, 1965-2003; Quarterly Economic & Statistical Review, Vol.20 No.3/4, Sept/Dec. 1998.

Zimbabwe has had persistent problems in restraining its budget deficit; the 1981-82 deficit was Z$524.1 million, while that of 1986-87 was Z$765.65 million, partly because of increased expenditure owing to the drought, which led to the introduction of supplementary budgetary expenditure appropriations in February 1984.

Today is no better. Zimbabwe revised its 2003 budget upwards in August 2003 by almost 90%, to free up cash to pay wages, import food and buy medicines in its hyper-inflationary economy. Finance Minister Herbert Murerwa asked Parliament to approve a supplementary budget of Z$672bn on top of the Z$770.3bn that was budgeted for the entire year. The supplementary budget showed that expenses by the ZANU (PF) government had risen 87.2% beyond what was planned.

The minister's statement was almost completely bereft of details on the state of Zimbabwe's economy, though it did reveal that manufacturing output had fallen 8.6% in the first four months of 2003.

Presenting the 2004 budget on November 20, the Finance Minister painted a grim picture, saying the economy would shrink by 13.2% at the end of 2003, while inflation would surge to 600% in December, reaching 700% early-2004. "Given a revenue of GDP ratio of 28%, revenues will be about Z$6.9 trillion. Total expenditures will amount to Z$8.74 trillion giving a deficit of Z$1.85 trillion, which translates to 7.5% of GDP — a standstill position compared to 2003 in the absence of significant international inflows."[192]

Presenting his eagerly-awaited monetary policy statement later that December, the new governor of the RBZ, Gideon Gono, said he would first take the scythe to money supply growth to reduce it from 500% by the end of the year to below 200% by the close of 2004. This came at a time when the southern African region was forecast to experience an average growth of 2.6%, while inflation would average 15.3%. Although President Mugabe and his government pinned their hopes of economic recovery on the agriculture sector, only Z$439.8bn was allocated to the Ministry of Agriculture. The Defense Ministry was allocated Z$661bn, even though its commitment in the DRC war had ceased. Murerwa earmarked a whopping Z$1.27 trillion for defense and security, although there is peace in the region. The figure was the third largest vote after the civil service wages bill (Z$3.18 trillion) and the Ministry of Education, Sport and Culture (Z$1.52 trillion). The meager housing vote of Z$10bn raised doubts about promises by Mugabe that the government would build a million houses in five years. (It costs about Z$15 million to build a basic four-room house.)

Fifteen per cent of the budget (a staggering Z$1.3 trillion) had been entrusted to the Finance Minister as an unallocated reserve, meaning that the government can spend it without parliamentary scrutiny — it can only be considered a special ZANU (PF) slush fund.

Economic analysts said Murerwa's budget had perennial structural deficits. It did not address three key issues, namely the skewed exchange rate, runaway inflation and the unrealistic interest rate regime. Murerwa failed to spell out how inflation would be brought down to the double digits he anticipated. The government hoped to raise resources from the domestic market, which was inflationary as it crowded out local players.

---

192. *The Hansard*, Harare 20 November 2003.

In March 1983, the government had reached agreement with the IMF for a stand-by credit of SDR300 million, plus a further SDR56.1 million under the IMF compensatory financing facility. Zimbabwe had already submitted to a 16.5% devaluation of its currency, in December 1982, and to import curbs, to meet the IMF's terms. However, following the supplementary allocations to the budget in 1983-84, and the government's failure to reduce the budgetary deficit for 1984-85, the IMF suspended disbursement of SDR125 million of the stand-by facility in August 1984. The budgetary deficit and external public debt continued to grow.

A five-year development plan (1986-90), announced in April 1986, envisaged real annual growth in GDP of 5%, with annual growth of 7% in the value of exports. Investment was to be encouraged by tax incentives, and government participation in industry was to increase. It was hoped that public debt servicing would decrease from the equivalent of 28% of export earnings to 18% during the period. In April 1987, however, the cost of debt servicing exceeded 35% of exports earnings.

*Table 14: Gross National Product per Head*

| GNP Measured at Average | Million US$ | Equivalent to US$ per Head |
|---|---|---|
| 1988-90 prices | 6,313 | 640 |
| 1990-92 prices | 5,896 | 570 |
| 1991-93 prices | 5,756 | 540 |
| 1992-94 prices | 5,424 | 490 |
| 1994-96 prices | 6,845 | 610 |
| 1996-98 prices | 7,214 | 620* |
| 1999 prices | 6,100 | 520 |

*\*Or US$2,489 per head, on an international purchasing-power parity basis.*
*Source: The Europa World Year Book 1987 to 2001, vol. II, London*

During 1980-90, GNP increased, in real terms, at an average annual rate of 2.6%, although GNP per head declined by 0.8% per year. Over the same period, the population increased by an annual average of 3.4%. The country's GDP as a whole increased, in real terms, by an annual average of 3.1% in 1980-91. However, GDP declined by 8% in 1992-93, owing to the effects of drought on the country's agricultural production. By the financial year ending June 30, 1992, there was a budgetary deficit equivalent to 9% of GDP.

During 1990-96, GNP per head decreased, in real terms, at an average annual rate of 1.1%. Over the same period the population increased by an annual average of 2.6%. The country's GDP increased, in real terms, by an annual average of 1.7% over the same period. Real GDP declined by 2.7% in 1999 and by 5.5% in 2000. In 2002, it declined by 11.9% and was estimated to decline by 15% in 2003. In contrast, Mozambique expected GDP growth of 8% in 2003.

In 1991, Zimbabwe recorded a visible trade surplus of US$48.1 million, while there was a deficit of US$489.3 million on the current account of the balance of payments. In 1990, the principal source of imports (20%) was South Africa, while the principal market for exports (12%) was the Federal Republic of Germany. In 1991, the principal source of both imports (28.9%) and exports (17.1%) was the Southern African Customs Union (which comprised South Africa, Lesotho, Botswana, Namibia and Swaziland). Other major trading partners were the UK, the USA, Botswana and Japan.

The principal exports in 1987 were minerals, tobacco, cotton lint and maize. The main imports were machinery and transport equipment, basic manufactures, chemicals and mineral fuels. The principal exports in 1991 were tobacco, metals and metal alloys. The main imports were machinery and transport equipment, basic manufactures, chemicals and mineral fuels.

In 1993, the country recorded a visible trade surplus of US$122.1 million, while there was a deficit of US$115.7 million on the current account of the balance of payments.

In 1994, the visible trade surplus equaled US$157.6 million, while a deficit of US$424.9 million on the current account of the balance of payments was recorded. In 1995, the principle source of both imports (41.2%) and exports (18.5%) continued to be the South African Customs Union. In 1997, Zimbabwe imported goods worth more than Z$17 billion compared with Z$16 billion in 1996 from the Customs Union, although more than 80% of the imports were from South Africa. Zimbabwe, on the other hand, exported goods valued at just over Z$4 billion in 1997 and Z$3.5 billion in 1996.[193]

At the end of 1992, Zimbabwe's external debt totaled US$4,007 million (of which US$2,783 million was long-term public debt). In that year the cost of debt servicing was equivalent to 31.9% of the value of exports of goods and services.

In the financial year ending June 30, 1994, the budgetary deficit was equivalent to 7.9% of GDP. End of 1993 external debt totaled US$4,168 million, of which US$3,021 million was long-term public debt. In that year the cost of debt servicing was equivalent to 32.3% of the value of exports of goods and services.

Furthermore, at the end of 1994, external debt totaled US$4,368 million, of which US$3,253 million was long-term public debt. The cost of debt servicing was equivalent to 26.9% of value of exports of goods and services. In the financial year ending June 30, 1997, the budgetary deficit was equivalent to 7.1%

---

193. *The Financial Gazette*, 30 July, 1998.

of GDP. Zimbabwe's external debt at the end of 1996 totaled US$5,005 million, of which US$3,338 million was long-term public debt, and the cost of debt servicing was equivalent to 21.2% of value of exports of goods and services.

On December 31, 1998, Zimbabwe's debt stood at Z$90 billion (US$2.37 billion) and was accruing monthly interest of over Z$1 billion; more than Z$2 billion was needed each month to service the debt. The country's domestic debt stood at Z$42.6 billion, as at the end of 1998. The total debt of Z$132.6 billion then accounted for 95% of GDP. In addition to Zimbabwe's domestic and foreign debts was the Z$29 billion in sovereign guarantees the government had issued in favor of borrowings by parastatals and private companies in which the government had substantial interest.[194] According to the country's central bank figures, local importers and holidaymakers in most cases immediately wiped out daily foreign currency inflows into the country. And, for the first time since independence in 1980, Zimbabwe failed to service its foreign loans on time in May 1999 because of a shortage of foreign currency, according to the World Bank.

In 1999, the country had a visible trade surplus of US$249 million, while there was a surplus of US$27 million on the current account of the balance of payments. During the same period the principal source of both imports (40.7%) and exports (12.6%) was South Africa. Other major trading partners were the UK, Germany, Japan and the USA. The principal exports in 1999, as in 1991, were tobacco, metals and metal alloys and the main imports were machinery and transport equipment, basic manufactures, chemicals and mineral fuels.

Statistics obtained from the Central Statistics Office in mid-November 2002 showed that Zimbabwe earned the equivalent of Z$66.4 billion from exports in 2001 but spent Z$95.5 billion on imports in the same period. The Z$29.1 billion deficit was attributed to declining output in the mining, agriculture and manufacturing sectors — the country's key foreign currency earners. Mineral output shrank by 25% between 1999 and 2001, and manufacturing by 7% in 2001, while agriculture fell by 11% during the same year.

There is not much sign of improvement since then. Revised figures from the Ministry of Finance showed that mining output would fall by 4.1% by the end of 2002, manufacturing by 11.9% while agriculture would suffer a massive 24.6% slump chiefly because of disruptions in commercial agriculture. While output in Zimbabwe's key export sectors was expected to continue falling, the country's

---

194. These corporations include ZISCO, Wankie Colliery, the Zimbabwe Minerals Development Corporation, the Industrial Development Corporation, Affretair, the Zimbabwe Defense Industries and the Development Trust of Zimbabwe.

import needs were rising. Zimbabwe's controversial land reforms disrupted commercial agriculture, a key export sector, which alone produces 60% of raw materials for the manufacturing sector and accounts for 40% of Zimbabwe's economy. Zimbabwe has had to import food because the reforms slashed domestic food production by over 60% in 2001-02.

The country is also dependent on electricity, fuel and raw material imports and could be forced to import other goods if the local manufacturing sector continues to shrink. According to a USAid-funded study by the CZI, manufacturing's contribution to the GDP dropped from 25% in 1989 to 14% in 2002. Manufacturing sector revenue declined from US$900 million in 1997 to US$263 million in 2002.

In its October 2003 Treasury report, the Ministry of Finance said that the current and capital accounts remained deficit accounts and were projected to deteriorate to US$1,130.2 million (Z$931 billion) and US$333 million (Z$274 billion) respectively, thus implying an overall foreign currency deficit of US$1,463.2 million (approximately 25% of GDP). The report also revealed that in 2000, the capital account had recorded a US$289 million deficit and a US$389 million deficit in 2001. For 2002, the ministry estimated that the account ended the year on minus US$218 million.

A budgetary deficit of Z$22,388 million, equivalent to 10.4% of GDP, was recorded in 1999. At the end of the same period the country's external debt totaled US$4,566 million, of which US$3,211 million was long-term public debt. In that year the cost of debt-servicing was equivalent to 25.3% of the value of exports of goods and services.[195] By November 2002, the country had an accumulative total of US$1.3 billion external debt, about Z$71.5 billion at the official exchange rate, but about $1.9 trillion on the parallel market.[196]

Meanwhile, at the end of August 2001, Zimbabwe's overdue obligations totaled SDR42.3 million (about US$53 million), including SDR18.9 million (about US$24 million) to the IMF's General Department, and SDR22.3 million (about US$29 million) to the Poverty Reduction and Growth Facility.[197] The country was experiencing high inflation — in excess of 70% — massive, soaring domestic and external debts, and a food crisis was looming. The rate of inflation averaged 32.3% annually in 1994-99. Consumer prices increased by an annual average of 20.1% in 1997, by 46.6% in 1998 and by 55.5% in 1999.

---

195. Europa World Year Book, Vol.II, 2002.
196. *The Daily News*, Harare, 15 November, 2002.
197. *Ibid.*, 27 September, 2001.

When in October 2001 the government re-imposed price controls, it had hoped to keep inflation below the three-digit figure, a psychological threshold that affects consumers and businesses alike. However, Zimbabwe's run-away inflation continued unabated, rising to 112.1% for the year to December 2001. Figures released by the Central Statistical Office (CSO) showed that the year-on-year inflation rate would continue to rise despite the imposition of price controls.

And as predicted, the year-on-year inflation rate for January 2003 shot to an all time high of 208.1%. By November, the figure stood at 619.5%, according to figures issued on December 17, 2003 by the CSO (it was 5% in neighboring South Africa). This was the single largest jump since the country's economy began its slide in 2000 (525.8% in October 2003). Of the 619.5% year-on-year rate of inflation in November 2003, increases in food prices accounted for 35 percentage points, drinks and tobacco went up by 49%, clothing and footwear by 21.9% while the worst was medical expenses which went up by 224% in a single month. In the past year, the CSO figures showed that cooking oil had gone up by 759%, shoes by 582%, public transport by 460% and cigarettes by 453%.

The public was concerned at the lack of action; consumer watchdogs had remained quiet in the face of the new price hikes. Moreover, it was inevitable that the inflation rate would continue rising as long as money supply growth continued unchecked.

Finance Minister Herbert Murerwa had pledged to slash inflation to 96% by the end of 2003, but his forecasts were over-optimistic given the government's loose monetary policy which encouraged consumptive borrowing. Murerwa had chosen to ignore negative factors that militated against his projections: the donor fatigue that cut off all the lines of credit which Zimbabwe had previously enjoyed; the drying up foreign exchange resources; and the food shortages that meant that every commodity available would be sold at exorbitant prices.

In its weekly economic highlights, dated January 11, 2002, the RBZ said: "High inflation has significantly eroded the value of money in circulation. In order to restore the real value of currency and hence the purchasing power of money, there is urgent need to bring inflation under control, and to aggressively reduce it to sustainable levels. This, of course, requires a credible disinflation program, consisting of a coherent set of anti-inflation measures."[198] The RBZ

---

198. The Reserve Bank of Zimbabwe, 11 January, 2002.

said that the acceleration in inflation during the past decade had led to a surge in consumers' demand for currency for conducting purchases.

Total currency, defined as notes and coins in circulation, rose from Z$1 billion in 1990 when inflation was 15.5% to Z$20.5 billion by the end of October 2001 — by which time inflation had risen to 97.6%.[199] The RBZ said the annual growth in total currency had risen sharply from 20% in 1980 to 146% by October 2001, indicating an increase in the public's demand for notes and coins. As a result, the public's preference for cash, as measured by the currency to deposit ratio, doubled from 6% in 1996 to 12.7% by October 2001.[200]

The default on payment of international debt further eroded the very limited creditworthiness and repute that still attached to Zimbabwe. The IMF and other lenders require that their borrowers can service their debts. It is this debt servicing that leaves the indebted countries even poorer. It is a vicious circle that leads many to speculate, again, as to the fundamental motivations that drive the IMF.

For every US$10 that the industrially developed countries send to the underdeveloped countries, US$110 goes straight back in the form of repayment of debts. In five years to 1999, Zimbabwe's expenditure on debt repayments rose from 5 to 10% of the country's GDP. The human cost is enormous. In almost all countries in Africa, a crushing burden of foreign debt results in government spending more repaying creditors than they spend on the infrastructure, health and education of their citizens. Inadequate public spending on social service provisions means that families must meet the costs of health and education out of their own pockets. A small fraction of what is spent on debt servicing could be used to eradicate infectious diseases and to provide primary health care. The struggling indigenous entrepreneur is forced to shoulder more transaction and production costs because external debt service has diverted resources away from activities, which create enabling environment for investment and development.

According to the Africa Forum and Network on Debt and Development (AFRODAD), sub-Sahara Africa's debt to both multilateral and bilateral creditors stood at almost US$370 billion (Z$20,350 billion) in October 2001.[201] This figure continues to rise, not because of any significant additional borrowing, but mainly as a result of the cost of servicing the debt. Approximately 30% of new aid money in sub-Saharan Africa is directed away

---

199. *The Daily News*, Harare, 22 January, 2002.
200. *Ibid.*
201. *Ibid.*, 26 October 2001.

from social services and redirected towards servicing debt payments to, mainly, the World Bank and the IMF.

The RBZ in its report for the period ending May 4, 2001 confirmed that Zimbabwe's external debt had soared to US$4.5 billion (Z$248 billion). The country was US$600 million in arrears, and by year's end the foreign debt arrears stood at US$700 million; it continued to build up during 2002 and were forecast to have ended the year at US$1.5 billion.. Figures released by the RBZ at the end of February 2002 showed that the government continued in its insatiable appetite for funds from the central bank. For the week ending February 22, the government's domestic debt stood at Z$220.9 billion up from Z$211.7 billion on February 8, 2002.

This means that, within a week, the government had spent more than Z$9 billion.[202]

The RBZ had earlier shown that advances to the government had skyrocketed from Z$10 billion on January 11 to Z$13.5 billion on January 18, 2002.[203] As of May 17, 2002 the government's debt had reached Z$279.8 billion. The debt had now been steadily increasing by more than Z$10 billion weekly. The RBZ said lending to banks declined, while net credit to the government increased. It said injections were mainly through Treasury Bills.[204] By the end of June 2003, the domestic debt was standing at Z$446 billion. Statistics released by the RBZ showed that the increase in domestic debt was driven by the government's use of its overdraft facility with the central bank. According to the Reserve Bank's figures, its advances to the government stood at Z$50.3 billion in the week ending May 16, up from zero in the week ending December 27, 2002. Outstanding government stocks declined by only one billion to Z$14.8 billion in the same period.

Economic analysts said the upsurge in domestic debt (Z$800 billion in December 2003) was a sign of a severe debt trap: the government was borrowing to repay its debts. Rather than financing ongoing and exhaustive expenditures, most of the funds were now being used for transfer payments and consumption purposes. Interest due on Treasury bills was at Z$173.5 billion (for TBs worth only Z$207.5 billion). The government's interest burden ballooned from Z$134 billion at the beginning of 2003.[205]

---

202. *Weekly Economic Highlights*, RBZ, 22 February 2002.
203. The Reserve Bank of Zimbabwe, 18 January 2002.
204. *The Daily News*, Harare, 7 June, 2002.
205. *The Financial Gazette*, 8 July, 2003.

In its weekly economic highlights of mid-February 2003 the RBZ said, "Since 1995, the stock of domestic debt has risen twenty two-fold from Z$24.5 billion to Z$369.2 billion by end of January 2003."[206]

According to statistics from the Ministry of Finance, Zimbabwe's total foreign debt was expected to grow to US$5.3 billion by the end of 2003, of which US$3.2 billion would be the principal debt and US$1.9 billion arrears.

A drop in the GDP was also forecast — the IMF said that according to its projections derived from data supplied by the government, the country's GDP would plunge from US$13.1 billion (Z$1 trillion) in 2003 to only US$4.5 billion (Z$3.7 trillion) in 2004. This meant that the country's total external debt would rise to a staggering 40.2% of GDP.[207]

The government in May 2003 started paying US$3 million towards clearing its outstanding arrears with the IMF, after promising the international lender that Zimbabwe was committed to settle her arrears. However, that was a lot to promise.

In the long run, the debt crisis has fuelled a vicious cycle of rising poverty, economic stagnation and increased social tension, contributing to processes which usually threaten to culminate in the collapse of a state. It is no surprise, therefore, that the World Bank and IMF, in 1996, agreed to search for solutions to debt problems like this.

The objective of the Heavily Indebted Poor Countries (HIPCs) Initiative was to reduce the external debt of the world's poorest, most heavily indebted countries —, of which 80% (33 out of 41) are in Africa — to sustainable levels. The Initiative would provide substantial debt relief to countries which implemented critical social and economic reforms as part of an integrated approach to lasting development.

On April 16, 1998 a campaign by the name of Jubilee 2000 was launched in Accra, Ghana with the aim to collect one million signatures from each African country to form a petition to present to donor countries in an effort to call for debt cancellation. According to world debt statistics, every African owes the lenders about US$330 at birth. The statistics further indicate that sub-Sahara African debt accounts for only one per cent of global trade, hence canceling the debt of the most indebted countries would be possible without hurting the global economy.

---

206. *Weekly Economic Highlights*, RBZ, 14 February 2003.
207. *The Daily News*, Harare, 10 September, 2003.

Jubilee 2000, whose concept was borrowed from the biblical Book of Leviticus which cites an ancient Jewish tradition whereby all debts are cancelled and slaves are set free, aimed to have debts cancelled by 2000. The campaign spread through Britain, Austria, Germany, and African nations such as Kenya, South Africa and Zimbabwe. The campaign estimated that unpayable debt was at least US$100 billion, though other sources put the figure as high as US$250 billion. In October 1998, the British Department for International Development said it would contribute £30 million over the next three years to help reduce the debt of some of the poorest African countries. The UK was pressing to ensure that by 2000 all eligible countries would at least have started the process that would lead to debt relief being received. In late January 1999, Chancellor Schroeder of Germany announced the Cologne Debt Initiative.[208]

One of the most ghastly consequences of being in debt is that a country loses its economic independence. It finds itself being coerced to adhere to any and every suggestion and demand from the IMF and Western creditors. Where French, Japanese and American farmers enjoy subsidies for their agricultural production, Zimbabwean farmers are denied such support and protection. Where American and European textile industries are protected from competition, African and Indian textile industries are forced to compete with the richest nations without similar protection.

Zimbabwe does not qualify for the HIPCs initiative; however, Zimbabwe could mitigate the effects of her relatively high stock of debt by more effective debt management. Proper debt management would provide cheap and concessional loans that could be productively invested in most viable projects that strongly support community needs and aspirations.

The issue of debt management in many underdeveloped countries, however, still remains obscure. The Jubilee 2000 campaign also attempts to shed some light on who are the policy-makers, what is negotiated, how is the debt portfolio managed, what data is available for the public, and what checks and balances are put in place.

In addition to debt, the balance of payments position is a mirror image of the economic status of that country over a period of time. When the balance of payments position is negative, it means that the country is consuming (importing) more than it can pay for. This was the case with Zimbabwe in 1997 when foreign currency reserves fell to dangerously low levels, at a time when foreign exchange inflows were also falling due to sluggish prices for the

---

208. The Financial Times, 21 Jan. 1999.

country's mineral and agricultural exports. The dwindling foreign currency reserves coupled with strong importer demand triggered an accelerated downward slide in the local unit, which has not stabilized, causing mayhem in the exchange rate market (more on that, below). Foreign investors sat on the sidelines, badly burned. Inside sources had it that foreign exchange reserves had reached a level of one month's cover.

Lack of foreign exchange has hindered the import of goods essential for industrial expansion, and a number of plans intended to rectify this shortage in the 1990s failed. Increasing budgetary deficits, met largely by domestic borrowing, were blamed for high levels of inflation in the 1990s. International aid was suspended during the latter months of 1999, including that provided by the IMF and the World Bank, owing to Zimbabwe's inability to comply with requirements for economic reform. The IMF was also concerned that expenditure figures for the war in the DRC that it had received from the Zimbabwe authorities were false, the true amount being up to ten times higher.

In April 2000, a number of white farmers refused to participate in the annual tobacco auctions, which were desperately needed to increase Zimbabwe's foreign exchange reserves, until there was a substantial devaluation of the currency. Several banks agreed with their demands. The government, however, feared that such a move would cost it dearly in terms of popularity and resisted until after its re-election in June. The Zimbabwean dollar was devalued twice in August, by a combined total over one-quarter. Revenue was also lost by the burning of the tobacco crop on some white-owned farms that had been forcibly occupied, although volumes increased in the tobacco auctions held in late 2000 (236m kilograms), and prices deteriorated less than had been predicted.

In March 2001, the IMF announced it would not grant Zimbabwe any further aid and in May it stated that Zimbabwe had not made any debt repayments since February. As a result, the IMF also removed the country from the list of countries eligible to borrow resources under the Poverty Reduction and Growth Facility in September. The World Bank had suspended aid in October 2000, and several Western donor governments suspended payments in 2000-01. As a result, in March 2001, the government obliged three-quarters of all export earnings to be paid into the RBZ, in an attempt to improve the country's foreign-currency position.

Zimbabwe has benefited from a well-developed infrastructure, mineral wealth and a highly diversified manufacturing sector. Thus, during the first phase of economic reforms, the country was operating on a base that was perceived as strong (although in real terms there were underlying structural weaknesses, well-disguised by the import-substitution-led industrialization strategy implemented during the UDI years). There was a sense of false security that made the independence government believe that the country could do without external help. However, lack of foreign exchange has hindered the import of goods essential for industrial expansion. It was hoped that this could be rectified through growth in the tourism industry, increasing exports of horticultural produce and, in 1997, the commencement of large-scale platinum mining, which was expected to contribute some 3.0% of annual GDP.

Nevertheless, in 1998 structural weaknesses were apparent from both a macro- and microeconomic perspective, well chronicled by the macroeconomic instability and low levels of supply response from private business. Zimbabwe's fiscal policy, to a large extent, failed to encompass stabilization, growth and distribution objectives, leaving the creators of wealth (the private sector) totally crowded out in the process of economic development. In June 1998, the Comptroller and Auditor-General disclosed that the government had over-borrowed on the domestic market by a whopping Z$78 billion and failed to collect more than Z$2 billion in revenue. Thus, the pace of capital accumulation was too slow on the back of savings and foreign exchange constraints.

The zimdollar is now just Monopoly money. Gone are the days when Zimbabweans cracked jokes about the Zambian Kwacha or the Mozambican Meticas, and questioned whether a ministry of finance even existed in Kaunda's Zambia.

*Table 15: The Falling Zimdollar*

| Year | £1.00 Sterling | US$1.00 |
|------|----------------|---------|
| Dec. 1970 | Z$1.720 | Z$0.720 |
| Jan. 1975 | 1.396 | 0.592 |
| Dec. 1981 | 1.384 | 0.719 |
| Dec. 1985 | 2.372 | 1.641 |
| Jan. 1990 | 3.661 | 2.270 |
| Jan. 1995 | 13.122 | 8.387 |
| Jan. 1996 | 18.549 | 10.839 |
| Nov. 1998 | 61.802 | 37.250 |
| Dec. 2000 | 82.170 | 55.070 |
| March 2003 | 1,288.242 | 824 |
| | | |

1- Z$51.24 (Dec. 2000)
Source: *Europa World Year Book, 1965-2001; Sagit Stockbrokers (Pvt) Ltd, Harare, 1998; Financial Gazette, 13 March, 2003.*

The crash of November 14, 1997 saw the zimdollar plummet by a record 75% against the US dollar. At independence, the zimdollar had been equivalent to US$1.40 (Z$0.71 = US$1). Now, the RBZ was forced to hike its rediscount rate twice in two months as the dollar crumbled, a crisis the government blamed on currency speculators. In November 1998, it was less than three US cents (Z$35 = US$1). Few people, locally and abroad, can comprehend how a nation with so much mineral wealth and other abundant natural resources, and hardworking people, could have gone down the drain so dramatically.

For a long time, the government has relied on domestic sources for funds to finance its recurrent expenditures, effectively pushing the private sector out of the financial market and driving interest rates upwards. Furthermore, the decline of foreign currency receipts caused by the retreating commodity prices, especially the waning competitiveness of tobacco, has a devastating effect on the economy.

Moreover, before the collapse of the zimdollar, the South African Rand had suddenly and unexpectedly depreciated heavily. Fearful that it would continue to do so, many Zimbabwean enterprises indebted to South African suppliers accelerated settlement of outstanding rand liabilities, thereby eroding some of Zimbabwe's relatively meager foreign exchange reserves.

Furthermore, recognizing that many of Zimbabwe's imports from her southern neighbor had a high import content and would therefore rise in price as a consequence of the Rand's depreciation, many increased their purchases from South Africa beyond usual levels, seeking to obtain the goods before price increases became effective. Payment of those higher than normal imports further eroded Zimbabwe's foreign exchange reserves.

However, as had all too frequently been symptomatic of Zimbabwean decision-making, rumor-mongering and ill-considered moves played a significant role in causing an exaggerated, largely unjustified money-market crash. As the dollar began its decline, panic led distraught debtors to rush to settle their foreign debts before the currency fell even further, creating a run on the foreign exchange reserves. In the process, the Reserve Bank of Zimbabwe believed that there was only one measure it could resort to in order to stabilize the currency, that being to raise the rediscount rate and thereby force up interest rates. The concept is a sound one, and is often effective;[209] however, the other economic repercussions of the further 3.5-percentage-point increase in the

---

209. in that the high costs of borrowings motivate delayed settlement of foreign debt and accelerated collection of export proceeds, whilst discouraging currency speculation and forward cover of liabilities.

rediscount rate were devastating. A very great number of Zimbabwean businesses were under-capitalized and subsisted only through reliance upon borrowings, and there were very few which could remain viable when debt servicing was at rates in excess of 40% of the debt.

Agriculture was already reeling from high input costs and inadequate commodity prices, in addition to a massive continuing interest burden; and that burden had now been exacerbated. Much of Zimbabwe's mining industry was in the same situation. Thus, the increase in interest rates must inevitably have contributed further to inflation and to diminished competitiveness in export markets.

At the end of September 1998, Finance Minister Cde Herbert Murerwa announced wide-ranging measures to relieve pressure on the battered dollar. Commercial and merchant banks' statutory reserves were increased from 20 to 25% of their capital, while their overnight foreign currency holdings were cut from US$5 million to US$2 million. In addition, no new licenses for foreign exchange bureaux would be issued; and strict limits were imposed on business transactions to stem an outflow of foreign currency. The crisis was little different from that experienced when the zimdollar crashed in November 1997: there were even worse problems for many companies, which were battling to control high input costs and trying to remain in business in the face of soaring lending rates[210] and declining consumer demand for their products. Price hikes of up to 60% killed demand for a range of locally-manufactured and foreign goods, as manufacturers tried to make up for the losses incurred during the state-imposed price freeze.

Imaginary and populist explanations,[211] and short-term solutions, were no longer able to make a dent. But still, the RBZ pursued the theoretically correct but practically disastrous course. Perhaps the RBZ could have directed its efforts towards encouraging the government to act to maximize exports and minimize imports. Since 1993, there had been periodic intimations by the government that export incentives would be introduced, and for over a year several ministers had repeatedly promised the re-introduction of incentives. But, with the exception of an inadequately implemented Export Processing Zones policy, the promises and assurances went unfulfilled. In like manner, more

---

210. In November 2003, banks quadrupled prime lending rates to 160% as compared to the rates in March.

211. i.e., blaming market speculators for the dollar's fall, accusing importers of panicking, and charging that exporters had driven the dollar lower by holding onto their receipts, hoping to cash in at lower rates.

would have been achieved by an upward tariff review of customs duties upon non-essential imports, in order to reduce imports.

In its weekly commentary for the week ended May 21, 1999, the Reserve Bank said: "Exports play an important role in the country's overall economic performance. Orientation of the economy towards more exports provides the much-needed foreign exchange to finance essential imports and also helps sustain domestic industry through expansion of markets. Focus should be on promoting export growth and ensuring an optimal mix in the structure of the country's export basket.... Zimbabwe's export market is still dominated by primary commodities with low value-addition and prone to fluctuations in international commodity prices. Pure manufactured exports, excluding ferro-alloys and cotton lint, only account for around 23% of merchandise exports." It further highlighted that agricultural and mineral exports aggregate 60.2% of total exports, and that secondary industry exports are 33.5% of total exports only, and suggested that "The country needs to restructure the export basket in order to sustain negative shocks on world commodity markets. A sustainable balance of payments position and exchange rate stability largely depend on the performance of the country's export sector.

"Poor performance of this sector implies that the country would have to rely heavily on foreign funding which is, however, not a sustainable path. Thus, industry should increasingly concentrate on value-addition, as well as development of new, competitive product ranges. In addition, exporters should be innovative and thrive for aggressive marketing initiatives. A vibrant export sector can, however, only be cultivated under a conducive environment of low fiscal deficits, low monetary growth, low inflation and, hence, an affordable cost of loanable funds. Stabilization of inflation is, therefore, crucial for sustained export growth."[212]

These points are entirely sound, but they are not comprehensive. An export-conducive environment also requires a deregulated economy or, at least, that such regulation is not counterproductive. Reacting to the constrained foreign exchange circumstances, the central bank intensified controls upon the repatriation of export proceeds. Since February 1998 (in order to prevent exporters or their customers from intentionally delaying export proceeds in speculation of further currency depreciation), exporters had been obliged by exchange control regulation to ensure that payment for export sales was received into Zimbabwe within three months of date of export. This is quite

---

212. The Reserve Bank of Zimbabwe, 21 May, 1999.

impractical and unrealistic, and resulted in a near-complete loss of export sales, with the result that Zimbabwe never enjoys the foreign exchange earnings, and the future of export ventures is put in jeopardy.

While the profits from currency speculation can be attractive, they are countered by the losses of interest earnings, or by interest commitments, in an economy where interest rates are extraordinarily high. Many of Zimbabwe's potential exports compete with those of other countries which are willing to extend credit to customers considerably in excess of 90 days, and Zimbabwe's regulations render this country's exports uncompetitive. The central bank has also been guilty of "disincentivizing" exports by its withdrawal of Foreign Currency Accounts (FCAs) from exporters in 1997. Most exporters do not only generate foreign exchange, but in so doing also incur foreign debt on the importation of production inputs, on export costs and the like. The absence of the former FCAs imposes upon the exporters exchange costs upon receipt of proceeds, and again upon subsequent purchase of foreign currency to meet external costs.

Furthermore, the government put new exchange control measures into effect in November 2002, requiring exporters to remit 50% of their proceeds to the RBZ, with the remainder also being held on their behalf by the central bank. Previously, exporters had to remit 40% of their proceeds and could trade the remainder on the lucrative parallel market for hard cash, where rates were more than 20 times the government-fixed Z$55 to US$1. However, under incessant pressure, the government eventually effectively devalued the official foreign exchange rate for key export sectors to just over half of its black market value against the US dollar. (As shown in the chart above, since December 2000 the exchange rate was Z$55 to US$1.) The government had decided to set a standard "export incentive" exchange rate of Z$800 to the US dollar for export earnings from sectors such as tobacco and gold. Until February 19, 2003, tobacco exporters were allowed to trade their foreign exchange earnings at US$1 for Z$99, while gold exporters were given Z$150. Depreciation was an assist, but even this was partially offset by increased costs of production inputs and by inflation.

While the Reserve Bank failed, in broad terms, to play its role in stimulating exports, the government after more than five years had still failed to align the Customs and Excise Act and the Sales Tax Act with the provisions of the Export Processing Zones Act, with the result that many of the incentives and benefits intended to attract EPZ enterprises were so substantially diminished as to eliminate the intended incentivization and discourage many enterprises from coming into being.

This negative characteristic was compounded by a Tax Department "witch-hunt" against EPZ ventures exploiting the employee tax-free fringe benefit provisions of the legislation. Those provisions had been made to encourage EPZs, and endeavors by the Department to tax the benefits, alleging them to be tax-evasionary, ran counter to the declared intents of the government. Similarly, the introduction of so-called export incentives in the Finance Act was markedly half-hearted on the part of government, and was inadequate to meet the needs of the economy.

Notwithstanding, in January 2003 alone, ten Zimbabwean companies applied for EPZ status, joining hundreds of local firms that have sought protection from the country's worsening economic crisis. There was growing interest from established companies to acquire EPZ licenses because of the favorable terms under which EPZ businesses operate. Companies within the export processing zone are entitled to a five-year tax holiday, a lower interest rate of 15% on bank loans, and exemption from paying duty when importing capital goods and machinery. The EPZ companies can now also borrow money at only 5% interest from a Z$25 billion revolving fund set up by the RBZ in 2002.

Although there had been a rise in EPZ applications, EPZs brought in a collective US$204.1 million (Z$168.51 billion) in 2002 but only US$60.7 million (Z$50.01 billion) had been recorded by August 2003. Analysts said this negative trend had been prompted by Zimbabwe's increasingly harsh operating environment. Nearly half of Zimbabwean industrial firms are on the verge of collapse because of government-imposed price controls, which have forced many companies to trade at a loss. Most manufacturing firms are struggling to import raw materials, machinery and spare parts because the acute foreign currency crisis, partly caused by a severe decline in Zimbabwe's export sector. Bankers said foreign currency reserves in the import sector diminished from about US$10.3 million in November 2002 to about US$600,000 in February 2003.[213]

Companies applying for EPZ licenses are expected to export more than 80% of their products. The EPZ Authority has in the past said that Zimbabwe's export receipts could rise by more than US$381 million annually if the government were to allow existing companies to operate under the export processing zone.

---

213. *The Zimbabwe Independent*, 7 March, 2003.

According to the World Bank, the implementation rate for approved projects in Zimbabwe is more than 60%, above the 30% average implementation rate for such projects in developing countries. US$137 million worth of projects have been approved since the inception of the EPZ program in 1996, while US$528 million in hard cash has been earned to date and 20,148 jobs created, according to figures from the EPZ Authority.

The suspension by the International Monetary Fund and other multilateral agencies of balance of payments support to Zimbabwe, because of differences with Harare over fiscal performance and its land reforms, has worsened the hard currency shortages. About 400 companies closed down in 2001, and 249 in 2002, due to the harsh operating environment. At least 900,000 jobs have been lost in the formal sector since 2000 because of the company closures, pushing unemployment to 80%, according to ZCTU.[214] Between December 2002 and April 2003, about 350 firms closed shop, leaving more than 350,000 workers without employment.[215]

In April 2003, the RBZ reported that Zimbabwe's capital account had virtually dried up following the suspension of foreign aid and development capital, coupled with unfavorable domestic and external conditions. (A capital account is a summation of investments, aid and credit coming into a country. It reflects the level of confidence the international community has in a country.)

While the situation in Zimbabwe has deteriorated, emerging markets and some Asian countries remain attractive to foreign investors because of brighter prospects for growth and higher returns on investments.

As if to add salt to the wound, Zimbabwe Electricity Supply Authority's load-shedding[216] had adverse effects on critical sectors of the economy, particularly mining, agriculture and manufacturing, which contribute at least 45% of GDP. In March 2003, ZESA was slowly being cut off by regional electricity suppliers because of its failure to clear arrears, resulting in the need for load-shedding. As of June 2002, ZESA owed US$24 million (Z$13.2 billion at the official exchange rate).[217] Statistics made available by the parastatal on June 19, 2003 show that the cash-strapped corporation, which was in the process of unbundling its operations to create four separate business units, had foreign currency arrears amounting to US$109.7 million. As of January 2004, ZESA's

---

214. *The Zimbabwe Standard*, 5 October, 2003.

215. *The Daily News*, 3 May, 2003.

216. Load-shedding is the reduction of electricity supplies at stipulated hours of the day due to a shortage of energy supplies.

217. *The Daily News*, 1 April, 2003.

foreign debt amounted to US$410 million. Top of the list is Hydro Cahora Bassa of Mozambique, which is owed US$31 million, South Africa's Eskom (US$20 million), Snel of the Democratic Republic of Congo (US$14 million), EDM of Mozambique (US$5 million), and Zesco of Zambia (US$4 million).[218]

ZESA was struggling to raise foreign currency needed to service the foreign debt. It was only logical for foreign suppliers to cut off supplies to ZESA because of the parastatal's failure to service its debts. Thus, industry continued to suffer losses incurred from disruptions in power supplies: workers were retrenched to reduce the wage bill, while some companies wound up operations. Research carried out in April 2003 showed that incessant power cuts were mainly hurting firms in the copper, glass and plastics manufacturing. As well as energy shortages, local industries were grappling with foreign currency shortages, high inflation (at 228%), liquid fuel shortages and shrinking markets. The CZI was quoted as having said, "Exports are going down as a result of production times being reduced. This would further worsen the country's already precarious foreign cash reserves."

In the agricultural sector, load-shedding was forcing farmers to reduce the number of hectares for winter maize and wheat. Zimbabwe normally grows between 85,000 and 100,000 hectares of winter crops, using overhead irrigation with water-pumping engines driven by electricity. Agricultural experts said that because of the power shortage only a quarter of the winter crop would be grown during the 2003 winter season. The country was already facing a serious shortage of wheat due to the destruction of the agricultural sector by the chaotic land reforms.

Ironically, in order to encourage farmers to plant winter wheat, the Minister of Agriculture increased the producer prices of the crop from Z$70,000 to Z$150,000 per tonne. The producer price of maize was also hiked from Z$28,000 a tonne to Z$130,000.

The construction industry is also hard hit. Some strategic companies that have closed down, causing a ripple effect, are Circle Cement, Zim Cement, Sino Zimbabwe and Portland Cement, which closed in February 2003 due to the foreign currency crisis. Cement, a major component in the construction industry, has been in short supply since the year 2002, after the government imposed price control restrictions on the commodity. The price of a 50kg bag of cement was gazetted at Z$511, but due to shortages and inflation, it was selling for Z$12,000 and on the black market for Z$16,500 as of the middle of October

---

218. *The Sunday Mail*, Harare, 1 February, 2004.

2003. Besides causing shortages on cement, price controls had resulted in the loss of over 20,000 jobs in the cement industry over the past two years.

The president of the Zimbabwe Building Contractors' Association, Mr. George Utaumire, said that considerable business had been lost due to the shortage of cement. Housing projects were shelved, leading to an increased housing backlog. He also said that membership of the association had dropped from 200 in 2002, to 70, as some companies failed to reopen in January 2003 after the annual shutdown. "More companies are likely to close shop this year," he said.

The rise in EPZ applications did not cover everyone, clearly. Although the reduction of the rates of corporate tax by 8–10 percentage points for companies achieving exports in excess of prescribed levels appeared significant, many exporters could not qualify as the measure of attainment was founded upon export volumes and not upon values. Thus, producers of a variety of products could well be exporting considerably in excess of 50% in value, but below that in volume, and therefore failed to qualify for the incentives. Moreover, the incentives only accrued to companies, and not to other exporters, and were of very little, if any, benefit to enterprises sustaining tax losses or who otherwise were not taxable. Even those who benefited only realized that benefit up to 18 months later.

Zimbabwe's precarious foreign exchange shortages continued to worsen, with exports bringing in only US$6.4 million (Z$352 million) on a cash basis for the period ending September 2001.

Import payments were mainly for machinery and equipment (US$2.6 million), manufactured goods (US$1.1 million), fuel and electricity (US$500,000), chemicals (US$400,000), and food (US$300,000).[219]

Zimbabwe's trade with fellow regional COMESA members continued to tumble with exports to Kenya collapsing by a staggering 83% in August 2003. Statistics released by the Ministry of Industry and International Trade indicate a precipitous degeneration of Zimbabwe's exports to the east African market. Exports to Kenya in 1997 totaled US$19.5 million before dropping to a paltry US$3.3 million. On the other hand, imports also dropped by 87% to US$2 million from US$15 million over the same period. This is despite Zimbabwe being one of Kenya's major trading partners in the southern African region. Zimbabwe holds the second position after South Africa as a source of imports for Kenya. Only two Zimbabwean companies, namely ZimRe Holdings and Econet Wireless, have

---

219. *The Daily News*, 11 October, 2003.

made inroads into the Kenyan market through tenders, while the diversified conglomerate Innscor Africa has already established itself in the fast-growing market with its popular fast-food brands.

Although Kenyan companies Africa Online and the Gweru-based Steelmakers have invested in Zimbabwe, the volume of trade needs to be increased as the range of tradable products is still comparatively low. Despite the fall, the balance of trade is in favor of Zimbabwe and is attributed to the nature of products traded in.

Exports to Zambia (Zimbabwe's second largest market) had also plummeted by about 80.4% to US$1.8 million in the first quarter of 2002, intensifying the foreign currency squeeze. This, plus problems in the fuel and transport sectors; the supply of energy, machinery and equipment, means that the regional market remains out of reach to most Zimbabwean companies.

Zimbabwe's currency took a further plunge towards its lowest trading record on the black market at the beginning of November 2002, due to what a leading economist said was panic buying by parastatals. Just a week before, the Zimbabwe dollar was trading at Z$800 against the US dollar and at Z$1,800 against the British pound. Trading was now at over Z$1,800 against the American greenback and Z$2,500 against the pound sterling and was expected to fall further. The Bulawayo parallel market was selling the rand for Z$250, up from Z$180, while the Botswana pula was selling at Z$280, up from Z$200 the previous week.[220]

Parastatals had flooded the black market to raise money to pay their debts and this had forced private companies involved in imports into panic buying of foreign currency. It should be noted that the fall of the dollar came a week after the IMF released a report urging the Zimbabwean government to act. The IMF report predicted that inflation in Zimbabwe could rise to 522% in 2003 if the government introduced no new economic measures.

The fall of the Zimbabwe dollar forced price increases on a daily basis in basic foodstuffs and imported goods — a move that hurt the already struggling ordinary Zimbabweans. The previous week, beef prices had gone up overnight by more than 100%, while the price of basic commodities was rising on a daily basis. If the dollar continued its free-fall, the remaining businesses that relied on imports would fold, adding to the unemployment and more widespread shortages of basic commodities.

---

220. *The Zimbabwe Independent*, 8 Nov., 2002.

Only a drastic devaluation of the Zimbabwean dollar could make a difference, now. Economists felt that if the president stood by his declaration that "devaluation is dead," then the country had no way to end the foreign currency shortages and repair the ever-rising exchange rate. Zimbabweans were waiting for the total collapse of the economy.[221]

More meaningful indicators of the gravity of the fiscal situation are hyperinflation, escalating money supply growth and offshore arrears. By the end of February 2003, total arrears stood at US$1.4 billion (Z$77 billion). Arrears to the IMF amounted to US$190 million while those owed to the World Bank were at US$186 million.[222] The suspension of Zimbabwe's voting rights in the IMF on June 6, 2003 worsened the country's international risk profile at a time it desperately needed foreign investment and aid to avert collapse. Another blow for the beleaguered Zimbabwean economy came on December 3, 2003, as the IMF began measures to expel Zimbabwe.

The decision was made after the country failed to make headway in clearing arrears on its debt (SDR164.9 million or US$233 million as of end of May) to the Bretton Woods institution. Withdrawal of its voting rights meant Zimbabwe would not vote on key decisions relating to IMF business. This also meant that Zimbabwe's credit rating, for a long time the envy of many a developing country, was reduced to junk status, a red flag to the international financier community.

One of the effects of the suspension was that any Zimbabwean company borrowing offshore was now subject to punitive interest rates, as offshore banks sought to rid themselves of any business exposure to the troubled country. Thus, a number of companies, including banking institutions which stitch up off-shore credit lines from correspondent banks, were racing to relocate their operations to neighboring countries, particularly South Africa, to circumvent the punitive rates being charged on Zimbabwean operations.

Zimbabwe first incurred arrears to the Fund in February 2001 and the country was declared ineligible to use IMF general resources on September 24, 2001. It was also removed from the list of countries eligible to borrow under the IMF Poverty Reduction and Growth Facility. Arrears alone were now 35% of GDP and total foreign debt, including arrears, exceeded GDP. Converted at a

---

221. The new governor of the RBZ introduced an auction system in January 2004, which constituted an effective devaluation of about 80% of the local currency from the official rate of Z$824 to US$1 to a weighted average rate of Z$4,196.58.

222. *The Daily News*, 7 March, 2003. (As of 31 October 2003 arrears to the IMF amounted to US$310 million.)

realistic exchange rate, Zimbabwe's GDP was probably in the region of US$4.5 to US$5 billion, meaning the economy was now smaller than those of Botswana and Mauritius.

### What Lies Ahead

In this crisis, essential measures that should be taken include:

Creation of an autonomous RBZ, which would curb financing of government expenditure;

Devaluation of the Zimbabwe dollar;

Increase in interest rates, coupled with accompanying measures to curb money supply growth;

Comprehensive liberalization of the economy to attract foreign trade and capital movements;

Urgent reduction of the cabinet and public sector, including reductions in the number of civil servants — especially soldiers;

Urgent establishment of an independent anti-corruption commission which should start a cleanup of both the public and private sectors;

Accelerated privatization of parastatals;

Collective bargaining to be accompanied by agreements on productivity; and

An orderly land-reform program in line with international norms where the rule of law applies.

However, these remedies are politically impossible, for several reasons.

Devaluation of the official exchange rate has been categorically resisted by President Mugabe himself, although the external value of the Zimbabwe dollar has been very unstable since 1997. The low-interest-rate policy has been counter-productive as it has only benefited the government, which has been able to borrow cheaply to meet its huge appetite for funds, and a few well-connected individuals who have been able to borrow for speculative purposes. The results have been high consumptive expenditures, which have been inflationary, and low levels of savings and investment, to the detriment of future growth.

The decline of national savings and investment levels over the past few years must be addressed. Having stood at levels of around 20.8% in 1995, the savings ratio had by 2000 fallen to 9%. In 2003, rates were estimated at below 8%. By contrast, successful newly industrialized nations such as South Korea, Malaysia, Singapore and Thailand have achieved growth and development through high savings rates of more than 30%.

This fall in savings rates has denied the economy resources for productive investment, at a time when both the public and private sectors required much higher levels of investment. The fall in savings and investment rates has been due to negative real deposit rates, caused by high domestic inflation of 525.8% and low nominal deposit rates of around 30% that have discouraged people from investing on a long-term basis. As a result, people have rearranged their asset portfolios towards stock and property markets and other non-productive activities as a hedge against inflation.

A substantial interest rate hike would burst the asset price bubble, bringing down highly-geared corporations and individuals, as well as several banks, in the process. Because members of ZANU (PF) heavies are engaged in the highly-geared sectors of the economy, a rational and responsible monetary policy is a non-starter.

More importantly, a sharp rise in nominal interest rates would jeopardize the government's land resettlement plans because it would make it impossible to provide credit to the new farmers at affordable rates.

Spending cutbacks are impractical, too, given the need to spend massively on land resettlement while also trying to keep pace with hyperinflation in terms of government consumption spending, wages and salaries. The impact of the fast-track land-reform program was to considerably reduce agricultural output as commercial farms immediately ceased to be productive units.

Lip service maybe paid to public sector reduction and privatization, but without foreign participation, privatization is unlikely to be successful.

Furthermore, with formal sector employment in 2002 no higher than at independence more than two decades ago, this is not the time for the government to be retrenching staff. In a vain attempt to hold onto power at any cost, the government would continue to spend money it does not have, funded by running the printing press, while also borrowing from the banks.

Successive finance ministers, and the outgoing Reserve Bank governor Leonard Tsumba, were guilty of creating the basis of a systematic financial sector crisis. Notes and coins in circulation increased 70% in the first eight months of 2002, while money supply reached 148.9% in November 2002 — twice as much as it was at the same time in 2001. According to figures presented to Parliament by Finance Minister Herbert Murerwa on August 21, 2003, annual money supply growth to April was 226%, largely on the back of high public sector borrowing requirements and high quasi-fiscal expenditures.

A headline in *The Herald* of March 5, 2003 announced that the government had launched "the much-awaited National Economic Revival Programme, which seeks to promote economic growth through home-grown solutions to various challenges facing the country." The new economic revival plan was underpinned on a two-tier nominal exchange rate of Z$824 to US$1 for all exporters and all sellers of foreign currency and Z$55 for government's official transactions, and other non-export sectors of the economy.

However, the NERP was the sixth such program to be hailed as the panacea for all the economic problems in the last twenty-odd years. We have had Zimcord, the five-year Transitional National Development Plan, Esap, Zimprest and the Millennium Economic Recovery Plan. Despite their inspirational names, all these programs failed to revive the economy. The problem is that the government does not have the political will to actually implement them.

Zimbabwe was relegated to the ranks of under-performers such as Ethiopia (one of Africa's poorest nations) and Bangladesh, according to the World Investment Report released at the beginning of September 2003 by the UNCTAD. In the foreign direct investment Potential Index that ranked 140 countries, Zimbabwe scored 0,075 to rank at 137, only ahead of Rwanda, the Democratic Republic of Congo and war-torn Sierra Leone who scored 0,044.

This ranking is guaranteed to frighten away few of the remaining investors thinking of coming to Zimbabwe. Thus, the economy was expected to register a decline by more than 9% in 2003 and this would be the fifth successive decline, as the economy last tasted a positive growth rate (2.9%) in 1998. All the productive sectors continued on a downward trend due the harsh macroeconomic conditions, although there were also problems peculiar to certain sectors.

The ZANU (PF) government and its free spending was the single biggest cause of the country's poor economic performance. Instead of the government curbing its reckless spending (most of it to buy political patronage), it branded those urging it to embrace fiscal discipline and austerity as enemies of the people. The huge national budget deficit spawned chronically high inflation which, compared to that of Zimbabwe's main trading partners, left a gaping difference, and that was the main force driving the economy down.

The country's already scarce foreign exchange reserves, which could have been used along with interest rate hikes to try to boost the economy at least for a short while, were down to the lowest levels ever, thanks to the government's decision to deploy troops, tanks and jets in the DRC. The country's hard cash earnings, already sapped by the poor performance of the export sector, were being burnt in the Congolese jungle. The zimdollar has been in free-fall because of the weak exporting capacity and the lack of balance of payments support from the IMF and other donor agencies.

Whereas it was easy for President Mugabe, in the past, to lay the blame for Zimbabwe's economic crisis on white commercial farmers, the opposition MDC, "Western conspiracies" or British Prime Minister Tony Blair, since the banknotes crisis in mid-2003 it has become patently clear that the main cause is the ZANU (PF) government. Furthermore, targeted sanctions imposed on Zimbabwe by the EU, USA and many members of the Commonwealth basically amount to nothing more than travel restrictions upon members of the government, senior public servants, and the hierarchy of the ruling party, and upon the funds of such persons held outside Zimbabwe; and thus have had no material economic consequences.

It was true that some aid programs had been discontinued, and others reduced. This occurred because the donors were made unwelcome by President Mugabe himself, who told them "to go to hell,"[223] and in many cases the aid had been abused, diverted to non-approved purposes, or hindered by interventions of the government, the ruling party and war veterans. Furthermore, beef exports to the EU had been stopped over fears about foot-and-mouth disease, which spread when war veterans cut fences. This situation did not occur as a result of political or trade sanctions.

Whilst some aid programs had ceased or been scaled down, others had been pursued and extended, e. g. the food aid that continued to be forthcoming from the very countries whom the government sought to blame. Britain donated £6.88m (US$11.6m) on October 23, 2003 to buy food for Zimbabwe's famished population and vaccines against potentially fatal childhood illnesses.[224] The Market Assistance Pilot Program funded by USAid to reduce urban vulnerability in Bulawayo was bringing 20,000 metric tonnes of sorghum into the country and on December 31, USAid announced a donation of 30,000 metric tonnes of sorghum, valued at US$12 million, for distribution by the WFP. In fact, not only had the US continued to give assistance to Zimbabwe, for humanitarian purposes, but it had markedly increased that assistance.[225] The European Commission (EC) announced at the end of November that it would make available some _7 million (US$8 million, at that time) in additional funding for

---

223. when the IMF withdrew its support in 1999.

224. *The Herald*, Harare, 24 October, 2003.

225. In 2000, the extent of assistance was US$13.6 million, which increased to US$21.3 million in 2001, and then increased dramatically in 2002 to US$148.3 million, whilst 2003 commitments are only marginally less, at US$138.4 million.

WFP food aid efforts in Zimbabwe. On January 20, 2004, the EC donated _20 million (US$25 million). The fresh donation brought to _52 million (US$60.5 million) the commission's contribution to alleviate food shortages in Zimbabwe since July 2003. It was said that this was sufficient to procure, deliver and distribute almost 160,000 tons of food to millions of Zimbabweans in need, and represented some 57% of tonnage requirements committed so far to the WFP food pipeline. The EC said,

> In committing these funds, the European Commission recognizes that the food security situation in Zimbabwe remains critical and that without the direct intervention of the international community, a significant proportion of the Zimbabwean population are at serious risk.

However, the Zimbabwe government cheerily suggests that the sanctions are to blame, seeking to continue to hoodwink the populace into looking elsewhere when in fact the country's economic calamities are almost entirely attributable to years of government corruption and misadministration.

Queues hundreds of people long have been almost a permanent feature around banks and building societies as people lined up in the hope of withdrawing their salaries, but often they are allowed no more than about Z$5,000 at a time to buy food and fuel, which are also scarce. The overriding cause of the banknote shortages is Zimbabwe's rampant inflation. It takes at least four times as many banknotes this year as last, just to buy the same volume and nature of goods. In addition, with many products no longer being available from traditional sources, including petroleum products, cooking oil and maize meal, a flourishing black market has developed, cash based, and generally charging far more than four times the previous prices.

The crisis might have been mitigated if the Reserve Bank of Zimbabwe had issued additional banknotes, but it was precluded from doing so — it had no foreign currency to import banknote security paper and ink.

The "hoarding" of banknotes only became a factor once the shortages were already very pronounced, and it never attained much magnitude as those who discontinued depositing their banknotes soon had to put them to use. Instead of constructively addressing the situation, with simultaneous expeditious release of new banknotes, containment of inflation and deregulation of the sort that would markedly obviate black market activity, the government issued regulations limiting withdrawals to Z$5 million,[226] nominally to prevent "hoarding" of cash; but this could only frustrate normal operations of cash-based businesses (and particularly larger businesses or those having numerous branches) — Z$5 million is nothing to big companies. The restricted size of cash transactions inevitably reduced trade volumes in an already sadly constricted economy.

On the eve of independence, the then Prime Minister Robert Mugabe addressed the nation. The following is an excerpt from that address:

"As we become a new people, we are called to be constructive, progressive and forever forward-looking, for we cannot afford to be men of yesterday, backward-looking, retrogressive and destructive.

"Our new nation requires of every one of us to be a new man, with a new mind, a new heart and a new spirit.

"Our new mind must have a new vision and our hearts a new love that spurns hate and a new spirit that must unite and not divide.

"That, to me, is the human essence that must form the core of our political change and national independence.

"Henceforth, you and I must strive to adapt ourselves, intellectually and spiritually, to the reality of our political change and relate to each other as brothers bound to one another by a bond of national comradeship.

"If ever we look to the past, let us do so for the lesson the past has taught us, namely, that oppression and racism are inequalities that must never find scope in our political and social system.

"It could never be a correct justification that because the whites oppressed us yesterday when they had power, the blacks must oppress them today because they have power.

"An evil remains an evil whether practiced by white against black or black against white.

"Our majority rule could easily turn into inhuman rule if we oppressed, persecuted or harassed those who do not look or think like the majority of us. Democracy is never mob-rule...."[227]

Two decades later, that frequently-reiterated pledge lies in tatters. The intervening years have seen mass murder, plunder, starvation, corruption, a partisan and politicized judiciary, army and police force, repeated efforts to crush the opposition and the white farming community, and economic collapse. Zimbabwe could not even come up with the money to print more money.

---

226. Specifically, the Presidential Powers (Temporary Measures) (Promotion of Banking Transactions) Regulations, 2003 (Statutory Instrument 171 of 2003). They prescribed daily banking of trade receipts, which can be expected to place the banking sector under unrealistic and excessive pressure, and many other counter-productive regulations.

227. The Prime Minister's TV Address to the Nation, 17 April, 1980.

Mugabe and ZANU (PF) have remained in the liberation-war trenches, fighting an invisible enemy.

To claim that "the sanctions imposed on the country have worsened the economic environment" is baseless. The fact is that no economic sanctions have been imposed upon Zimbabwe by any of the international community; only, some have withdrawn aid which they previously provided for Zimbabwean development. Even those who have withdrawn that aid have continued to provide humanitarian aid such as food, and funding to combat HIV/AIDS. The very countries that are attacked by Zimbabwe's politicians for having imposed targeted sanctions are foremost in supplying aid for humanitarian purposes, and that aid has effectively supplied Zimbabwe with significant inflows of foreign exchange or of import requirements and have therefore effectively contributed to the economy and relieved the Treasury's fiscal burden.

None of those countries has discontinued or barred trade with Zimbabwe, and the few who have imposed constraints upon investment in Zimbabwe have only done so because the current Zimbabwean economic environment renders Zimbabwe an unattractive investment destination and thus, with or without sanctions, little investment is, or will be, forthcoming.

It is of economic consequence that Zimbabwe has been cut off by the IMF and the World Bank. But that rupture is not primarily based on politically motivated sanctions. Zimbabwe's default in debt-servicing was the proximate cause for the suspension by the IMF. Similarly, the World Bank's constitution bars it from providing funding to any country whose arrears with the bank exceed stipulated limits.

The government and President Robert Mugabe, in particular, continue to play with smoke and mirrors, refusing to face reality and take the drastic steps necessary for economic recovery.

# APPENDIX I.

*Table 16: The Presidency and Ministers' Annual Salaries and Allowances (in Z$)*

| CATEGORY | JULY 1998* | JULY 2003** |
|---|---|---|
| 1. President Robert Mugabe | | |
| (a) Salary | 307,200 | 20,200,000 |
| (b) Cabinet allowances | 120,000 | 7,770,625 |
| (c) Housing Allowance | 80,000 | 5,180,417 |
| 2. Vice Presidents (2) | | |
| (a) Salary | 280,000 | 18,400,000 |
| (b) General allowances | 50,000 | 3,235,714 |
| (c) Housing Allowance | 40,000 | 2,548,571 |
| 3. Cabinet Ministers | | |
| (a) Salary | 213,000 | 16,500,000 |
| (b) General allowances | 22,000 | 1,682,225 |
| (c) Housing Allowance | 40,000 | 3,058,592 |
| 4. Governors | | |
| (a) Salary | 213,000 | 16,237,332 |
| (b) General allowances | 22,000 | 1,655,095 |
| (c) Housing Allowance | 40,000 | 3,009,264 |
| 5. Speaker of Parliament | | |
| (a) Salary | 213,000 | 17,300,000 |
| (b) General allowances | 22,000 | 1,764,855 |
| (c) Housing Allowance | 40,000 | 3,208,826 |
| 6. Deputy Ministers | | |
| (a) Salary | 180,000 | 14,023,872 |
| (b) General allowances | 12,000 | 922,925 |
| (c) Housing Allowance | 40,000 | 3,076,416 |
| 7. Deputy Speaker | | |
| (a) Salary | 180,000 | 14,023,872 |
| (b) General allowances | 12,000 | 922,925 |
| (c) Housing Allowance | 40,000 | 3,076,416 |
| 8. Members of Parliament | | |
| (a) Salary | 110,000 | 11,249,640 |
| (b) General allowances | 12,000 | 1,215,234 |
| (c) Constituency Allowance | 2,196 | 222,388 |
| 9. Chairpersons of: | | |
| Parliamentary Legal Committee | | 12,479,856 |
| Public Accounts Committee | | 12,479,856 |
| 10. Chief Whip | | 12,479,856 |

*Source: *Government Gazette, July 1998.*
*** Statutory Instrument 147 of 2003.*

# Appendix II. Government Composition

THE GOVERNMENT: MARCH 1975

HEAD OF STATE
President

CABINET POSTS
1. Prime Minister
2. Deputy Prime Minister and Minister of Finance
3. Minister of Roads and Traffic, Transport and Power
4. Minister of Foreign Affairs and Defense
5. Minister of Internal Affairs
6. Minister of Information, Immigration and Tourism
7. Minister of Justice, Law and Order
8. Minister of Health, Labor and Social Welfare
9. Minister of Commerce and Industry
10. Minister of Local Government and Housing
11. Minister of Agriculture
12. Minister of Education
13. Minister of Lands, Natural Resources and Water Development
14. Minister of Mines
15. Minister of Public Service and Co-ordination

*Source: The Europa World Year Book 1975, vol. II, London.*
*NB: Every Ministry has a Deputy Minister.*

THE GOVERNMENT: MARCH 1982

HEAD OF STATE
President: Rev. Canaan Sodindo Banana (took office 18 April 1980).

THE CABINET
1. Prime Minister, Minister of Defense and Public Works:

    Robert Gabriel Mugabe

2. Deputy Prime Minister:

    Simon Vengayi Muzenda

3. Minister of Economic Planning and Finance:

    Dr Bernard Thomas Chidzero

4. Minister of Foreign Affairs:

    Witness Mangunda Pasichigare Mangwende

5. Minister of Justice:

    Simbi Mubako

6. Minister of Labor and Social Services:
   Kumbirai Kangai

7. Minister of Justice, Legal and Parliamentary Affairs:
   Eddison Jonas Mudadirwa Zvobgo

8. Minister of Home Affairs:
   Herbert Ushewokunze

9. Minister of Local Government and Housing:
   Enos Chamunorwa Chikowore

10. Minister of Lands, Resettlement and Rural Development:
    Moven Enock Mahachi

11. Minister of Trade and Commerce:
    Richard Chemist Hove

12. Minister of Agriculture:
    Dennis Norman

13. Minister of Information, Posts and Telecommunications:
    Dr Nathan Marwirakuwa Shamuyarira

14. Minister of Manpower Planning:
    Frederick Shava

15. Minister of Industry and Energy Development:
    Dr Simba Makoni

16. Minister of Water Resources and Development:
    Simbarashe Mumbengegwi

17. Minister of Mines:
    Tapfumaneyi Maurice Nyagumbo

18. Minister of Transport:
    Masimba Masango

19. Minister of Health:
    Oliver Munyaradzi

20. Minister of Education and Culture:
    Dr Dzingai Mutumbuka

21. Minister of Works: Vacant

22. Minister of Roads and Traffic:
    Daniel Ngwenya

23. Minister of Youth, Sport and Culture:
    Ernest Kadungure

24. Minister of Natural Resources and Tourism:
    Victoria Fikile Chitepo

25. Minister of National Supply:
    Enos Nkala

26. Minister of Women's Affairs:
    Joyce Teurai Ropa Nhongo

Ministers of State in the Prime Minister's Office:

27. Emmerson Dambudzo Mnangagwa

28. Dr Sydney Tigere Sekeramayi

29. Speaker of Parliament: Didymus Mutasa

Source: *The Europa World Year Book 1982, vol. II, London.*
NB: *Every Ministry has a Deputy Minister.*

THE GOVERNMENT: MAY 1990

HEAD OF STATE
President: Robert Gabriel Mugabe (took office 31 Dec. 1987, re-elected March 1990)

THE CABINET
1. Vice-President:

Simon Vengayi Muzenda

2. Senior Minister in the President's Office (without portfolio):

Joshua Mqabuko Nkomo

3. Senior Minister in the President's Office for Political Affairs:

Didymus Mutasa

4. Senior Minister in the President's Office for Finance, Economic Planning and Development:

Dr Bernard Thomas Chidzero

5. Minister of Foreign Affairs:

Dr Nathan Marwirakuwa Shamuyarira

6. Minister of Justice, Legal and Parliamentary Affairs:

Emmerson Dambudzo Mnangagwa

7. Minister of Defense:

Richard Chemist Hove

8. Minister of Home Affairs:

Moven Enock Mahachi

9. Minister of Local Government, Rural and Urban Development:

Joseph Msika

10. Minister of Lands, Agriculture and Rural Resettlement:

Witness Mangunda Pasichigare Mangwende

11. Minister of Information, Posts and Telecommunications:

Victoria Fikile Chitepo

12. Minister of Labor, Manpower Planning and Social Welfare:

John Landa Nkomo

13. Minister of Industry and Commerce:

Kumbirai Kangai

14. Minister of Energy, Water Resources and Development:

Herbert Ushewokunze

15. Minister of Mines:

Jonas Christian Andersen

16. Minister of Transport and National Supplies:
    Dennis Norman
17. Minister of Health:
    Dr Timothy Stamps
18. Minister of Community and Co-operative Development:
    Joyce Teurai Ropa Mujuru
19. Minister of Public Construction and National Housing:
    Enos Chamunorwa Chikowore
20. Minister of Environment and Tourism:
    Herbert Muchemwa Murerwa
21. Minister of Higher Education:
    David Ishemunyoro Karimanzira
22. Minister of Education and Culture:
    Fay Chung

Ministers of State in the President's Office
23. Dr Sydney Tigere Sekeramayi (National Security)
24. Eddison Jonas Mudadirwa Zvobgo (Public Service)
25. Simbi Veke Mubako (Regional and International
    Organization Co-ordination)
26. David Kwidini (Sports Co-ordination)
27. Joseph Culverwell (National Scholarships)
28. Tichaendepi Masaya (Finance, Economic Planning
    and Development)
29. Vacant (Youth)
30. Brig.-General Felix Muchemwa (National Service)
31. Speaker of Parliament: Nolan Makombe

PROVINCIAL GOVERNORS
32. Manicaland: Bishop Joshua Towndie Ngoweni Dhube
33. Mashonaland Central: Joseph Ngandi Kaparadza
34. Mashonaland East: Rwizi Grafton Ziyenge
35. Mashonaland West: Mudhomeni
    Nyikadzino Chivende
36. Masvingo: Dzikamayi Callisto Mavhaire
37. Matabeleland North: Welshman Mabhena
38. Matabeleland South: Mark Nuda Dube
39. Midlands: Tranos Makombe

*Source: The Europa World Year Book 1990, vol. II, London.*
*NB: Every Ministry has a Deputy Minister.*

THE GOVERNMENT: MAY 2000

HEAD OF STATE
President:
Robert Gabriel Mugabe (took office 31 Dec. 1987, re-elected March 1990, March 1996)

THE CABINET
1. Vice-President:
   Simon Vengayi Muzenda
2. Vice-President:
   Joseph Msika
3. Minister of Defense:
   Moven Mahachi
4. Minister of Home Affairs:
   Dumiso Dabengwa
5. Minister of Justice, Legal and Parliamentary Affairs:
   Emmerson Dambudzo Mnangagwa
6. Minister of Finance and Economic Development
   Herbert Murerwa
7. Minister of National Affairs, Employment Creation and Co-operatives:
   Virginia Thenjiwe Lesabe
8. Minister of Public Service, Labor and Social Welfare:
   Florence Lubalendlu Chitauro
9. Minister of Local Government and National Housing:
   John Landa Nkomo
10. Minister of Lands and Agriculture:
    Joyce Mujuru
11. Minister of Industry and Commerce:
    Nathan Marwirakuwa Shamuyarira
12. Minister of Mines, Environment and Tourism:
    Simon Kaya Moyo
13. Minister of Information, Posts and Telecommunications:
    Chenhamo Chakezha Chimutengwende
14. Minister of Foreign Affairs:
    Dr Isack Stanislaus Goreradzo Mudenge
15. Minister of Higher Education and Technology:
    Dr Ignatius Morgan Chiminya Chombo
16. Minister of Education, Sports and Culture:
    Gabriel Machinga
17. Minister of Health and Child Welfare:
    Dr Timothy Stamps

18. Minister of Transport and Energy: (vacant)

19. Minister of Rural Resources and Water Development: (vacant)

20. Minister without Portfolio:

    Eddison Jonas Mudadirwa Zvobgo

21. Ministers of State in the President's Office:

    Cephas Msipa

22. Ministers of State for National Security:

    Dr Sydney Tigere Sekeramayi


Ministers of State:

23. Tsungai Hungwe

24. Sithembiso Nyoni

25. Oppah Rushesha-Muchinguri

26. Planning Commissioner: Richard Hove

27. Speaker of Parliament: Cyril Ndebele


PROVINCIAL GOVERNORS

28. Manicaland: Kenneth Vhundukayi Manyonda

29. Mashonaland Central: Border Gezi)

30. Mashonaland East: David Ishemunyoro Karimanzira

31. Mashonaland West: Peter Chanetsa

32. Masvingo: Josaya Dunira Hungwe

33. Matabeleland North: Welshman Mabhena

34. Matabeleland South: Stephen Jeqe Nyongololo Nkomo

35 Midlands: Lt.-Col Herbert Mahlaba

*Source: The Europa World Year Book 2000, vol. II, London.*
*NB: Every Ministry has a Deputy Minister.*

THE GOVERNMENT: APRIL 2003

HEAD OF STATE
President:
Robert Gabriel Mugabe (took office 31 Dec. 1987, re-elected March 1990, March 1996, March 2002)

THE CABINET
1. Vice-President:
   Simon Vengayi Muzenda
2. Vice-President:
   Joseph Msika
3. Minister of Special Affairs in the President's Office:
   John Landa Nkomo
4. Minister of Defense:
   Dr Sydney Tigere Sekeramayi
5. Minister of Home Affairs:
   Kembo Mohadi
6. Minister of Justice, Legal and Parliamentary Affairs:
   Patrick Antony Chinamasa
7. Minister of Finance and Economic Development
   Herbert Murerwa.
8. Minister of Public Service, Labor and Social Welfare:
   July Moyo
9. Minister of Local Government, Public Works and National Housing:
   Dr Ignatius Morgan Chiminya Chombo
10. Minister of Lands, Agriculture and Rural Resettlement:
    Dr Joseph Made
11. Minister of Industry and International Trade:
    Samuel Mumbengegwi
12. Minister of Mines and Minerals Development:
    Edward Chindori-Chininga
13. Minister of Energy and Power Development:
    Amos Midzi
14. Minister of Environment and Tourism:
    Francis Nhema
15. Minister of Foreign Affairs:
    Dr Isack Stanislaus Goreradzo Mudenge
16. Minister of Higher Education and Technology:
    Simbabrashe Mumbengegwi
17. Minister of Education, Sports and Culture:
    Aeneas Chigwedere

18. Minister of Health and Child Welfare:
    Dr David Parirenyatwa

19. Minister of Transport and Communications:
    Witness Mangwende

20. Minister of Rural Resources and Water Development:
    Joyce Mujuru

21. Minister of Youth Development, Gender and Employment Creation:
    Elliot Manyika

22. Minister of Small and Medium Enterprises:
    Sithembiso Nyoni

Ministers of State in the President's Office
23. Jonathan Moyo (Information and Publicity)

24. Nicholas Goche (National Security)

25. Paul Mangwana (State Enterprises and Parastatals)

26. Thenjiwe Virginia Lesabe (Vice-President's Office)

27. Flora Buka (Land Reform)

28. Speaker of Parliament: Emmerson Dambudzo
    Mnangagwa

PROVINCIAL GOVERNORS
29. Manicaland: Oppah Muchinguri

30. Mashonaland Central: Elliot Manyika (acting)

31. Mashonaland East: David Ishemunyoro Karimanzira

32. Mashonaland West: Peter Chanetsa

33. Masvingo: Josaya Dunira Hungwe

34. Matabeleland North: Obert Mpofu

35. Matabeleland South: (vacant)

36. Midlands: Cephas Msipa

*Source: The Europa World Year Book 2003, vol. II, London.*
*NB: Every Ministry has a Deputy Minister.*

# Bibliography

### Books

Astrow, André, Zimbabwe: A Revolution That Lost Its Way, Zed Books, 1983

Barber, William J. The Economy of British Central Africa: A Case Study of Economic Development in a Dualistic Society. London: OUP; Stanford UP, 1916.

Blake Robert. *A History of Rhodesia*. New York: Knopf, 1977.

Bond, Patrick and Manyanya, Masimba, Zimbabwe's Plunge, Exhausted Nationalism, Neoliberalism and the Search for Social Justice, The Merlin Press, 2002.

Budge, Sir E.A. Wallis, *The Dwellers on the Nile*, London, 1926;

*A History of Egypt*, 8 Volumes, London, 1902;

*The Egyptian Sudan*, Vol. 1-2, London, 1907;

Short History of the Egyptian People, London 1914;

*Egypt*, London, 1925.

Collins, Desmont. *The Human Revolution from Ape to Artist*, Phaidon, Oxford, 1976.

Davidson, Basil *A History of East and Central Africa*, Doubleday, Anchor Books.

Dumbutshena, Enoch. *Zimbabwe Tragedy*. Nairobi: East African Publishing House, 1975.

Durevall, Dick and Mlambo Kupukile, Trade Liberalization and Foreign Exchange Management: Zimbabwe 1990-1993, Stockholm, 1994.

Fagan, Brian M. *Southern Africa during the Iron Age*, Thames and Hudson, London, 1965.

Fage, J.D., *A History of Africa*, London, 1988.

Gale, William Daniel. The Years Between 1923-1973. Half a Cebtury of Rhesponsible Government in Rhodesia. Salisbury: H.C.P.Andersen, 1973.

Graham Boynton, *Last Days in Cloud Cuckooland: Dispatches from White Africa*, Jonathan Ball Publishers, Johannesburg, 1998.

Hall, R.N. and Neal, W.G., *The Ancient Ruins of Rhodesia*, Methven, London, 1902.

Hanna, Alexander John. *The Story of the Rhodesias and Nyasaland*, 2nd ed., London: Faber & Faber, 1965 (First pub., 1960).

Hirsch, Morris I. A. Decade of Crisis: Ten Years of Rhodesian Front Rule (1963-1972). Salisbury: Peter Dearlove, 1973.

Hommel, F., Die vorsemitishen Kulturen in Aegypten und Babylonien, Leipzig, 1882.

Hope, Christopher. Brothers Under the Skin: Travels in Tyranny, Macmillan, 2003.

Ilsley, Lucretia L. Rhodesia's Independence Struggle: The Role of Immigrants and Investors. New York: Andronicus Pub. Co., 1976.

Jackson, John G., *Introduction to African Civilizations*, Citadel Press, Secaucus, N.J.07094.

Leakey, Dr. L.S.B., Progress and Evolution of Man in Africa,

MacNaughton, Duncan, *A Scheme of Egyptian Chronology*, Luzac and Co., London, 1932

Mason, Philip. The Birth of a Dilemma: The Conquest and Settlement of Rhodesia. London: OUP, 1958.

Maspero, G., *Dawn of Civilisation*, London, 1894.

Struggle of the Nations, London, 1896.

Passing of the Empires, London 1900.

Morgan, J.J.de, *Les Premiéres Civilisations*, Paris, 1909.

Mtshali, B. Vulindlela. *Rhodesia: Background to Conflict*. London: Lesli Frewin, 1968.

Newberry, P.E. and Gastang, J., *Ancient Egypt*, Boston, USA, 1904.

Osler, Sir William, *Evolution of Modern Medicine*, London, 1921.

Palmer, Robin H. *Land and Racial Domination in Rhodesia*. London: Heinemann, 1977.

Palmer, Robin & Neil Parsons. The Roots of Rural Poverty in Central and Southern Africa. London: Heinemann, 1977.

Phillipson, David W. *African Archaeology*, Cambridge, 1985.

Ranger, Terence O. *Aspects of Central African History*. London: Heinemann, 1968.

*The African Voice in Southern Rhodesia, 1898-1930*. London: Heinemann; Nairobi: East Afr. Pub. House, 1970.

Ransford, Oliver. The Rulers of Rhodesia: From Earliest Times to the Referendum. London: J. Murray, 1968.

Samkange, Stanlake. *Origins of Rhodesia*. London: Heinemann; New York: Praeger, 1969.

Shamuyarira, Nathan M. *Crisis in Rhodesia*. London: Andre Deutsch; Nairobi: East Afr. Pub. House, 1967.

Sinclair, Paul J.J. *Space, Time and Social Formation*, Uppsala, 1987.

Sioveking, Ann. *The Cave Artista*, Thames and Hudson, London, 1979.

Sithole, Ndabaningi. *African Nationalism*. 2nd ed. London: OUP, 1968. (First pub., Cape Town: OUP, 1959).

Smith, Ian D., *The Great Betrayal*, Blake, London, 1997.

Thompson, Leonard M. African Societies in Southern Africa: Historical Studies. London: Heinemann, 1969.

Vambe, Lawrence. An Ill-Fated People: Zimbabwe Before and After Rhodes. London: Heinemann, 1972.

From Rhodesia to Zimbabwe. London: Heinemann, 1976.

## Reports

*Ancient Mining in Rhodesia*, Summers, R., (Salisbury, National Museums of Rhodesia, Memoir No.3, 1969)

*Breaking the Silence: Building True Peace*, compiled by the Catholic Commission for Justice and Peace (CCJP) and Legal Resources Foundation, 1997

*Civil War in Rhodesia*, compiled by the CCJP in Rhodesia, 1975, republished 1999.

*Country (Zimbabwe) Reports on Human Rights Practices – 2003*, US Bureau of Democracy, Human Rights and Labour, Washington D.C. February 25, 2004.

Economic Intelligence Unit Report, 1989-1991, SIDA, Sweden.

*Election 2000*, Volume One, CCJP, 2000.

First Five Year Development Plan (vol 1), Harare, 1986.

*Global Development Finance 1999*, World Bank, Washington, April 1999.

Human Development Report 1997.

*Institute of Directors Zimbabwe*, Direct Report, September 1999.

*Man in the Middle (The): Torture, Resettlement & Eviction*, compiled by the CCJP in Rhodesia, 1975, republished 1999.

*Media Under Siege*, Media Monitoring Project Zimbabwe, Harare, December 2003.

*Movement for Democratic Change Manifesto*, Zimbabwe, August 1999.

Not Eligible: The Politicization of Food in Zimbabwe, Human Rights Watch, New York, 24 October, 2003.

*National Democratic Institute (NDI) for International Affairs Report*, Washington, May, 2000.

*National Youth Service Training: An Overview of the Youth Militia Training and Activities in Zimbabwe*, Solidarity Peace Trust, Johannesburg, 5 September, 2003.

*Pre-colonial Goldmining in Southern Zambezia: A Re-assessment*, Phimister, I.R., African Social Research (1976), [III], xxi, 1-30.

*Neutrality in Humanitarian Assistance: A Case Study from Zimbabwe*, Overseas Development Institute, UN, 2004.

*Not Eligible: The Politicization of Food in Zimbabwe*, Human Rights Watch, New York, 24 October, 2003.

Presidential Land Review Report, The, Harare, 2003.

Study of Economic Integration in Southern Africa, African Development Bank, Oxford, 1993.

Thompson Report on the City of Harare (The), June 1999.

*UNCTAD Annual Report*, New York, September 1998; September 2003.

Who is Responsible? A Preliminary Analysis of Pre-election Violence in Zimbabwe, The Zimbabwe Human Rights NGO Forum, Harare, June 2000.

Zimbabwe: A Framework for Economic Reform (1991-1995), GZ, Harare, 1991.

Zimbabwe: At 5 Years of Independence, Nehanda Publishers, Harare, 1985.

*Zimbabwe: Danger and Opportunity*, International Crisis Group (ICG), 10 March, 2003.

Zimbabwe: In the Party's Interest?, African Rights, June 11 1999.

*Zimbabwe: Rights Under Siege*, Amnesty International, 3 May, 2003.

*Zimbabwe's Land Reform, An Audit of the Public Perception*, Mass Public Opinion Institute, Harare, December 2003.

### Periodicals

Africa Analysis

*Africa Confidential* (fortnightly), London

*Afrika News Network*, Copenhagen, Denmark

Africa News Online

BBC Online Network

*Business Day*, Johannesburg, SA

*Commerce* (monthly), Harare

The Daily Mail, London

The Daily News, Harare

*Direct Report*, Institute of Directors Zimbabwe, June 1999-September 1999, Vol.4 No.3

*Economic Review* (quarterly), Zimbabwe Financial Holdings, Harare

*The Economist* (monthly), London

*The Europa World Year Book*, Vol II, Europa Publications Limited, London

The Financial Gazette (weekly), Harare

*The Hansard*, Harare, 1980-2003

*The Herald* (daily), Harare

*i'Africa News Network*, Copenhagen, Denmark

IMF, International Finance Statistics, New York

The Insider, Harare

Journal of the South African Institute of Mining & Metallurgy, Huffman, T.N. 'Ancient Mining and Zimbabwe', 1974.

The Mail & Guardian (daily), Johannesburg, SA

*Metro* (daily), Stockholm

*New African* (monthly), London, Sept. 1994

Panafrican News Agency Online

*P.M. News*, Lagos, Nigeria

Quarterly Digest of Statistics, CSO, Harare

Quarterly Economic and Statistical Review, (Reserve Bank of Zimbabwe), Harare

*Sapa-IPS*, Harare

Southern African Economist (monthly), Harare

Southern African Political and Economic Monthly, Harare

Southern Press, Canada

*Star Tribune*, Minneapolis, Minnesota

Statistical Yearbook, UN, New York

*The Sunday Mail* (weekly), Harare

UN Integrated Regional Information Network

UN, International Trade Statistics, New York

UN, National Accounts Statistics, New York

UN, Statistical Yearbook, New York

Wall Street Journal, New York City.

Weekly Economic Highlights, RBZ, Harare

*The Zimbabwe Independent* (weekly), Harare

Zimbabwe Investment Review (monthly), Harare

The Zimbabwe Standard, (weekly), Harare

The Zimbabwe Mirror (weekly), Harare

*ZIMFEP Annual Report*, Govt. Printers, Harare

Zimtoday. Com (monthly)

# INDEX

## A

A1 model 255, 256
A2 model 252, 255, 256
Abuja Agreement 136, 259
ACP-EU 127
Affirmative Action Group 219, 220, 222, 236
Affretair 300
Africa Forum and Network on Debt and Development 303
Africa Resources Investment 216, 217, 218, 219, 220
Africa Resources Ltd 217, 218, 232
Africa Unity Square 154
African Associated Mines 229
African Daily News 59
African Development Bank 202, 270, 274
African National Congress 18, 28, 29, 32, 50, 91, 93, 129, 156
African National Council 28, 93
Agricultural Bank of Zimbabwe Limited 280
Agriculture, Ministry of, 247, 249, 297
Ahidjo, Ahmadou 156
AIDS 61, 176, 275, 325
AIPPA 68, 100, 122, 123, 131
Air de Paris 184
Air Harbour Technologies 141, 183, 184
Air Zimbabwe 166, 167, 225, 277, 278, 280, 281
Airzim 281
Algeria 101, 106, 179, 271
Alliance of Manufacturers and Exporters 226
Amakhosi Productions 65
Amani Trust 110, 111, 120, 121
ammonium nitrate 257, 262
Amnesty International 103, 131
ANC. See African National Congress 18, 50, 156
Anglo American Corporation 217, 229, 261
Anglo-American plan 29
Anglo-Portuguese Convention 13
Anglo-Rhodesian Settlement Proposals 21, 27, 90

Angola 101, 106, 181
Annan, Kofi 103, 184
Appellate Division 22
Argus Press 60
ARI. See Africa Resources Investment 216, 217, 218, 219
asbestos 68, 229, 243, 290
Asians 24, 28
asset disposal 285, 287
Associated Newspapers of Zimbabwe 100
Astra Holdings 274, 281

## B

Babayane 13
Banana, Canaan 38, 39
Banda, Kamuzu 93, 166
Bangladesh 321
Bank of Credit and Commerce International 185
banking crisis 239
Bantu 6
BBC 21, 90, 108
Beehive Management Services 229
Beira 291
Belgium 159
Ben-Menashe Ari 67, 123
Bill of Rights 19, 40, 51, 67, 78, 83, 85
Bindura Nickel Corporation Limited. 217
Bingaguru 13
Birwa 15
Bitcon (Pvt) Ltd 189
Blair Tony 322
Boka, Roger 170, 238, 239
Bosnia 180
Botswana 8, 60, 101, 156, 161, 166, 181, 186, 191, 192, 198, 259, 299, 317, 319
Brezhnev, Leonard 160
British Department for International Development 306
British Order-in-Council 14, 245
British Parliament 17, 23

British Privy Council 19
British South Africa Company 1, 12, 13, 14, 15, 16, 59, 205, 245
BSAC. See British South Africa Company 1, 12, 13, 14, 15, 16, 59, 205, 245
Bubiana conservancy 262
Burkina Faso 101, 106
Burundi 106
Business Extension and Advisory Services 227
Buxton Committee 16

### C

Cabinet 25, 32, 35, 39, 41, 49, 67, 69, 71, 73, 77, 83, 84, 128, 166, 174, 183, 186, 188, 190, 191, 202, 218, 232, 251, 254, 273, 274, 279, 285, 286, 327
Cambodia 109, 121
Cameroon 101, 156, 181
Campfire 275
Canada 31, 128, 179, 180, 226, 227
Capital FM 61
CAPS Holdings Limited 287
Carter, Jimmy 31
Castro, Fidel 61
Catholic Church 42, 67, 129, 136, 146
CDC Capital 283
cement industry 283, 315, 316
censorship 37, 59
Central Intelligence Organization 111, 202, 287
Central Mechanical Equipment Department 161
Central Organ for Conflict Prevention, Management and Resolution 101
Central Statistical Office 291, 302
Central Statistical Office. See CSO 291, 302
Changamire 9, 10
Chavunduka, Gordon 223
Chavunduka, Mark 53, 55, 57
Cheda, Misheck 260
Chehesai Transport (Pvt) Ltd 192
Chidzero, Bernard 241, 263
Chikerema, James 28, 62, 63, 93
Chiminya, Tichaona 98
Chimurenga 14, 65, 66, 91, 110, 245, 294, 295
Chimurenga music 65
China 109, 201
Chinamasa, Patrick 55, 76, 98, 99, 151, 185, 243
Chinamora dynasty 11
Chinhoyi Battle 27
Chirau, Jeremiah 20, 30
Chitepo, Herbert 20
Chiyangwa, Philip 142, 219, 222, 230, 236, 237
Choto, Ray 53, 55
City Council 187, 188
Civil Protection Unit 178
Clay Products 229
Clinton, Bill 101

Coghlan, Charles 15, 16
Cold Storage Company. See CSC 207, 225, 251, 272, 274, 281
Cold War 103, 183
College of Chiefs 27
Cologne Debt Initiative 306
colonial constitutions 2
colonial laws 2, 59, 68
colonial power 36, 47, 248, 250
colonial regimes 103
Coltart, David 48, 99, 107
commercial agriculture 209, 257, 301
Commercial Bank of Zimbabwe 218, 220, 225, 280
commercial banks 165, 194
Commercial Farmers' Union 45, 249
commercial farms 45, 90, 110, 112, 113, 246, 247, 251, 259, 274, 320
commercialization 205, 207, 225, 274, 281, 282, 288
Commissioner of Police 39, 169
Commissions 28, 29, 31, 32, 35, 37, 38, 42, 67, 75, 79, 80, 81, 82, 83, 85, 86, 87, 88, 99, 122, 129, 136, 146, 147, 162, 173, 174, 175, 180, 199, 275, 322, 323
  Chanakira 188
  Chidyausiku Constitutional 76
  Chihambakwe 175
  Delimitation and Electoral Supervisory 36
  Dumbutshena 175
  Electoral Supervisory 37, 44, 70, 133, 136
  EU 180
  Land Tenure 175
  Public Service 82, 169
  Sandura 60, 174, 191
Cotton Company of Zimbabwe 218, 219, 280, 287
Council of Chiefs 25, 31, 34, 35, 40
Credit Guarantee Facility 236
credit rating 283, 318
Crown Colony 16
CSC 207, 238, 283, 287
CSO 302
Cultural Revolution 109
customary law 41, 76
CZI 223, 224, 227, 301, 315

### D

da Sousa 13
Dabengwa, Dumiso 52, 95, 98, 117, 138, 156, 190, 216
Dairy Marketing Board 280
Dairyboard Zimbabwe Limited 218, 280, 282,

284
Dairyboard Zimbabwe Limited. See DZL 218, 225, 280, 287
Dande 9
DDF 170, 171, 189
death penalty 42
Declaration 19, 22, 31, 33, 68, 136
Defense Forces 34, 38
Delimitation of Constituencies and Electoral Districts 22
Delta Corporation 274
Demobilization Fund 168, 175
demobilization payments 92
Department of Immigration 199
Department of Social Welfare 201
Derelict Land Board 247
Development Trust of Zimbabwe 198, 300
diamonds 233
Dickens & Madison 67
District Development Fund 169
District Development Fund. See DDF 169
domestic borrowing 266, 282, 307
domestic credit 271
domestic financing 280
domestic market 206, 291, 297, 308
domestic saving 207, 282, 288
Dongo, Margaret 43, 96, 97, 98, 102, 117, 140, 149
donor agencies 183, 258, 266, 272, 322
Douglas-Home, Alec 27
DRC 90, 165, 197, 259, 273, 297, 307, 321
droughts 7, 191, 196, 207, 258, 259, 262, 283, 295, 296, 298
Dukwe camp 60
Dumbuseya 15
Dumbutshena, Enoch 102, 175
Dunlop 229
Duty Deferment Facility 189
DZL 218, 280, 282, 284

**E**

East Asia 216
Econet 185, 186, 187, 237, 238, 316
Economic Structural Adjustment Programme 3, 172, 263
Economic Structural Adjustment Programme. See ESAP 172, 263
Election Directorate 44
Elections
    by-elections 120, 130
electoral college 24, 30, 34
Electoral Commissions Forum 126
electoral law 36, 101, 125, 133, 134
electoral process 42, 71, 96, 101, 114, 115, 127, 129, 133, 136
Elklit, Jorgen 134
Emergency Powers 37, 59, 67

Emergency Powers (Security Forces Indemnity) Regulations 37, 59, 67
Empretec Zimbabwe 227
Energy and Power Development, Ministry of 193
Enhanced Communications Network 185, 238
Enhanced Structural Adjustment Facility 269
Enterprise Services for Southern Africa 234
Environment and Tourism, Ministry of 202, 249
EPZ 208, 209, 312, 313, 314, 316
Ericsson International AB 185
ESAP 3, 172, 263
Eskom 315
Ethiopia 167, 321
EU Commission. See commissions 180
European Community 289
European Investment Bank 270, 274
European Parliament 180
European Union 103, 112, 127, 128, 163, 168, 240, 270
Evangelical Fellowship of Zimbabwe 127, 146
exchange rate 155, 193, 196, 264, 267, 269, 294, 297, 301, 307, 311, 312, 314, 318, 319, 321
Exchequer, the 26
export earnings 292, 295, 298, 307, 312
export growth 296, 311
export markets 285, 310
Export Processing Zones 206, 209, 310, 312
Export Processing Zones. See EPZ 206, 209, 310, 312
export promotion 2, 296
export receipts 292, 313
Export Revolving Fund 296
export sector 301, 311, 312, 313, 321

**F**

Famine Early Warning Systems Network 258
Far East 258, 291
farm occupations 248
Fearless Talks 27
Federal Republic of Germany 299
Federation of Rhodesia and Nyasaland 17
Fidelity Printers and Refineries 197
Fifth Brigade 37, 65, 95, 137, 146, 147
Financial Holdings. See Finhold 219
Finhold 219, 281
First Banking Corporation 233
First National Building Society 240
Food and Agriculture Organization 178
foreign aid 180, 263, 274, 314
foreign capital 207
foreign currency 165, 177, 193, 194, 231, 237, 257, 259, 262, 265, 271, 277, 280, 283, 288, 289, 290, 300, 301, 306, 309, 310, 312, 313, 314, 315, 317, 318, 321, 323
Foreign Currency Accounts 312

foreign direct investment 321
foreign exchange 193, 194, 195, 237, 238, 245, 261, 264, 267, 270, 271, 273, 274, 276, 283, 285, 290, 295, 302, 306, 307, 308, 309, 310, 311, 312, 316, 321, 325
foreign missions 163, 164, 165
foreign reporters 123
Forestry Commission 281
Fort Hare 165
France 31, 104, 153, 265, 276
franchise 16, 27, 234, 246
Franchise Association of Zimbabwe 234
Front for the Liberation of Zimbabwe 93
Frontline Presidents 29, 93
funding 42, 43, 86, 138, 141, 220, 227, 228, 242, 243, 248, 257, 259, 269, 273, 275, 285, 288, 311, 322, 325

**G**

G-15 Summit 166
Gabon 101, 166
Garwe, Paddington 67
Gaza kingdom 11
GDP 202, 206, 244, 245, 261, 266, 270, 272, 273, 276, 279, 282, 283, 286, 289, 290, 291, 292, 294, 295, 296, 297, 298, 299, 300, 301, 303, 305, 308, 314, 318
General Plantation and Allied Workers Union of Zimbabwe 258
Geneva Conference 29, 32
Germany 31, 69, 265, 276, 300, 306
Gezi Training Centre 120
Gezi, Border 117, 120, 144, 147
Ghana 79, 101, 153, 181, 263, 305
Gibraltar 27
GMB 139, 178, 279, 283
GNP 294, 298
Gokomere 5, 8
Government Tender Board. See GTB 70, 184, 185, 207
Grain Marketing Board. See GMB 139, 281
Gramma Records 232
Great Zimbabwe 5, 6, 7, 9, 10
Green Bombers 120, 122, 126, 131, 135
Grobler Treaty 12
Groupe Accor of France 280
GTB 207, 208, 237
Gubbay, Anthony 43, 50, 65, 250
guerrilla bases 27
Guinea Bissau 106
Gukurahundi 92, 115
Guruhuswa region 9, 10

**H**

Harare 5, 8, 11, 17, 43, 45, 53, 54, 58, 61, 65, 66, 68, 76, 80, 96, 97, 98, 101, 102, 103, 104, 105, 108, 109, 111, 112, 116, 117, 121, 123, 124, 125, 126, 130, 131, 132, 136, 138, 141, 146, 147, 148, 149, 153, 154, 158, 161, 162, 163, 164, 165, 167, 168, 170, 178, 180, 184, 187, 188, 191, 192, 193, 198, 203, 204, 208, 221, 226, 227, 234, 235, 236, 246, 248, 249, 251, 252, 254, 258, 263, 275, 279, 281, 288, 289, 291, 297, 301, 303, 304, 305, 308, 314, 315, 322
Harare Polytechnic 191
Harid, Eric 70, 199, 200, 201
Hartley Platinum Project 290
Hasedat Corporation 198
Heavily Indebted Poor Countries 305
Heroes Acre 95
High Court 22, 31, 37, 45, 55, 56, 57, 59, 67, 96, 98, 99, 100, 118, 126, 130, 133, 144, 169, 171, 174, 185, 188, 242, 250, 251, 260
HIV 275, 325
Hong Kong 258
House of Assembly 24, 25, 26, 30, 31, 33, 34, 35, 38, 39, 40, 41, 42, 87
Housing Guarantee Fund 169
Huggins, Godfrey 17, 50
human rights 24, 33, 51, 52, 58, 61, 65, 66, 67, 68, 69, 78, 82, 103, 104, 105, 106, 108, 110, 128, 129, 130, 132, 134, 136, 149, 271
Human Rights Forum 123, 129
humanitarian crisis 257
Hungwe, Charles 144
Hwange Power Station 268
hyperinflation 271, 318, 320

**I**

IBDC 181, 182, 221, 222, 223, 225, 236, 239, 244
IBWO 182, 220, 221, 223, 239, 240
IMF 3, 179, 240, 248, 249, 263, 264, 265, 266, 267, 269, 270, 271, 272, 273, 274, 275, 276, 277, 282, 283, 285, 288, 298, 301, 303, 304, 305, 306, 307, 317, 318, 322, 325
import payments 316
import substitution 289
imported goods 157, 230, 299, 317
independence government 36, 51, 59, 60, 67, 68, 97, 168, 194, 228, 235, 246, 277, 308
Independent Broadcasting Authority 46
independent journalists 123
Independent Journalists Association of Zimbabwe 100
India 79
indigenization 2, 162, 167, 205, 207, 208, 210, 211, 212, 216, 218, 219, 220, 221, 222, 224, 227, 228, 230, 234, 235, 236, 238, 239, 240, 243, 278, 281, 285, 286
Indigenous Business Women's Organization. See IBWO 182, 220, 221
Indigenous Commercial Farmers' Union 253
indigenous companies 206, 207, 208, 211
indigenous investment 2, 212

Industrial Steel and Pipe 230
Industry and Commerce, Minister of 141, 170
Industry and International Trade, Minister of 226
inflation rate 202, 276, 294, 302
Information and Publicity, Minister of 47, 99
Information, Posts and Telecommunications, Minister of 46, 47, 135, 185
Innscor Africa 317
Institute of Development Studies 159
insurance companies 227, 280
interest rates 105, 189, 203, 209, 211, 226, 228, 230, 264, 266, 273, 276, 277, 290, 291, 294, 297, 309, 310, 312, 313, 318, 319, 320, 321
Interfin 165
Internal Settlement 32
international aid 179, 181
International Airport 141, 153, 184, 203, 204
international community 128, 136, 177, 181, 212, 250, 283, 288, 314, 323, 325
International Conference Centre 66
international contracts 180
International Covenant on Economic, Social and Cultural Rights 177
International Criminal Court 135
International Development Association 225
international donors 69, 90, 259, 275, 285
International Finance Corporation 217, 234
international loans 283
international market 181, 292
international media 101
International Monetary Fund 3, 179, 240, 248, 249, 263, 264, 265, 266, 267, 269, 270, 271, 272, 273, 274, 275, 276, 277, 282, 283, 285, 288, 298, 301, 303, 304, 305, 306, 307, 314, 317, 318, 322, 325
International Monetary Fund. See IMF 314
international monitors 113, 119
international observers 126, 137
international recession 294
international treaties 22, 190
International Union of Socialist Youths 103
Italy 104, 159, 289
Ivory Coast 101, 181, 259

**J**

Jamaica 166
jambanja 108
Japan 159, 207, 265, 276, 299, 300
job stayaways 41
Joint Parliamentary Assembly 127
joint-venture projects 226
Jongwe Press 144
judiciary 26, 30, 37, 44, 50, 56, 57, 68, 72, 80, 83, 131, 134, 148, 151, 157, 175, 242, 256, 324
Justice for Agriculture 257
Justice, Legal and Parliamentary Affairs, Min-

ister of 39, 43, 98, 118, 218

**K**

Kalahari 9
Kangai, Kumbirai 139, 150
Kanto & Immerman 100
Kasukuwere, Saviour 192, 222
Kaunda, Kenneth 28, 29, 155, 308
Kenya 6, 79, 101, 106, 158, 179, 181, 186, 306, 316
Khmer Rouge 109
Kim Il Sung 167
Kingdom Bank 220
Kings Haven Hotel 232
Koran 143
Korean-trained force 92
Kushinga Phikelela College 150

**L**

Lancaster House Agreement 33, 38, 247
Lancaster House Constitution 2, 32, 33, 35, 36, 37, 45, 56, 69, 74, 116
Land Conference 248
Land redistribution 246
Land reform 47
Latin America 263, 264
Law Society 83, 100
Legal Resources Foundation 78, 146
legal system 41, 157
Legislative Assembly 15, 16, 18, 21, 23
Legislative Council 15
Lemba 15
lending agencies 277
lending rates 310
Lesotho 106, 153, 299
liberation war 66, 67, 125, 144, 150, 249, 289
Liberty Party of Zimbabwe 94
Libya 104, 184, 193
Libyans 169, 252, 253
Lippert Concession 14
Liquor Licensing 68
Lobels Bread (Pvt) Ltd 231
Lobengula 12, 13, 14
Local Government and National Housing, Ministry of 169
logging rights 198
London 13, 17, 20, 24, 25, 32, 61, 89, 104, 108, 110, 123, 135, 136, 166, 171, 185, 237, 245, 248, 268, 289, 298
Lotshe Hlabangana 13
Lusaka Accord 32
Luxembourg 159, 180

**M**

M&S Syndicate 243
maize production 256

major currencies 165, 208, 292
majority rule 17, 18, 23, 26, 29, 38, 324
Makamba, James 194, 237
Makoni dynasty 10
Makoni, Simba 10, 12, 120, 138, 264, 285
Malawi 17, 93, 181, 191, 259
Malaysia 166, 183, 200, 215, 258, 319
Malaysian Corporation 183
Malta 30
Malta Talks 30
Mandela, Nelson 106, 156
Manifesto 107
Manyika kingdom 13
Mapfumo, Thomas 65, 66
Market Assistance Pilot Program 322
martial law 22, 54
Marxism-Leninism 49, 63, 160
Marxist ideology 137
Masire, Katumile 156
Matobo Hills 5
Mauritius 101, 181, 191, 228, 319
Mavhaire, Dzikamai 71, 116, 138, 145, 146, 147, 148, 150, 151, 152, 281
Mbeki, Thabo 105, 128, 130, 156, 271
Mbire region 10
MDC 48, 53, 98, 99, 102, 104, 105, 106, 107, 108, 109, 111, 112, 113, 115, 116, 117, 118, 119, 121, 123, 124, 125, 126, 129, 130, 131, 132, 133, 134, 135, 136, 142, 155, 177, 188, 242, 250, 322
Media Defense Fund 47
Media Institute of Southern Africa 46, 47, 100
Meldrum, Andrew 123
Mexico 103
Mfecane invasions 11
Micro Business Development Corporation 223
Middle East 166
military hardware 200, 274
Millennium Economic Recovery Plan 212, 321
mineral exports 290, 311
mineral reserves 289
Mines and Minerals Development Department 197
Mines, Environment and Tourism 117
mining industry 232, 289, 310
mining output 300
Minister Without Portfolio 85
minority rights 33, 34
Misconduct Statutory Instruments 199
Moffat Treaty 12
Mohammed 215
monetary policy 297, 302, 320
money market 214
money supply 272, 297, 302, 318, 319, 320
Morocco 106
Movement for Democratic Change. See MDC 48, 67, 102, 104, 107, 119, 155
Movement for Independent Electoral Candi-

dates 97
Moyo, Jonathan 76, 80, 99, 100, 117, 187, 252
Mozambique 20, 113, 129, 179, 198, 259, 260, 294, 299, 315
Mshete 13
Msika, Joseph 139, 144, 148, 162
Msipa, Cephas 162, 230
Mtukudzi, Oliver 66
Mudede, Tobaiwa 88, 243
Mudenge, Stan 138, 165
Mudzuri, Elias 126, 130, 188
Mugabe, Innocent 253
Mugabe, Leo 141, 142, 184, 204, 230, 237
Mugabe, Robert Gabriel, 125
Mugabe, Sabina 141
Mujuru, Solomon 149, 156, 185, 228, 232, 237, 238
multinational corporations 180, 218, 235, 239
Multi-Party Consultative Conference 77
Munhumutapa Empire 9
Munyathi Mining Limited 287
Murerwa, Herbert 111, 143, 145, 171, 176, 184, 218, 283, 296, 297, 302, 310, 320
Musarurwa, Willie 60, 61
Mushandirapamwe Hotel 89
Mutare rebellion 143
Mutasa 10, 12, 13, 138, 139, 148
Mutasa dynasty 10
Mutasa, Didymus 10, 12, 13, 138, 139, 148
Muzenda, Simon 138, 140, 143, 146, 147, 152, 155, 156, 220
Muzorewa, Abel 20, 28, 29, 30, 32, 33, 36, 37, 42, 60, 89, 93, 102, 112, 175
Mzilikazi 12

**N**

Namibia 69, 73, 77, 129, 181, 299
National Affairs, Employment Creation and Co-operatives, Ministry of 42, 116, 138
National Aids Council Trust Fund 176
National Assembly 84, 85, 87, 141
National Blankets 144
National Constitutional Assembly. See NCA 69
National Convention for Change 77
National Democratic Institute for International Affairs 114
National Economic Consultative Forum 103, 190, 219, 226, 292
National Economic Revival Programme 320
National Housing Fund 169
National Investment Trust 218, 220, 233, 280, 285
National Investment Trust of Zimbabwe 220
National Merchant Bank of Zimbabwe 219
National Oil Company of Zimbabwe. See NOCZIM 192, 240

National Railways of Zimbabwe. See NRZ 95, 192, 277
national reconciliation 92
National Social Security Authority. See NSSA 172
National Sports Stadium 154
Native Africa Investment 230
Native Purchase Areas 245
Native Registration 50
Native Reserves 245
Ncube, Welshman 48, 67, 76, 94, 106, 107, 115, 223, 233
Ndebele amity 12
Ndebele War 14, 245
Ndebele, Cyril 52, 148
NEPAD 130, 271
Net Two 185, 186, 237
Net*One 286
New Partnership for Africa's Development. See NEPAD 130
New Zealand 69, 128, 254
Ngavavongwe Records 232
NGO 45, 110, 221
Nile 6
Nitram 92
Nkomo, Joshua 17, 20, 28, 29, 32, 36, 39, 40, 50, 92-95, 137, 147, 152, 185, 198, 237, 238, 331
Nkomo, John 187, 256
nomination papers 76, 135
Non-Aligned Movement 153
non-governmental organization. See NGO 45, 111, 171, 178, 258
North Korea 92, 121, 137, 154, 167
Norwegian Agency for International Development (NORAD) 224
Notarial Deed of Trust 220
NRZ 192, 278, 280, 281, 283, 286, 288
NSSA 172, 219, 285
Nyandoro, George 93, 155
Nyarota, Geof 60
Nyerere, Julius 95, 108, 156
Nyika Investments 228

**O**

OAU Charter 106
Obasanjo, Olusegun 130, 271
off-shore facility 271
Oil Blending (Pvt) Ltd. 287
oil companies 231, 287
Old Mutual 231
Olivine Industries 281
Ombudsman 35, 38, 70, 83
OPEC 184
Organization of African Unity 93, 101
Owen, David 29, 30, 32

**P**

parallel market 177, 193, 194, 195, 197, 276, 301, 312, 317
Parliament 17, 21, 22, 23, 24, 27, 31, 32, 33, 34, 37, 38, 39, 40, 41, 43, 44, 47, 48, 49, 50, 52, 65, 67, 69, 70, 71, 72, 73, 74, 75, 77, 79, 80, 82, 83, 84, 85, 87, 95, 98, 101, 102, 117, 118, 122, 124, 128, 132, 133, 134, 135, 136, 138, 141, 142, 143, 144, 145, 146, 148, 149, 151, 156, 160, 162, 164, 167, 169, 170, 171, 184, 203, 215, 235, 241, 247, 249, 250, 251, 269, 279, 281, 296, 320, 327
parliamentary elections 81, 108, 133, 135
parliamentary privilege 151
party youths 139, 150
Patriotic Front 1, 29, 30, 31, 32, 36, 93
patronage system 241
Paweni, Mashata 175, 191
Pensions and Provident 225
petrofin bills 279
petroleum products 291, 323
Pinochet, Augusto 104, 134
Pioneer Column 14
politburo 40, 137, 138, 141, 142, 148, 149, 152, 156, 181, 254
Political Affairs Ministry of 42
political parties 22, 42, 43, 44, 68, 71, 72, 78, 81, 85, 102, 114, 117, 152, 178, 210
    African National Congress 18, 28, 29, 32, 50, 91, 93, 129, 156
    African National Council, ZANU, ZAPU, etc. 28, 32, 36, 38, 39, 40, 50, 60, 91, 92, 93, 94, 95, 112, 125, 137, 148
    African National Council, ZANU, ZAPU, etc. See also ZANU, ZAPU. 1, 20, 29, 32, 35, 36, 38, 40, 42, 43, 48, 50, 58, 59, 60, 63, 67, 68, 69, 70, 71, 72, 73, 74, 75, 76, 78, 80, 81, 85, 86, 87, 89, 90, 91, 92, 93, 94, 95, 96, 97, 98, 99, 102, 104, 105, 106, 107, 108, 109, 110, 111, 112, 113, 114, 115, 116, 117, 118, 119, 120, 121, 123, 124, 125, 126, 129, 131, 133, 135, 136, 137, 138, 139, 140, 141, 142, 143, 144, 145, 146, 147, 148, 150, 151, 152, 153, 155, 156, 160, 170, 173, 176, 177, 181, 182, 188, 189, 191, 192, 194, 197, 203, 212, 215, 216, 217, 232, 236, 240, 243, 244, 247, 248, 251, 252, 253, 254, 255, 258, 271, 272, 281, 286, 288, 296, 297, 320, 321, 322, 325
    Dominion Party 50
    Forum Party of Zimbabwe 102
    FROLIZI 93
    Movement for Democratic Change 48,

67, 102, 104, 107, 119, 155

National Democratic Party 17, 50

Rhodesian Front 19, 21, 22, 24, 25, 50, 55, 59, 67, 91, 246

United African National Council 91, 102

United National Federal Party 32

United Parties 42, 43, 44

Zimbabwe Union of Democrats, See also ZUD 76, 102

Zimbabwe Unity Movement, See also ZUM 77, 95

Portugal 294

Portuguese colonial empire 20

POSA 68, 122, 124, 131, 132

Post Office Savings Bank 172

Posts and Telecommunications Corporation. See PTC 46, 186, 225

Potential Index 321

poverty 63, 105, 159, 180, 205, 206, 207, 210, 211, 240, 242, 248, 267, 271, 305

Poverty Reduction and Growth Facility 301, 307, 318

Precious Stones 67

presidential amnesty 93

presidential pardon 72, 96, 242

Presidential Powers (Temporary Measures) 41, 48, 49, 64, 65, 84, 103, 324

price controls 193, 195, 196, 264, 270, 273, 302, 313, 316

PricewaterhouseCoopers 179

Private and Voluntary Organizations Amendment 45

private investment 206

private sector 161, 171, 198, 205, 208, 211, 212, 215, 225, 226, 227, 242, 264, 268, 272, 275, 279, 281, 282, 286, 287, 292, 308, 309, 319, 320

privatization 2, 3, 159, 183, 205, 206, 207, 212, 220, 225, 233, 268, 272, 273, 274, 278, 279, 280, 281, 282, 283, 284, 285, 286, 287, 288, 292, 319, 320

Privatization Agency of Zimbabwe. See PAZ 233, 279

privatization programme 273, 283, 284, 287

Privileges and Immunities 59, 148

Privy Council 22

procurement procedures 200, 207

producer prices 257, 315

productive investment 205, 207, 210, 320

Protected Areas 59

protected villages 20

provincial leadership 139, 142

PTA Bank 270, 274

PTC 46, 185, 203, 241, 279, 281, 286

public assets 278

Public Construction and National Housing,

Ministry of 169, 202

public expenditure 102, 160, 267

public funds 42, 86, 179, 274, 281

public offerings 278

public petitions 74

Public Prosecutor 83

public resources 171, 282

public sector 190, 205, 207, 224, 272, 278, 282, 292, 319, 320

Public Service and Social Welfare, Ministry of 172

Public Service Association 78

public spending 202, 303

public transport 193, 242, 288, 302

Pungwe Water Project 108

Purchase Areas 26, 246

purchasing power 302

**R**

raw materials 195, 244, 258, 261, 265, 301, 313

RBZ 238, 240, 270, 271, 272, 297, 302, 303, 304, 305, 307, 309, 310, 312, 313, 314, 318, 319

RBZ governor 238

Registrar of Banks and Financial Institutions 238

Registrar-General 44, 88, 218, 243

Renamo 39, 129

Reserve Bank of Zimbabwe. See RBZ 277, 283, 303, 304, 309, 311, 323

Rhodes, Cecil 12, 13, 14, 16, 59

Rhodesia 1, 16, 17, 18, 19, 20, 21, 22, 23, 24, 27, 28, 33, 36, 59, 64, 68, 87, 93, 136, 154, 213, 294

Rhodesia Railways 294

Rhodesian Printing and Publishing Company 60

Richards, Ivor 29

riot police 61, 99, 108, 124, 132, 139

Road Motor Services 288

rock paintings 5

Rowland, Tiny 243

Rozvi 8, 10, 15

Rudd Concession 12, 13, 14

Rufaro Stadium 53, 105

rule of law 55, 56, 57, 64, 68, 96, 100, 101, 102, 113, 128, 130, 157, 271, 277, 319

Rural Resources and Water Development, Minister of 170

rural voters 90

Russia 179

Rwanda 6, 106, 180, 321

**S**

SADC 125, 128, 129, 153, 190, 229, 231, 234, 264, 289

Sahara 106, 303, 305

Salaries Service Bureau 201

Salisbury 17, 27, 28, 29, 32, 33
Sandawana 68, 197
Security Council 29, 31, 197, 295
Sedar-Senghor, Leopold 156
See British South Africa Company 1, 12, 13, 245
Seed Co. 231
Selous Scouts 20
Sese Seko, Mabutu 179
settlement talks 2, 30
Shamuyarira, Nathan 93, 141, 142, 148, 292
share allocations 280
Sheikh Yamani 184
Shona 5, 6, 7, 8, 9, 10, 11, 12, 13, 14, 15, 65, 95, 108, 182, 246
Shona chiefdoms 11, 15
Sibanda, Gibson 102, 105, 106, 139, 152
Sierra Leone 106, 321
Singapore 200, 319
Sithole, Edison 59
Sithole, Ndabaningi 20, 28, 29, 30, 32, 93
Sithole, Tommy 60, 61
Small Enterprises Development Corporation 225
small-medium enterprises. See SMEs 224
SMEs 224, 227
Smith regime 50, 56, 67, 194, 213, 246, 277
Smith, George 55, 169
Smith, Ian 19, 20, 21, 22, 27, 28, 29, 32, 36, 37, 38, 55, 56, 59, 87, 89, 109
Soames, Arthur, Lord 33, 91
Social Dimension Fund 172
socialist economy 92, 263
socialist experimentation 263
socio-political systems 2
Sofala 6, 7, 8, 10
Solta (Pvt) Ltd 188
Somalia 106
Somvech 188
Sotho groups 9
South Africa 6, 12, 15, 24, 28, 37, 38, 45, 60, 68, 69, 70, 73, 77, 79, 94, 105, 106, 120, 123, 127, 128, 129, 130, 133, 134, 136, 153, 156, 165, 181, 191, 215, 217, 219, 230, 233, 253, 260, 271, 276, 290, 294, 299, 300, 302, 306, 309, 315, 316, 318
South Korea 181, 200, 319
Southampton Life Assurance Society of Zimbabwe 219
Southern Africa Development Community. See SADC 125
Southern African Customs Union 299
Southern Rhodesia 13, 15, 16, 17, 18, 19, 21, 23
Southern Rhodesia Order-in-Council 21
Soviet Union 62, 266
Stalinist dictatorship 268
Standard Bank of London 186
state assets 278
state enterprises 205, 206, 212, 274

state farms 248
state of emergency 22, 24, 37, 39, 41, 82, 88
State terrorism 134
Stevens, David 98, 99
stock control 210
stock-feed producers 258
Sudan 106
Super ZAPU 60
Supreme Court 37, 39, 41, 42, 43, 44, 45, 50, 51, 53, 55, 56, 57, 59, 61, 65, 83, 100, 134, 185, 250
Supreme Sales and Hire 230
Sussex University 159
Svosve 10, 248, 249
SW Radio Africa 61
Swaziland 106, 299
Sweden 185, 268
Switzerland 128, 167
syndicates 158, 233
Systems Technology 232

T

TA Holdings 249
Tamoil 193
Tanaka Power 232
Tanzania 20, 156, 158, 166, 181, 263
tariff adjustment 284
Tawara 9
tax evasion 158
tax havens 159
technical assistance 231, 275
technological development 200
Tekere, Edgar 76, 102, 137, 191
TeleAccess Communications 232
Telecel 185, 186, 194, 204, 237
telecommunication services 47
TelOne 286
tender system 49, 66, 181, 207, 212
Tete 9
textiles sector 291
Thailand 258, 319
Thatcher, Margaret 32
Tiger Talks 27
Tobacco 109, 176, 240, 259, 281
tobacco 154, 176, 177, 213, 239, 244, 245, 248, 255, 259, 260, 261, 265, 272, 273, 283, 292, 299, 300, 302, 307, 309, 312
Tobacco Growers Trust 176
Tobacco Research Board 281
Togo 101
Torwa 9, 10
Transitional National Development Plan 212, 295, 321
Transnational Holdings Ltd 219
Transparency Front 80
Transparency International 159, 180, 190
Transvaal Boers 12

Treasury 167, 201, 208, 272, 280, 282, 301, 304, 325
Treasury Bills 304
Tredgold, Robert 50
Tribal Trust Lands 26, 213, 246
tributary provinces 10
Tripartite Negotiating Forum 257
Trust Merchant Bank 220, 228
truth commission 107
Tsumba, Leonard 238, 239, 272, 320
Tsvangirai, Morgan 53, 62, 67, 97, 105, 106, 107, 108, 121, 123, 125, 133, 134, 153, 242
TTL Board 22
Tungamirai, Josiah 140, 150, 232, 236
Tunisia 101
Turner and Newell 229

**U**

UCLAF 180
UDI 19, 21, 22, 27, 56, 59, 194, 206, 213, 229, 291, 293, 294, 308
Uganda 6, 69, 79, 101, 113, 158, 181, 259, 260
UK 22, 31, 134, 184, 220, 249, 294, 299, 300, 306
UN 29, 30, 31, 64, 79, 81, 103, 129, 163, 167, 197, 245, 291, 295
UNCTAD 179, 321
UNDP 129, 227, 248
Unilateral Declaration of Independence. See UDI 1, 19, 23, 55
Union Carbide 228
United Merchant Bank 238, 272
United States Agency for International Development. See USAID 224
United Tours Companies 231
unity accord 37, 40, 93, 94, 95, 137, 148
Unity Day 94
universal adult suffrage 30, 34
University of Aarhus 134
University of Zimbabwe 39, 97, 106, 191, 223
USA 121, 123, 135, 166, 249, 265, 289, 299, 300, 322
USAID 224
USAid 275, 301, 322
Utete, Charles 174, 254, 255, 261

**V**

Vance, Cyrus 32
Vasco da Gama 166
Vehicle Inspection Depot 199
venture capital 207, 211, 226, 228
Venture Capital Company of Zimbabwe 227
Victoria Falls Conference 28, 29
Vietnam 258
VIP housing scheme 169
Vorster, John 28

**W**

Walton Investments (Pvt) Ltd 229
Wankie Colliery 283, 300
War Victims' Compensation Fund 172, 174
Washington DC 114
WestLb 283
Westminster system 84
WFP 178, 258, 322
White Paper 43
White Voters' Roll 31
Wildlife and Environment Zimbabwe 262
wildlife industry 262
Willowgate scandal 60, 116
Women in Business 221
World Bank 179, 181, 182, 225, 234, 235, 240, 249, 263, 264, 266, 270, 271, 275, 276, 288, 296, 300, 304, 305, 307, 314, 318, 325
world markets 272
world trade 159
WS Craster 287

**X**

Xosas 6

**Y**

Yamani, Hani 184
Young Turks 107
Young, Andrew 29, 30
youth brigade 92
Youth League 93, 147, 236
YTL International 183

**Z**

Zambezi 6, 7, 9, 213
Zambia 17, 20, 113, 153, 181, 213, 260, 279, 294, 308, 315, 317
Zambia Investment Centre 260
Zambuko Hillary Clinton Centre 221
ZANLA forces 20
ZANU (PF) 1, 20, 29, 32, 35, 36, 38, 40, 42, 43, 48, 50, 58, 59, 60, 63, 67, 68, 69, 70, 71, 72, 73, 74, 75, 76, 78, 80, 81, 85, 86, 87, 89, 90, 91, 92, 93, 94, 95, 96, 97, 98, 99, 102, 104, 105, 106, 107, 108, 109, 110, 111, 112, 113, 114, 115, 116, 117, 118, 119, 120, 121, 123, 124, 125, 126, 129, 131, 133, 135, 136, 137, 138, 139, 140, 141, 142, 143, 144, 145, 146, 147, 148, 150, 151, 152, 153, 155, 156, 160, 170, 173, 176, 177, 181, 182, 188, 189, 191, 192, 194, 197, 203, 212, 215, 216, 217, 232, 236, 240, 243, 244, 247, 248, 251, 252, 253, 254, 255, 258, 271, 272, 281, 286, 288, 296, 297, 320, 321, 322, 325
ZAPU 32, 36, 38, 39, 40, 50, 60, 91, 92, 93, 94, 95, 112, 125, 137, 148

ZBC 46, 61, 62, 98, 114, 185, 286
ZCTU 39, 41, 57, 61, 62, 97, 102, 104, 105, 132, 136, 152, 269, 277, 314
ZESA 183, 268, 277, 279, 281, 283, 284, 286, 314, 315
ZIANA 60, 150, 225
ZIDCO Holdings 144
ZIMASCO 217, 228, 232
Zimbabwe Broadcasting Corporation 46, 61, 286
Zimbabwe Conference on Reconstruction and Development 295
Zimbabwe Congress of Trade Unions. See ZCTU 39, 190
Zimbabwe Cycle 230
Zimbabwe Defense Forces. See Defense Forces 119, 201
Zimbabwe Defense Industries 300
Zimbabwe Development Bank 226, 274
Zimbabwe Development Corporation 287
Zimbabwe Electricity Supply Authority. See ZESA 183, 284, 314
Zimbabwe Enterprise Development Programme 223
Zimbabwe Freedom Movement 135
Zimbabwe Human Rights NGO Forum 111, 112, 121, 131
Zimbabwe Indigenous Economic Empowerment Organization 223
Zimbabwe Indigenous Security Association 208
Zimbabwe Institute of Mass Communication 60
Zimbabwe Inter-Africa News Agency. See ZIANA 60
Zimbabwe Investment Centre 260, 267
Zimbabwe Iron and Steel Company. See ZISCO 277
Zimbabwe Mass Media Trust 60
Zimbabwe Minerals Development Corporation 300
Zimbabwe Miners' Federation 197
Zimbabwe Mining and Smelting Company. See ZIMASCO 217
Zimbabwe Music Corporation 232
Zimbabwe National Army 104, 135, 146, 168, 228
Zimbabwe National Chamber of Commerce 80, 223
Zimbabwe National Liberation War Veterans Association 139
Zimbabwe National Network for People with HIV/AIDS 176
Zimbabwe National Vulnerability Assessment Committee 178
Zimbabwe Newspapers (Pvt) Ltd 264
Zimbabwe People's Convention 80
Zimbabwe Programme for Economic and Social Transformation 267

Zimbabwe Reinsurance Corporation 218, 274, 280
Zimbabwe Republic Police 101, 104, 132, 193
Zimbabwe Revenue Authority 198
Zimbabwe Sun Hotels 231
Zimbabwe Teachers' Association 78
Zimbabwe Tobacco Association 176, 262
Zimbabwe United Passenger Company 288
Zimbabwe-Rhodesia 32, 33, 36, 175
Zimchem Refineries 287
ZimPost 241, 286
ZimRe 233, 280, 284, 316
ZimRights 134, 136
ZimTrade 227
ZINATHA 223
ZIPRA 20, 37, 92, 94, 95, 168
ZISCO 277, 279, 283, 300
Ziwa 5, 7, 8
ZNCC 223
ZSE 231, 233, 268
ZUD 76, 102, 115, 117
Zulus 6
ZUM 95, 96, 102
Zumbo 9
Zvinavashe, Vitalis 122, 156
Zvobgo, Eddison 39, 72, 75, 77, 85, 138, 140, 146, 150, 162, 188

Main.
28.95

320.96891 CHIKUHWA
Chikuhwa, Jacob W. (Jacob
Wilson), 1940-
A crisis of governance :
Zimbabwe

PORTLAND PUBLIC LIBRARY
5 MONUMENT SQUARE
PORTLAND, ME 04101

| MAY 2 3 2005 DATE DUE | | |
|---|---|---|
| NOV 0 5 2005 | | |
| APR 2 5 2006 | | |
| | | |
| | | |
| | | |
| | | |
| | | |
| | | |
| | | |

Printed in the United States
24313LVS00002B/70-78